The German Army on Vimy Ridge 1914 – 1917

In loving memory of my father

Bill Sheldon 1921 – 2002

One of nature's gentlemen and
A life long admirer of Germany,
Its music, its culture and its language.

The Author

Dr. Jack Sheldon retired from the British Army in 2003 after a thirty-five year career as a member of the Queen's Lancashire Regiment. He is a graduate of the German Command and Staff College in Hamburg and he held numerous international appointments, including that of Military Attaché Berlin.

For the past eight years he has been living in the Dauphiné Alps of southeast France, researching and writing his acclaimed German Army in The Great War series. These have already become the standard works on the subject for both the specialist and the general reader.

Jack Sheldon, a member of the British Commission for Military History, the Douglas Haig Fellowship and the Western Front Association, is in demand for his expertise on all aspects of the German military during the First World War.

By the same Author:

The German Army on the Somme 1914 -1916, *(also in paperback)*
The German Army at Passchendaele, *(also in paperback)*
The German Army on Vimy Ridge 1914 – 1917, *(also in hardback)*
The German Army at Cambrai
The German Army at Ypres 1914
The German Army on the Western Front 1915

The Germans at Beaumont Hamel *(Battleground Europe Series)*
The Germans at Thiepval *(Battleground Europe Series)*

All are available through www.pen-and-sword.co.uk

The German Army on Vimy Ridge 1914 – 1917

Jack Sheldon

Pen & Sword
MILITARY

Published in 2008
and re-printed in this format in 2013 by

Pen & Sword Military
an imprint of
Pen & Sword Books Ltd
47 Church Street
Barnsley
South Yorkshire
S70 2AS

ISBN:- 978-1-78346-184-4

Printed and bound in the UK by CPI Group (UK) Ltd, Croydon, CRO 4YY

Pen & Sword Books Ltd incorporates the Imprints of Pen & Sword Aviation,
Pen & Sword Family History, Pen & Sword Maritime, Pen & Sword Military, Pen
& Sword Discovery, Wharncliffe Local History, Wharncliffe True Crime,
Wharncliffe Transport, Pen & Sword Select, Pen & Sword Military Classics, Leo
Cooper, The Praetorian Press, Remember When, Seaforth Publishing
and Frontline Publishing.

For a complete list of Pen & Sword titles please contact
PEN & SWORD BOOKS LIMITED
47 Church Street, Barnsley, South Yorkshire, S70 2AS, England
E-mail: enquiries@pen-and-sword.co.uk
Website: www.pen-and-sword.co.uk

Contents

Foreword

My first visit to the Western Front took place nearly a quarter of a century ago. I was then a postgraduate student working on a MA thesis, and having read so much on the subject, to finally be able to see and walk the ground had a profound impact on me. What struck me was the very incongruity of such terrible events having taken place in such a peaceful pastoral setting as the Somme. In most places the only indication of a warlike past were the presence of war memorials and beautifully kept Commonwealth War Graves Commission cemeteries. Not so Vimy Ridge, which we visited either *en route* to the Somme or on our way back (time has blurred the precise sequence of events). The atmosphere here was somehow sinister. The trenches at Beaumont Hamel, having been grassed over, were partially tamed by nature. At Vimy Ridge the trenches, permanently preserved in concrete, had an angular and threatening brutality.

The sheer closeness of the rival trench systems also came as a shock. It is one thing to read about their proximity in the scholarly comfort of a university library, quite another to stand there and gain a sentry's eye view of the enemy front line. I also went down into the Grange tunnel, which led me to suspect that the soldiers who sheltered there must have regarded it with a curious feeling in which claustrophobia and safety were mingled. And then up to the Canadian monument, which struck me then – as it still does – to be remarkably handsome. Certainly, it contrasts starkly with the building-block ugliness of the Memorial to the Missing at Thiepval. From the Canadian memorial, the view over the Douai plain shows more clearly than any map why Vimy Ridge was an important military objective, and why so many soldiers from Germany and the French and British Empires fought and died there.

My first visit to Vimy Ridge – and I have returned countless times since – left me with a nagging frustration. I wanted to know more about the other, non-Canadian soldiers who served there, the Moroccans who came close to capturing the Ridge in May 1915 and who are commemorated on a memorial there; the British who held the sector in 1916 before the Canadian Corps arrived; and not least, the men on the other side of No Man's Land. In the mid-1980s, works in English covering these topics were few and far between. Now, thanks to Jack Sheldon's work, the Germans on Vimy Ridge have a voice.

Jack Sheldon is exceptionally well qualified to write this book. Fluent in the German language, he brings his training as a professional soldier to bear on the subject (he retired as a colonel having previously graduated from the German General Staff course at the *Führungsakademie* in Hamburg). Following the pattern established by his previous books on the Germans on the Somme and at Passchendaele, he exploits primary sources and regimental histories to provide a richly-detailed work which will be absolutely invaluable to military historians. But this is no mere compilation of sources; Jack Sheldon also provides some penetrating analysis. He is painting on a broader canvas than in his previous books, covering from the German perspective the fighting in the area throughout the war. While the events of April 1917 on Vimy Ridge are familiar, the actions in 1914 and 1915 are almost unknown to Anglophone audiences, the fighting in 1916 scarcely less so. Jack Sheldon succeeds brilliantly in bringing these neglected but lethal actions to life. Of the many vignettes he uses, perhaps my favourite is *Offizierstellvertreter Hugo Gropp's* gripping account of the mine warfare that was endemic on Vimy Ridge, which ends with the wonderfully bathetic comment, 'Five words appear in the Army Communiqué, 'We have exploded a mine successfully'.

However, with the 90th anniversary commemorations of the capture of Vimy Ridge still fresh in people's minds, it is the discussion of April 1917 that will gain the most attention. Jack Sheldon debunks several key myths pertaining to this battle. It is not true to say that the Canadians took the Ridge after British attacks had failed – the British had made no attempt to capture it (and one might add, the Canadian Corps was in a very real sense 'British' in 1917, modern nationalist myth-makers not withstanding). Neither was 'Vimy Ridge as good as impregnable' – the Germans faced a number of problems in holding it. Nonetheless, in some places the defenders resisted the assault remarkably effectively; so much so that, after analysing the lessons of April 1917, 'the German army went into the Third Battle of Ypres convinced that it had a working answer to Allied tactics and the power of the gun.'

The German Army on Vimy Ridge 1914–1917 is an important book that continues the move away from simplistic accounts of the fighting on the Western Front. Everyone with an interest in the First World War owes Jack Sheldon a debt of gratitude for his scholarship and his painstaking work. More than anyone else writing in English in recent years, he has given the ordinary German soldier of the First World War a human face. That is not the least of his achievements.

Gary Sheffield
Centre for First World War Studies, University of Birmingham
December 2007

Introduction

The name Vimy Ridge instantly conjures up visions of the great Canadian National Memorial which stands proudly on Hill 145, commemorating the seizure of the Ridge during the opening phase of the Battle of Arras in April 1917. Yet Vimy Ridge is so much more than Hill 145 and its history far more complex and heroic than its ultimate capture alone – dramatic though that undoubtedly was. One of the best places to view and appreciate its full extent is from the road between La Gueule d'Ours and Willerval, three kilometres east of the village of Vimy. From there the tactical significance of its extension to the southeast of Farbus becomes clear. In fact, the high ground runs for fourteen kilometres, all the way to the Scarpe; its overall length being such that it took the combined efforts of both the Canadian Corps and XVII Corps to capture it in its entirety.

In all, Vimy Ridge and the surrounding area were fought over on four major occasions during the war. The first of these occurred during September and October 1914, when desperate French defensive measures held the German advance in the Arras area during the so-called 'Race to the Sea'. There was constant skirmishing and some intense fighting, especially on the Lorette Spur to the west of Souchez, during the following winter; then spring and autumn 1915 saw the launch of two large scale offensives by the French Tenth Army, which aimed to recapture the Ridge and break the German lines in Artois. Both failed at enormous cost to both sides, but the French army in particular, which suffered a total of 150,000 casualties during the major fighting alone, was especially badly hit and morale suffered proportionately.

It is important to stress the dimensions of these 1915 battles, because it was then that the French army, in a series of massive battles of extraordinary savagery (which have totally disappeared from popular memory), took on formations of the German army at the height of their powers and succeeded in so damaging the defensive posture of the German army and cramping it for space west of the Ridge that the final assault of April 1917 was made possible. In addition, the outstanding performance of the Moroccan Division on 9 May 1915 should never be forgotten. Due to failures elsewhere within the French Tenth Army, its precarious hold on Hill 145 was smashed by German counter-attacks, but it remains a feat of arms comparable with the finest achieved anywhere on the Western Front during four years of war.

The need to reduce the pressure on the French army led to the British army assuming responsibility for Vimy Ridge from March 1916 then, in the November of that year, their costly battles for Courcelette and Regina Trench behind them, the men of the Canadian Corps began to depart the Somme and take over the lines from which they would ultimately launch the fourth of these assaults which would lead to the Victory at Vimy and, for many, the emergence of Canada as a proud nation state. The quiet period when British units manned the trenches from Souchez to Arras has given rise to one of the strangest myths about Vimy Ridge, one that needs to be scotched firmly at the outset.

Statements, both written and spoken, about the victory, regularly make much of the fact that Canadian troops succeeded where the French and the remainder of the British army had failed. Some authors even choose to spell out the losses allegedly suffered by the British army in the attempt to take the Ridge; one recent estimate putting the number at 100,000 (almost one quarter of the total number of casualties suffered during the Battle of the Somme). It is true that the arrival of British units put an end to Vimy Ridge being the quiet 'live and let live' front it had become since the fighting died away in October 1915, mining and counter-mining increased in intensity and, in the wake of Operation *Schleswig Holstein* in May 1916, the then Commander of the British IV Corps, Lieutenant General Sir Henry Wilson, did press for additional resources to allow him at least to restore the ground lost. He was overruled by Sir Douglas Haig, whose priority then and throughout 1916 was the Battle of the Somme. There was *never* the slightest attempt to capture Vimy Ridge between the French offensive of autumn 1915 and the triumph of the Canadians in April 1917 and the casualties suffered in this sector, though not insignificant, were very slight compared with those on the Somme. The most costly period was 22–24 May 1916 when British losses in killed, wounded and missing were about 2,500 and the Germans roughly half that figure.

Whilst on the subject of myth, it is important also to dispose of the notion that Vimy Ridge was as good as impregnable. One of the main reasons why the German army fought so hard to maintain the front as far to the west of the Ridge as possible, despite the loss of the Lorette Spur which meant that large lengths of it could be observed by the Allies, was to overcome the unpalatable, but inescapable, geographical fact that the Ridge itself was, from autumn 1915 onwards, extremely vulnerable to determined attack. It was, for example, only 700 metres wide at its narrowest point near Hill 145. Long before the Somme battles, the German army was well aware of the need for depth in defence – especially here at Vimy Ridge where placement of the gun lines was exceptionally difficult. Given the range of contemporary guns and restrictions on the barrel elevation of the field guns, being forced to place some of these critical weapons to the east of the Vimy Ridge greatly affected their usefulness.

It was not even easy to construct the infantry positions scientifically. A *Zwischenstellung* [Intermediate Position] was developed to the rear of the three lines of the First Position, but parts of it were not well placed. The Second Position, for want of anything better, had to be dug along the base of the eastern slopes of Vimy Ridge, which was obviously a totally unviable location once the crest line was lost to the defence. As a result, well before the battles of April 1917, work had begun on a Third Position some kilometres to the east of the Ridge.

Running north – south past Sallaumines, Méricourt, Acheville and Fresnoy to Oppy and Gavrelle, it provided a fall–back position for the defence; one which was resorted to by mid April 1917, but it was in no way comparable to the heavily wired and concreted defences of the Hindenburg Line to the south.

The only hope for the defence in early 1917 was to hold the First Position in sufficient strength to be able to fend off an Allied attack until operational reserves could be rushed forward. This front-loading of the defence, which led to a high density of German divisions holding the line between Lens and the Scarpe, went against all the lessons learned on the Somme, but there was no obvious alternative. Worse still, the dugouts, originally produced when the First Position was further west, were mostly clustered in the front line trench itself. This left them vulnerable to destructive fire and meant, in the event of Allied penetrations, that large numbers of defenders were vulnerable to being encircled – precisely what happened on 9 April 1917.

It was not that the German chain of command was unaware of these difficulties. Ludendorff was briefed in person about the issues at Headquarters I Bavarian Reserve Corps in mid-March 1917. The problem was that pressure of events on the Somme the previous year had led to Sixth Army, like all other non-engaged formations along the northern half of the Western Front, being starved of manpower and resources. As a result it had proved to be impossible to dig sufficient dugouts further back and the ill-placed ones had to be used. Every effort was made by incoming troops to better the situation, but the winter weather, bombardments and Canadian pressure all militated against significant improvement.

That said, the active patrolling policy within the Canadian Corps in the early part of 1917 was something of a two-edged sword. It may well have made the defenders edgy and contributed to the wearing down of their morale but, inevitably, the very frequency of patrols and raids caused the defenders to pay great attention to measures designed to avoid being surprised and to develop highly efficient means of alerting their artillery, as the Canadians found out to their cost on numerous occasions. The capture of German troops may have helped the Allied intelligence staffs to build up a picture of the defences, but there can be little doubt that any gains in this area were offset entirely by the quantity and quality of intelligence extracted by German interrogators from Allied prisoners. In the case of the Canadian Corps, there was an additional negative factor. These raids were costly, accounting for a considerable proportion of all casualties suffered by the Canadians in the Vimy area. The losses during the raids of 13 February and 1 March 1917 alone, for example, amounted to 150 out of 900 and 687 out of 1,700 participants respectively; whilst between 20 March and the opening of the offensive on 9 April, there were Canadian raids every night, at a cost of approximately 1,400 casualties.

It may be a coincidence, but the 4th Canadian Division, which appears to have pursued the most active raiding policy and to have suffered the worst of the casualties (including those associated with the catastrophic failure on 1 March 1917) as a result was also the formation which had the biggest problems achieving its objectives on Vimy Ridge – despite having the least distance to advance. Could the loss of comparatively large numbers of high quality junior officers and NCOs and increased wariness on behalf of men, who had been called on to carry out too many frontal assaults already, have diluted their aggression and the quality of their minor tactics?

Major General Arthur Currie, Commander 1st Canadian Division and rightly regarded as the best of the generals that Canada produced during the First World War, was known to be against raiding for the sake of it. As a result, his casualties before the main battle were slight and the advance of his men on 9 April 1917 was carried out with speed and panache, despite the need along the way to deal with isolated pockets of resistance, all of which had to be subdued by the use of section and platoon attacks.

Interesting to note, the Germans had a number of negative comments to make about the standard of tactics used by the attackers at Vimy Ridge when they came to analyse the reverse and to draw the lessons from it. This may seem odd, in view of the fact that the German defenders were comprehensively defeated; but there may be something in such statements, other than expressions of institutionalised bravado.

Much of the battle was over very quickly. Guns and infantry positions were overrun and large numbers of prisoners were taken. But between 9 and 12 April 1917 this operation cost the Canadian Corps some ten thousand casualties, which somebody or something, other than just misdirected Allied fire, must have caused. It is known from the German records that general wastage, sickness and high casualties amongst the infantry during the build up to the battle meant that most front line sub-units were down to strengths of eighty men or fewer when the assault was launched. In some places the defence, therefore, could only put up one man for each four or five metres of front – an apparently hopelessly weak position; yet the survivors must have fought hard.

It is known, for example, from analysis of the records for Reserve Infantry Regiment 261, defending Hill 145, that its forward defence was initially conducted by only four weak companies – from north to south 9th, 11th, 1st and 3rd. In other words, the First Position was manned by 3rd Battalion in the north and 1st Battalion in the south. The 2nd Battalion was in brigade reserve throughout and, with the exception of 5th Company, which lost seventeen men killed in the defence of the *Zwischenstellung* [Intermediate Position], had hardly any casualties at all. So during the battle for the key terrain, a total of eight understrength companies, four in the ground holding role and four responsible for counter-attacks, held off the entire 4th Canadian Division efforts in Sector *Fischer* for nearly two days at a cost of 190 men killed or missing believed killed, approximately 430 missing (presumably captured) and about 250 wounded and evacuated. Given that Canadian losses in killed and wounded were considerably higher this represents a *local* outcome very much in favour of the defending troops. In the end the remnants of Reserve Infantry Regiment 261 were ordered back from their exposed final positions on the eastern edge of the crest line, which certainly explains why the name *Vimy* was in pride of place on the regimental banner after the war, why there was a considerable haul of medals following the battle and why, lessons learned and applied, the German army went into the Third Battle of Ypres convinced that it had a working answer to Allied tactics and the power of the gun.

Jack Sheldon
Vercors, September 2007

jandl50@hotmail.com

Author's Note

The Germans never differentiated between English, Scottish, Irish or Welsh soldiers and units, referring to them all as Engländer. This usage was frequently extended to contingents from the Dominions as well. Engländer *has been translated throughout as 'British' for troops from the United Kingdom and usually adjusted where other nationalities were involved.*

German time, which was one hour ahead of British time, is used throughout the book.

Acknowledgements

This book, like the previous ones in the series, could not have been written without the use of the huge legacy of German regimental histories, generally written during the interwar period as a labour of love by former serving officers on behalf of their regimental associations. The care with which this was done in so many cases goes a long way to overcome the handicap of the lack of the Prussian archives, which were largely destroyed at the end of the Second World War during a bombing raid on Potsdam. Of fundamental importance in the writing of this book, however, is the fact that so much of the fighting on Vimy Ridge during the thirty months it was in German hands, was carried out by Bavarian troops, under Bavarian commanders – latterly right up to Army Group level. This means that staggering quantities of primary source material are available for study in Munich and I am most grateful to the Director and Staff of the *Kriegsarchiv* for all their help during the research process.

My special thanks are due to Professor Gary Sheffield for contributing the Foreword. Professor Sheffield, through tireless effort over many years, has forced us to re-evaluate many of the long-standing interpretations of the Great War and the field of study has been much enriched by his contributions. My editor, Nigel Cave, has once again kept me firmly on track and I am grateful to him, as I am, too, for the expert advice and material help I have received from Lieutenant Colonel Phillip Robinson RE of the Durand Group concerning mining under Vimy Ridge. Nevertheless I am conscious that, in tackling this technically complex subject, I may have introduced some errors, which are entirely my responsibility.

Canadian Great War expert Ted Wigley cleverly solved the mystery of the name under which the deserter Otto Ludwig Dörr served in the Canadian army and generously passed on the information to me via Chris Wight. Mick Forsyth kindly assisted with suggested translations of obscure German words and supplied me with a most useful glossary of German mining terms. I am also grateful to Eddy Lambrecht for his assistance in obtaining photographs. My wife Laurie has once more prepared the maps and helped me greatly through her love and support. The friendly team at Pen and Sword Books have all made the process of seeing the book through to publication a pleasure and I thank them all. Every effort has been made to avoid infringing copyright. Should this have occurred by some accident, I would ask that my sincere apologies be accepted.

CHAPTER ONE

The Capture and Consolidation of Vimy Ridge and the Surrounding Area

At the end of September 1914, as part of the attempt to unlock the temporary stalemate on the Western Front by moving the focus of operations north, the German XIV Reserve Corps was heavily engaged in an attempt to advance on the axis Bapaume – Albert – Amiens. As increasing French resistance caused the advance to slow, then stall, it was clear that not only had this attempt to outflank the French army failed, but that a risk was developing further north that the French might turn the tables and carry out an outflanking manoeuvre of their own. Five German cavalry divisions (Guards, 2nd, 4th, 7th and 9th) were already heavily engaged with French cavalry and infantry formations as they attempted to secure the open flank. Meanwhile, reports from agents were being processed by the German High Command that French and British formations in unknown strength were assembling in the Arras – Lille area, that the railway network between Lille, Douai and Arras had been secured and that the rough line Orchies – Douai – Arras had been occupied by enemy pickets.

There could no longer be any doubt that a serious attempt was underway to outflank the German army away to the north of where Sixth Army was currently operating. Counter-measures were set in train urgently. As a preliminary step 1st Guards Infantry Division and IV Corps were deployed to the north of XIV Reserve Corps, with the twin objectives of relieving the pressure there and freeing up part of the cavalry for use elsewhere. Away to the south, I Bavarian Reserve Corps, commanded by General der Infanterie von Fasbender, was withdrawn from Lorraine and rushed north via Luxemburg, Liège, Namur and Mons towards Cambrai and Valenciennes; the aim being to concentrate swiftly then to launch forward via Douai in an attempt to outflank the left wing of the French army.

By midday 30 September, about half of the formations of I Bavarian Reserve Corps had arrived. Generalleutnant Alfred Göringer's 1st Reserve Division detrained in Cambrai and Lourches, whilst 5th Bavarian Reserve Division, commanded by Generalleutnant Friedrich Freiherr Kreß von Kressenstein, was assembling in Denain and Valenciennes. At 11.30 am I Bavarian Reserve Corps ordered the divisions to march off immediately with every available man, with the aim of doing everything possible to reach Douai by that evening. By 1.00 pm 1st Reserve Division was on the march northwest from Cambrai and heading towards Douai with five battalions (Bavarian Reserve Infantry Regiment 3 complete and 1st and 2nd Battalions Bavarian Reserve Infantry Regiment 12) and the reserve engineer company; the move being supported by 2nd Battalion Bavarian Reserve Field Artillery Regiment 1. The elements of 5th Bavarian Reserve Division which had arrived in Denain, namely Bavarian Reserve Infantry Regiment 6 and 1st and 2nd Battalions Bavarian Reserve Infantry Regiment 7 set off towards Auberchicourt, there to assemble, prior to moving off at 3.30 pm towards Douai, which lay to the west.

The commander of 5th Bavarian Reserve Division despatched its organic cavalry (Bavarian Reserve Cavalry Regiment 5) forward in a screening manoeuvre as far as the Scarpe bridges in Marchiennes and Vred, then advanced along its axis, with two battalions from Bavarian Reserve Infantry Regiment 7 north of the road to provide flank protection. The adoption of this formation paid off when, later in the day, the French put up strong resistance in and around Lewarde, about six kilometres from Douai. Not until 8.00 pm did 2nd Battalion Reserve Infantry Regiment 6 succeed in ejecting the enemy from Lewarde, so the entire division bivouacked for the night in the village and surrounding localities. 1st Bavarian Reserve Division also managed to close up to within about six kilometres of Douai by the evening, having had to fight to drive the French out of the villages of Cantin and Roucourt and so having lost several hours. Further to the rear almost all the remaining units of the corps had arrived, so its formations were well placed to carry out its overnight orders: 'The Corps is to capture Douai and the heights to the west of the town tomorrow.'[1]

The plan envisaged 5th Bavarian Reserve Division advancing from the east, with 1st Bavarian Reserve Division approaching the town from the southeast. Whilst the inner regiments fixed the defence in Douai, the flanking formations would sweep in wide arcs around Douai: 5th Bavarian Reserve Division to the north, 1st Bavarian Reserve Division to the south, prior to closing the ring around the town to the northwest at Esquerchin. In the event the distances involved were simply too great and there was too much resistance; the regiments found themselves repeatedly involved in skirmishes for minor places and no single unit reached Esquerchin that day. Nevertheless the manoeuvre succeeded in bringing about the fall of Douai. Fighting continued in the built up area until nightfall, by which time large quantities of equipment and 900 Frenchmen, including nine officers, had been captured. By the following day the number had increased to about 2,000, most of whom were men of the 5th, 6th and 7th Territorial Regiments. It was alleged by the German attackers that they were fired at in Douai by civilians. Generalleutnant Hurt, commander of 9 Bavarian Infantry Brigade, immediately imposed a fine of 300,000 Francs on the town, which was speedily paid by the authorities.

Hauptmann Motschenbacher 3rd Battalion Bavarian Reserve Infantry Regiment 6 [2]

"Towards 3.00 pm the battalion reached the Dechy – Douai road, to the west of Dechy. The advance guard bumped into a minor roadblock, comprising several wagons pushed together. It was defended by a group of French cycle troops, who withdrew in the direction of Douai after a short exchange of fire. Because the situation was unclear I halted the battalion and sent a report to Brigade giving its location and details of its route. This report was received with some surprise by Brigade, because of the amount of ground the battalion had covered. Greater enemy resistance had been expected. Nevertheless the Brigade ordered a continuation of the march to Douai and, despite minor skirmishes, the troops arrived at the railway overpass to the east of Douai. It was not possible to advance any further for the time being. The enemy had placed a group of wagons armed with machine guns on the edge of Douai, where they could bring fire to bear on the road.

"When the advance stalled I moved to the head of my troops, taking up a position with my staff in the firing line in the courtyard of a factory, beneath its tall chimney. We could easily observe the armoured wagons, but our rifle fire seemed to have little effect on them. In order to minimise infantry casualties, I called for artillery support. I did not have the impression that we were up against particularly determined troops and felt that a few shells would dislodge them and clear the way for us. The first shell arrived and struck the centre of the high chimney about half way up, taking a large piece out of it. Splinters rained down on us, covering us liberally with red brick dust. As a result of this we kept one eye on the chimney in case it was going to collapse on us and the other on the armoured wagon. Luckily the artillery battalion commander arrived on the scene and I was able to point out both the wayward impact of the shell and the armoured wagon. Fortunately the next rounds were on target and the armoured wagon disappeared.

"In the meantime night had drawn in and we launched our assault. With rifles at the ready and bayonets fixed, the troops forced their way through the city gates and into the town. Every likely or actual target was hit by extremely heavy fire. The extraordinarily loud sounds in the narrow streets, which were lined by tall buildings, certainly had the effect of forcing the French defenders to pull back hastily, but it had such an effect on the nerves of our victorious troops that it acted almost like a drug and made command and control from difficult to impossible. Gradually the excitement died down and rapid progress was made to the market place, where we paused and re-grouped before pushing on through the town in a westerly direction.

"In the meantime night had fallen. The leading platoon bumped up against a column of abandoned wagons in one of the darkened streets. Once more fire was opened along the street as the enemy fled and hammered against the walls of house from which fire was coming. Everywhere there was the hellish din of battle. Finally the situation quietened down. The French seemed to have disappeared; the streets and houses appeared to be as quiet as the grave. Of course this was not the case, so strong patrols were used throughout the night to maintain contact with the companies which had been pushed out in a line to picket the western edge of the town, whilst the remainder of the battalion settled down along the main street or in the courtyards of the adjacent houses.

"Up until midnight reports kept coming in that French soldiers, who were sheltering in various houses, wished to surrender. There were several hundred of them. The prisoners were assembled in the church which had never had so many visitors. Once I had reported to brigade headquarters in the town hall and informed them about the large quantities of men and materiel that had been captured and where the picket line had been established, I went at about 2.00 am to the battalion command post. This had been established in the villa belonging to the Douai Public Prosecutor. I greeted him, calmed him down and, through him, his extremely anxious wife. A loud laugh drew me into the kitchen. There the twenty five year old son of the house, smartly dressed in a cutaway jacket and striped trousers, was sitting on the kitchen stool grinding coffee for the bold Bavarian Reserve Sixth. They had certainly earned a cup."

There being no time to lose, despite this success, I Bavarian Reserve Corps ordered a continuation of the advance for 2 October. 1st Bavarian Reserve Division was to advance via Brebières to St Laurent, whilst 5th Bavarian Reserve Division was to march via Izel and Oppy to Bailleul. This would mean that the corps was concentrated and deployed about four kilometres from Arras. Although the corps only knew for certain that the French 70th Reserve Division was on the march from the northwest in the direction of Bailleul, it appeared to take for granted that St Laurent and Bailleul would be reached, because it went on to direct how long the formations were to pause in those places, prior to continuing the advance on Arras. Subsequently the French 70th Reserve Division operations plan was captured and the Germans were able to reconstruct exactly what the French intentions had been.

The French 70th Reserve Division, commanded by General Fayolle, which was still on the march in the direction of Lens, had been directed to deny its left flank to threats from Douai, to advance towards Gavrelle and Fresnes and to link up to the right with the French 77th Division under General Barbot,[3] which was concentrating in the area of Neuville Vitasse to the south east of Arras. Both divisions had been rushed north from the Vosges front and their actual employment on arrival had only been decided at the last minute.[4] In order to carry out this order, the French 139 Brigade was despatched towards Fresnes, via Bois Bernard and Neuvireuil, whilst maintaining a strong flank guard to cover its left. The French 140 Brigade was directed to march southwest towards Gavrelle from Bois Bernard. Once they reached Fresnes and Gavrelle, the main bodies of these

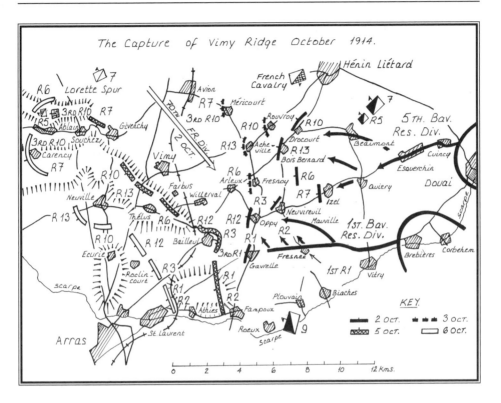

formations were to pause during the evening of 2 October and to push forward an outpost line to the south.

All these manoeuvrings meant that the on 2 October two French columns, each in brigade strength, were advancing in parallel from north to south whilst, simultaneously, two German columns, each in divisional strength, were moving from east to west. The French were trying to screen off Arras and the Germans to get there first. There could only be one result for these converging forces. The French 139 Brigade was going to bump straight into the 5th Bavarian Reserve Division, followed closely by the clash of the French 140 Brigade and the 1st Bavarian Reserve Division. In order to follow the course of events, the experience of the 5th Bavarian Reserve Division will be covered first. In the absence of cavalry reinforcements, it was left to the weak divisional cavalry regiment to attempt to scout out to the north and west. Furthermore, the division had to provide its own rearguard, earmarking 2nd Battalion Bavarian Reserve Infantry Regiment 7 and 1st Battalion Bavarian Reserve Infantry Regiment 13 for the purpose. The leading elements of 9 Bavarian Reserve Brigade had barely reached Esquerchin when the threatening situation to the north forced the divisional commander to strengthen the flank guard, commanded by Major von Grundherr, thus removing 3rd Battalion Bavarian Reserve Infantry Regiment 6, the remainder of Bavarian Reserve Cavalry Regiment 5 and 3rd Battery Bavarian Reserve Field Artillery Regiment 5 from the advance.

By about midday leading elements of 9 Bavarian Reserve Brigade had reached the western edge of Quiéry la Motte and the main body of 11 Bavarian Reserve Brigade was at Esquerchin, but then French resistance began to increase. Three French batteries galloped into position near a copse northwest of Izel and began bringing down concentrated fire on both the German advance guard and main body. An attempt by 2nd Battery Bavarian Reserve Field Artillery Regiment 5 to bring down counter-battery fire from a position just to the north of Quiéry la Motte foundered instantly; it was shot to pieces. Its commander, Hauptmann Ruff, and many of his gunners were killed. As if this was not enough, French skirmishers emerged from Drocourt and advanced towards the German columns, which had no choice but to deploy to meet the threat. Bavarian Reserve Infantry Regiment 7 (less its 2nd Battalion) worked its way forward to within 500 metres of the French lines at Izel and the two remaining battalions of Bavarian Reserve Infantry Regiment 6 extended this line to the north under heavy fire until it could challenge the copse where the three French artillery batteries were operating.

In the meantime 11 Bavarian Reserve Brigade pushed northwest towards Beaumont from Esquerchin, collected part of the flank protection party and pressed on towards Drocourt and Bois Bernard to the west. This manoeuvre was also supported by the rearguard, which was moved to the north to prevent enemy cavalry interfering with the thrust of the brigade towards the west. The move came not a moment too soon. The two battalions were quickly in action, successfully countering a determined French attack from the direction of Hénin Liétard. At more or less the same time, about 4.00 pm, Bavarian 9 and 11 Brigades launched attacks, which were immediately successful. Bavarian Reserve Infantry Regiment 7 fought its way into Izel and Bavarian Reserve Infantry Regiment 6 captured the copse to the northwest, together with three guns and six ammunition wagons. At 4.45 pm, Bavarian Reserve Infantry Regiment 13 stormed and took the heights 1,500 metres east of Bois Bernard, whilst Bavarian Reserve Infantry Regiment 10 captured Beaumont Station.

At 7.00 pm Bavarian Reserve Infantry Regiment 10 took Drocourt and a little later. Bavarian Reserve Infantry Regiment 13, assisted by Bavarian Reserve Infantry Regiment 6, entered Bois Bernard (whose capture was not completed until the following morning).[5] As a result of this action, the storming of the area of Fosse 1, Drocourt by Bavarian Reserve Infantry Regiment 10 and the capture by Bavarian Reserve Infantry Regiment 6 after heavy street fighting of the village of Fresnoy, the front line on 3 October now ran Drocourt – Bois Bernard – Fresnoy.

Wehrmann Georg Preiß 4th Company Bavarian Reserve Infantry Regiment 6 [6]

"Although it was already going dark, we had to capture the wood to our front. Working our way forward in tactical bounds, we worked our way forward and we had soon reached the woodland with only light casualties. Thanks to the full moonlight, we could see the village of Fresnoy en Gohelle about 500 metres away. It was to be a bloody battlefield for us. Not a sound could be heard coming from the village, so we front line soldiers knew only too well what that meant. A dead horse was lying between the edge of the wood and field. A comrade of mine and I were settling down to spend the night behind it, when at 12.30 am we received orders that the village was to be captured. We deployed silently, fixed bayonets and, linking with the company on our right, we set off in the direction of the village.

"When we had closed up to only about eighty metres, we heard shouts of 'Hoorah' off on the right flank. Simultaneously there was an enormous burst of firing. It was the most violent we had ever experienced and we threw ourselves down on the ground, some behind stacked sheaves of corn. The French continued to fire from time to time and we replied in kind. About 5.00 am orders arrived that we were to withdraw some distance because our artillery was going to bring the village under fire. This was far from easy in the hail of fire the French were bringing down and a number of our brave comrades fell. At around 7.00 am our gunners started firing on the village. It was a tremendous spectacle. As soon as the first shells started to fall, the French immediately broke for the rear.

"For many of them, however, it was already too late. A second assault led to the capture of the village unopposed. As we entered the village we saw how heavy the casualties had been on both sides. Many of them were German, but a great many more were French. We spent the rest of the day and the next night in the village, but there was no question of sleep. The following morning we headed off again, capturing Arleux, Farbus and Thélus, with varying degrees of difficulty."

Down to the southeast, Bavarian Reserve Infantry Regiment 7, the advance guard of Bavarian 9 Brigade, could make no progress against Neuvireuil, being pinned down by small arms fire from the French infantry and the fire of a French heavy battery somewhere near Acheville. It was forced to dig in midway between Izel and Neuvireuil. Meanwhile, 1st Bavarian Reserve Division had pushed forward from Brebières, beginning at 8.00 am. Taking the lead was 1 Bavarian Reserve Brigade, commanded by Generalleutant von Kneußl; following up Generalleutnant von Graf's 2 Bavarian Reserve Brigade. Because its right flank was protected by 5th Bavarian Reserve Division and its left by IV Corps and the 9th Cavalry Division operating in the valley of the Scarpe, the division was able to close right up on Fresnes without having to give battle. By 11.00 am, however, it was beginning to clash with enemy patrols. Furthermore, although the situation to the north and northwest was unclear, it was obvious that 5th Bavarian Reserve Division had run into problems and had been delayed. There was nothing for it but to press on, putting out flank protection to the north. This was done, but the main body, advancing further towards the outskirts of Gavrelle, suddenly came under small arms and artillery fire from Oppy. Hurriedly deploying, the units and formations of 1st Bavarian Reserve Division soon found themselves drawn into a battle which lasted for hours and caused them serious casualties. Pinned down by small arms fire from the edges of the villages of Oppy and Neuvireuil and taking casualties from constant HE and shrapnel fire from the direction of Arras, the troops could only stick it out and await the arrival of 5th Bavarian Reserve Division, but of that formation there was still no sign.

By 4.45 pm, the divisional commander had decided to direct the remaining four battalions of 2 Bavarian Reserve Brigade to advance via Mauville Farm and capture Neuvireuil and Oppy. The torrent of French fire made these orders extremely difficult to carry out. It was not until 9.00 pm that Bavarian Reserve Infantry Regiment 3 captured Neuvireuil and, despite the joint efforts of 3rd Battalion Bavarian Reserve Infantry Regiment 12 and 2nd Battalion Bavarian Reserve Infantry Regiment 3, it was almost midnight before Oppy fell. 1st Bavarian Reserve Division then went into hasty defence in the area Neuvireuil – Oppy – Gavrelle- Fresnes and, during the late evening, contact was finally established with 5th Bavarian Reserve Division along the road towards Izel. It meant that the Corps orders had not been fulfilled. Instead of reaching the line St Laurent – Bailleul, only the line Drocourt – Gavrelle, somewhat to the northeast, had been achieved. On the positive side, however, the Corps had held the attack of the French 70th Reserve Division on its flank and forced it back to the northwest. It had failed to get through to Arras, the way to which now appeared to be clear.

Oberst Max Helbling Bavarian Reserve Infantry Regiment 2 [7]

"Suddenly, at 11.45 am came an order from Division: 'Stand to your arms! Enemy infantry are advancing against our right flank from the direction of Neuvireuil and are already very close' . . . In no time at all, the 3rd Battalion (Foerst) was involved in a fire fight with French *chasseurs*. The 2nd Battalion (Haselmayr) was next to follow up, echeloned to the right. The 8th Company swiftly extended the line of the 3rd Battalion whilst 5th and 7th Companies became involved in a costly battle with a new enemy battalion-sized group, which was occupying a clump of five trees on the enemy left flank. The 6th Company (Molenaar), together with the Machine Gun Company remained at Mauville Farm, where the regimental headquarters had also been hastily established. The farm provided excellent observation, but was under constant enemy artillery fire . . .

"Despite maintaining a sharp look out, nothing could be seen of the 5th Bavarian Reserve Division and no information was received from that source. As a result the regiment sent mounted men to Izel to link up and obtain situation reports. Because the regiment was coming under very accurate fire from the French *chasseurs*, Seuffert's Battery, from battalion Reuß, was brought into action near Mauville Farm. Having been briefed exhaustively by the infantry regiment commander, the battery homed in on the *chasseur* battalion by the clump of trees from the rear, avoiding bracketing the target as the fire was adjusted. Once on target a few well-directed salvoes obtained a decisive result by completely destroying the French *chasseur* battalion. At that, the 5th and 7th Companies launched an assault, taking the objective and hanging on grimly until 5th Bavarian Reserve Division arrived later . . .

"Now it was possible to make out that the 5th Bavarian Reserve Division was involved in heavy fighting around Izel. After careful observation, a well-camouflaged group of French artillery was detected. Battalion Reuß was summoned and directed onto the target by the regimental commander. In an instant the fire had a dreadful effect. The French artillery raced westwards, one gun at a time, past a mill located between Izel and Neuvireuil, but each in turn was engaged by our artillery and infantry and all the guns were destroyed or abandoned. Although it was not clear to them at the time, a powerful blow had been struck on behalf of 5th Bavarian Reserve Division, making things much easier for them subsequently.

"Now, however, a force of French infantry, in a strength of about two regiments, launched forward from the direction of Neuvireuil. The regimental commander, who was co-located with the artillery commander and his observers, directed that the increased French artillery fire which was falling on and around Mauville farm and which had already killed Reserve Leutnant Molenaar, commander of 6th Company, was to be ignored. Instead, the guns were to be trained on the French infantry and were to engage these troops when they deployed. When, at about 2.00 pm, at least one full-strength French infantry regiment deployed and began what they thought was a covered flanking manoeuvre we waited until they were approaching the place where their artillery had been destroyed earlier, then the regimental commander ordered the artillery to spring the trap.

"The effect of this fire from a flank was indescribable. As though caught by an electric shock, the red-trousered troops scattered, fleeing for all they were worth in the direction of Bois-Bernard to the north and towards the mill, all the time pursued by a storm of shells and shrapnel rounds. This action came as a rare, but brilliant, success for the regiment and our artillery. Having cleared the way for the 5th Bavarian Reserve Division it could now harvest the fruit of this action. At about 5.00 pm the flank of this division (Brigade Hurt) advanced unmolested via the mill towards Neuvireuil. The intention of the French XX Corps to hit the German IV Corps hard in the flank by means of three columns: right via Bailleul, centre and strongest, via Neuvireuil and left via Izel was brilliantly wrecked by the advance of the Reserve Corps, coupled with the victorious fight of 1 Bavarian Reserve Brigade and the forward thrust of 5th Bavarian Reserve Division.

"Nevertheless the French made desperate attempts to delay the left flank of 5th Bavarian Reserve Division, by means of artillery concentrations, but the effect was only partial and temporary and the northern flank of this division continued to advance . . . [8]

Unsurprisingly, the orders for 3 October were for the vigorous continuation of the advance on Arras. In order to facilitate progress, artillery units were moved forward during the night and the four cavalry divisions operating in the valley of the Scarpe (Guards, 4th, 7th and 9th) were given deception and supporting roles. On the assumption that these army cavalry formations would intervene to the north, the intention was to swing the divisions of I Bavarian Reserve Corps once more round to the west. 5th Bavarian Reserve Division was given as its objective the line Vimy-Thélus, 1st Bavarian Reserve Division the line Thélus – St Laurent. These advances were predicated upon effective cavalry intervention in the north, followed by probing attacks to the south to unhinge the French defences. No such thing happened. The cavalry were slow off the mark, which meant that the infantry of I Bavarian Reserve Corps was tied down protecting the gains of the previous day or countering fresh threats further to the north until 3 October was well advanced then, when the cavalry finally worked its way to the north, a combination of intensive urbanisation and the operations of the French defenders prevented them from getting forward.

Finally, 7th Cavalry Division arrived in the area of Beaumont in mid-afternoon and was able to assist 9 Bavarian Reserve Brigade to advance on and capture Méricourt, which was finally secured by Bavarian Reserve Infantry Regiment 7 at about 7.00 pm. Once this brigade had begun to move it was possible for other regiments of the 5th Bavarian Reserve Division to commence operations. By 3.30 pm Rouvroy was captured by Bavarian Reserve Infantry Regiment 10 and Acheville fell to Bavarian Reserve Infantry Regiment 13 about 4.00 pm. However an attempt at 7.00 pm by Bavarian Reserve Infantry Regiment 6 to launch an assault on Arleux from a distance of about 500 metres failed, despite the fact that all three battalions of the regiment were once more concentrated and deployed in the attack. In a disappointing day for the German army, the sole gains were the three villages listed above; the line Arleux – Bailleul – Point du Jour was still firmly held by the French.

Oblivious to the increasing exhaustion of the infantry regiments, orders arrived late on 3 October that the advance was to be continued. These can be summed up succinctly as, 'Get forward! Continue the advance throughout the night! Set off immediately!' Already the previous night General von Falkenhayn was becoming frustrated at the turn of events. He had fully expected to make rapid progress westwards in this area and it was simply not happening.[9] The weary troops did their best to comply. Despite continual exhortations, local geography and the presence of stiffening French resistance reduced the ability of the cavalry which could not operate effectively to the north, so 'Group Hurt' on the extreme right flank took on the task of flank protection, in addition to pressing forward from Méricourt to Avion. 'Group Samhaber' was given Vimy as its objective. It had proved impossible on 3 October for the regiments of 5th Bavarian Reserve Division to maintain continuity along its front and this tendency increased on 4 October. There was a gap of four kilometres between the two objectives ordered and the only consolation was the thought that, with French forces established on Vimy Ridge, the gap was completely overlooked; it could only have been filled at the price of high casualties due to artillery fire. Instead the aim was for the division to concentrate once more further to the west.

On receipt of his orders, Generalleutnant Hurt despatched 3rd Battalion Bavarian Reserve Infantry Regiment 10 to capture Avion. Unfortunately and not entirely surprisingly, the battalion got lost in the dark, so the same mission was given at 5.00 am to 1st Battalion Bavarian Reserve Infantry Regiment 7, which succeeded in launching its attack at 6.00 am and capturing Avion after a brief battle. The reminder of the brigade arrived at 8.00 am and the advance continued. As soon as the head of the column emerged from Avion French fire intensified. There was small arms fire from the front and artillery fire from the direction of Lens and Givenchy. The advance appeared to be about to stall, but Generalleutnant Hurt issued fresh orders to Bavarian Reserve Infantry Regiment 7 and its companies pressed on. Despite being under continuous heavy artillery fire the regiment pushed forward, working its way as far as the Lens-Arras road by midday. It then took over five hours to progress a further 400 metres to the west of the road where, as it began to get dark, the men collapsed, exhausted.

At that precise moment a 5th Bavarian Reserve Division liaison officer, Hauptmann Gürtler, arrived on the scene, bearing an urgent order from the divisional commander that the heights around Givenchy were to be captured at all costs that night and bringing a message from the Kaiser to the Army High command, in which he sent his greetings to the troops and expressed the wish to receive further reports of success that day. The regimental officers got their weary men back on their feet and the advance continued; pushing on past the copse where the French defence had been conducted so obstinately earlier in the day until, after a nightmare struggle, the wooded hill between Souchez and Givenchy, which became known as the *Gießlerhöhe* was finally cleared and wrested from its French defenders at around 2.30 am on 5 October.

As dawn approached the remainder of 'Group Hurt' arrived, having left Avion at about 4.30 am. Its units paused briefly on the edge of a wood to the south of Liévin, then 3rd Battalion Bavarian Reserve Infantry Regiment 10 swung south-west towards the wood about one and a half kilometres north east of Souchez [Bois de l'Abîme on the modern map]. Bavarian Reserve Cavalry Regiment 5, however, moving independently, had pushed on through the darkness in a westerly direction through the largely built up area, being observed somewhat sceptically by the local inhabitants as they moved silently along darkened streets.

At one critical point, Leutnant Hesselberger, who could speak French, calmed the situation by shouting out, 'We are British cavalry. There is no cause for alarm!' By 10.30 pm they were established on the heights to the west of Angres and went into bivouac. It had been an eventful advance.

Major Karl von Grundherr zu Altenhan und Weyerhaus Bavarian Reserve Cavalry Regiment 5 [10]

"It was 6.00 pm [4 October]. The buildings on the slopes to the east of Eleu could only be made out with difficulty. Our route took us past the southern outskirts of Lens. An axis was designated and an objective selected on the high ground to the east of Eleu. Leutnant Hesselberger and a few troopers were sent ahead to scout the route. The regiment followed up close behind the leading group and, moving partly through the outskirts of Lens and partly through the open ground crossed by railway tracks, arrived at the Vimy – Lens road. A barricade was swiftly dismantled. The leader of the scouts had reported that the hill was unoccupied and then ascertained from some of the inhabitants who came out of their houses that there was no enemy in the vicinity. By now it was completely dark and trees and bushes cast deep shadows.

"The regiment ascended the hill to the east of Eleu. A local inhabitant was seized. It was felt that because he was carrying a lamp on a pole that his activities were suspicious. To our front a light was flashing in a factory building which was supposed to contain a patrol of French Cuirassiers, One young leutnant requested permission to go and deal with it, but our objective was Angres, so we pressed on forward. Leutnant Hesselberger, who spoke French perfectly, took command of the advance guard, commandeering the services of various French workers as involuntary guides and, in this manner, we made our way along long rows of houses or workers' dwellings to the Lens – Liévin road. We made our way easily along the cobbled roads. There were lights on in the houses in Liévin and some of the inhabitants stood there gaping at us from their doors. The commander of the advance guard shot questions at them from time to time. They were generally scared to death and answered fearfully, giving mixed and confused responses.

"Asked if there were any Prussians about, they were eventually persuaded that we were a British cavalry unit and some of the bolder ones volunteered the information that French cuirassiers and artillery had ridden the same way earlier, but that they were not accompanied by infantry. We could not deviate from the route. One house followed another, so there was nothing for it but to ride on. Liévin and Angres have grown together, so the road seemed to be endless. A road in Angres led off to the right and, in the moonlight, we could make out stacks of straw, so we headed off up the hill. After a short move over open country we found ourselves to the north of Angres. This was our objective. The squadrons settled down in amongst the stacks of straw. One third of the regiment was on sentry duty, another third settled down with their arms ready to hand and the final third tended the horses. Small patrols were despatched to reconnoitre towards the road Souchez – Aix-Noulette and the area of Angres.

"Spahis were reported to the right and a gun battle opened up to our front. Both events were symptomatic of our edginess and exhaustion. The Spahis turned out to be locals moving about with baskets on their heads and the pickets to the front had engaged groups of workers who were making their way to work in Liévin. On the other hand, off to the left, lights could be seen on the heights south of the Souchez river and there was the sound of small arms fire right through until the early hours. It was now important to report to 'Group Hurt' that we had safely arrived on our objective, without coming into contact with the enemy. Leutnant Hesselberger and Kriegsfreiwilliger Hensolt both volunteered to ride back along the dangerous route with the report. Leutnant Hesselberger takes up the story: 'Together with Kriegsfreiwilliger Hensolt I rode back, arriving in the burning village of Avion, which had been assaulted a little earlier, about midnight. The general and his staff were located here. It was with a huge sigh of relief that I was able to deliver my report, but it was also a source of pride and satisfaction that the information which had been eagerly awaited was received so enthusiastically. The immediate outcome was that the infantry received orders to advance on Angres, being informed that the cavalry were already there . . .

"My return to the regiment was a whole lot less comfortable. It was far from heartening to be encouraged constantly to ride on by a series of stretcherbearers, who were carrying wounded men back for treatment. In any case we had no choice. The advancing infantry were engaged in fire fights with enemy infantry all around in the woods and streets, so it was essential that I got back to report this to the regiment. Bullets whizzed past us in all directions. My companion, who was of a philosophical bent, threw out the rhetorical question as to whether it was preferable to be hit by a German or French bullet. I did not stop to consider the implications of the question further, but spurred my horse into a gallop and carried on down the road a good pace. We were extremely pleased, and not just because of our report, to return to the regiment unscathed at about 4.00 am.'

"Dawn began to break and soon our victoriously advancing infantry arrived in our position, having driven the enemy before them, making us once more the bait in the mousetrap as they did so, but their arrival meant we could breathe easy and greet the new day of battle with fresh courage."

Aided by the continuation of the advance by the units of 'Group Hurt', the remaining two Groups from 5th Bavarian Reserve Division also made useful progress during the night 3/4 October. At around 3.00 am 'Group Samhaber' launched an attack on Acheville. In the course of a fierce battle, during which Oberst Hörst, commander of Bavarian Reserve Infantry Regiment 13, was severely wounded, the entire locality was secured during the hours of darkness. Even before daybreak, the first French positions, 400 metres west of Acheville, were captured and, by 7.30 am, the second French position was also taken. Maintaining the momentum, Bavarian Reserve Infantry Regiments 10 and 13 pressed on, until the advance wavered about 8.30 am approximately 800 metres short of the railway embankment to the east of Vimy.

At this precise moment a Corps ordered was received stating that, because the enemy appeared to be withdrawing, 5th Bavarian Reserve Division was to push on vigorously. In fact the underlying assumption was quite wrong; on the contrary, the French resistance was continuing to increase and Bavarian Reserve Infantry Regiments 10 and 13, whose men were utterly exhausted, simply could not get forward. To advance against the railway embankment and Vimy Ridge behind it, in broad daylight and without artillery support, seemed to offer no hope of success and there they remained all day. A divisional order arrived at 5.00pm, directing them to advance and capture the ridge and *Telegraphenhöhe* [Telegraph Hill = Modern Hill 139] behind it, but even that could not galvanise the men into action. Eventually reports began to spread (later confirmed by divisional headquarters) that the Kaiser had arrived at Corps Headquarters and sent greetings to the Bavarians and the hope that hills 140 and 132 would be captured.[11]

At that the Division despatched a fresh order; the attack was to be carried out 'at all costs' – a phrase that seemed to crop up far too frequently in orders at that time. Large supplies of wine had been seized earlier in Bois Bernard. This was distributed and, at 10.00 pm, the assault began. By 10.30 pm the railway embankment was in German hands. Pushing on in the darkness, the main mass thrusting to the south of Vimy, the heights were stormed. It was difficult to maintain direction in the dark, Hill 140 (La Folie) was by-passed accidentally and, instead, the troops found themselves reorganising on *Telegraphenhöhe* – allegedly to shouts of 'Hurrah for the Kaiser!' Fortunately for the Germans, the French army had evacuated both Telegraph Hill and Vimy itself.

The third Group of 5th Bavarian Reserve Division, 'Group Leibrock', based around Bavarian Reserve Infantry Regiment 6, also had a successful twenty four hour period between midnight 3/4 and midnight 4/5 October. Having launched an attack on Arleux at 2.00 am 4 October, one hour later the place was securely in German hands. The advance then continued, at the cost of considerable casualties, until Willerval was reached at 8.30 am. Although the railway embankment and Farbus were almost within touching distance, this attack also stalled until the evening of 4 October when, the divisional order and message from the Kaiser having been received by Bavarian Reserve Infantry Regiment 6, that attack was resumed as it went dark. Initially only 1st Battalion Bavarian Reserve Infantry Regiment 6 was involved, but as units to the north began to move forward, the 2nd and 3rd Battalions advanced, first against Farbus, which was quickly taken, then *Telegraphenhöhe* shortly after midnight.

5th Bavarian Reserve Division had certainly achieved considerable success that day; its front had been pushed a considerable distance to the west. Nevertheless, with the exception of *Telegraphenhöhe*, the French still controlled Vimy Ridge. In contrast, 1st Bavarian Reserve Division made no worthwhile progress at all. Bavarian Reserve Infantry Regiment 3 launched repeated assaults, but all withered away with many casualties in the face of resolute French small arms fire. Bailleul, in particular, was defended obstinately and the Germans could make no impression on it. It was as though a defensive ring had been thrown around Arras and that Bailleul had been earmarked as a crucial bastion of the defence. A gap began to develop between 1st Bavarian Reserve Division and 5th Bavarian Reserve Division, which of course was thrusting forward to the north of Arras.

On 5 October the hope was that the German cavalry would be able to press forward, overcoming French resistance and that 7th Cavalry Division would be able to make a further attempt to fall on the French left flank and rear. In the north, once Generalleutnant Hurt was informed that the cavalry had arrived nearby, he issued orders at 4.10 am 5 October that Bavarian Reserve Cavalry Regiment 5, supported by 10th Company 3rd Battalion Bavarian Reserve Infantry Regiment 10, was to advance and take Hill 165, Notre Dame de Lorette. By 6.00 am these forces were established on the Lorette Spur around the chapel, being joined later that morning by 11th Company. The occupation of this key feature may have occurred bloodlessly, but whilst the remainder of the brigade completed its concentration in the area bounded by Angres, Souchez and Givenchy, the Lorette Spur came under heavy French artillery bombardment from an arc running from northeast to northwest. For months to come the area would be under fire day and night.

5 October was the day that General Foch arrived to coordinate the operations of all the French forces north of the Oise. There was an immediate change in policy. Until that time, the French Tenth Army had been content to impose delay on the German invaders, yielding ground as slowly as possible. Foch insisted that every effort be made to seize the initiative.[12] Without any further delay the French infantry began to react. Hasty counter-attacks were conducted by French units from the area of La Folie against the Bavarians to the south east. Both sides settled down to a fire fight which lasted for several hours. No impression was made on the German troops and gradually it began to appear that the French, conscious that they had been outflanked on both sides, were beginning to pull back towards the west. Two large groups in approximately regimental strength [i.e. each over 2,000 men] were observed withdrawing through Neuville St Vaast and to the south of Carency. Vimy Ridge had obviously been evacuated. This ridge, the defence of which was to cost so much during the coming months, was

taken without a fight and the Corps was quick to issue orders for a follow up behind the retreating French formations. Hurt's formation was to advance along the line Souchez – Carency – Camblain, whilst that of Samhaber was directed via Neuville St Vaast – St Eloi towards Acq.

At around 2.00 pm, 2nd Battalion Bavarian Reserve Infantry Regiment 7 set off via Ablain for Carency, where it came under heavy French artillery fire and the advance ground to a halt in the eastern part of Carency. The remaining two battalions of Reserve Infantry Regiment 7 took up position on the heights to the south of Carency at about 6.00 pm and went firm there for the night. Reserve Infantry Regiment 10 from Group Samhaber concentrated in and around Souchez whilst, up on the Lorette Spur, Reserve Cavalry Regiments 5 and 10 and 2nd Battalion Reserve Infantry Regiment 10 took up hasty defence as leading elements of 7th Cavalry Division, whose advance had been severely delayed during the day, began to arrive. Only at that point could it be said that the cavalry was in a position to carry out its flank protection duties. In fact the assault on Carency was far from straightforward as this account by a member of Bavarian Reserve Infantry Regiment 7 shows clearly.

Hauptmann Schaidler 2nd Battalion Bavarian Reserve Infantry Regiment 7 [13]

"At 11.00 pm 4 October the regiment stormed Givenchy. The advance was continued after a short pause and, in a constant running battle, by 2.00 am 5 October the French had been cleared out of both our objective, the wood northeast of Souchez and the hill between Souchez and Givenchy, both of which were firmly in the hands of the regiment. At the entrance to Givenchy the courageous commander of 3rd Battalion, Hauptmann Lothar Schmidt, was killed by a rifle bullet.[14] For months to come a simple cross erected between trees marked the place where Hauptmann Schmidt and Leutnant Volkart were buried together . . . The battalion, which was reduced by now to nine officers and 500 men, was reorganised into two full strength companies and occupied the copse two kilometres to the north of Souchez. There was heavy field artillery fire from the northeast and northwest. The remaining regiments of the division had a firm grip on the Lorette Spur, Vimy and the heights to its west and the woods to the east of Thélus. There they repulsed heavy counter-attacks by French colonial troops, driving them off with bloody casualties.

"About 10.00 am the enemy began to withdraw, leaving behind only strong rearguards, covered by plenty of artillery. It was essential not to let them escape unscathed. The Reserve Corps directed that energetic efforts were to be made to hinder the enemy withdrawal so, to 5th Reserve Division, despite its heavy casualties and the general exhaustion of its troops, fell the decisive task on the right flank of advancing to the line Carency – Mont St Eloi. Group Hurt, our regiment, together with 3rd

Battalion Bavarian Reserve Infantry Regiment 10, some cavalry, an artillery battalion and supporting engineers set off in the early hours . . . As it became light, lines of enemy infantry appeared to the south of Givenchy and were immediately brought under rapid fire. In addition, our artillery, too, fired into the rear and flanks of the enemy who were pulling back westwards from Souchez. It was not until 8.00 am that the French artillery began to bring down fire against the summit and eastern slopes of the Lorette Spur.

"Around midday the 1st and 3rd Battalions received the mission of advancing via Cabaret Rouge to the heights south of Carency. The battalions came under small arms fire from the direction of Souchez, but this did not halt the forward movement and, by just after 5.00 pm, they had captured the hill to the south of Carency and the copse to its southeast. At 11.30 am the 2nd Battalion was tasked to advance on Carency Station via Ablain. Just as the leading elements arrived on Hill 125 to the north of Carency, a hail of artillery fire from hidden positions in the direction of Villers au Bois forced them to take cover then pull back towards Ablain. Simultaneously, columns and lines of enemy infantry, with Spahis in their white coats to the fore, launched forward against Carency and Hill 125. It was an unforgettable sight, but a most dangerous situation.

"Swiftly reaching a decision and in order to prevent his left flank from being cut off, Reserve Hauptmann Christian Langheinrich directed Henneck's 5th Company to occupy the copse to the north of Carency, front facing the village. At the same moment he heard that the companies which had been despatched to Hill 125 were falling back on Ablain. Without stopping to ponder, Hauptmann Langheinrich directed part of Henneck's company to race to the aid of the few sections which were trying to take cover behind stacks of straw against the hail of artillery fire. Under the command of the tried and tested Unteroffizier Hofmann of 7th Company, these few sections and the depleted Henneck company, Hauptmann Langheinrich quickly established a thin firing line, whose well-aimed fire temporarily brought the French advance to a standstill. The battalion had no machine guns, nor any artillery support.

"Oberleutnant Henneck, the sole remaining officer, assumed command of the troops on Hill 125, whilst Hauptmann Langheinrich, ignoring the torrent of enemy fire and his own exhaustion, hurried off to Ablain, there to rally the remainder of his battalion and to lead them forward again onto Hill 125, where they all dug in. It was entirely due to the forceful personality of Hauptmann Langheinrich, assisted only by the last two officers of his battalion, Oberleutnant Henneck and Leutnant Hertel, that the vital Hill 125 was held and, as a result, all French thrusts against the right flank of the brigade came to nothing . . . This day of battle had cost our regiment a further four officers and 165 junior ranks . . . For his outstandingly courageous personal behaviour and decisive leadership as the battalion commander, Hauptmann Langheinrich was made a Knight of the Military Max Joseph Order.[15]

In summary, it is fair to say that the closer the advance drew to Arras, the more French resistance grew and the harder it became to make progress forward. On *Telegraphenhöhe* some of the units of Group Samhaber had been fully occupied all day long, repulsing repeated French attacks and, around 7.00 am, major attacks were launched by Zouave forces to the north of Thélus, against Bavarian Reserve Infantry Regiments 10 and 13. All were beaten back with bloody casualties, but delay was imposed so that when, in response to the corps order to advance, elements of Bavarian Reserve Infantry Regiments 10 and 13 attempted to renew the advance and gain the line of the road leading to Neuville St Vaast, French forces located in Thélus put up such a sharp defence that the men of Reserve Infantry Regiment 13 had to turn in that direction and became involved in a heavy battle for that place. According to German accounts the French lost heavily during this action, which may explain why the subsequent move against Neuville St Vaast was straightforward.[16]

In the event the French only imposed a delay and, by 6.00 pm, Bavarian Reserve Infantry Regiment 13 was able to move on Neuville St Vaast. Possession of this village was not disputed and by 11.00 pm Bavarian Reserve Infantry Regiment 13 was able to move in; enemy rearguards having taken up fresh positions at La Targette. Although the final action of the day was bloodless, the regiment had taken some casualties earlier in the day, including Oberleutnant Gollwitzer, adjutant of 1st Battalion, who was the first of their officers to be killed in the Vimy area.[17] Further to the south and equally key in terms of opening the way towards Arras, were the battles being fought by 1st Bavarian Reserve Division in the Bailleul area. Eventually, by the evening of 5 October, the way was clear for the advance to be resumed on a broad front the following morning and orders were issued to that effect by corps headquarters. Group Hurt was directed once more to aim for Camblain, with flank protection intended to be provided by the Army Cavalry. There was some scepticism about the ability of the delayed cavalry to carry out this function, but Generalleutnant Hurt was certainly pleased to have the opportunity to drive forward from his dominating, but exposed, positions on the Lorette Spur.

It was clear from the outset that possession of this particular feature was a mixed blessing. On the one hand it provided excellent points of observation; on the other its steeply wooded slopes, especially from the north and east, which provided excellent covered approaches for attackers and were difficult to engage with artillery fire, made it hard to defend – especially because the French artillery could concentrate fire on it from all sides. However, because to give up the Lorette Spur, would necessarily also involve the relinquishment of the entire triangle Ablain-Carency-Souchez, the decision was made to continue to hold it. Despite the desirability of pressing forward in this important area, events conspired to prevent it. By the early morning of 6 October 1914, the cavalry had still not closed up and, although 1st Reserve Division had made some progress down around Bailleul and Point du Jour, it was still lagging; there could be no question of a further advance for the time being. Instead, at 6.00 am, the corps issued fresh orders that 5th Reserve Division was to provide flank protection whilst all available corps units and formations swung round to assault Arras.

In order to carry out these instructions, Group Hurt had to seal off Ablain and Carency to attacks from the west and also to block all the roads leading from the north. The result of this was that the Lorette Spur remained in the divisional front line. Group Samhaber was given the task of striking in a southerly direction, taking the crossroads one kilometre to the north of Ecurie then, leaving flank protection out to the west, to drive on Arras. 1st Reserve Division was tasked to conform to this plan by assaulting Arras from the west and initially occupying the line Roclincourt – St Laurent. IV Corps and the Guards Corps were also directed to join in the attack on Arras from positions further to the south. In the meantime Generalleutnant Hurt ordered 2nd and 3rd Battalions Bavarian Reserve Infantry Regiment 6 to advance onto the Lorette Spur and to dig in facing north. This was duly achieved with very little interference from the French and one battery of Bavarian Reserve Field Artillery Regiment 5 followed up, taking up a position to the west of the road. Elsewhere it was a day of mixed fortunes for the German cavalry from 7th and 9th Divisions, but at least the combined efforts of Bavarian Reserve Infantry Regiment 6 and some of the units of 7th Cavalry Division ensured that the positions on the Lorette Spur were maintained throughout the day; this despite constant probing by infantry patrols and the fact that the Spur was under constant French artillery bombardment from gun positions to the north, southwest and south.

Generalleutnant Hurt was considerably exercised by the risk and likely cost of holding onto the exposed positions on the Lorette Spur and met up at 6.00 pm with the commander of 5th Bavarian Reserve Division, the magnificently named Generalleutnant Friedrich Freiherr Kreß von Kressenstein, to discuss the situation. The divisional commander decided that the spur was to be retained and there, for the time being, matters rested. Simultaneously, elsewhere all efforts at advancing on Arras were subject to increasingly determined French resistance. The Group Hurt flank guard, commanded by Oberstleutnant Beyerlein and dug in on the western edge of Ablain, had been engaged heavily throughout the afternoon by French attacks launched from both northwest and southwest and, such was the concern about the way the situation was developing, with its attendant risk that the French army might be able to thrust forward into the unoccupied gap between Carency (Group Hurt) and La Targette (Group Sambaber), that Generalleutnant Hurt pulled together his brigade reserve (3rd Battalion Bavarian Reserve Infantry Regiment 7 from Souchez and half of 1st Battalion Bavarian Reserve Infantry Regiment 6 from the northern sector of the Lorette Spur, which seemed to be least at risk) and sent them to occupy the gap to the southeast of Carency. This small force was withdrawn to Souchez once more when it went dark.

Group Samhaber, fresh from its success at Neuville St Vaast, attempted early on 6 October to carry out its previous orders and advance on St Eloi. Moving past La Targette, which had been evacuated also by the French, Bavarian Reserve Infantry Regiment 13 quickly came under fire when it was about 600 metres to the west of La Targette from dug in French units near Berthonval Farm. This forced them to deploy and then to dig in as artillery fire from the west started to come down heavily from about mid-morning. This fire remained a problem until a heavy howitzer battery on the heights around La Folie brought under fire first the church tower in St Eloi and then the infantry positions around Berthonval Farm. At that the French infantry pulled back hurriedly, but by then the fresh orders, directing Bavarian Reserve Infantry Regiment 13 to advance towards Ecurie, had arrived. This caused them to swing down towards the south to join forces with Bavarian Reserve Infantry Regiment 10, which was already on the move past La Targette, only to discover that Maison Blanche contained strongly entrenched French forces.

Not surprisingly the attack stalled at once and the remainder of the day saw occasional exchanges of small arms fire and not much else. A false report from artillery observers on the heights around La Folie that German troops (presumably the Guards, who were known to be operating to the south) had been seen advancing into the outskirts of Arras led to an order to the division at 6.00 pm that the advance was to be resumed, but this was rescinded some two hours later and Bavarian Reserve Infantry Regiment 10 spent some time trying to link up with troops from 2 Bavarian Reserve Brigade, who were meant to be in the Ecurie area. In fact they had not succeeded in reaching that place.

Following the heavy fighting around Bailleul, which had cost them a great many casualties, units of 2 Bavarian Reserve Brigade had bivouacked for the night west of the Bailleul – Vimy railway embankment. Then on the morning of 6 October, leaving Oberst von Retzenstein in command of 3rd Battalion Bavarian Reserve Infantry Regiment 3 and 2nd Battalion Bavarian Reserve Infantry Regiment 2 holding the high ground to the west of Bailleul, Oberstleutnant von Passavant assembled 1st Battalion Bavarian Reserve Infantry Regiment 3 and 3rd Battalion Bavarian Reserve Infantry Regiment 12 in the Thélus area, prior to setting off about 9.00 am in a southerly direction towards Roclincourt. Because this involved traversing open ground swept by artillery fire, the advance made only faltering progress. Their problems were further exacerbated by the fact that they had received neither food, nor even water, for the past two days.

Of course, supplying the troops with rations, water and ammunition was intensely difficult throughout the period when the situation was fluid. For days at a time some of the troops found themselves living off the land. Local inhabitants were frequently quite helpful in this respect, providing food fairly readily, in return for little more than a roughly chalked sign on their front doors; 'Gute Leute, bitte schonen' [Good people, treat with consideration]. When anything was requisitioned it was a strict rule that a receipt had to be given to enable those involved to reclaim the cost later. Naturally this offered an opportunity to humorists within the regiments; Infantry Regiment 15 reporting that on one occasion it entered a cowshed and found a cow in one of the stalls with a note tied to its horn, 'Two litres of milk taken from this cow. Signed: Müller, Gefreiter'.[18]

The commander of 2 Bavarian Reserve Brigade, Generalleutnant von Graf, informed the divisional commander, Generalleutnant Alfred Göringer, about the precarious logistical situation during the early afternoon of 6 October but, in view of the need to conform with the 5th Bavarian Reserve Division advance south of Neuville St Vaast, General Göringer ordered that the advance was to continue – which it did, but painfully slowly. By nightfall leading elements were still 1,200 metres short of Roclincourt. The relatively small numbers of advancing troops and the wide areas to be covered meant that there were numerous gaps between formations and units, which the French defenders exploited to cause high casualties to the Bavarians. Nevertheless, once night fell, the advance continued through the night, enabling the German troops to close to within 500 metres of the French positions around Roclincourt and about 300 metres short of the Bailleul – Arras road near a second place named Maison Blanche.

Despite the unpromising results achieved on 6 October, the Army High Command, unwilling to accept that the opportunity of breakthrough had passed, once again issued ambitious orders for 7 October. Their aim was to advance to the north of Arras as far the line Petit Servin – Mont St Eloi – Maroeuil and so go a long way towards outflanking Arras to the north. Simultaneously, it was hoped that assaults by 1st Bavarian Reserve Division from the east, IV Corps from the southeast and Guards Corps from the south would lead to the fall of Arras. Unfortunately, not even the arrival of XIV Corps on the right flank, which was intended, finally, to resolve the flank protection difficulty, enabled the objectives of the day to be realised. Quite apart from general exhaustion, much of the momentum of the various assaults was dissipated by the need constantly to plug gaps or counter fresh threats. In addition, the French had been making superhuman efforts to reinforce this threatened area and, during the day on 7 October, fresh troops were thrown into the battle.

On the I Bavarian Reserve Corps front, Group Hurt managed in the north to hold its positions in the face of determined attacks, but there was no question of being able to advance them in any way. Furthermore 2nd and 3rd Battalions Bavarian Reserve Infantry Regiment 6 took a serious pounding from the French artillery fire which continued to land throughout the day on the Lorette Spur, then some of its companies moved temporarily later that day, west towards Carency. An eyewitness from Bavarian Reserve Infantry Regiment 6 captures the order and counter-order of the difficult days.

Wehrmann Georg Preiß 4th Company Bavarian Reserve Infantry Regiment 6 [19]

"During the evening of 7 October we advanced towards Carency, about a forty five minute march from Souchez, where we dug in, about 100 metres from the village and were harassed by French fire constantly. Here the battalion commander, Hauptmann Hofmann,[20] was wounded in the head (he died several days later in Douai). We were only too pleased when night fell and the firing eased somewhat. Towards midnight we pulled back into the village of Carency and were billeted in a farmyard. Because of the shooting we were only able to move back in a series of dashes. It was far from comfortable in our farmyard where we had to bed down in an open-sided barn. After a few hours we were ordered to move into the garden of the farm where some men of Bavarian Reserve Infantry Regiment 10 had been digging in.

"We took over the digging duties, but we also had to continue to fire at the enemy in order to keep them quiet. Towards dawn we pulled back to Souchez and our positions were taken over by Bavarian Reserve Infantry Regiment 7. We were given some coffee in Souchez, then we moved via Ablain St Nazaire for the first time onto the Lorette Spur. This was crowned by a small pilgrims' chapel; otherwise it was covered in fields of grain. To the west we could see a large leafy wood and we entered it. We were greeted by a few shots, but otherwise all was quiet. Later we shot up a strong French patrol moving on the northwest slope. Towards evening we retraced our steps along the heights, past the chapel and down to Souchez."

Group Samhaber, which had been ordered to continue its advance on Mont St Eloi, simply failed to make any impression whatever on the French defenders. The same was true of the efforts by 1 Bavarian Reserve Brigade to make further progress in the Roclincourt area. The French Tenth Army had issued orders the previous night to X Corps and Barbot's Division that they were to hold on to their newly entrenched positions 'at all costs' – that phrase again! The orders were clearly obeyed; the front was beginning to solidify, just as it had on the Somme a few days previously – and for much the same reasons.[21]

Despite the obvious lack of progress of the previous forty eight hours, the orders for 8 October were essentially the same. There was official acknowledgement that Roclincourt posed a particular obstacle to any attempt to outflank Arras from the north, so a special operation in regimental strength was mounted against it at 4.00 am. The units involved were 1st and 2nd Battalions Bavarian Reserve Infantry Regiment 3 and 3rd Battalion Bavarian Reserve Infantry Regiment 12, supported by two engineer searchlight troops and two four gun assault batteries of artillery, which were deployed right forward amongst the infantry. Despite this carefully prepared attack, it quickly became clear that the days of easy advances were over and that even hastily entrenched positions were a substantial obstacle to assaulting troops. Some ground was gained temporarily down towards the Bailleul – Arras road, but the attempt on Roclincourt itself had to be abandoned. Casualties had been high. 3rd Battalion Bavarian Reserve Infantry Regiment 3, for example, was reduced to 240 riflemen by the end of the day.

The experience at Roclincourt was repeated elsewhere up and down the line that day. Although numerous attempts were made to get forward, the story was always the same. The assaults dashed up against French resistance, which seemed to be increasing by the hour. Elements of Bavarian Reserve Infantry Regiment 6 tried to advance from the Lorette Spur west towards Petit Servin but, clashing with French troops in hasty defensive positions, they were forced to halt and dig in as best they could. The hope remained that 13th Infantry Division and XIV Corps to the north would make some progress and thus force the French to pull back to conform, but this simply did not happen. As if to underline the increase in French resistance and a determination to pull back no further, the would-be German attackers suddenly found themselves during the afternoon the subject of a general French attack, which was launched along the entire front from Ablain to Neuville St Vaast.

This development triggered, in turn, the emergency move forward of all available German reserves within range of the battlefield to seal up the gaps. Bavarian Reserve Infantry Regiment 2, for example, rushed forward from Vimy, via Givenchy, in an advance to the southwest in order to fill a dangerous gap between Groups Hurt and Samhaber. It arrived in the nick of time to help beat off a French attack against Bavarian Reserve Infantry Regiment 13 on the right flank of Group Samhaber. Similarly, a threatening situation on the left flank, where Bavarian Reserve Infantry Regiment 10 was located, was only averted by the timely arrival forward of 1st and 2nd Battalions Reserve Infantry Regiment 12, which had been located at Farbus and now moved swiftly via Thélus and the south of Neuville St Vaast to counter a French advance from the Maroueil area.

The afternoon battles created a minor crisis at Carency, where a violent French attack, launched by the French 43rd Division, forced back men of 3rd Battalion Bavarian Reserve Infantry Regiment 10 and caused the loss of the western outskirts of the village. The leading battalion of 13th Infantry Division, 2nd Battalion Infantry Regiment 15, which was marching through Souchez, was re-directed by Generalleutnant Hurt to force march forward to Carency. Reacting well, this battalion was in action at Carency in less than one hour – a very considerable achievement. Whilst men of 2nd Battalion Bavarian Reserve Infantry Regiment 1 were also rushing forward from Vimy, 2nd Battalion Infantry Regiment 15 succeeded in restoring the situation at Carency and capturing two officers and ninety men from the French 31st *Chasseurs*. For the time being the position was secure and, in the meantime, the main body of 13th Infantry Division had arrived and was deploying onto the Lorette Spur and the surrounding area.[22] The French were disappointed by this setback, but freely acknowledged that their attacks had been countered by, 'a resolute enemy, who stood and fought hand to hand'.[23]

That night the forward German positions were held (from north to south) by 13th Infantry Division (Aix Noulette), elements of Jäger Battalion 11 and one Pionier Company (Lorette Spur), Bavarian Reserve Infantry Regiment 6 (Bois de Bouvigny), 1st Battalion Bavarian Reserve Infantry Regiment 7 (western edge of

Ablain), 2nd Battalion Infantry Regiment 15 (between Ablain and Carency), 3rd Battalion Bavarian Reserve Infantry Regiment 10, 2nd and 3rd Battalions Bavarian Reserve Infantry Regiment 7 and 2nd Battalion Bavarian Reserve Infantry Regiment 1 in and around Carency, Bavarian Reserve Infantry Regiment 2 in the gap southwest of Carency and west of La Targette, Bavarian Reserve Infantry Regiments 10 and 13 west of La Targette, north of Maison Blanche and south of Neuville St Vaast. 1st and 2nd Battalions Bavarian Reserve Infantry Regiment 12 were to the north of Ecurie, 1st and 2nd Battalions Bavarian Reserve Infantry Regiment 3 north and east of Roclincourt and 3rd Battalion Bavarian Reserve Infantry Regiment 1 down towards the valley of the Scarpe. In reserve and at high readiness to move were the 3rd Battalions of Bavarian Reserve Infantry Regiments 3 and 12.

The significance of this detailed description of the line held and the forces deployed to do so is that the battles of the previous few days had brought to an end the war of movement in the Arras area. The line solidified in a less-than-ideal manner and there began positional warfare in this area, despite numerous attempts during the next few days to find a means of unlocking the French defences. All such moves were in vain, as men on both sides dug in where they found themselves. Already by 9th October the German army was conducting reliefs in the line – mainly to restore some order to the jumbling of units and formations which the confused nature of the fighting had caused. This process of reorganisation took a week to complete and, once it had been, the forces which were to man the front line in this area during the coming weeks settled down as follows: Lorette Spur, 13th Infantry Division then, from north to south, 5th Bavarian Reserve Division commanded by Generalleutnant Freiherr Kreß von Kressenstein and comprising 9 Bavarian Reserve Brigade (Generalleutnant Hurt) with Bavarian Reserve Infantry Regiments 6 and 7 and 11 Bavarian Reserve Brigade (Generalleutnant Samhaber) with Bavarian Reserve Infantry Regiments 10 and 13. To the south, Generalleutnant Göringer's 1st Bavarian Reserve Division was made up of 2 Bavarian Reserve Brigade (Generalmajor von Graf) with Bavarian Reserve Infantry Regiments 12 and 3 and 1 Bavarian Reserve Brigade (Generalmajor von Kneußl) with Bavarian Reserve Infantry Regiments 2 and 1.

As the autumn days shortened, I Bavarian Reserve Corps, which was to play such a significant part in the Vimy area during the coming months, found itself responsible for the Arras front from Ablain to Athies. However, the fact that overall responsibility for the Lorette Spur had been ceded to 13th Infantry Division did not mean that it suddenly became a quiet place, or that the Bavarians had ceased totally to be involved there. As early as 9 October, French troops of 43rd Division, XXI Corps, mounted a serious counter-attack against it, which involved men of the Bavarian artillery in extremely close-quarter fighting. At approximately 4.00 am, 6th Company Infantry Regiment 55, commanded by Leutnant Lieber, had been ordered forward to relieve 3rd Company Bavarian Reserve Infantry Regiment 6 around the chapel and to hold it against all assaults.

[24] By 6.00 am, when the relief in the line was not yet complete, an entire battalion of the *Chasseurs Alpins* launched forward against their lines. Fighting was hand to hand on the left (southern) flank; elsewhere the French closed up to eighty metres distance. The situation for Leutnant Lieber and his men was critical.

Hauptmann Freiherr von Guttenberg Bavarian Reserve Field Artillery Regiment 5 [25]

"As dawn broke on 9 October, the enemy launched a strong counter-attack from Bouvigny Wood. Because of the wide frontage of the division, the Spur was only held by a weak force of friendly infantry, mostly comprising one company of the Marburg Jäger Battalion [Jäger Battalion 7, 13th Infantry Division] of the neighbouring division which had just arrived to our right. From our own regiment 1st and 3rd Batteries were occupying fire positions in a dip on the southern slope of the Spur, just on the northern edge of Ablain. The sound of rapid small arms fire could be heard coming from the summit, but otherwise the artillery knew nothing of the overall battle situation. Hauptmann Prunner, the battalion commander, therefore despatched Vizefeldwebel Gudden to find out what was going on above us. Having reached the top, he found himself swept up in the infantry battle. The enemy infantry had established themselves in a hedgerow about 100 – 200 metres to the front of the thin line of Jägers.[26] Only from their muzzle flashes could they be located. Both sides engaged each other vigorously.

"Vizefeldwebel Gudden was fortunate enough to be able to make his way as far as the walls of the chapel, where the company commander informed him that he had no chance of holding the summit unless he received immediate artillery support. The company had no machine guns. Moving as quickly as he could, Gudden retraced his steps to the batteries. Whilst still on the spur, he met up with Oberleutnant von Spruner, commander of 1st Battery, who was carrying out another reconnaissance on his own initiative. Blurting out his information, Gudden described the situation, adding desperately that it would be impossible to haul guns up the steep slope. He was immediately contradicted by Oberleutnant von Spruner. 'If it has to be done, then somehow we shall do it! Now go and report to Hauptmann Prunner and tell him that efforts must begin immediately to neutralise the enemy infantry from below. If not it will be all over before I can get my guns up the hill!'

"Racing down the hill as fast as he could, Gudden passed on his report and Hauptmann Prunner directed two guns of 3rd Battery to engage at maximum elevation. The distance as the crow flew was 350 metres, but the guns opened with shrapnel at 800 metres, because the friendly infantry (invisible from below) was located 100 metres forward of the crest and the enemy a further 200 metres away. Once more Gudden rushed up the steep slope, equipped with a yellow signal flag, which he used to direct the fire, by means of hastily agreed signals, onto the hedgerow. Naturally all the flag waving attracted a hail of small arms fire, which Gudden ignored and he managed to take cover in the lee of a stack of straw. Very soon the first shrapnel balls were lashing the enemy hedgerow. Although the initial bursting point was rather high, the fire still caused the enemy infantrymen to take cover. Their fire slackened and most of it went high. Individual riflemen could be seen through gaps in the hedge pulling back to Bouvigny Wood.

"In the meantime long tow ropes had been fastened to two guns of 1st Battery and, by dint of extreme exertion, they were hauled up the steep slope. The leading gun, pulled by about twenty gunners, was placed in position by Oberleutnant von Spruner personally. The enemy's heads were still being kept down by the fire of 3rd Battery, so they did not notice the gun until it was already in a firing position. It immediately attracted a great concentration of small arms fire, but the daring crew ignored it and the orders were given. 'Load! Open sights! Rapid fire!' It was just as had been practised against moving targets on the range so often and in no time shells were crashing into the hedgerow. The enemy were so busy engaging the first gun that they did not notice the second one taking up position beside the stack of straw and opening fire against a concentration of enemy located in undergrowth further to the right.

"It was not long before the gunners gained the upper hand. The enemy small arms fire died away then fell silent. All those who did not remain behind killed or wounded hared back into the protection of the wood. Oberleutnant von Spruner chased them all the way back with gunfire. Our jägers leapt to their feet to watch what was going on, shouting, thankfully: 'That support arrived in the nick of time!' The danger that our little group of infantrymen would be overrun had been avoided for the time being. Our control over the Lorette Spur had been asserted. But the danger was far from over for the guns, which had already had two men killed and two wounded. The enemy artillery, having observed the action of the guns on the summit, brought down a hail of fire from covered positions against them. Given fresh courage by their supporting artillery, the enemy infantry launched forward once more from Bouvigny Wood. There were casualties and, with the right hand gun crew reduced to one gunner, Oberleutnant von Spruner himself took over as gunlayer. Whilst the infantry rushed ammunition forwards, he and the gunner fired round after round at point blank range, so rapidly that the enemy attack was halted between fifty and one hundred metres away.

"However, by now the storm of enemy artillery fire was so intense that our own infantry could hold on no longer and was forced back to the extreme edge of the crest. It was the greatest misfortune that the stack of straw now caught fire and the fire spread rapidly to the wheel of the gun. In these circumstances there could be no question of continuing to fire so, temporarily, Oberleutnant von Spruner pulled his few remaining men back. Such was the respect afforded to the gunners by the enemy that there was no immediate attempt to follow up and, for the time being, the guns remained isolated between the lines. Oberleutnant von Spruner was, however, not willing to let matters rest like that. By nightfall all the preparations had been made for the recovery. Replacement wheels were brought forward from the horse lines; everybody was briefed carefully about their individual tasks. Tow ropes and tools were prepared.

"As it went dark a courageous little band, commanded by Oberleutnant von Spruner, set off up the Lorette Spur, complete with wheels and tools. The stack of the straw was still burning brightly, lighting up the half-collapsed gun. It was questionable, given the bright illumination, if it would even be possible to approach the gun. But the unbelievable worked. Even though the enemy was so close that the sounds of talking and the clang of digging tools could be heard clearly, they noticed nothing of the daring operation. As a first step the undamaged gun was recovered and rolled as quietly as possibly down the slope. At the same time willing hands, guided by the armourer, worked to repair the damaged gun. Brightly lit up by the fire, a replacement wheel was fitted and the gun was borne off in triumph to be rolled down the hill as well.

"That same night strong infantry reinforcements arrived and were able to re-occupy the area of the chapel and the terrain either side of it. The dominating and vital high ground was secure once more. Everyone involved received recognition later . . . Oberleutnant von Spruner, to whose decisive intervention, unswerving determination and outstanding leadership the successful outcome of the operation on the Lorette Spur could be attributed, later received the highest recognition – the Military Max Joseph Order. Unfortunately he did not live to receive the honour; he died in May 1915, having been mortally wounded the day previously."[27]

Wehrmann Georg Preiß 4th Company Bavarian Reserve Infantry Regiment 6 [28]

"Meanwhile Prussian troops had moved onto the heights. They were jägers from Marburg and they occupied part of the spur. We continued on our way to Ablain. The night was quiet, but towards 6.00 am bullets began rattling against the roof of our barn. We stood to our arms immediately and headed back onto the spur through thick fog, to take up our positions in the line just in front of the chapel. A field track led away diagonally past a stack of straw. This is where battle was joined and it was hot while it lasted. As the fog lifted we saw that the French had pressed up very close. We found that we could get a very clear picture of the enemy in our sights, so most of our hits were head shots. A good many of the French raced back to the wood to take up positions, but we stayed in the open. Matters became more serious as the French received reinforcements and their artillery increased the rate of fire.

"At this point two Bavarian guns were towed up onto the hill. One went into position near a stack of straw, the other a little further down the slope by a track. Fire was immediately opened at eighty metres range and the effect on the target was good. However we could not benefit for long. A French aircraft appeared and, despite the fire, flew low over our positions. A short while later we came under very heavy artillery fire; so heavy in fact that we could see nothing because of the smoke and hear nothing because of all the explosions. The 2nd Battalion was moved up, because our ranks had been thinned considerably. I watched as Hauptmann Schilling, out in front, led his men forward and then fell.[29]

"Towards midday the fire slackened somewhat. Many of our comrades lay, still holding their rifles, but killed by head wounds. I was just about to run back to the Prussian Jägers who were manning the Second position, when we were hit by a concentration of shrapnel, which caused a terrible number of wounds. At that everyone pulled back rapidly into the so-called *Schlammulde* [Mud Hollow], where many wounded were lying on the ground. An uninjured man and I carried the poor chaps back to a point where they could be recovered under the cover of darkness. We ourselves were then relieved by Prussian troops and said goodbye for the time being to the blood-soaked Lorette Spur, where so many of our brave comrades lay."

Naturally there was no immediate acceptance of the fact that the war of movement had come to an abrupt end in the Arras area. During October I Bavarian Reserve Corps continually issued orders such as that on 7 October, 'Roclincourt is to be captured tonight by 1st [Bavarian] Reserve Division.' Nothing came of the attack and much the same was true when, on 14 October, the Corps heavy artillery was directed: 'To prepare the capture of Arras.' Still the orders multiplied and their urgent tone increased. On 19 October the Corps ordered, 'On 20 October, 1st [Bavarian] Reserve Division is to capture Roclincourt, the high ground around Maison Blanche[30] and St Laurent East.' An intensive effort ensued and three days later, on 23 October, the farm buildings of Maison Blanche and the eastern part of St Laurent were captured. After a further two days of bloody house-to-house fighting, the western sector of St Laurent was also taken, but nothing ever came of the attempts to seize Roclincourt or St Nicolas; whilst Arras itself remained a distant dream.

Every effort was made, nevertheless to maintain the offensive spirit and to seek out every possible tactical advantage as this report concerning a patrol conducted on 16 October shows.

Gefreiter August Bühler 2nd Company Bavarian Reserve Infantry Regiment 6[31]

"Even though in general our position had attained their final layout and would not change much, nevertheless numerous operations aimed at pushing our lines forward at particular paces were undertaken. On 16 October, for instance, we found ourselves deployed near to Carency and next to the Arras road. Because no reports concerning the enemy had been received for the past two days, 2nd Company was ordered to send a patrol forward about 500 metres into No Man's Land. I was designated patrol commander and took two reliable comrades with me. One was Hofmann from Fürth and the other was a man who had become separated from Bavarian Reserve Infantry Regiment 11.[32] Because the lie of the land prevented us from observing over it and because we had no idea where the enemy positions were, we crawled forward 400 metres then, about 100 metres further on, we came across a row of corn stacks.

"We discovered that the area was unoccupied and the same thing applied to a sunken road leading away to the left. Leaving our comrade from the 11th behind, I made my way with Hofmann carefully along the sunken road. After about 100 metres we arrived at an acacia copse. 500 metres away we could make out an enemy picket, comprising about two sections. We pushed on until we were about 100 metres behind and to one side of this picket. Here we came under fire from a line of French infantry about 300 metres away. My comrades were then wounded and could not move, so it was left to me alone to return to the battalion and report. Concern about the fate of my comrades caused me to volunteer to go and recover them. Fog descended and, under its cover, I was able to go forward and bring back Hofmann, the father of four children. He was wounded in four places.

"The other comrade was nowhere to be found. He had disappeared. It turned out that he had managed to make his own way back and was back with the company by the following day. On the basis of my report Bavarian Reserve Infantry Regiment 7, which relieved us two days later, was able to advance its front by about 500 metres."

Strenuous French efforts transformed the area into one great mass of defensive works, which were garrisoned by a constant stream of colonial reinforcements. As early as 12 October, the order from Tenth Army had been, 'To continue to reinforce and improve the positions, but to be ready at all times to undertake a vigorous offensive.'[33] Although this did not remain the policy for very long, at that Zouaves, Turcos and troops from Senegal combined to work to deny any further progress in this area to the German invaders. As the days went by, further factors came into play. It was essential, for example, for the Bavarians to maintain the pressure, in order to ensure that no French troops could be withdrawn from this front and be rushed to the north where the battles around Ypres were in full swing. On 29 October I Bavarian Reserve Corps expressly drew attention to this when it stated: 'Tomorrow the decisive assault begins along the fronts of Fourth and Sixth Armies. 1st Bavarian Reserve Division is to ensure through constant threats of an attack that the enemy remains fixed to its front.' Naturally the division conformed to its orders but, having been in action constantly for weeks, it needed a break as the month of November opened, so attention turned to the sector of 5th Bavarian Reserve Division.

For the coming weeks the main German effort was directed against Ecurie and the line of the modern N 17 road leading towards Arras from Petit Vimy. This did not simply amount to a change in divisional responsibility. The development of lines of trenches meant that siege tactics began to be employed and the German troops began to sap their way forward, digging narrow zig-zag trenches forward from the front line trenches towards the French positions. At intervals a short trench would be dug parallel to the French lines. These served the dual purpose of acting as listening posts and also providing points from which the work of sapping forward could be protected. The work of digging itself was protected as far as possible by use of sandbags and infantry shields.[34] Once all the sap heads had reached a feature of some tactical significance, attempts were made in conformity with classic siege warfare tactics to join them up to form a new continuous trench, which would serve either as the start line for an assault, or provide the basis for a new round of sapping. Very quickly the entire area to the west of Vimy Ridge became cross-crossed with an astonishingly dense web of defensive works, with names such as the 'Labyrinth.'

In reality it usually proved impossible to create these new parallels, because they attracted the attention of the French artillery, which generally bombarded them until they were unrecognisable. Nevertheless it was generally possible to develop the sap heads sufficiently to permit local attacks to take place and they were used a great deal as the starting points for mining operations which quickly spread up and down the line in this area. A successful mine blast could almost always be exploited, either to advance the front line or to seize a section of enemy trench. Of course all this digging and engineering work attracted unwelcome enemy attention, so such activities came to be restricted to the hours of darkness or days of poor visibility. There were also limitations to what could be achieved. Some manpower had to be kept back to ensure that the main German defences continued to be developed so as to resist possible French assaults. The construction of the second trench of the First Position and communications trenches to link them added further to the complications of the overall system and to the length of trench to be maintained during bad weather.

During this first winter, the prevailing view on the German side was that the second line was to form the man defensive line. In most places it was situated 200 – 500 metres in rear of the front line and was usually manned by the support troops. At this stage of the war it did not amount to a continuous line. Instead it comprised a line of mutually supporting strong points, which were sited about 100 – 250 metres apart to exploit natural features and to be capable of all round defence whenever possible. They were equipped with deep dugouts and stocks of ammunition food and water. They were also heavily wired as stocks of barbed wire became available. In the event of an attack, the idea was that a proportion of the support troops would rush forward to reinforce the front line garrison, but in this event, reserves from further to the rear would also be moved forward to replace them. This method of operation also had the advantage that it eased the roulement of the men of a particular regiment through the different roles of forward troops, stand-by and reserve.

Much the same was occurring all along the Western Front during the first winter of the war, but because of the significance of Vimy Ridge, the Lorette Spur and possession of Arras, development along these lines was particularly swift in this area. Within weeks all manner of engineer stores had been moved up and placed in position, along with a wide variety of trench mortars, searchlight detachments and observation balloons. The main problem, however, was a lack of artillery and scarcity of ammunition for those guns that were deployed. It limited the scope of offensive operations and later, in 1915, was blamed for the reverses suffered by the German army on this sector, despite the fact that the situation was much the same for the French army at the time. Meanwhile the troops did what they could with what they had to hand and November 1914 was marked by a series of limited assaults on the Ecurie sector.

These began on the night of 4/5 November with an attack on a cluster of French trenches immediately west of the Petit Vimy – Arras road. Commander 5th Bavarian Reserve Division prefaced his orders with the remark, 'The harder and sooner we attack Ecurie, the less the enemy will be inclined to dare to bring up fresh troops.' He also emphasised that the assaulting troops were to concentrate on getting forward, regardless of progress on their flanks. The maximum number of troops was pressed into service for this operation. This included a group of reinforcements for Bavarian Reserve Infantry Regiment 7, who had been hoping to have a quiet evening drinking some of the supplies of beer which had accompanied them from Germany, but it was not to be.

Reserve Leutnant Georg Will 2nd Company Bavarian Reserve Infantry Regiment 7 [35]

> "Today [4 November] the men who had arrived with me were allocated to companies. I was detailed to join the 2nd Company, which was already forward manning the position. As a result I was to await the arrival of the company in Vimy, but things turned out differently. News of the arrival of fifteen hectolitres of beer had spread rapidly. Everyone was delighted and was looking forward to a pleasant evening. Already by 8.00 pm the officers of the 3rd Battalion had assembled, a barrel of *Meisel* light beer had been tapped and was ready to be served when, at 8.30 pm, Hauptmann Lienhardt entered the room and announced, 'Gentleman, I am sorry, but our evening of beer drinking, which we had been so looking forward to, cannot go ahead. We must leave at once. The

battalion is to be formed up at the western exit of the village ready to move off at 9.00 pm.' That was the first surprise!

"The battalion marched off, a party of forty men for the 1st Battalion, with me at its head, brought up the rear of the column. The night was pitch black and it was raining. My little group belonged to nobody. That became instantly clear when we entered Neuville. The other companies simply disappeared in all directions and we were left standing about aimlessly in the street. To add to the problems shells were landing on the village and our artillery was replying. We newcomers could hardly tell the difference between the firing signatures and the crash of shells exploding. Suddenly an unknown officer appeared and advised us to disappear off the street with all speed. We took cover in a barn. In an outhouse we also discovered a cellar which some of us immediately pressed into service. The remainder stayed in the barn and slept on the floor.

"What was happening? Elements of our division, amongst them some of the companies from Bavarian Reserve Infantry Regiment 7 had launched an attack along the Arras road which was directed against Ecurie. Some trenches were stormed, but were quickly lost again. On 5 November I was ordered to take my men to La Targette. The brewery there was in use as a casualty collection point. There, for the first time I saw Stretcherbearers Hertel and Limmer in action. They were responsible for bringing in casualties and giving them first aid. It was very cramped in the overflowing cellar. Around midnight we located a more comfortable billet in another cellar. We threw ourselves down on some piles of material and went to sleep.

"Suddenly there was a suspicious noise. We could hear French voices on the cellar stairs. Had we fallen so quickly into the hands of the French? However it was a bloodless meeting. The 'enemy' were three women from the village who also sought shelter in the cellar. As day dawned the whole area was blanketed in a thick layer of fog. Men, who had made their way here after the attack, appeared from all directions. I was ordered to assemble every man in La Targette and to lead them forward onto the positions which were only a few hundred metres to our front. The utmost speed was essential because the fog could lift at any moment. Initially we moved along the road, then we took to the trenches, before finally following a wet communication trench which led to the front line.

2nd and 7th Companies were totally intermingled, so my men took up positions in the narrow wet trenches wherever there was room. Offizierstellvertreter X was in command of 2nd Company, but he was in a dreadful state – a completely broken man. The 7th Company was commanded by Offizierstellvertreter Krauß who was in full control of his emotions. That same evening the entire company was withdrawn to

Neuville, where we slept in a cellar. Marx had been hit in the calf by a shell splinter and was not fit for duty. I took over from him until the return from hospital of Leutnant Kühn. We spent the next few days here or manning the forward positions. The journey forward took about thirty five minutes and we always moved rapidly during reliefs, because the route was constantly under small arms fire. The company occupied Trenches 16, 26 and half of Trench 6. In all this was a frontage of about 500 metres and the company strengths varied between eighty and ninety men."

During the night 4/5 November, the regiments of the division had carried out their orders to the letter. On the left flank Bavarian Reserve Infantry Regiment 10 broke into the French front line on a 100 metre frontage and held it against constant attempts by French colonial troops, alternating with artillery concentrations, to recapture it. There they stuck it out, despite mounting casualties, whilst others sapped furiously forward to link up with them. This was an extremely slow process because the saps kept being smashed by the French artillery. Finally, on the night of 20/21 November, it was possible to launch another attack which gained a further 100 metre section of trench. This was reinforced the following night as engineer stores were brought forward, but it was a terribly slow business. Bavarian Reserve Infantry Regiment 12 took over from Bavarian Reserve Infantry Regiment 10 at the end of the month and launched a further attack on 6 December, which captured the last of the French positions close to the main road.

Two days later Bavarian Reserve Infantry Regiment 13 succeeded in taking a 400 metres section of trench located between the Petit Vimy – Arras and Souchez-Arras roads then, on 8 December, Bavarian Reserve Infantry Regiment 10 launched another attack to the east of the Souchez – Arras road and captured the farm of Maison Blanche,[36] This was quite a feat of arms. The farmhouse had been captured temporarily on 5 November, but had to be evacuated once more after French counter-attacks. In the intervening period the farm had been developed into a strong point and surrounded by trenches. The men of Bavarian Reserve Infantry Regiment 10 now developed the farm further, digging substantial dugouts and turning it into a small fortress. The salient so produced became known as the *Scharfes Eck* [Sharp Corner].

Despite these gains, it is important to realise that such was the intensity of fighting that after five weeks of battle the German front had only been advanced between 100 and 200 metres. Ecurie was still 500 metres away at the closest point and the French had pulled back closer to the village, where they were strongly entrenched. It was a small return for so much effort. The work of sapping forward went on, being countered, as before, mainly by the French artillery. As the weather deteriorated further the attacks on Ecurie (which never fell) stalled. On the German side it was gradually realised that if they could not counter the French artillery, there was little that the infantry could achieve alone and unaided. Time and again desperate calls for help either went unanswered by the artillery or were followed by only a token response. One of the ironies of this policy was that some of the very few shells fired actually began the destruction of the chapel of Notre Dame de Lorette.

4th Battery Field Artillery Regiment 58 had been moved forward onto Hill 119 (later known as The Pimple), west of Givenchy on 19 October. It was under strict orders from the highest level only to engage particularly valuable targets and under no circumstances to fire at the chapel on the Lorette Spur. It became clear, however, that the chapel was being used by the French as an observation point. Gradually, as trenches snaked towards it, a machine gun and one or more snipers began operating from it. The German infantry began to press for it to be shelled and eventually, a week later, permission was granted, if a good target presented itself. Finally, at 12.30 pm 24 October, 4th Battery opened fire when a large number of Frenchmen were seen gathered in and around the chapel. By an extraordinary fluke, the very first ranging shell went straight through the roof of the chapel.[37] Tiles flew in all directions, the windows blew out and clouds of dust, followed by large numbers of French soldiers emerged. After that all restrictions were off and over the next few weeks this attractive building in its marvellous setting was reduced to dust and rubble.

In early November a commanders' conference was called at which it was announced in strictest confidence that it would not be possible for the foreseeable future for the German guns to engage either French artillery or observers. There was an almost total lack of shells. What ammunition there was would be reserved for infantry targets and only those which appeared to be important and could be hit with reasonable certainty. It was also impressed on commanders that, on no account, was this information to become known to the German infantrymen, who were having daily to endure the sight of their construction work repeatedly being smashed by the French gunners. In an attempt to provide some semblance of protection, small calibre infantry guns were concentrated in places where they could bring enfilade fire to bear on the French trenches. General von Fasbender also caused strenuous efforts to be made to identify sharp shooters and snipers within the infantry battalions and to equip them with good quality rifles fitted with sniper sights.

These initiatives did have some effect. It certainly became very difficult for the French soldiers to risk moving about in daylight if they wished to avoid being shot but, regardless of how effective the measures were, they could not compensate for the lack of artillery support. By the end of November the First Battle of Ypres was coming to a close and, with its termination, the daily battles around Arras also died away as both sides took stock of the novel situation and adopted measures to cope with the deteriorating weather.

Reserve Leutnant Georg Will 2nd Company Bavarian Reserve Infantry Regiment 7 [38]

"Day by day the weather got worse. Rain, rain – rain without end! In the trenches a layer of sodden sticky clay built up, which had to be dug out daily. When it all became too much we threw great fascines down, but these of course made the trenches shallower and we had to start digging out once more in very difficult conditions. Even the companies notionally at rest had to come forward at night and help with the digging. It was an endless task, which offered no prospect of success. After twenty four hours the trenches were in a worse condition that they had been previously. There were twenty to forty centimetres of water in the trenches – if only it had been water! Instead it was thick clinging mud through which, in the end, it was impossible to move. Yet men had to live in these conditions, to drag or push each other out and were forced to move by traversing along the collapsing walls of the trenches, moving slowly like the larvae of massive insects. Ration and carrying parties and relieving troops took to moving across country. They feared the mud of the trenches more than the bullets of the enemy and most of the troops simply did not bother to eat or drink.

"Of course these men were expected to fight when the enemy came. They were still soldiers, even though they looked more like mobile lumps of clay and were more in need of help than able to fight. None of the weapons were operational; the bolts could not be worked backwards and forwards. Repeatedly reliefs had to be arranged in order to cope with weapon problems. In the meantime they were kept wrapped in sand-bags, which were also used as coverings for the legs. Despite all this the sentries had to stick it out in the mud and water. For a long time I regarded it as fun. No hole was too deep or bog too wide for me to cross. Neither mud nor water could dampen my spirits. No man in the company was filthier than me and that cheered the men up. Whenever we crawled through a hole we scraped the worst of the mud off each other using our bayonets or spades.

"The enemy did not leave us alone either. The *Chasseurs Alpins* were superb shots. They were even prepared to aim at the weapon slots in the infantry shields. Our men gave the enemy snipers nicknames. One minute 'Sepp' might be firing; the next 'Emil'. Despite all the strain, they never lost their sense of humour and they were inured to death. 'They have just shot another.' said the sentry, jerking his thumb at Halenke who had been killed by a bullet through the heart . . . A communication trench linked the sunken road and our trench. Directly opposite the junction there was a black wooden cross set into the trench wall. It bore the names of three of the fallen of Bavarian Reserve Infantry Regiment 6. Hanging from it, despite the wind, the weather, the rain and the storms, was a note handwritten in pencil: 'Farewell my dear brother. Your brother, Georg.' I would never forget the sight of this simple wooden cross. We could not recover the bodies of the fallen to the rear. We buried them where they were killed."

The French were the first to take the initiative. The fact that the men of 5th Bavarian Reserve Division had seized Vimy Ridge and the Lorette Spur was intolerable to them. The salient created by the German possession of the Lorette Spur, coupled with French superiority in artillery, meant that this feature and the immediate surrounding area were obvious targets for attention. Throughout early December probing attacks were made all around Carency and the Spur itself, as the French attempted to locate weak points in the defence. This was intended to be a serious attempt to recapture lost key terrain. Tenth Army was reinforced with six groups of heavy artillery and gave as objectives for these operations, 'The heights west of Givenchy-en-Gohelle, Cote 140 [Hill 145], La Folie farm and *Telegraphenhöhe*,'[39] which was nothing less than ambitious, but planning and preparation was thorough; General Pétain submitting to the army commander General de Maud'huy, a detailed proposal for an attack in strength, intended to force a swift penetration in the area of Hill 145.[40] In general these attacks were held and not much progress was made, but in a particularly sharp night action, launched by elements of the French XXXIII Corps on 6 December, which degenerated into vicious hand-to-hand fighting close to the western side of the village of Carency and when no fewer than one officer, two Senior NCOs and seventy five junior ranks were captured, Unteroffizier Sigmund Bonnet, Offizierstellvertreter Sylvester Reichelt and Wehrmann Gustav Wedler of 4th Company Bavarian Reserve Infantry Regiment 6 were all awarded the Bravery Medal in Gold for their heroism.[41]

A period of relative calm followed these failures but, on 12 December, Tenth Army issued fresh orders for a resumption of the attack, which was aimed primarily against the line Hill 145 – La Folie and was the responsibility of XXXIII Corps. In order to prevent the German defenders from concentrating their reserves against only one threat, there was to be a general assault along the full length of the Tenth Army front and a special effort by XXI Corps against Souchez and Givenchy-en-Gohelle.[42] In the event the offensive operations, launched on 17 December, when a sharp increase in artillery fire signalled the start of another French attempt to recapture the Vimy Ridge and the approaches to it, failed yet again to make significant progress anywhere. Instead the fighting broke down into localised, individual battles for key points and localities. The Adjutant of 9 Bavarian Reserve Brigade, who had been sent forward by Generalleutnant Hurt to find out what was going on, became involved personally in the battle.

Hauptmann Füchtbauer Adjutant 9 Bavarian Reserve Brigade [43]

"The French forced their way to the front line trench in sub-sector 9 b, which stuck out further forward than the rest. Whilst the company commanders of 4th and 9th Companies met to arrange a counter-stroke in the strong point located in the third trench, parties armed with home made hand grenades launched immediate attacks from the second trench of sub-sector 9 a and from the front line trench of the sector of

Bavarian Reserve Infantry Regiment 7 against the enemy who had made a lodgement in 9 b. It should be noted that the home made grenades worked well, but had to be lit with a cigar . . . [I] met up with the assault group in 9 a. By means of shouts and signals we linked up with the assault group from Bavarian Reserve Infantry Regiment 7.

"Displaying cold blooded courage a brave Vizefeldwebel, who was commanding the Reserve Infantry Regiment 7 assault group, threw one grenade after another into 9 b, in order to add weight to [my] calls for surrender. After the third repetition this is what happened and the French gave up. With that the connection between Strong Point 9 and Carency was re-established. There remained only the need to parade the prisoners on the road and to move them at the double to Carency. The whole episode seemed to leave the French at a loss what to do, because from their positions, which were densely manned and close by, came not one single shot – which is more than can be said about their artillery!"

After several days of continuing artillery fire, which claimed numerous lives and wounded many more, thoughts began to turn towards Christmas. Up on the Lorette Spur however, fighting raged through until 22 December, by which time the fighting of the past few days had claimed the lives of over 1,000 French soldiers, whose bodies lay unburied between the positions. The French intention had been to continue with their operations but, due to thick fog on 23 December, the decision was made to suspend them until 25 or 26 December.[44] After the heavy fighting of the past weeks, it was important for morale of the German troops for Christmas to be marked in the traditional way, but it was clearly not possible for all the rifle companies holding the line to be able to celebrate on the same day. As a result, some were withdrawn from the trenches early, so as to be ready to man the forward positions over the Christmas period.

Reserve Leutnant Georg Will 2nd Company Bavarian Reserve Infantry Regiment 7 [45]

"We held our company Christmas celebrations on 23 December. Real German Christmas trees arrived from the Homeland and there were lots of presents, which were arranged on tables around the Christmas tree. At 3.00 pm the company assembled and Kühn gave a short speech. The bearded warriors were moved to tears by this and some could not control their voices during the singing of 'Silent Night'. French women and children stood outside our circle, staring in amazement at this strange spectacle. On 24 December we marched forward into the positions so that the forward companies could also celebrate Christmas. In Avion, La Coulotte, Givenchy and even Souchez, lit Christmas trees could be seen through the windows. Wherever we went in these foreign places, the German Christmas Eve was being observed.

"The Christmas spirit ruled in the trenches too. The communication trench was impassable, so we moved cross country and not a shot was fired. We could not take this peaceable situation for granted, however, and the utmost vigilance and readiness was ordered. At midnight the entire trench garrison sang 'Silent Night'. The French did nothing to disturb us; instead, coming from the right hand corner of the wood was the sound of a French carol. The night passed quietly. Dense fog made it impossible to see anything, so I patrolled forward. Taking a rifle from the left hand listening post, I crawled very close to the enemy trench. There was not a sound or sign of movement; they obviously wanted to enjoy a quiet Christmas as well. There were large stacks of unthreshed grain in front of our positions, one of which was set on fire. This lit up the night sky and made observation easier.

"The peaceful situation lasted until midday on 26 December. Suddenly a man burst into our dugout, exclaiming breathlessly, 'The French are approaching our trench – and they are not carrying weapons!' It was true. There, in front of Bavarian Reserve Infantry Regiment 6, there were large groups of men and the same was happening in front of our 1st Company. Our men followed the example of the French and the troops met up between the positions. The French and German soldiers conversed as best they could, but sign language was the main means of communication. Cigarettes were exchanged. It was almost as though a truce had been arranged. Even the officers participated in the fraternisation. On our left flank there was nobody to be seen. The French could not see what was going on. One of our number rather carelessly got up onto the parapet and was promptly shot through the chest.

"The fraternisation did not last long. Our artillery, having spotted the gatherings, fired shrapnel into the area. We were furious about this disturbance, saying that if we had actually needed them, they certainly would not have spotted anything. Some of the poor devils manning our trenches still nursed thoughts of peace. Once more Gefreiter Hofmann left our trenches and went over to the French. He did not return. The French artillery now opened up, bringing down such a weight of fire that we thought there was going to be an attack. It did, in fact, happen and the French forced their way into Trench 10 of Bavarian Reserve Infantry Regiment 6 for a short period, but they could not hold on to their gains."

The Lorette Spur continued to be the focus of French attention in the closing days of the year. Fog had prevented a resumption of the French assault on 25 or 26 December, but on 27 December, the French artillery brought down a barrage of concentrations of fire along the entire front from the Spur down as far as the Petit Vimy – Arras road, although this was followed only by assaults on the Lorette Spur and the Carency sector, where Bavarian Reserve Infantry Regiment 6 suffered casualties of twenty killed and seventy five men wounded, most of them from the 1st Battalion, which had been in support and which conducted a successful counter-attack to throw back the French *Chasseurs Alpins* who had

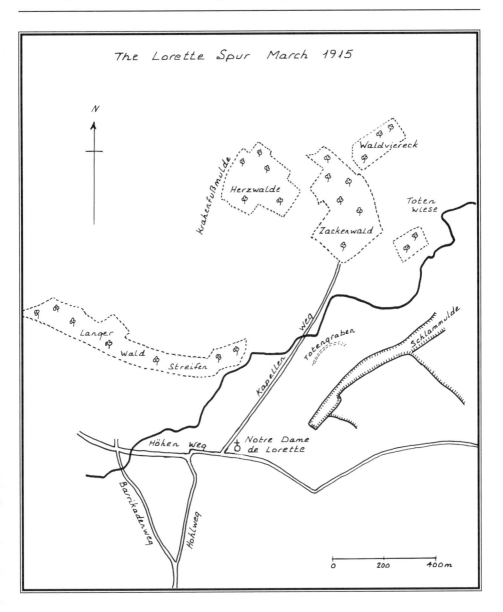

The Lorette Spur   March 1915

attacked slightly further to the southeast than they had on 17 December. The focus of the attack meant that the operation also involved troops of Bavarian Reserve Infantry Regiment 7.

Reserve Leutnant Georg Will 2nd Company Bavarian Reserve Infantry Regiment 7 [46]

"News arrived: 'The French are attacking Carency and the Lorette Spur.' At 3.30 pm an order arrived: 'Enemy has broken into Trenches 22 and 23. No more details available. 1st Battalion Bavarian Reserve Infantry Regiment 7 is to use hand grenades to eject the enemy.' That was simple and direct. The only problem was that, at first, nobody had the slightest idea how to go about it. The battalion commander himself said, 'I do not know either, but it has got to be done.' The 1st Company under Reserve Oberleutnant Bohnsack was to advance via Trench 14 to Trench 22 and the 2nd Company under Fries to march via Carency to Trench 22. In five minutes the companies were ready to move off. Every man was armed with grenades. The grenades were fine examples of their unholy origins; they had been home made by our *Pioniers*. Comprising a jam tin attached to a wooden handle, they had to be lit with a match or a burning cigar. However, even the simplest soldier knew what to do with them.

"At the western exit of Souchez Fries ordered us to halt. He then threw some grenades himself for practise and fired up the company with a few rousing words. 'Men do your duty. The Fatherland expects it of you. None of you has more to lose than I do. I am the father of six children. I left my dear wife and children to obey the call of the Fatherland. So let us go with God for King and Fatherland!' With these words the Kriegsfreiwilliger, who was already over fifty years old, embarked on his first and yet extremely difficult mission. With such a leader none of his men hesitated. The approach route was under fire. Most of the shells passed over the road and crashed into the slope behind, but one landed amongst Kuhn's platoon at the rear of the company. Hühne led the centre platoon and I commanded the leading platoon.

"Fries was familiar with neither the route, Carency, or the position itself, but he was still the man for the moment. It was difficult to move through the hollow. I showed him the way and we hurried forward. Every ten paces we had to pause, the company lying down in one long line in the morass, as shells whistled overhead. No sooner had the shells crashed down than we were struggling back to our feet as quickly as the sticky mud would permit us and we picked our way forward until we had to throw ourselves down in the filth once more. We suffered no casualties and, just as it went dark, we reached Trench 22 which was full of men from Bavarian Reserve Infantry Regiment 6, so we could not approach the break in point this way.

"We turned so as to launch our attack cross country. Fries was always in the lead, pushing forward like a man years younger. Side by side with him were a group of particularly stout hearted men: the old Matthes, the courageous Wührl and several others. Eventually we gained the trench and took cover in a shelter bay. Here we began to roll it up, but it was far from easy: the enemy had established themselves firmly and they poured fire at us. Lighting the grenades was a complete nightmare. There we were with dirty wet hands: half-frozen; in the dark; trembling with the tension of a close-quarter battle; and we were meant to strike matches and throw grenades. It was never going to be easy.

"Despite all, we *had* to do it. Fries, not being content with advancing along the trench, climbed out of it, so that he could throw grenades from above. The rest of us threw from within the trench, whilst others passed us grenades. Space was lacking, so it was impossible for many of us to work at one time. Fries had a lit cigar clenched in his lips and each time he crawled further forward then threw. I managed to drop my box of matches. So I had to borrow his cigar each time I needed to light a grenade. Advancing along the trench was simply gruesome. Wounded and dead lay on the floor and we trampled them into the morass. In the small sap, bodies were piled up. We could hardly distinguish friend from foe in the dark. It was indescribably chaotic.

"We pressed on and kept shouting to the 1st Company who were deployed to the left, in order to establish contact, but it was all in vain. The three commanders: Oberleutnant Bohnsack, Reserve Leutnant Heckert and Vizefeldwebel Heigele had all been knocked out in the first rush.[47] The fighting went on until morning, but by then the trench was clear of enemy. Before then I had left the battle. As I threw a grenade, I was shot twice through the arm. Initially I only felt a heavy blow and was unsure whether a bullet or a fragment had caused warm blood to flow out of my sleeve. I was able to make my way back to the previous shelter bay, where Würhl gave me first aid and heaved me up out of the trench. Here I lay on my back and used my legs to push myself backwards. In that fire there could be no question of moving upright. The mud built up around my shoulders, spilled onto my chest and filled the pockets of my jacket.

"The batman of Reserve Leutnant Marx had a serious wound in his thigh, but slid back in the same way, despite the fact that he could only push with his good leg. We took a short break by a stack of straw, fortifying ourselves with a large swig of schnaps, which did us a great deal of good. We then made our way back through the hollow to the aid post at Carency East, where we found Vizefeldwebel Hühne with two bad arm wounds. My companion had a wound in the rear of his thigh into which you could put two fists, yet he had worked his way all the way back to Carency East unaided. The aid post was overflowing with seriously wounded men. The doctor advised all of us who could walk to make for Souchez and get our wounds dressed there. He himself was swamped. So off I strode . . . The 2nd Company lost forty two men, of whom twelve were missing, either dead or trampled into the mud. Some were still being discovered months later. Dead men were stumbled over, sometimes a boot or an arm was seen sticking out of the mud and occasionally the filthy stink of a rotting corpse was noticed. All were victims of 27 December."

Despite all the French attacks, which by 15 January 1915 had cost them total casualties of 7,771 casualties, of whom 1,939 were killed and 758 missing,[48] at the turn of the year German troops were still holding on to this exposed sector. This was doubtless to the satisfaction of the Kaiser, whose New Year message to his troops included the ringing phrase, 'The territory in which the German Eagle has sunk its claws, the territory which has been sanctified by the blood of German soldiers, must remain German.'[49] The close proximity of the French and German trenches around Carency led to a German-speaking French soldier sending Bavarian Reserve Infantry Regiment 6 a somewhat coarser and less complimentary New Year greeting.

Reserve Leutnant Gruber Bavarian Reserve Infantry Regiment 6 [50]

"Our trenches were so close that we could shout to one another. On this occasion a French soldier shouted across, 'You stupid Bavarians. You are nothing but eaters of black pudding and sauerkraut!' It turned out that he was a former waiter from the restaurant in the *Stadtpark* in Nuremberg. On another occasion, when he started in on a long speech criticising the Kaiser, the Crown Prince and our officers and threatened to slit their throats we drowned him out by singing a few Bavarian songs. The French vented their anger at this by loosing off a few shots."

In the meantime pressure continued to be applied especially on and around the Lorette Spur. The French inhabitants were evacuated from Souchez on 12 January and from Ablain the following day. There were suspicions that there was a security risk all the time that local inhabitants were living so close to the front line, because they might have been passing information to the French army. Equally important, however, was the amount of effort it took to keep them under observation and to ensure that the means to feed them were available. So, in the event, it all became too much of a burden for the German defenders and the French population of these places was transported to the rear in a fleet of ambulances.[51] There could, however, be no evacuation for any of the front line soldiers in the Vimy area. As 1915 opened, all they could do was to hang on, battling to maintain their positions despite appalling weather, deep mud and the constant wastage caused by incessant sniping and artillery fire. During the early months of that year, 5th Bavarian Reserve Division alone was suffering an average of ten killed and twenty wounded on quiet days and many more during attacks. It was an inauspicious start to what was to be a year of major battles.

Notes
1. Bezzel: History Bavarian Reserve Infantry Regiment 6 p 27
2. *ibid.* pp 30 – 31
3. General Barbot was later killed on 10 May 1915 during the fighting for the Hill 119 (The Pimple). His dying words were said to be, 'Beautiful . . . Glorious day . . . Victory.' General Ernest Jacques Barbot is buried in an individual grave (Carré L14, Rang 1, No. 19277) at the French National Cemetery at Notre Dame de

Lorette and a statue to him in a dramatic pose, dressed in the uniform of the *Chasseurs Alpins,* stands in Souchez.

4. *Les Armées Françaises dans la Grande Guerre, Tome Premier, Quatrième Volume* p 186 & 189. On arrival in the Arras-Lens area, the two divisions were formed into a provisional corps under the command of General d'Urbal.

5. Stammberger: History Bavarian Reserve Infantry Regiment 13 p 11

6. Bezzel: *op. cit.*pp 48 – 49

7. Dellmensingen: *Das Bayernbuch vom Weltkriege* pp 107 – 109

8. The day cost Bavarian Reserve Infantry Regiment 2 heavy casualties. It suffered six officers killed and eleven wounded (two of whom subsequently died). 167 junior ranks were killed and 345 wounded (of whom thirty eight died later). Of the officer casualties, Hauptmann Dr. Fritz Röder is buried at the German cemetery at Neuville St Vaast B17, G 851. Reserve Leutnant Theodor Molenaar is buried in the *Kamaradengrab* of the German cemetery at St Laurent- Blangy, as are Vizefeldwebel Josef Hebauer, Vizefeldwebel Artur Lange, Vizefeldwebel Stephan Reichhold, Wehrmann Georg Schuster and Vizefeldwebel Richard Schuster.

9. Reichsarchiv: *Der Weltkrieg 1914 – 1918 (Fünfter Band)* p 180

10. Dellmensingen: *op. cit.* pp 109 – 111

11. 5 Oct 14 was a day of crisis for the German High Command. It had become clear that, far from thrusting into a wide empty gap in the French defences, the opposing forces were now fairly evenly matched. No formation was close enough to be brought into action to reinforce north of Arras for several days. As a result the opportunity for a decisive breakthrough was running into the sand. Heated discussions between Falkenhayn and Generalmajor Konrad Krafft von Dellmensingen, Chief of Staff Sixth Army, provided the former with an opportunity to vent his frustration at the way the advance was stalling. Dellmensingen retorted by pointing out the facts of the evolving situation and the men parted, agreeing only that somehow the main weight of the cavalry to the north had to be committed decisively to the battle without further delay. It never happened; the troops may have been ordered, 'to force a final decision', but exhortations alone no longer sufficed and the advance reached its high water mark that day. See Reichsarchiv: *Der Weltkrieg 1914 – 1918 (Fünfter Band)* pp 183–187.

12. *Les Armées Françaises dans la Grande Guerre, Tome Premier, Quatrième Volume* p 222

13. Dellmensingen: *op. cit.* pp 104 – 105

14. Hauptmann Lothar Schmidt is buried in the *Kamaradengrab* of the German cemetery at St Laurent - Blangy.

15. This was a rare distinction for a junior officer. In all only 237 were awarded during the war.

16. Stammberger: History Bavarian Reserve Infantry Regiment 13 p 11

17. Oberleutnant Wilhelm Gollwitzer is buried in the *Kamaradengrab* of the German cemetery at St Laurent-Blangy

18. Riebensahm: History Infantry Regiment 15 p 71

19. Bezzel: *op. cit.* pp 48 – 49

20. Hauptmann Lorenz Wilhelm Hofmann succumbed to his wounds on 18 October 1914. His body was later repatriated to Germany and he is buried in the war cemetery at Sulzbach-Rosenberg Block E Row XI Grave 25.

21. *Les Armées Françaises dans la Grande Guerre, Tome Premier, Quatrième Volume* p 229

22. Riebensahm: History Infantry Regiment 15 p 73
23. *Les Armées Françaises dans la Grande Guerre, Tome Premier, Quatrième Volume* p 230
24. Poetter: History Infantry Regiment 55 p 15
25. Dellmensingen: *op. cit.* pp 111 – 113
26. In fact, as has been noted, there were also elements of Infantry Regiment 55 in position around the chapel of Notre Dame de Lorette.
27. Oberleutant Alfred von Spruner, one of only 237 recipients of the Knights Cross of the Military Max Joseph Order, was mortally wounded on 9 May 1915 on the first day of the French Neuville St Vaast – Carency offensive. He has no known grave.
28. Bezzel: *op. cit.* pp 49 – 50
29. Hauptmann Wilhelm Schilling is buried in the *Kameradengrab* of the German cemetery at St Laurent-Blangy.
30. This refers to the second 'Maison Blanche' located near the Bailleul – Arras road.
31. Bezzel: *op. cit.* p 57
32. Bühler is wrong about this. The man was from the 11th Jäger Battalion.
33. *Les Armées Françaises dans la Grande Guerre, Tome II* p 24
34. These shields, which feature a loophole for a rifle, turn up frequently as battle-field debris to this day. Almost invariably they are described as 'sniper shields', but in fact these simple protective devices were available on very wide issue within the infantry.
35. Meier-Gesees *Vater Wills Kriegstagebuch* pp 11–13
36. This Maison Blanche was located near to the present day German military cemetery of Neuville St Vaast/Maison Blanche.
37. Windthorst: History Field Artillery Regiment 58 p 58
38. Meier-Gesees *Vater Wills Kriegstagebuch* pp 19–21
39. *Les Armées Françaises dans la Grande Guerre, Tome II* p 160
40. *ibid.* pp 166–167
41. Bezzel: *op. cit.* p 59 This was an extraordinary event. The Bravery Medal in Gold was the highest award available to junior ranks in the Bavarian army and only 1003 were awarded throughout the entire war.
42. *Les Armées Françaises dans la Grande Guerre, Tome II* pp 169–170
43. Bezzel: *op. cit.* p 60
44. *Les Armées Françaises dans la Grande Guerre, Tome II* p 181
45. Meier-Gesees: *op. cit.* pp 27 – 29
46. *ibid.* pp 29 – 33
47. Neither Oberleutnant Bohnsack (who died of a serious stomach wound), nor Vizefeldwebel Heigele have known graves, but Leutnant Traugott Heckert is buried in the *Kamaradengrab* of the German cemetery at St Laurent-Blangy.
48. *Les Armées Françaises dans la Grande Guerre, Tome II* p 189
49. Kriegsarchiv München HS 1992/3
50. Bezzel: *op. cit.* p 63
51. Zahn: History Infantry Regiment 111 p 93

CHAPTER TWO

The Battles of Spring 1915

hroughout the first four months of 1915 the front from the Lorette Spur to the Scarpe was never quiet. Within the limits of munitions and manpower, trench warfare was incessant. Particular dates, such as 16 – 17 January and 3 – 5 March 1915, stood out as occasions when the fight for the Lorette Spur was particularly intense, but it is impossible to look back on this period and to isolate genuinely quiet periods. As a result a steady flow of casualties was evacuated to the rear and the totals mounted with the approach of spring. As May opened, artillery fire crashed down all along the front from Armentières to Arras, increasing in power and weight day by day. Nevertheless, opinions were divided on the German side about what this meant. Several divisions considered that the French forces opposite them had made insufficient preparations for an assault to be imminent.[1] In some places the French front line trenches were a few hundred metres from the German First Position and no efforts seem to have been made in places to dig closer jumping off trenches. Bad weather hindered air reconnaissance and the Allies, in any case, enjoyed air superiority, all of which contributed to the tactical surprise which the French army achieved when it launched forward on a broad front on 9 May, with the firm intention, above all, of capturing Vimy Ridge and breaking through to the east. If the French were to have established themselves on the crest, they would have been able to dominate the Douai Plain with observation and fire.

The troops of the French XXXIII Corps, deployed to the west of Vimy Ridge, were left in no doubt about the significance of what was about to be launched:

"After a campaign which has lasted for nine months, it is high time we made a decisive effort to break through the enemy lines and, as a first step, eject the Germans from French soil. The moment is favourable. Never before has the army been stronger, or inspired by better morale. The enemy appear only to have stationed a few divisions to our front; our forces are four times more numerous than theirs. At our disposal is the strongest force of artillery which has ever been deployed on the battlefield. This is not a *coup de main* operation. It is not a case of capturing a few trenches; rather it is a matter of hitting the enemy extremely violently, defeating them and pursuing them with unparalleled determination and endurance, regardless of the strain, hunger, thirst and suffering involved."[2]

From the beginning of the major French Spring Offensive, Neuville St Vaast was a primary focus of the battle. It is effectively impossible to overstate the ferocity of the artillery bombardment and the sheer savagery of the fighting which followed here. When the blow fell on 9 May 1915, the full fury of five French corps of General d'Urbal's Tenth Army descended on the two divisions of I Bavarian Reserve Corps, which had been in the line by then for months.[3] The German High Command had taken risks in this area, so although by dint of hard, self-sacrificial defence the 1st Bavarian Reserve Division was able, more or less, to maintain its positions, this was not the case for the critical sector from the Lorette Spur to La Targette defended by 5th Bavarian Reserve Division. In addition to the steady toll of casualties suffered by this division, it had had to release two of its best regiments (Bavarian Reserve Infantry Regiments 6 and 13)[4] to stiffen two other newly raised Bavarian divisions. They were replaced by the Prussian Landwehr Regiment 39, which fought gallantly, but was not a like-for-like replacement.

As a result on 9 May considerable ground was gained between Carency and Neuville St Vaast and the garrisons of two villages, Neuville St Vaast especially, because it acted as a forward bastion barring the way to the prize of Vimy Ridge, came in for immensely rough treatment. It is quite possible that the French chain of command was expecting to have to fight extremely hard to make progress in this area because, without any doubt, they let a golden opportunity slip through their fingers when, on 9 May, troops of the Moroccan Division of XXXIII Corps overran the troops of Landwehr Regiment 39[5] and forced their way onto Hill 145 of Vimy Ridge, where the Canadian National Memorial now stands, but were thrown back off it within a few hours by means of desperate German counterattacks, launched by the local reserves (primarily units of Bavarian Reserve Infantry Regiment 7), which rushed to the scene.[6] Bearing in mind that the capture of the ridge was one of the three main objectives which General Foch had been given, this was a poor performance.

In his report of 8 August 1915, sent to the Commander in Chief, General Joffre, Foch blamed the failure on the way the reserves were handled:

> "One point, in particular, which concerns 9 May is worthy of discussion. It would appear that the Moroccan Division, having initially captured Hill 140 [*sic* = modern Hill 145], was unable to hold on to it because neither XXXIII Corps, nor Tenth Army, was in a position to reinforce what it had achieved; this was due to the fact that reserves did not arrive promptly and, perhaps more important, the lack of a properly developed concept for the deployment of reserves. In point of fact, at the moment the assault began, the XXXIII Corps reserve comprised one brigade of the Moroccan Division deployed as follows: One regiment (8th Zouaves) at Mont St Eloi, three kilometres behind the front, one regiment (4th Tirailleurs) at Acq, six kilometres behind the front. This reserve was used in dribs and drabs: three battalions of 8th Zouaves were sent into battle at 1.00 pm, half a battalion of 4th Tirailleurs at 3.30 pm and a further half battalion at 4.00 pm. These reserves were sent forward to assist in consolidation and to repel an expected counter-attack, not to

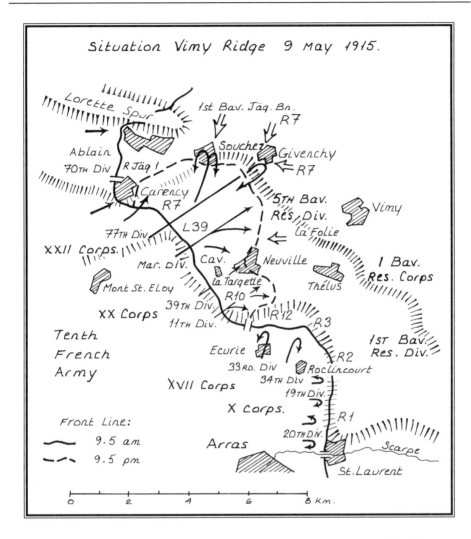

exploit what had been gained. The closest Army Reserve (18th Infantry Division) was twelve kilometres behind the front at Béthonsart . . . The error of holding reserves too far away was common to all levels of command on 9 May . . . In summary, commanders at all levels do not seem to have envisaged the possibility that an attack could be pressed four kilometres in an hour, as was that of the Moroccan Division." [7]

For good measure Foch, who was quoted in the French Official History, also blamed the British First Army:

"The delayed arrival of the reserves was not the sole reason why we only obtained an incomplete result. The attack of Tenth Army was supposed to benefit from an attack to the north carried out by the British First Army, but this operation, which was preceded by a completely inadequate artillery bombardment, stalled almost completely on the 9th, then petered out and was not resumed until the 16th. This failure, followed by inaction from the period 10th to 15th, allowed the Germans to concentrate against Tenth Army all the forces which had arrived newly in the area . . . " [8]

From the start the battles for Ablain, Carency and Neuville St Vaast were notable for a wild, close-quarter intensity, which was remarkable even by Great War standards. Some flavour of experience of these days in mid-May was captured after the war by Bavarian Reserve Infantry Regiment 10, whose 2nd and 3rd Battalions fought and died in and around the village of Neuville St Vaast as the offensive opened.

"Right in the front line, Reserve Oberleutnant Habenicht, commanding 9th Company, was sitting in his newly constructed dugout when he looked at his watch. It was 10.00 am. 'How many have you counted so far?' '2,000, Herr Oberleutnant,' replied his orderlies. '2,000,' muttered the officer, '2,000 since 7.30 am on this tiny piece of ground!' Seconds later the dugout swayed violently or, rather, it was heaved up into the air, just as though it had been hoisted by a giant hand. 'That was a mine that they have just exploded,' bawled Offizierstellvertreter Lobherr, commander of the left hand platoon. A second huge explosion followed. The survivors scrambled out of their dugouts, shouting, 'We are all going to be blown up!' but they retreated quickly because it was no longer possible to count the impact of incoming shells. Red hot shell fragments, clods of earth, sandbags and other debris flew in all directions, pouring down the steps to the dugouts where the defenders, hardly visible because of the fumes and smoke, waited grimly.

"Lobherr kept a look out himself, but could only risk taking swift glimpses; the scythe of death was swinging dangerously close. All of a sudden, at 11.45 am, all was still – just as if an engine had been switched off. 'Here they come,' he roared, 'everybody out of the dugout!' About fifteen men, their senses reeling, raced to climb the dugout steps. Looking out, their eyes lit upon enemy infantry in immense numbers: several battalions, line after line of them, twelve ranks deep, were approaching at an easy pace, not expecting to meet any opposition. To the right, they had already passed us, but over there . . . ! Without orders the defenders opened up a rapid fire, reaping a rich harvest; demanding a high price for this piece of territory. Finally a few German shrapnel rounds burst above the masses! Behind us a French machine gun could be heard as it opened up.

"What is happening over there in trenches 8 and 10? There was nothing to be seen, but we could hear isolated shots. To our front the French had gone to ground, unwilling to advance against us; held in check by a handful of riflemen. How long could it last? 'Shall I go over to the 12th [Bavarian Reserve Infantry Regiment of 1st Bavarian Reserve Division]?' asked Gefreiter Schwarz. 'But you are wounded in the arm!' He was not listening; he had already rushed off. Zig-zagging through the fire like an eel, miraculously he made it back. 'They cannot spare anything. They need every man to save their own skins!' Offizierstellvertreter Lobherr went over himself, but also returned empty handed. Then the Oberleutnant himself followed. He got as far as a sandbag barricade, piled high with German corpses, then was unable to traverse a stretch of trench which was under artillery fire and had to return without having accomplished anything.

"Alone, cut off and left to their own devices, they faced certain defeat. The ammunition began to run out, so they were left with no choice. That night, under the cover of darkness, they pulled back. In the lead were the wounded, who were followed by the remainder of the little garrison carrying all their weapons and equipment. Orientating themselves by the light of weapons flashes and flares, they slipped through the French lines and linked up with 4th Company Bavarian Reserve Infantry Regiment 12. They were the very few men of the gallant 3rd Battalion to break through to the rear. A dark veil of destruction had descended on many others . . .

"The situation had had similarly tragic consequences in the dugout of the battalion commander, Hauptmannn Seekirchner. From the early morning a series of messages arrived, each of them bearing worse news than the last. No sooner had trenches been cleared out than they were flattened again. Was our artillery actually firing? We could see and hear as good as nothing from it amidst the storm of enemy fire, then the last telephone lines which linked the commander to the companies and the artillery were destroyed. Now began a dreadful, nerve-wracking time. It was awful to have to remain there, unable to influence events or to counter our likely fate. Here was a commander cut off from his troops, but still weighed down by a heavy responsibility for them. The Hauptmann stared into the dense wall of smoke which enveloped the forward trenches. Everything humanly possible had been done. Suddenly small arms fire cracked overhead. It came as a marvellous relief. A few short minutes passed, marked by hope and apprehension too. A few men raced past the dugout shouting, 'Here come the French!'

"Nobody wanted to believe it, but when Leutnant Jena, who had been wounded, arrived bearing the same news, there was no longer any doubt. The battalion adjutant, Leutnant Fritsche, Leutnant Diener, (commander of the assault pioneers) and some orderlies hastily constructed a sandbag barrier in front of the dugout. The adjutant peered over it. 'Here they come! Great masses of them! They have already pushed past us to the left and right!' In the circumstances an attempt to continue to offer resistance would have been pointless. The battalion staff pulled back through an enormous weight of artillery fire and linked up with Major Brunner, the sector commander – but they were all alone; without any troops. It was a tragedy for the defence." [9]

In the meantime, back in Neuville itself, 4th and 6th Companies commanded by Reserve Leutnant Weißker and Reserve Oberleutnant Fischer were in support and ready to move. 5th and 7th Companies were located in Vimy and the 1st Battalion was in reserve in Acheville. In the early morning the regimental commander, Oberst Sämmer, ordered an increased state of alert then, at 9.00 am, despatched the uncommitted remainder of 2nd Battalion forward to Neuville and directed 1st Battalion to move to Vimy. Reserve Leutnant Besch, adjutant of 1st Battalion, was up on a roof observing events. He noticed that some of the German soldiers were pulling back followed by large red flags with, behind them, French infantry. At that the officers and men of sector headquarters took up fire positions then poured an immense weight of fire into the advancing French troops. The attack stalled and 5th and 7th Companies were thrown into the fight. In the course of a bitterly contested battle, the garrison of Neuville was pushed back into the northeast corner of the village and several guns were lost.

One of the reasons for the loss of guns was that at the time some of the artillery batteries were operating well forward, either just behind or in amongst the defending infantry. Elements of 1st Battery Field Artillery Regiment 50 were deployed in and around Ablain as the offensive opened.

Leutnant Belzer 1st Battery Field Artillery Regiment 50[10]

"My section was located in Ablain, deployed to counter any attack directly and dug in behind and amongst the infantry. I had the strictest orders that I was only to open fire if Ablain was attacked directly. It was essential that nothing was done to betray our positions and cause the village itself and its advanced infantry outposts to be engaged systematically. I woke at 7.00 am on 9 May. It was a beautiful Sunday morning, the rising sun shining down for the last time on thousands of warriors. We felt refreshed and uplifted by this sunshine. After I had washed and made some coffee I began my rounds. The forward gun was being serviced in the farmyard . . .

"I wanted to visit the other section of the battery, commanded by Reserve Leutnant Pattenhausen and located 900 metres southeast of Ablain by the Mill at Malon [Malaine] on the banks of the Carency river. I noticed immediately that there was an unusual amount of shell fire . . . hardly had I reached the sugar refinery than there was a series of extremely heavy detonations in the village and huge louds of smoke rose from the centre of Ablain. It was becoming rather uncomfortable and I decided to return. I was amazed to be met by a stream of infantrymen, who were seeking cover in the ditches either side of the road. Meanwhile the artillery fire continued to increase, concentrating on the single road through the village. Numerous houses were already destroyed and flames leapt up from others as I hurried back along the road.

"When I reached the barricade, I was blocked by a collapsed house and noticed that the screens erected to cut out the view from the Lorette Spur had been blown over. Every movement in the village could now be observed. Covered in dust and sweating I arrived at the forward gun. Thank God, the telephone line was still working. The section was brought to alert and the Mill section briefed about the situation. I moved to the command post of 1st Battalion Infantry Regiment 109 where we stood and watched as two assault columns up on the Lorette Spur emerged from their trenches to advance on the left flank of Infantry Regiment 111. Something had to be done at once and I raced back to my position. The guns had been dug in to face the most likely threat against Ablain, but now the threat was emerging from a totally unexpected direction.

"The guns were hauled out of their pits and manhandled into position on a slight rise near the *Mairie* [town hall]. The height difference between gun and target was seventy metres; the range about 850 metres. Normal barrel elevation could not cope with this. Only when the sights were placed at 1,200, did we obtain the correct angle. After eight rounds we had a stoppage when a locking bar broke and the spare was in the armourer's chest. We were terribly exposed in the open to enemy small arms fire, so we rushed to drag the gun away and temporarily bury the sights and the breech mechanism . . . I then directed that the Belgian 'Revolver Gun', manned by Foot Artillery men and located in the town hall go into action, taking over from the damaged gun . . .

"The propellant powder of these old shells produced such enormous quantities of smoke that there could be no question of observation from the gun position itself. Fortunately, after a few rounds had been fired, the firing pin broke. Frankly, this captured weapon with its utterly useless ammunition was more trouble than it was worth. It was now all down to the gun near the church. I directed its fire by telephone from the forward gun position but, because no movement could be seen in the enemy trenches, I soon ceased fire. This was about 10.00 am. At that time a fragmented message arrived from the Mill section. All that could be made out, before the line went dead was, 'The French are . . .' Probably the handset had been destroyed before the French arrived. Whatever the case, the section had obviously been overrun and could no longer offer resistance . . . "

Belzer's description of the hectic scenes of desperate activity around Ablain cover the remainder of the events of the next few days in considerable detail. Bearing a charmed life, he was everywhere, causing guns to be repaired, re-distributing ammunition and bringing fire down, often at extremely close range, until, eventually, ground was ceded in this sector and the entire battery was relieved some days later. During the afternoon of 9 May, he witnessed the gallant charge of the French Moroccan Division onto Hill 145 and played a small part in repelling it.

Leutnant Belzer 1st Battery Field Artillery Regiment 50[11]

"At 1.00 pm the southern end of the heights which are arranged like a horseshoe around Givenchy were attacked by the enemy. The breakthrough between Carency Copse and Neuville allowed French assault troops – blacks from Senegal and Foreign Legionnaires [*sic*] to advance in the direction of Souchez – Hill 123. Once this line was attained the fate of the crest line Hill 119 [The Pimple] – Hill 140 [Hill 145] was as good as sealed. Almost the entire artillery of the Corps was now under small arms fire. By the deployment of every man and round available, these wild hordes were thrown back from the crest. That was decisive. The three guns in Ablain were able to play a full part, by engaging the retreating enemy in the flank. At a range of 3,200 metres we caused the enemy heavy losses. It was not until they reached the dip along the line of the Souchez – Arras road that they could escape our fire.

"Simultaneous to this operation, the enemy had launched a subsidiary one which, with a bit more effort, would have succeeded. Through the temporary occupation of Souchez, the enemy had managed to cut off the advanced posts Lorette Spur – Ablain – Carency from all possible support. Spotting the danger at once we launched an immediate counterstroke with two companies that threw the enemy back to the line of the Souchez cemetery. This meant that we once more had the use of the road to Ablain and, although it could not be used by day because it was under constant fire, it did allow some support to get through at night."

At mid-morning 9 May, led by Major Schäzler, men of 1st Battalion Bavarian Reserve Infantry Regiment 10 rushed forward to reinforce the Neuville St Vaast area and 4th Company under Leutnant Schludi succeeded in taking up positions before the village to provide protection for a battery that was in extreme danger of being overrun. The remainder of 1st Battalion launched a counter-attack. This did not succeed in recapturing the entire village, but it did bring the French advance to a halt. Furthermore, with the exception of one battery, all the guns which had been lost previously were back in German hands. Reinforcements arrived during the afternoon. These were insufficient to permit the counter-attack to be pressed further forward, but the French were also prevented from advancing further. A gallant attempt was made by a party under Offizierstellvertreter Seeburger to recover the lost guns. The attackers reached the battery position, but their attack was then broken up by heavy fire.

By the end of 9 May, the French attack had definitely been held within Neuville St Vaast, despite the loss of the forward positions. Early on the morning of 10 May, the French launched another attack in great strength against the battered German defences. House to house fighting broke out; there were repeated attacks and German counter-attacks but, fundamentally, the French could at that time make no more impression on the village. Heavy attacks continued during the next few days. These led to serious French losses and a rising toll of German casualties, but no more ground was lost so, by 15 May when Bavarian Reserve Infantry Regiment 10 was relieved, the immediate crisis appeared to be over in Neuville St Vaast but, equally, it was quite evident that in the coming days the French would continue to press hard in this sector.

On 10 May 1915, the main priority for the German chain of command was to take steps to recapture all the positions which had been lost the previous day. One attack order after the other was issued, each of which stressed the need to restore the situation and laid down the boundaries for each of the units and formations arriving to reinforce the troops already deployed. None of these attacks achieved very much. To begin with, the overall situation was far from clear. The confused nature of the fighting had led to considerable mixing of units and sub-units. There had been particularly high officer casualties and, whether killed captured or wounded, the result was the same. Many command appointments were not filled. Large numbers of the reinforcing troops were unfamiliar with the ground. They arrived late, exhausted or in the wrong place. There was insufficient artillery to support the troops already in place adequately, so support of the newly-arrived units was particularly problematic.

Throughout the day there were desultory attempts to advance the German positions, but all failed to make any significant progress and, by the evening of 10 May, orders were issued that all efforts were to be directed to the development and holding of the current line. As was to be expected the French army renewed its attacks with the utmost vigour but, the momentum having gone out of the attacks, the German lines gaining in strength and reinforcing artillery arriving behind the threatened sector almost by the hour, the result was a huge rise in French casualties for very slight additional gains. The front from Souchez to Neuville remained under intense pressure, but was held successfully. The gaps in the defences north and south of Hill 123 were closed off on 11 May, two companies of 3rd Battalion Landwehr Infantry Regiment 39 having counter-attacked the southern slopes of this feature during the evening of 10 May. There were still areas which were causing concern; all efforts to plug the gap between Souchez and the *Artilleriemulde* [Artillery Hollow – to the north of the Lorette Spur] continued to be in vain and the situation in and around Carency was grave. Such was the appalling nature of the fighting on the Lorette Spur that the greater part of the trench system west and south of Carency had been lost on 9 May and the remaining positions were only maintained with the utmost difficulty in the face of continuous French attacks in strength. By the evening of 10 May the remnants of Reserve Jäger Battalion 1 and 3rd Battalion Bavarian Reserve Infantry Regiment 7 were fighting grimly to retain a hold on the last few sections of trench in German hands. Emergency calls for assistance in the form of reinforcements, small arms ammunition, grenades and food were met back in Souchez, where Major Düwell, the commander of Bavarian Reserve Jäger

Battalion 1, sent forward a company of Infantry Regiment 109 during the night 10/11 May and followed this up at about midday on 11th with a further two platoons of Infantry Regiment 111.[12] The following night Oberstleutnant Esche of Landwehr Infantry Regiment 39 made his way forward to Carency at the head of two composite companies and took command. It was too little, too late. At 9.00 am a massive three hour bombardment, involving the use of 23,000 shells, crashed down on the village, to be followed by an all-out assault against the company of Infantry Regiment 109, which was occupying Trench 105 to the north of Carency. This attack first broke into the position, then cut off the survivors and the way was open for an assault on the village from three sides.

This overwhelming French attack was countered by the remainder of three companies of Reserve Jäger Battalion 1, with six machine guns, two platoons of 10th Company Infantry Regiment 111, a weak company of Landwehr Infantry Regiment 39, a battalion from Infantry Regiment 109, one howitzer and a single remaining gun of 5th Battery Bavarian Reserve Field Artillery Regiment 5. During desperate fighting during the next two days, the remainder of the garrison was all killed or captured and the fate of Oberstleutnant Esche and his men was never determined with any accuracy. They were missing and Carency had fallen.[13] The German commanders had no choice but to pull back their line.

By about 13 May, the initial impetus of French attacks began to ebb away in the northern sector. The sheer intensity of the fighting during the previous ninety six hours had taken its toll and the weather worsened until squally rain storms dominated and reduced most of the battlefield to one great squalid swamp. Not for nothing were the French soldiers nicknamed, 'The mud men of Artois'. That is not to say, however, that the offensive was over: far from it. At 2.00 pm on 15 May an extraordinary weight of fire began to fall on Souchez. There was a brief pause around 4.00 pm, then it came down, worse than ever, until 6.00 pm. Survivors later recalled that they had never previously experienced such a bombardment. The trees in the grounds of the chateau were reduced to matchwood, the chateau itself collapsed completely and the chapel was reduced to a heap of ruins. The enemy trenches were seen to be full of men, but no attack followed. It was a complete mystery, but some ascribed it to the particularly powerful response by the German guns.

Further to the south the battle still raged around the area of the Labyrinth, centred about 1,500 metres south of Neuville. The fighting had been especially severe here on 9 May when the initial French penetrations had been made and a week later there was no sign of any let up. Both sides were well aware that this area was the key to possession of Vimy Ridge and neither would yield. The French strained every sinew to secure both the village and the Labyrinth and so be in a position to assault the ridge from this direction, but the German troops in Neuville, under the command of Major Brunner, were well aware what was at stake. They hung on grimly to the northern half, engaging day and night in the bloodiest variety of street fighting from house to house. At times different parts of the same building were in the hands of both sides as the fighting swung to and fro from the cellars to the attics. Buildings and street barricades changed hands constantly and the confused nature of the battle meant that men were constantly being taken prisoner and released once more.

Casualties on both sides mounted alarmingly as every barricade, ruin and shattered building was disputed and, meanwhile, major attacks continued all around the area, hammering in on the northwest corner and the southern and western edges of the village. Under constant artillery fire the defenders struggled to maintain their positions. Occasionally they were able to snatch a short break in the so-called *Neuville-Grotte* [a major underground shelter], where the supporting troops waited in readiness, but for the majority sleep became a thing of memory as every moment of the night was taken up repairing and shoring up the defences – especially on the threatened eastern edge of the village. Pionier companies (4th Company Bavarian 2nd Pionier Battalion, 3rd and 5th Companies Bavarian 4th Pionier Battalion and 1st Bavarian Reserve Pionier Company) were rushed forward to work on these defences, which they did with great heroism, despite being under incessant fire.

Unteroffizier Goldfuß 1st Bavarian Reserve Pionier Company [14]

"On 9 May 1915 the French succeeded in wrecking our positions around Neuville St Vaast with drum fire and forcing their way into our trenches. A stop line was swiftly created in Neuville, which was located about three kilometres behind the front line. Our company played a leading part in this action. By bringing down heavy fire on us during the days that followed the enemy hoped to drive us completely out of the village, where they had already established some footholds. On 12 May we were subjected to a crazy weight of fire. Guns of all calibres poured fire onto our positions, concentrating especially on the village. Massive 280 mm shells crashed down, sending up great clouds of smoke and collapsing entire houses at a stroke. Small calibre guns, the so-called *Hollerbüchsen*, [15] made a terrible racket. Their shells passed so close over our parapet that they frequently carried sandbags away and cost the lives of many a true comrade.

"Whilst under this fire, I constructed a sandbag barricade in a sunken lane which led into the village. The enemy let us finish our work in peace then, suddenly, brought down such a concentration of fire that in no time flat the barricade had been blown away once more. After the fire had been going on for three hours, the enemy suddenly lifted it to the rear and onto approach routes and roads. Then we could see the French attacking towards us; black they were, with grim, snarling faces. To the left of the sunken road our infantry beat off the attack. Back in the sunken road we calmly let the black devils close up on us then. Together with four more engineers I dashed up to the right to a position about twenty metres away. There we let enemy by pass us, so we could hit them from behind.

"Throwing as one, we hurled five grenades at them. These burst right amongst them and in seconds they were all dealt with. We then rapidly rebuilt the barricade. About two hours later enemy soldiers began working their way towards us. Unfortunately we were now out of hand grenades, so they were able to work their way forward and take cover in some buildings. Some even forced their way past the barrier, but we immediately finished them off in hand-to-hand fighting. It was not long before our position became serious. The scoundrels, who had taken cover in the buildings, brought heavy small arms fire down on us. One of my comrades was killed and two others wounded. In the nick of time, thank heavens, we were re-supplied with hand grenades, which cheered we engineers up considerably.

"Great! We began throwing once more and our grenades certainly had the desired effect. The [vacated] houses were occupied by our infantry and we engineers finished off the barricade. The enemy tried everything with their guns and mortars to drive us back from the positions we were maintaining, because we were making their further advance extremely difficult, but it was all in vain! We engineers were determined not to be driven back. Once during the night, at 2.00 am, we heard the sound of hooters and shouted commands coming from the enemy trenches *Allons! Allons!* [Let's go!]. A violent attack was launched with much shouting, but not a man got into our position and not one returned to his starting point. Yet again we rebuilt our barricade and we went on holding it until finally we were relieved and were able to leave this hellish cauldron."

Frequently the efforts of the engineers were in vain as the French artillery engaged each of their efforts to close the gap between the village and the cemetery by means of a trench. The number of wounded to be cared for increased enormously until eventually the *Neuville-Grotte* was full to overflowing with them. Enormous efforts were made to evacuate them under the cover of darkness; the carrying parties coming forward with fresh supplies and removing individuals as and when they could. There was a shortage of every type of supply – especially drinking water, but the troops managed to endure the intense pressure for eight days and nights in succession. It was an outstanding performance by Bavarian Reserve Infantry Regiment 10 as a whole and three commanders in particular: Oberst Sämmer, Major Brunner and Hauptmann Hitzler.

Sämmer, the regimental and sector commander, moved his headquarters forward to Neuville during the first morning, so as to be able to direct the battle more closely and then spent the entire week at the focus of the fighting with his men. Major Brunner, commanding officer of 1st Battalion Bavarian Reserve Infantry Regiment 10, was the man whose inspirational leadership on 9 May meant that the garrison of Neuville held the first ferocious French assaults. He then went on to lead the fighting at the head of a *Kampfgruppe* [Battlegroup] Brunner, which took under command all reinforcements which made it forward to the threatened area. Then there was Hauptmann Hitzler who, together with the men of 3rd Battalion Bavarian Reserve Infantry Regiment 12, fought his way forward at the critical moment on 9 May and remained to defend the northwest sector of Neuville against all attacks, until his death on 14 May when he was mortally wounded by a shell splinter. These three men and the men they led put up a first class defence against the odds and were rightly proud of what had been achieved, albeit at the price of seventy five per cent casualties in some of the companies.[16]

As the full scale of the battle became clear and the reserves which were near at hand had all been drawn in to the fighting, it was necessary for the German chain of command to look further afield for reinforcements. At the time the front of XIV Reserve Corps was calm, so 26th Reserve Division, responsible for the front line down south on the Somme from Serre to the Albert – Bapaume road, was called upon to supply troops. A comprehensive reorganisation of the front saw Reserve Infantry Regiment 99 withdrawn from the line around Beaumont Hamel and three of its four Battalions, together with the staff of 52 Reserve Infantry Brigade, despatched north to assist. Strenuous efforts by German defenders on the ground had prevented the French, who had continued to drive forward with the utmost élan and determination, from getting established on the heights just to the west of La Folie, but the position was precarious in the extreme as the French continued to press forward against Neuville St Vaast. In command of 3rd and 4th Battalions Reserve Infantry Regiment 99, Major Gerhard von Meerscheidt-Hüllesem was ordered to take command of the sector and to relieve the hard-pressed defenders, who by now were at the end of their tether.

During 15 and 16 May the battalions of Reserve Infantry Regiment 99 gradually assumed responsibility for the village, which was outflanked to the north and south. As the companies moved forward they had to yield constantly to the streams of exhausted and seriously wounded men moving towards the rear and also to absorb the descriptions of the desperate nature of the position and the fighting from their NCO guides. Eventually the relief was complete and, as French aircraft circled constantly overhead and the roar of the artillery and mortars never ceased, the front line was manned by the 3rd Battalion: from north to south 12th, 9th, 10th and 11th Companies, who clung to positions in gardens, sunken roads and wrecked buildings. The war diary of 10th Company recorded the move as follows; [17]

"After many hold ups, we finally arrived at the entrance to Neuville, which was barricaded with wagons. The closer we approached the centre of the village, the greater the desolation. We picked our way carefully across the rubble. Passing the *Felsenkeller* [Rock Cellar – a common name for a solidly constructed mined dugout], we linked up with the battalion. Climbing over piles of rubble we entered a garden, through which an almost flattened communication trench ran. Then we bore away to the left, through a house and, climbing over collapsed beams and more rubble, we crossed the road, passing several half-charred corpses. Gradually the communication trench improved. A member of Infantry Regiment 40 met us and led us off down a shallow trench. The trench had several shallow shelter scrapes along its walls, but they looked as though the rain was about to collapse them. Before the relief was complete a huge fire fight broke out and there were heavy explosions, probably mortar rounds, in our immediate vicinity. No attack followed, however – probably due to our aggressive returning of the fire."

Reserve Infantry Regiment 99 succeeded in holding its precarious positions in Neuville St Vaast for several days, but it was felt that unless something could be done to relieve the deep outflanking of the village, it would not be tenable in the long term. 115th Division, therefore, ordered a counter-attack to be launched by troops of Infantry Regiments 40, 136 and 171, together with three detachments of Reserve Infantry Regiment 99, with the aim of expanding the German position in the southeast sector of the village. Despite all the stress and strain of the last few days, Reserve Infantry Regiment 99 managed to produce 300 volunteers under Major Karst, commander of 3rd Battalion, to take part in this attack. One of the detachment commanders later wrote a detailed report about it to Oberst Friedrich Grall, the regimental commander.

Leutnant Arnold 3rd Battalion Reserve Infantry Regiment 99 [18]

"Reserve Infantry Regiment 99 was required to produce three one hundred-man columns under the command of Petri, Martin and me. We received the order to this effect in Neuville the night before the assault, together with the additional information that detailed divisional orders would not be available before the following morning. In the meantime we were to organise the assault troops, which were to be drawn from volunteers. The difficulties caused us in carrying out this order in the short time available may only really be appreciated by somebody who was actually deployed in the witches' cauldron which was Neuville. Forming groups of volunteers from men deployed in a village that was totally wrecked by gun fire, was constantly under fire from three sides, where the men were scattered in locations varying from an underground cave that held about 700 men and was difficult to reach, to isolated cellars scattered throughout the village, to obtain men who were almost exhausted from the preceding days of house-to-house fighting was a task whose fulfilment demanded the utmost commitment.

"During the night I succeeded in assembling my men so that I could provide them with the necessary inspiration for the operation. The following morning, at about 10.00 am, we received orders from Division via Major Karst, commander of the 3rd Storm Detachment of Reserve Infantry Regiment 99. In accordance with the orders the storm columns were divided into three waves. Our regiment formed the second wave. The task of the first wave was to break in. The second was to consolidate and hold, whilst the third was available in support. One hour before the assault began a battalion of mortars was to destroy the point to be attacked. On 22 May, at exactly 7.00 pm, the mortars opened fire but, unfortunately, this did not have the desired effect. Almost all the rounds dropped short, landing close to my column and burying some of my men alive. It was certainly not a happy sight for us to watch the mortar bombs missing their targets; in particular because we had been told, 'The mortars will do all the work. The infantry simply has to march forward.'

" . . . At exactly 8.00 pm I led my men forward in the assault along the line of a collapsed communication trench, with the aim of pushing on through a previously designated gateway into the area round the town hall. Unfortunately it was not possible to find the column to my front and the same was true later of the supporting column. As a result I was thrown back on my own resources. The gateway that we had to break through gave onto a crossroads that was under heavy fire from all sides. As a result we lost many a brave lad. My engineer leutnant, who was to have constructed an obstacle, was killed at once. It was a moment for decisive action. With or without an obstacle we had to get across the street and into the French houses. I collected together a little group of men and, together with them, forced a way across the road and into the houses.

"Unfortunately we had a considerable number of casualties here as well. Hirsche got a bullet though the foot, so that left me with no officers; Leutnant Stamm, my second officer, having been killed the previous night. Altogether twenty men crossed unscathed, for the remainder the weight of small arms fire made it impossible. Now we got down to work. We cleared six houses with hand grenades and took six prisoners. Then it was a matter of preparing the open windows for defence; a task to which the prisoners contributed greatly. Naturally the French concentrated all their fire against us but, with the few grenades we had brought across, we managed to keep them at bay. In the meantime it was 8.30 pm. We had no sandbags and no grenades left. In addition I had no idea about the progress of the attack to my left, the progress of which was intended to remove the threat to my rear.

"A patrol I had sent out previously returned to report that the area around the town hall was swarming with enemy soldiers. I was now more or less cut off. I immediately despatched two messages to regimental headquarters requesting support, hand grenades and other stores. We had to use a French water bottle to throw the messages across the road to my men on the other side. They arrived safely, but unfortunately no support arrived. At 3.00 am an order from Infantry Regiment 40 reached me to give up street fighting, because the situation was so unfavourable. With heavy hearts, we had to abandon the houses whose capture had cost us such heavy losses."

The situation was much the same to the south in the Labyrinth, where Bavarian Reserve Infantry Regiment 12 bore the burden of the French offensive, launching one counter-attack after another in the vain attempt to close the gap which the French had forced in their First Position and to hold on grimly to their forward positions on their right flank which were threatened from three sides. After three days of desperate fighting, the commander of I Bavarian Reserve Corps delegated to 1st Bavarian Reserve Division the discretion to withdraw from this endangered place, but it was felt that if this firm shoulder fell, it would become impossible to hold Neuville and that therefore the way to Vimy Ridge via Neuville and Thélus would be opened up, so the decision was taken to hold. This was all the more bold because at that time there were absolutely no troops in reserve within the Corps which could be sent to bolster the forward positions.

Working together, the staffs of 1st Bavarian Reserve Division and 2 Bavarian Reserve Brigade brought together a scratch force comprising 1st Battalion Bavarian Reserve Infantry Regiment 12, the Assault Pioneer Detachment of Bavarian Reserve Infantry Regiment 12, 1st and 3rd Companies Bavarian Reserve Infantry Regiment 3 and one platoon of engineers from 3rd Battalion Bavarian Pionier Battalion 18 and launched it on 12 May in a grinding counter-attack towards the so-called *Lossow-Arkaden*. The engineers managed to re-take about 150 metres of the *Arkaden*, but the French in turn recaptured it. Benefiting from a constant stream of reinforcements from the rear, the French troops continued to press their attacks in this area. Bavarian Reserve Infantry Regiment 12 was attacked from the south and from the rear by the French launching from the *Lossow-Arkaden*, but the defence held firm, despite the fact that the assaults were repeated each day up to six times across the same ground; the French having to withdraw time and again to the protection of the *Arkaden*.

Some ground was gained along the line of the road towards Thélus, however. During the evening of 11 May the German garrison was driven out of the cemetery after an intense bombardment of several hours duration, leaving the French to inherit an appalling scene of desolation, where the corpses of the newly killed German soldiers were intermingled with the remains of villagers long since dead, whose graves had been smashed by the fire. Rushing to the rescue, the men of 3rd Battalion Infantry Regiment 93 of IV Corps saved the day.[19] Having been held on call in Bailleul throughout 10 May, they were alerted shortly after midnight the following night. Marching rapidly through the night, they received orders in Vimy to relieve elements of Landwehr Regiment 39 and Infantry Regiment 40. This they achieved by 6.00 am 11 May and so prevented any further advance towards Thélus for the time being. Reinforced in turn by 1st and 6th Companies Infantry Regiment 157, 11th and 12th Companies Infantry Regiment 93, they held on under constant heavy artillery fire until 15 May, when they moved to relieve the worn out men of 2nd Battalion Bavarian Reserve Infantry Regiment 12, who were holding positions to the west of the Vimy – Arras road.

The battle for the Lorette Spur continued unabated and formations of 117th Division were warned to move forward and relieve the hard-pressed defenders from 28th Infantry Division. It was none too soon. In six days of fighting, Grenadier Regiment 110 alone had lost 150 men killed, 432 wounded and 396 missing. Infantry Regiment 106, for its part, was as good as wiped out. It had suffered 311 killed, 898 wounded and 240 missing.[20] During the late afternoon of 18 May, Major Mund, commander of Infantry Regiment 157, assembled all the officers of the regiment in a derelict café in Givenchy to brief them and issue his orders, which concluded with the words, 'Gentlemen the situation is extremely difficult. Nevertheless the positions must be held at all costs. The honour of the regiment demands that we achieve this regardless of how serious the casualties are.'[21] Returning to their companies and battalions, the troops lost no time in preparing to depart.

Major Guhr 2nd Battalion Infantry Regiment 157 [22]

"Once the companies had arrived in Givenchy they marched forward to their individual sectors. The night was pitch black and although the route followed a broad road, it was easy to stray off course. Columns moving in the opposite directions and numerous vehicles of all types completely blocked the road. The enemy maintained a rapid rate of fire, not only with his artillery, but also with small arms so, as a result, a constant stream of projectiles passed overhead. Altogether it was a slow and terrible advance. At long last we closed up on Souchez. One shell hole after another slowed our progress. It was raining cats and dogs, the pathway underfoot was wet and slippery and the air was fouled by the stink of corpses. Still we pushed on gradually, the battalion staff moving well in front of the remainder of the battalion: Stabsarzt Eppenstein, Leutnant Rumpf, the clerks and runners and I. Suddenly my legs shot out from underneath me and I found myself at the bottom of a crater lying in a repulsive, quivering, stinking mass. I had fallen right into the body of a horse in an advanced state of decomposition. My companions could only with difficulty conceal their *Schadenfreude*[23] at my sorry situation and my accompanying profanities.

"Finally we arrived at Battalion Headquarters, which was located in the cellar of a house in Souchez. The staff of Reserve Infantry Regiment 10, which was already located there, advised us to move out, because the entire place was flooded. Acting at their word, we decamped to a covered culvert just to the north of the sunken road in Souchez. On the way there Stabsarzt Eppenstein disappeared into the very same shell hole as I had previously. His was a rather less grisly experience than mine had been; nevertheless I in turn experienced the same feeling of *Schadenfreude*. A dressing station was established in a home for the disabled in Souchez, whilst the staff set itself up in its gloomy hole. In the meantime the companies had reached their new locations.

"In the morning there was a sharp increase in artillery fire, followed by a storm of small arms fire. A tour of inspection as dawn broke that day revealed that the positions were in ruins. All the trenches had been flattened! There could be no command and control because all the telephone links had been cut and the weight of fire prevented the runners from moving. Feeding was out of the question. The troops could not stand up and expose themselves because of the risk, so it was completely out of the question to contemplate issuing rations."

Once the deployment was complete, 1st Battalion Infantry Regiment 157 had moved through the area of Infantry Regiment 111 and taken over the sector in the *Schlammulde* [Mud Hollow] from 2nd Battalion Reserve Infantry Regiment 22. 3rd Battalion Infantry Regiment 157 linked up with 1st Battalion Infantry Regiment 111 and occupied the eastern part of Ablain as far as the cemetery. 1st Battalion Infantry Regiment 157 continued down to the Souchez river, then eastwards along it as far as the southern exit of Souchez. It was a very constricted and vulnerable battlefield. Everywhere could be seen the traces of the battles which had been raging for weeks. Trenches and dugouts were wrecked and, down near the Souchez river, the remaining trenches had over fifty centimetres of water and mud in them and the dugouts were flooded. Delivery of rations was erratic because heavy shelling prevented the field kitchens from setting up near the front and there were no usable links between the companies.

The tactical situation was also poor. Pressure of the constant battles meant that many defensive positions had been dug where the fighting had stopped, leaving them vulnerable to fire from a flank or even to the rear in some cases. The wire obstacle, where it still existed, was strung with the rotting corpses of men long dead: Germans and both black and white French troops lay sprawled and intermingled, filling the air with an appalling stench. Command and control was almost impossible; virtually all the telephone links had been destroyed and their repair was almost beyond human capacity. Despite the difficulties, the incessant French assaults, launched repeatedly over the same ground, were beaten back, though sometimes only after the most desperate hand to hand clashes. Improvement in the French positions on the Lorette Spur meant that almost the entire position was under constant enemy observation, but somehow the defence held for a while.

A further massive French effort on 21 May enjoyed more success. The defence was pushed back, a two-company counter-stroke failed to make any meaningful progress and the line had to be re-established precariously following the line of an unmade track along the northern edge of Ablain. Trenches were pushed forward to the Lorette Spur and the new position did at least provide some flank protection and prevented further French penetrations in this area for the time being. The 2nd Battalion Infantry Regiment 157 had suffered very heavy losses during this fighting, but the situation was restored when elements of Reserve Infantry Regiment 202, Jäger Battalion 13 and Reserve Jäger Battalion 12 were rushed forward, enabling the battered Infantry Regiment 157 companies to drop back into support.[24]

Still the French pressure was maintained in an unrelenting manner. Additional reinforcements, some of them from Grenadier Regiment 109, Bavarian Reserve Infantry Regiments 11 and 22 and the newly-formed Reserve Infantry Regiment 201, were thrown into the battle and, eventually, the surviving remnants of Infantry Regiment 157, who had been deployed in Ablain, were fully relieved. Meanwhile the battle continued and other companies of the regiment continued to suffer badly. Officer casualties were particularly high, demonstrating how important the personal example of the junior commanders was in holding the strained defences together. Leutnants Börger and Millarsch of 8th Coy were killed on 25 May, as was Reserve Leutnant Strzibny of 12th Company on 27 May.[25] Leutnant Pätzold of 11th Company was severely wounded on the same day. Some idea of the harsh nature of this battle and the appalling conditions under which it was fought may be derived from the following account by a platoon commander who was deployed in Ablain.

Feldwebel Geburek 8th Company Infantry Regiment 157 [26]

"Gradually morning drew closer and, with it, the time for my with-drawal to the dugout I had been allocated on the edge of the village, near the church. Some sentries who occupied reasonable positions in the ruins of walls remained on duty to observe. The remainder of the platoon, some sixty five men, including the machine gun crew, had to make their way back carefully to the dugout without being spotted. This manoeuvre was highly successful, but it was extremely difficult to accommodate sixty five men in a poorly constructed dugout with space for forty at the most. This dugout had been built in the most basic manner. It was only meant to house a few men, so there was no provision for ventilation or any other amenity. Worse, it offered only cover from view and was merely proof against splinters or small arms fire. Any artillery shell would have gone straight through the weak wooden ceiling.

"The only solution was for me to grip the situation rigidly and to cram each man into the smallest space possible. It was now broad daylight and there could be no question of moving elsewhere. It was not simple to arrange, but with goodwill much had already been achieved elsewhere; it could be done here too and speed was essential. So equipment was stacked in one corner, rifles in another near the exit and each man sat down between the legs of another. It worked. The worst consequences of being thus crammed together were not clear at first. They flowed from it being a hot and dry season of the year. The few observation slits in the walls and the door, which was tucked away in a corner, permitted hardly any air to enter; a particular problem for the sixteen men wedged under or on the beds against the rear wall. To begin with it was not so bad, because the morning was still cool. But as the sun got up and the enemy artillery fire increased, it became more and more unpleasant.

"Already at 5.00 am two men were wounded, one of whom suffered concussion, due to pieces of tiles being flung off the ruins of the church when a heavy mortar bomb fell on them. We had no choice, but to keep them with us. Any movement and the enemy would have been able to direct the fire right at us, because we were in full view of [troops on] the Lorette Spur. As the day wore on our thirst increased, but despite having been promised it, we had received no water. The universal stink of corpses made this problem even worse. We were steadily being driven mad by it. We shared what little we had, but it was really too little in the awful circumstances and the foul air. Such was the lack of oxygen that every twenty minutes we had to swap over the men on and under the beds with those sitting near to the door. The only way was to scramble over the heads and shoulders of the sitting men.

"Jam tins made the rounds constantly so that men could relieve themselves. At one point three enormous rounds impacted just in front of the dugout, causing everything to shake violently; fortunately there were no worse consequences. The hands of our watches crawled at a snail's pace towards the hour of relief, but we had to stick it out until 9.30 pm, a full nineteen hours. It was only by harsh means that I could maintain discipline then, when I later ordered the dugout to be cleared, I discovered to my horror that two of my men had suffocated where they lay on the beds; these brave lads had succumbed just before the hour of relief came, but the sight of their corpses hurt us all terribly. It would have been far better to have been blown into small pieces by a shell than to have died in these conditions.

"Nevertheless fate had been kind to us. It was far worse for our comrades from the other two platoons. They had taken cover in three normal cellars. In one of these cellars was my company commander, Leutnant Börger, together with forty two other men. At about 9.30 am a large mortar round penetrated the cellar and buried everything under a mound of rubble. A second cellar which contained twenty men suffered the same fate as the first. I did not find out about these events until I went to look for orders that evening. I searched for the house, but could not find it: it had collapsed completely. I could, however, hear the groans and whimpering of the wounded coming from beneath the rubble. I immediately set two sections to work with spades. They managed to recover five men seriously wounded, but all the remainder were dead.

"The night following this dreadful day was relatively quiet in comparison with the usual racket. I reported the situation to Battalion Headquarters by telephone and in writing and later received adequate supplies of food and water from them. I also split my men into smaller groups in order to prevent a repetition of the previous disasters. All the time, we maintained a good lookout from the forward trench in order to avoid being surprised. All these measures paid off, because despite large quantities of artillery fire coming down, we suffered no more significant casualties during daylight hours. The following night we were relieved. Our replacements arrived at 12.30 am; whereupon, exhausted, we began the dangerous march to the rear. Far behind the front, arriving in dribs and drabs, the remnants of the company gathered together. At 4.15 am on 27 May, we reached our quarters in Lens and thereby hoped to have prolonged our lives by forty eight hours: because that was the amount of time we had been allowed for rest and recuperation, provided that there were no alarms during that time (which was often the case)."

Despite the unceasing French pressure and the gradual forcing back of the German lines, there was the utmost reluctance to yield any more terrain north west of Souchez and one formation after another continued to be deployed forward to the area.

Reserve Leutnant Joachim Freiherr von der Goltz 8th Company Infantry Regiment 142 [27]

"The Lorette Spur! That was the place we fed with our blood; that was the place of our greatest suffering and our greatest source of pride. It was the month of May, scented by lilacs and cherry blossom, marked by waving narcissi and nodding cowslips. The musketiers were occupying rest quarters, lying in the grass and sunning themselves. In the distance could be seen the gentle blue outline of a hill over which the sun was setting. Suddenly there was a flash, then another, all accompanied by a rumbling roar and clouds of smoke. These grew in size until the entire hill was crowned by one great column of dust and smoke. It was the evening 'blessing' on that place of memory, the Lorette Spur!

"It was the end of May: *The regiment is to return to the Lorette Spur! Departure tomorrow at 7.00 am.* 'Lads, act like men', urged the Leutnant during roll call. That was easy. We were men all right. During his briefing to the officers of the 2nd Battalion the commander said, 'I can see from the light in your eyes that I need do nothing extra to inspire your courage . . .' Did we really have shining eyes? Well the commander certainly said so and we loved him for it, even when he was cursing and angry. He continued, 'The regiment has been given a mission of honour . . .' Beaming eyes all round – yes, really. These were officers he could trust.

"Friday evening the head of the battalion column arrived at Souchez. Can it really be Souchez? There used to be a house over there. That cellar over there where a section of us used to shelter is now flooded. That dead horse never used to be there – nor that corpse in field grey either. That undamaged house: it stinks abominably now, but last winter it kept us warm. That was then! We reach the cross roads. Is it going to be the *Schlammtal* [Mud Valley – just to the north of the Lorette Spur]? No we are off to the sugar refinery [located due west of Souchez]. Oh well, it cannot be any worse. We reach the outskirts of Souchez. Flares go up and shells are already falling. The stretcherbearers come rushing over. Yes we are back at the Lorette Spur.

"Battalion order: *At 2.00 am 5th and 8th Companies are to assault the sugar refinery*. A hand grenade dump has been established forward. Each man files past and collects five grenades. A wehrmann clenches his fist, 'They will soon know that we are back!' The battalion disappears down into a communication trench. Corps Order of the Day in June: 'The regiment, acting with unshakeable bravery and high courage, defended the Lorette Spur once more against all assaults of an enemy who enjoyed overwhelming strength . . .'

"The regiment was relieved. Lorette Spur, you bloody bride of the regiment! Farewell Lorette Spur!"

Goltz had personal reasons in plenty to remember this dreadful period of desperate, close-quarter fighting from 27 May to 7 June which cost the regiment eighty three killed, 332 wounded and 334 missing. During a fierce day of attack and counter-attack on 1 June, his position overrun by a large French assault, he only survived by feigning death and lying immobile for fifteen hours in a small shell hole only eighty metres from the French position.

French pressure was also beginning to tell further south where, at the cost of dreadful casualties, the French troops became firmly established in the area of the Neuville cemetery, just to the south of the road in the direction of Thélus. Feeding in more men and further developing the location into a strongpoint, the French were able, not only to complete the capture of Neuville later, but also to threaten the viability of the Labyrinth. In these unfavourable circumstances, in early June the regiments of the 15th Infantry Division found themselves entraining from their positions many miles to the south, to relieve the hard-pressed defenders at this primary focus of the battles. First to deploy was Infantry Regiment 161, whose 1st Battalion was launched straight into an attack. Their objective was a French salient east of *Lossow-Arkade*. Supported by hand grenade teams and numerous flamethrowers, 2nd Company Infantry Regiment 161 prepared to attack.

Gefreiter Wagner 2nd Company Infantry Regiment 161 [28]

"We were all nervous and were thinking, 'Is this assault going to work?' During the afternoon I went on sentry, in order to get to know the ground across which that evening I should have to cross in a few short bounds, but what drew my attention was the presence in the French trench of several machine guns, all pointing at our platoon position. Leutnant Großmann called me over to him again at 7.30 pm, asked me what it looked like and whether I thought the attack was going to succeed. In all seriousness, I told him no, but stressed at the same time that, naturally, I would give it everything that I had got. Just before 8.00 pm he gave me several cigars and asked me to stay as close as possible to him during the attack, because it was impossible to say how things would turn out.

"The hour of the attack drew ever closer, our shells whizzed over our heads at high speed, but not one single one landed on the positions thirty metres to our front; they all came down further away. Things got much busier in the French trenches. They stood shoulder to shoulder and waited for us to launch ourselves at them. At the last minute our platoon was allocated a flamethrower, which was intended to support our attack. However, no sooner had the operator sent the first few bursts towards the enemy trenches, than he was hit. Furthermore all the black smoke filled up the sunken road, so that our view of the enemy was completely blocked.

"Simultaneously a hail of machine gun fire opened up on us, which made it difficult to exit the sunken road. To my left Leutnant Großmann was shot through the head. My mate from Saarbrücken who, like me, had already brought down fire on the enemy trenches, was also shot through the head and was killed instantly. What good was our weak rifle fire against the overwhelming fire of machine guns? All our firing in this sector was completely pointless. The company commander, Leutnant Klein, stood in the sunken road, utterly traumatised, miserable and mourning over his comrade Großmann. He did not give one single word of command."

This particular attack faltered and failed immediately, but although the tactical situation was much the same for the troops tackling the attack on the *Tsingtau-Graben* [Tsingtao Trench, with its echoes of pre-war service in China] some measurable progress was made elsewhere in the Labyrinth.

Gefreiter Weiß 6th Company Infantry Regiment 161 [29]

"At exactly 8.00 pm 3rd Company left the sunken road and 6th Company, which formed the second wave, occupied it. During this process an Unteroffizier and several men were killed due to carelessness. They had secured hand grenades to their belts. One carried by the Unteroffizier caught in the barbed wire and exploded, setting off the remainder and blowing him and several others to bits. Unfortunately, right at the beginning, the brave company commander, Leutnant Spürk, who always led from the front, was hit in the head by a bullet and collapsed, severely wounded. With that the 3rd Company attack stalled and the assaulting troops flooded back into the sunken road. Now it was the turn of 6th Company, commanded by Reserve Leutnant Böhm and Sergeant Bittkow and joined by the remainder of 3rd Company to renew the attack.

"Leutnant Böhm and my section commander, Gefreiter Löffelsend, pressed hard, with great daring, towards the sandbag barricade in the communication trench but, before they could reach the enemy obstacle, they were brought down by shots to the head at a range of ten metres. We leapt forward over them and closed up on the enemy. A hand to hand fight ensued. At that point, Sergeant Bittkow, who had led his platoon across open ground, came to our assistance. We fought hard with our bayonets and were able to avenge our beloved Leutnant and courageous section commander Löffelsend. The French, who had set up a machine gun behind their barricade, defended themselves bravely, but it availed them nothing. We killed most of the crew.

"These men belonged to the French 69th Infantry Regiment. The flamethrower in the advanced sap was unable to support us. Even with a favourable wind, its range was only fifteen metres and the barricade was about twenty five to thirty metres away. The captured Frenchmen were then conducted back to the sunken road and the captured trench prepared for defence. As we worked to deepen the trench, we discovered that the French had been burying their dead in the foot of the trench. Our senses reeled as our spades constantly hit the remains of corpses."

In its after-action report the regiment summarised these events as follows:

"Despite being confronted by a hail of artillery, mortar and machine gun fire, a vigorous frontal lunge towards the *Tsingtau-Graben* succeeded in gaining the enemy trench. The flamethrowers worked well, but smoke blowing back into the faces of the assaulting troops caused some problems. In and around the *Tsingtau-Graben,* a bitter close quarter battle, with hand grenades and, in the case of the French, chemical filled grenades, broke out. 1st Battalion Infantry Regiment 161 took eighty prisoners and captured two machine guns and four mortars. Several counter-attacks in considerable strength, which continued until 11.00 pm, were beaten off."[30]

An eyewitness from 1st Company was closely involved with the grenade fighting and also found himself confronting a completely novel weapon.

Fahnenjunker Maas 1st Company Infantry Regiment 161 [31]

"On the left flank there were two captured mortars, around which a violent battle with hand grenades developed. The hand grenades had been made by the engineers. They were just old jam tins, filled with explosives and nails and equipped with a piece of fuze. They had to be lit with a cigar or a match and be thrown immediately. The mortars were, unfortunately, lost: largely due to the fact that our grenades were so poor and unreliable. Worse we had never seen or even heard of them before. Nevertheless we succeeded in blocking off the trench with sandbags.

"In the late evening the fighting tailed off considerably and I detailed sentries for the night. I settled down on the firing step with another man and slept until it began to get light. When I woke up, I noticed that my neighbour was still sleeping and it was not until I took a closer look that I realised that I had spent the night next to a sitting corpse. There was another dead man sitting elsewhere in the trench, his fingers clasping the rosary which hung around his neck. Close by, bodies lay heaped up, all of them German. During the night further supplies of hand grenades had arrived. In order to improve the situation at the barricade, I selected a place for myself off to one side, where I could observe the effect of our grenades and so direct the throwing so as to ensure that they actually landed in the enemy trenches.

"At that somebody drew my attention to a French trench periscope. I scrambled down from my dangerous vantage point to continue the observation with the periscope. I had not raised it more than a hand's breadth above the parapet, than it was smashed by a shot. That was a pity, but far better than if I had been hit myself. It was during these days that I first came across gas, which was contained in the French gas grenades.[32] Sometimes there was such a stink of gas that we had to evacuate a large length of the trench. At the barricades the battle with grenades continued without a break. In order to ensure that our men were still holding on at the barricade on our left flank, I had, on occasion, to pass through the gas affected trench. Pressing a handkerchief to my nose I passed through the area safely. The gas at that time was not really dangerous. We had no casualties, but we were confronted with a completely unknown weapon, against which we had no defence at that time."

On 23 May elements of Infantry Regiment 160 found themselves advancing via Farbus and Thélus to take up positions in *Tsingtau-Graben*, which was located right along the forward edge of the Labyrinth. They were required urgently; the previous day, their sister regiment Infantry Regiment 161 had lost heavily during desperate fighting to take this important position.

Unteroffizier Pape 6th Company Infantry Regiment 160 [33]

"On Whitsunday we had a church parade early in the morning. This was followed by a cheery get-together, when we celebrated the recent round of promotions which had just been announced and had a chance to meet up with friends from the other battalions. Whilst this was in full swing, we were suddenly alerted. About 2.00 pm we marched off; the 2nd Battalion heading straight for the front line. After a very, very strenuous march we arrived on the position at 4.00 am. All the approach trenches were under heavy fire. Unteroffizier Hendrichs was killed on the way and two other men were wounded.

"We relieved elements of Infantry Regiment 161 who had stormed the position the previous day. The 6th Company sector was very awkward. Although the entire trench system here bore the name 'The Labyrinth', it really applied in full to our company sector. Infantry Regiment 161 had pushed forward from the French-held, originally German lines, an area bounded by two communication trenches and approximately 100 metres wide, a salient which stuck out 100 metres in front of the remainder of the German forward position. The communication trenches leading forward and the continuation of the position left and right had been sealed off by both sides with sandbag barricades. As a result the company had French troops extremely close on both flanks and to the front. If the French succeeded in passing the barricades, the company would have been cut off, because no other communication trenches ran to the rear.

"The utmost alertness was essential, therefore. The sentries were constantly in position, with bayonets fixed and hand grenades prepared for throwing. Any careless movement, or even loud talking, sparked off an exchange of hand grenades. The company, operating on the principle that it would throw two or three hand grenades for every one thrown by the French, remained masters of the situation. Because of the inter-mingling of the trenches there was as good as no artillery fire. We occupied a slight rise in the otherwise flat landscape and so, during this beautiful clear weather, had excellent views of the surrounding area. To our left we could see the church spires in Arras. To our half right there was a marvellous view of Bouvigny Wood, out of which the towers of Mont St Eloi, so very picturesquely placed, greeted us defiantly.

"We could, in addition, make out the villages, which at that time were constantly being mentioned in the Army Communiqués: Ablain, Carency, Neuville and Souchez. Ninety degrees to the right lay the Lorette Spur, which was almost constantly cloaked in smoke and dust. The chapel was a desolate heap of ruins, which, during pauses in the battle, could be made out clearly with a telescope. Behind was Vimy Ridge, a wooded strip which [concealed] countless German batteries. During the nightly defensive fire missions it took on a ghastly beauty. The following day, the second of the Whitsun holiday, we learned about Italy's entry into the war. It happened like this: on the right flank of the company a piece of bread with a note attached was suddenly thrown over the barricade. Written in German script in German was the following announcement: 'German Soldiers! Italy has declared war on you today. There is no point in fighting on. Come over to us. We regard you as courageous soldiers and you will be well treated. Remember that at home you have wives and children, parents and fiancées. If you like a German-speaking Frenchman, who is also the father of family, can negotiate with you.'

"Hand grenades were our reply to this disgraceful suggestion. As soon as it went dark, accompanied by laughter and shouts of 'Hello!' we called, 'we want to speak to the German-speaking Frenchman!' Nobody appeared but the company of our battalion, which was located behind our right flank, captured a French soldier that night. As it got light we noticed that he had the same regimental number as us. So here two 160th Regiments faced one another. Whether this man was the father of a family, I never found out. Our company held the position right up until the moment when we were relieved. As a result we were somewhat more fortunate than the relieving company of another regiment which, during an attack a few days later, all went into French captivity."

So much for the confused fighting for the Labyrinth; 1,500 metres to the north, 8th Company Infantry Regiment 160 found itself confronting the French strong point around Neuville cemetery at close quarters.

Unteroffizier Kring 8th Company Infantry Regiment 160 [34]

"The company occupied a sunken road, about ten metres wide and five to six metres deep. In the centre of the position the fallen lay around in great heaps. The side facing the French was steep and dotted with sentry positions. In one such position, a sentry lay in a huddle; killed by a shot to the head. The blood had flowed down the slope of the sunken road and had gathered in a pool on the base of the trench. It needed strong nerves to live with these sights constantly and not to fall victim to our fears. There could be no thought of burying the dead; the crews of the French captive balloons kept a sharp lookout and even the slightest movement brought down French defensive artillery fire. The stench of corpses was so strong that, at times, it was almost impossible to breathe.

"From the sunken road, a short flight of stairs led to a section of trench which opened out into a sap running across to the French positions. This section of trench was barely as deep as a man, but the attempt to dig it deeper foundered because we kept coming across corpses and had to halt our work. To the right, more or less in the centre of the section of trench, was a completely flattened area. A bayonet, holding down a field post card was stuck into the wall by its entrance. It read: 'Here lie thirty two courageous German engineers'. The sap was about three to five metres from the French and was about one metre deep. Here a section remained on duty for a full twenty four hours at a time before it could be relieved. The slightest noise meant that hand grenades flew back and forth. There was no way back by day. This is where the French threw over a note, informing us that the Italians had declared war on us. Their kindly invitation to us to desert between 8.00 and 9.00 pm was not followed up. We gave them thanks for their invitation by sending over some hand grenades.

"No food arrived in the forward area, so we were very hungry, but our thirst was even worse. Hardly any of us had anything left to drink. Even the contents of the water bottles of the fallen were drunk, if there was anything left in them. Our thirst became insupportable, so I decided to go to Vimy and fetch some drinking water and departed, carrying as many water bottles as I could. I squelched my way back through the communication trenches, taking cover from time to time. By sheer luck I bumped into our field kitchen, which was set up behind the railway embankment in Vimy. The cooks asked me in amazement where the other ration carriers were. The catering officer explained that they had been in position since 8.00 am waiting for us. I was, and remained, the only man from the company who came to collect rations.

"As a special treat there was a piece of bacon for each man. I began by filling myself completely, packed two sandbags full of bacon, filled all the water bottles with coffee then, with messages of good cheer ringing in my ears, I set off for the front once more. This time things did not go so well. Two sandbags crammed with bacon and all those filled water bottles slowed me down, but worse was to come in the communications trenches. I kept getting caught up every few moments. In several places the French artillery fire had flattened the trench and these points were under constant machine gun fire. What was I to do? Taking a quick decision, I threw over the sacks of bacon, followed by the bottles. French machine guns promptly opened fire. As soon as the strips of bullets were used up, I hared across.[35] In this way I was able to arrive at my company with all the food and drink intact. I was greeted with great enthusiasm."

It was much the same story of attritional struggle to the north, where the companies of Infantry Regiment 114 were defending against thrusts in and around the *Schlammulde*. During the night 4/5 June, 8th Company was moved forward and its 3rd Platoon found itself defending a position near the so-called *Marokkaner-Wäldchen* [Moroccan Copse].

Offizierstellvertreter Seliger 8th Company Infantry Regiment 114 [36]

"The trench which ran from the *Schlammulde* to the *Marokkaner-Wäldchen* resembled nothing so much as a line of craters strewn with corpses. Only the final thirty metres leading to the copse could be recognised as a trench and, as such, be used as a defensive position. It was my job to occupy these thirty metres and a further forty within the copse with the thirty three riflemen of my platoon. Although there was a gap of about 250 metres yawning between the left flank of my platoon and the remainder of 8th Company, the right flank had linked up with a platoon from Reserve Infantry Regiment 201. To the right of this platoon, however, was another gap of 200 metres. Because the distance to the enemy lines was very short – in some instances a mere stone's throw – these two gaps offered the enemy extremely favourable points for attacks. The morale of my men was particularly affected by the presence in the trenches of large numbers of dead and seriously wounded men from the companies which we had relieved.

"During the night the gaps were occupied by listening posts. At dawn on 5 June, the French brought down murderous artillery fire all along the entire position. The section of trench just outside the copse, which I had occupied with two sections, came in for particularly severe treatment. The weapons mostly involved were two light field guns which, firing over open sights, brought down an appalling weight of fire and caused us casualties on the extreme left flank. About 10.00 am a heavy gun joined in, as did two mortars. In order to avoid unnecessary casualties I concentrated the platoon into the section of trench inside the copse, which was not under such heavy fire. Only Unteroffizier Gaugel and two men remained on the left flank to maintain observation.

"During the afternoon the black troops opposite launched an attack. They worked their way forward like cats through the undergrowth on the floor of the copse, whereas outside the copse they intended to thrust through the unoccupied sector. The attack withered away with bloody casualties in front of our position and the same fate befell repeated attempts during the afternoon. We received useful fire support from the right flank of 2 Platoon during the attack. Taking a swift decision, the right hand section of Unteroffizier Midderhof launched itself into the unoccupied gap and, together with Gaugel's section, prevented any penetration there.

"The failed attacks were followed by a renewed heavy bombardment with artillery and mortars then, about an hour later, the French launched a further attack. This time it was not directed primarily against the *Marokkaner-Wäldchen,* but rather against the *Schlammulde* Position. Although my platoon succeeded once more in fending off the black troops, a section of trench in the *Schlammulde,* which stuck out forward, was captured and two sections went into captivity as a result. The strength of my platoon was down to only nineteen men, each of whom had only seventeen bullets left. In the event of a further attack, the situation did not look rosy. It was important not to let it come to that so, as the silence became suspicious, I fired an unbroken series of red flares so as to bring our 210 mm howitzer, which was accurately zeroed in on the enemy trenches in the copse, into action. I achieved my intended effect because there was not another serious attack. Here and there, there were brief exchanges of fire in the copse wherever the black troops attempted to creep up on our positions."

Reserve Leutnant Mußler 10th Company Infantry Regiment 114 [37]

"A Landsturmmann was on sentry duty during the morning of 6 June. There was a sudden enemy artillery concentration and, in the course of this, both his legs were blown off above the knee. In extreme pain his screams were dreadful and he shouted for help. But there were no bandages suitable for his wounds and no medical orderlies anywhere nearby.

Whenever the fire slackened, one of us would crawl over to where he was dying to comfort him and to exhort him to be patient, but then duty would call us back to our own posts. Abandoned and alone, his fight with death drew from him utterly heartrending shrieks. A medical orderly hurrying by said that he simply had insufficient dressings to tackle such serious wounds; the poor man was simply going to die.

"It was impossible to consider evacuation to the rear in broad daylight. During the afternoon the wounded man seemed to recognise the hopelessness of his position. Now he shouted endlessly: 'Do me a final mercy; shoot me dead.' It wounded us to the heart; we could not hold back our tears, but under a higher law we were prevented from acceding to his request and giving him the *coup de grâce* he sought. Just as the final rays of the sun were setting, he gave out a muffled death rattle. After twelve long hours of struggle, he had yielded his soul to God."

When eventually the regiment was relieved and left this dreadful place the overall experience had been so intensely dispiriting and the casualties so high that there was no cause for celebration. As they left the place their thoughts kept returning to their comrades who had been killed:

"Despite the fact that the June sun rode high in the clear blue sky and that at night a sea of stars shone down on the earth in great beauty, the place that they lit up was abysmally ugly. The burning sun made fearful sights even more gruesome and its warmth, which normally brings forth life, simply accelerated the rate of decomposition of human beings who only the day before had been full of life. Truly this was a place of skulls; a Golgotha – but one which lacked the shining act of propitiation which alone could bring deliverance." [38]

The early days of June saw 1st Bavarian Reserve Division still under considerable pressure in the area of the Labyrinth. Infantry Regiment 153 was sent to reinforce the division and soon found itself relieving the hard-pressed troops in the Labyrinth and trying to come to terms with the close quarter battle in the maze of trenches. Reacting to the loss of a section of trench by 6th Company Infantry Regiment 153 the previous day, a concerted counter-attack by the 2nd Battalion was launched to re-establish the position during the early morning of 11 June. Assaulting from the north, with support from other elements of 6th Company operating to the south, the attack successfully restored the situation and recaptured a machine gun which had been lost the day before. During this attack Ersatzreservist Männel of 3rd Company[39] distinguished himself to such an extent that he was awarded a special hand-made watch which had been presented to the regiment as an award to be given to a member who especially distinguished himself in the field. The watch was the work of the noted maker W. Richter of Altenburg. The regimental commander later wrote to Richter explaining what had been done to earn it.

Lens, 9 August 1915

Dear Herr Richter,

When I assumed command of the regiment, His Highness the Duke handed to me the valuable watch, which you donated to the Regiment when it first marched away to the war, in order that I should be able to fulfil your desire for it to be presented to an especially worthy recipient. During the very serious battles around Neuville St Vaast, when hundreds of members of the regiment performed extremely well, Ersatzreservist Kurt Männel of the 3rd Company of the Regiment was absolutely outstanding. He played a leading role during the savage battle with hand grenades on 11th June, standing up on the parapet, stripped to his shirt-sleeves in order to be able to throw better and from there threw one grenade after another into the ranks of the attacking Frenchmen. His complete disregard of death was an example to all who observed him and it was very much thanks to him that victory was ours. He was wounded in the hand that same day, but has now been released from hospital. He had already been awarded the Iron Cross, so today I have presented him with your watch and trust that, in so doing, I have carried out your wishes. I shall be sending an appropriate report to His Highness the Duke.

> Koenemann
> Oberstleutnant and Commander
> 8th Thuringian Infantry Regiment 153[40]

The endless French pressure all along the front meant that, by the end of the first week in June, time was running out for the German defence of Neuville St Vaast. Prior to this time, however, the High Command had confirmed in various ways its view that: 'The position in Neuville must be held at all costs.' 'We must be clear that here we are holding perhaps the most important point on the Western Front.' 'We cannot afford to yield a single foot of ground. Here we stand and here we must die.' The difficulty was that ceaseless French determination and pressure had rendered the task beyond any human capacity to achieve. The Saxon Infantry Regiment 107 of the newly-created 58th Infantry Division, which had been closely involved in repeated deployment ever since the beginning of the spring battles, found itself back in the wreckage of Neuville as June opened. Experienced front line officers from the regiment carried out detailed examinations of the situation on the ground and, convinced that there was no further merit in trying to hold Neuville against the incessant attacks, made every effort to persuade the chain of command to abandon the unequal struggle.

According to the history of Infantry Regiment 107,

> "The village was one great mass of stone and rubble. Not one house, not one wall, was undamaged. On the streets craters of immense size

overlapped one another, whilst in between lay piles of debris, collapsed walls and an indescribable tangle of beams and roof timbers . . . heavy mortars crashed down through roofs, ceilings, floors and cellars, reducing them to ruins. One cellar after another was buried . . . explosive gases from the shells mixed with chalk dust from the collapsing walls and the smoke of burning beams . . . in vain the front line called constantly for artillery support, but cloaked by clouds of smoke and dust, the signals could not be seen. Every attempt to report the situation to the rear withered away in the enemy defensive fire and many volunteer runners were killed . . . "[41]

Limited permission to pull back was granted, but only on the understanding that the regiments involved would have to be prepared at any time to launch counter-attacks against the village in order to prevent the French from consolidating their advantage. The time for such an operation to be launched with any realistic hope of success was already past and, just as the final scenes of the battle were about to played out, the regimental commander felt that he had no alternative but to make the case for withdrawal officially:

Oberst Löffler Commander Infantry Regiment 107 [42]

"Defending that part of the village of Neuville which is still in our hands is costing a disproportionate number of casualties. I am duty-bound to state my conviction that, in the face of the strenuous enemy efforts, it will be impossible to defend in the long term. With the exception of the extreme left flank, in Neuville we hold only one single position. It is out of the question to create cover or communication trenches to the rear; it being completely impossible to break through the masses of stone of the collapsed houses either above or below ground. The single trench line has to be manned in sufficient strength for the purpose and all the time it is being subject to the entire weight of fire of the super-heavy artillery pieces and mortars which are directed against the northern sector of Neuville. In a planned fashion, step by step, this fire is destroying, in addition to our position, all the previously available underground shelters, or preventing their use by collapsing the entrances.

"Only two usable deep shelters remain and neither has a covered approach. All movement is impossible by day and when attempted by night causes large numbers of casualties. No matter how much work is done, it will be impossible to halt the continuing deterioration in the situation. Apart from the actual casualties, the troops are suffering from the depressing realisation that the expenditure of their very last reserves of energy is achieving nothing. The situation will only be containable in the *Abschlußstellung* [Final Protective Position – located a little to the east of the village] if, as is to be expected, the enemy continues to press on with their exertions in Neuville. In view of the recent order for the withdrawal of the regiment from Neuville, it is my duty, in the interests of the troops who will follow, to make this report."

Men of Infantry Regiment 107, 3rd Battalion Reserve Infantry Regiment 120 (also part of 58th Infantry Division) and Infantry Regiment 160 of 15th Infantry Division were rushed forward to block any further forward French movement in this critical sector and were also launched forward in a series of limited counter-attacks which, at enormous cost, achieved very little progress, made unsustainable minor gains and spelled the end for Neuville St Vaast, which fell definitively into French hands on 8 June. One small chink of light was the fact that determined work by Reserve Infantry Regiment 120 managed to enabled them to carve a way through to a completely encircled company of Infantry Regiment 107, which was then able to carry on the final hours of defence of the village.[43]

The French infantry had resisted vigorously, French artillery fire was extremely heavy and, most devastating of all, mistakes made by the German artillery, whose support to the sector had been erratic in previous days, led to huge concentrations falling on the German survivors of the attacks. It was the final straw. That day Infantry Regiment 28 reported during the morning, 'Infantry Regiment 160 has been forced back by our own artillery fire. Our own left flank is being brought under enfilade fire by the advancing enemy, located on the northwest edge of Neuville but, thanks to our support, the enemy has been driven back.' This was followed at 4.00 pm by a further report: 'The two right flank companies of Infantry Regiment 160 have disappeared. They have either been captured or have withdrawn. The northwest edge of Neuville is occupied by French troops who are digging in.'[44]

Unteroffizier Nölle 4th Company Infantry Regiment 160 [45]

"During 6, 7 and 8 June, the remains of the village of Neuville St Vaast, near Arras and just a few kilometres from the hard-fought-over Lorette Spur and Souchez, were featured constantly in the Army Daily report. 4th Company Infantry Regiment 160 was holding the last of the houses still in German hands. Of course it is important to understand that these were houses in name only; in fact half their roofs had gone and they threatened to collapse at any moment. The Frenchmen, who had established themselves in cellars, barns etc. on the other side of the road, made various attempts by night to throw us out completely but in this they did not succeed. There were wild exchanges of hand grenades, interspersed with small arms fire. Because the positions were totally entangled, there could be no question of artillery fire.

"Just as dawn was breaking there were further daring thrusts by the French and, because of the restricted fields of fire, we had to save our skins by defending in several directions simultaneously. As far as possible we did this with our rifles in order to conserve hand grenades. Word quickly spread about the arrival of an order, 'The Company may pull back to the trenches of the 28th behind the village.' The availability of this legal possibility to pull back out of the appalling rubble of houses and collapsed roofs and to withdraw to the rear, coupled with severe forward pressure being exerted by the French, produced something like panic amongst the men. We NCOs did everything in our power to counter this tendency to carry out the order immediately; first, because the sight of fleeing opponents would have given French morale a considerable boost and second, because it would have led to a disaster, with everyone being shot down or captured.

"Sanitäts-Gefreiter Bommes, the tried, tested and universally admired bearded Landsturmmann, had an excellent influence at this moment. In civilian life he was a lay brother in his order's hospital in Trier . . . He was also a poet who could produce first class verses about the company. Now he saw to it that the withdrawal, although slowed considerable by the piles of rubble from wrecked walls and roofs everywhere, took place securely. In the meantime Offizierstellvertreter Fink, commander of 1 Platoon, assisted by four or five NCOs, including the highly daring Gefreiter and Officer Cadet Lehmacher from Oberkassel, near Bonn, held the French in check. Unteroffizier Möhn from Dietz received a serious wound in the upper arm caused by a grenade splinter. This was unfortunate, because he was the best grenade thrower in the company, having already proved himself in close-quarter battle in Champagne and Ailly Wood.

"We now ran out of hand grenades; there were no machine guns and with a few rifles we had no chance of holding this lot back. I bawled at Grundmann, the one remaining musketier who was hanging on forward with us, that I would guarantee him the Iron Cross (which at that time was still a real incentive!) if he gathered up a few sacks of grenades from the company as it fell back. This he managed to do, even though he had to brave a hail of small arms fire as he raced across open ground to collect the much-needed sacks. We were once more able to throw, until the entire company, with the exception of those killed during this battle, were safely out of the trap. A little while later, to our great joy, Grundmann did indeed receive the Iron Cross for his daring performance. Of the 120 men with which we entered Neuville, afterwards we numbered no more than forty five."

The fall of Neuville opened new possibilities for the French offensive, which their commanders were anxious to exploit. Analysis of operations on 9 May and on subsequent days had enabled General Foch to draw certain lessons and, in preparing for a major new assault on 16 June, he was determined to remedy earlier faulty dispositions and tactics. Writing in his report of 8 August 1915, Foch stated:[46]

"Before 9 May the hope was that if operations were continued without interruption both by day and night, the enemy would be prevented from reacting and the result would be to throw the enemy lines into confusion. Operations conducted after 9 May, however, seemed to indicate that the only results were obtained through the dash of the initial attack and that once it was held, it was necessary to remount a completely fresh assault. Everything had to be done, therefore, to ensure that this attack was given the impetus which would permit maximum penetrations to be made. This was the guiding principle for the attack of 16 June.

"Thus it was that the reserves were to follow hard on the heels of the assaulting troops. Their number, as well as those of the front line forces, had been augmented. The heavy artillery had been reinforced and, on 16 June, Tenth Army fired twice as much heavy calibre ammunitions as was used on 9 May . . . It was decided that the second attack, just like the first, would be preceded by several days' bombardment; the aim being to demolish or destroy all passive obstacles [to progress].

"It was decided, in addition, during the days before the attack to simulate the start of the attack by increasing the weight of fire from time to time, but that, on the day of the attack itself, there would be no immediate preparation of the attack; no change to the cadence of the firing. This, it was hoped, would surprise the enemy for the short time it would take to jump off into their positions."

In the event, surprise was not achieved. The French had telegraphed their intentions, countermeasures were put in place early and large amounts of artillery ammunition were stockpiled forward by the German defenders. On 10 June, for example, the artillery commander of 15th Infantry Division, writing formally to his divisional commander, drew attention to the probable enemy intentions:

Generalmajor von Fritsch Commander 15 Field Artillery Brigade [47]

"All the indications lead to the conclusion that the French are planning to try to break through in overwhelming strength from Neuville via the line Thélus – La Folie to Vimy. This attempted break through could take place at any moment . . . If it were to succeed then all the artillery, both heavy and light, deployed around Vimy and La Folie would be lost and beyond saving . . . I regard the move to the rear of the entire divisional artillery as necessary and to be carried out immediately . . . Naturally my entire position on this would be negated if one or two fresh divisions were to be launched immediately in an energetic offensive, designed to forestall the French breakthrough [attempt].

No such forces were available, but other emergency measures were put in place and, with four to five days at their disposal, these were unusually thorough. On 16 June, down near Roclincourt, for example, men of Reserve Infantry Regiment 99 were manning forward positions when the renewed French offensive broke over them. They were well aware about what was to happen. They had watched as the French pushed forward a sap to within sixty metres of their lines and had endured what, for that period of the war, was yet another massive bombardment, with a total of 300,000 shells being fired along the front north of Arras. As dawn broke a great deal of activity was observed in the French trenches, the artillery fire increased in weight as the morning went by, reaching a peak after 11.30 am, when suddenly there was an enormous explosion as a mine was blown. To shouts of 'Here they come!' the German defenders tumbled out of their dugouts and manned what was left of their front line trench.

For the defence, too much damage had been done to the position; too many men had become casualties and the attack was launched in overwhelming force with great élan. Quickly a penetration was made at the junction between the 7th and 8th Companies but, acting in accordance with their standard operating procedures, the defenders lost no time in barricading the trenches, sealing the flanks of the breach and preparing to resist any attempt to roll up their trenches. Immediately men of the 5th and 6th Companies began to move forward into a blocking position to prevent the penetration from developing into a breakthrough. German artillery fire crashed down on the lost section of trench and to the front in an attempt to hinder the move of reserves, but the pressure on the defence was immense. Ammunition ran short and casualties began to mount. Leutnants Schulten and Thom were killed as they rallied their men[48] and Reserve Oberleutnant Müller was hit by shell splinters. Before long command of 7th Company devolved onto Unteroffizier Sklarski who, himself wounded in the head by a bullet which had cut a groove in it, provided leadership for the rapidly shrinking band of defenders, as they waited for help to arrive and the dugouts filled up with the wounded.

It was a similar story in the 8th Company sector, where attempts to seal off a broad gap in the defences had led to wild hand to hand fighting, with no quarter given on either side. Some idea of the confused nature of the battle was provided later by one of the 7th Company platoon commanders:

Offizierstellvertreter Hinkel 7th Company Reserve Infantry Regiment 99 [49]

"We were ready to defend ourselves with bayonets and spades when I noticed, a long way off to the right, a line of infantryman firing at the French trenches. It was our side! I tied a large piece of sacking to my rifle and waved it. The only result was that five or six German rifles sent bullets into the sacking just by my head. So I lowered both my skull and the flag! Once more we had to wait. In the meantime our 210 mm howitzer landed shells over there, throwing up baulks of timber and sandbags. Two or three rounds landed with extraordinary accuracy in the French trenches and amongst their men. We carried on waiting. Suddenly the French brought down fire on our support trench. Our second last grenade flew destructively into their section of the trench. I stood by the barricade; the last of the grenades laid out and prepared to throw, when bayonets suddenly lunged at it, pushing it over. When the first Frenchman spotted me, he jumped and spun round. The others pressed forward and I threw the last grenade into the mass of bodies. The area was full of dead and wounded men. Now to move right! It was impossible to see five paces for all the dust and smoke. We bawled '99th, *Hurra!*' so as not to be taken for the enemy. Hand grenades were thrown. Were they French or German? We raced into a dugout. What good were spades and bayonets against hand grenades! Nerves on edge, unable to contribute, we waited for capture, death or relief."

Fortunately the courage of Gefreiter Spindler, who raced through the storm of fire and bursting grenades and shells, enabled him to link up with men from Bavarian Reserve Infantry Regiment 3 to explain the situation. Gradually the counter-attacks by the Bavarians, the supporting companies and 4th Battalion Reserve Infantry Regiment 99, which had been in reserve, began to tell and the situation was restored, but not before further grievous losses had been suffered. Hauptmann Leiling, commander of 14th Company, whose name is indelibly linked to his underground constructions in the Beaumont-Hamel – St Pierre Divion area of the Somme, played an inspirational role at the head of his company, which played a key role in bringing relief to 7th Company.

Hauptmann Franz Leiling 14th Company Reserve Infantry Regiment 99 [50]

"The entire trench was full of Frenchmen, as were all the dugouts. In the meantime 2 Platoon had arrived. Together with elements of 1 Platoon, it opened fire at hundreds of Frenchmen who leapt out of our trenches and rushed back to their own ones. They were brought down in masses. The other part of 1 Platoon mopped up to the left . . . as far as the left flank of 8th Company. At that point they met up with Hübner's platoon from 15th Company. 14th Company alone took between eighty and ninety prisoners. Both officers and men of Bavarian Reserve Infantry Regiment 3 expressed wonderment and joy at the way my men advanced. 3 Platoon had by now arrived and was sent off down the trench to the right. Casualties within 14th Company amounted to nine killed, one missing and twenty one wounded."

On a day of great gallantry on both sides, Reserve Unteroffizier Gröning of 15th Company came in for high praise for his courageous conduct. He described his own actions in a later report.

Reserve Unteroffizier Gröning 15th Company Reserve Infantry Regiment 99 [51]

"A major gave me the personal task of taking a small group of men, advancing rapidly up a sunken road to the front line and rolling up the enemy once I arrived. Quickly I assembled a courageous sixteen-man team. Because the sunken road was under heavy fire I ordered them to follow me rapidly, but individually. We arrived in the sector of 9th Company Bavarian Reserve Infantry Regiment 3, where I met up with Oberleutnant Bonnegut and a Bavarian leutnant, who was defending a barricade with some of his men. Naturally they were highly delighted to greet our arrival. Oberleutnant Bonnegut gave me a quick briefing: the trench to the left was full of Frenchmen. There was no time to delay for thought. 'Up and at 'em!' was the order of the day.

"The barricade was dismantled and we found ourselves confronted by another. The enemy put up strong resistance, but our hand grenades did not miss their targets and this barricade, too, was soon taken. It was an appalling sight, because we had to force our way over a great heap of enemy corpses. We fought our way past a further five barricades and so rolled up the enemy. We could now hear German voices. What could it be? The 14th Company had rolled up the trench from the right! We were over-joyed; all the more so because we had freed our comrades from their difficult situation and especially because we had not suffered many casualties. Meanwhile reinforcements in the shape of a platoon from 6th Company under Leutnant Nehlig arrived on the scene. Our liberated comrades joined in and, together, we brought the fleeing enemy under heavy fire as they flooded back to their own positions. No Man's land was strewn with bodies and on 17 June we cleared 123 dead Frenchmen from one section of trench."

In this area the recapture of the German front line decided the battle in favour of the defence, but the cost to Reserve Infantry Regiment 99 had been high; the 2nd Battalion alone suffering casualties of seven officers and 257 junior ranks killed, wounded or missing. Up on the Lorette Spur, Infantry Regiment 27 of 7th Infantry Division deployed forward late on 14 June to relieve the exhausted men of Reserve Infantry Regiment 202. Following the heavy earlier battles, there were no trenches and hardly any dugouts available. From positions in the craters the forward companies, with Reserve Infantry Regiment 22 to their left and Infantry Regiment 165 to the right, looked out over a No Man's Land that was frequently no more than 100 metres wide and attempted to protect themselves from the incessant artillery fire: no easy task in the circumstances when digging was a near impossibility. Nevertheless, each night attempts were made to dodge the flares and to improve the positions. It meant that very little sleep was to be had and the work was extremely frustrating. No sooner had some progress been made than the result was flattened or wrecked by French fire the following day.

Finally, following a particularly heavy bombardment, the French launched a major attack against the sector in the early afternoon of 16 June – rather later than the one launched further south against Roclincourt.

Gefreiter Stolingwa Machine Gun Company Infantry Regiment 27 [52]

"On 16 June at 1.00 pm, the French lifted the drum fire to the rear. For us that was a clear sign: the enemy was about to attack. Things got lively in our trench. Armed with weapons and hand grenades we rushed to our positions. Charging like maddened, bloodthirsty animals, the French columns hurled themselves at us. Most of them were black. Powerfully supported by our artillery, we succeeded in bringing down accurate fire from machine guns and rifles and so brought the wild hordes to a standstill."

Attacking in three company-sized waves under the cover of smoke and 200 metres apart, the French troops crashed against the centre and left flank of Infantry Regiment 27, where they were brought under heavy small arms fire by 10th and 12th Companies, before closing to grenade and bayonet fighting range. The French soldiers who forced their way into the forward position were mostly cut down but, as five sections from 9th and 11th Companies rushed forward through the heavy protective bombardment with ammunition, grenades and water to bolster the defence, a group (underestimated as comprising sixty to eighty Frenchmen) established themselves in a pocket of resistance, which was not removed until Infantry Regiment 165 launched a counter-attack that evening; a determined immediate counter-stroke led by Feldwebel Leutnant Porath of 9th Company Infantry Regiment 165 having been earlier shot to a standstill.[53]

Reserve Leutnant Recknagel 11th Company Infantry Regiment 27 [54]

"On 16 June Angres lay under heavy fire, through which the 11th Company had to hurry in order to go to the aid of the pressed 10th Company. Having been tasked by Hauptmann Lange, I rushed forward to orientate myself. It was no longer possible to talk in terms of a position. I found the garrison dotted around here and there in the remains of the trenches. These men were totally apathetic and so ground down by the effects of the fire that they had to be pummelled or shaken in order to get through to them. This was a completely different war from that which was being waged in front of Arras itself. The ploughed up ground resembled a mountain landscape and the wounded could only be transported to the rear under cover of darkness. Our fallen and the many dead Frenchmen, a high proportion of whom had first been buried by shell-fire and then dug up again in the same way, spread a fearful stink of corpses. Only with great difficulty could they be recovered [for burial in the rear]. It is nothing short of a miracle in that heat and with that enormous plague of flies that no epidemics broke out."

It fell to 3rd Battalion Infantry Regiment 165 to launch the counter-attack during the evening of 16 June and its commander, Major Gruson, directed 11th Company, reinforced by a platoon from 6th Coy to carry it out. This was far from straightforward; first, because the French artillery continued to bring down a protective barrage round the newly gained section of trench and, second, because the number of French troops was far higher than had been estimated. Fortunately, acting on his own initiative, Reserve Leutnant Hey had launched his own attack at the head of 12th Company and this made steady progress as it grenaded its way towards the captured trench. Gradually more German troops were fed in, so that eventually the French were being squeezed by elements of 6th, 9th, 11th and 12th Companies. When the French commander was killed, shot down by Reservist Jäger of 12th Company, resistance collapsed. One officer and 203 other ranks were captured, along with two machine guns then, later in the evening, Reserve Leutnant Wille of 11th Company, whose platoon had been assigned the task of consolidating the recaptured trench, took another French captain prisoner.

Once more the French attack had failed, but the cost to the defence had been high. Thirty two members of Infantry Regiment 165 had been killed and 57 wounded. Of these eighty nine, forty four were from 12th Company alone. The battalion commanding officer later summed up the events of the day in his after-action report, drawing attention in this extract to the performance of several key figures:

Major Gruson 3rd Battalion Infantry Regiment 165 [55]

> "Reserve Leutnant Hey distinguished himself through his extraordinary zeal and energy. Tirelessly, he inspired his men to greater courage and to hold on in the face of heavy drum fire. He also displayed personal courage as he conducted a reconnaissance and during the battle with hand grenades. Hauptmann Walter [commander 11th Coy Infantry Regiment 165] also behaved bravely as he calmly prepared and conducted the counter-attack. The conduct of Reservist Jäger was absolutely outstanding. He was wounded by a shell just as the operation was ending. Reserve Assistenzarzt Dr Meinhof, the battalion medical officer, who was responsible for medical care in the front line, must also be specially mentioned, as must other medical personnel: Sanitäts-Unteroffizier Wenzel of 12th Company, who reacted instantly to calls for help, despite the drumfire and who was hit immediately and Krankenträger Lampe who, without orders, rushed out to him immediately."

Although this counter-attack had relieved pressure on the right flank of Infantry Regiment 27, there was another penetration on their left flank, near the boundary with Infantry Regiment 26. Once more a fairly large group of French colonial troops were in possession of a length of trench. A wide gap opened up between Infantry Regiments 26 and 27 and could not be closed because of the weight of French fire, which increased until it forced the Infantry Regiment 26 companies which were holding the *Schlammulde* to withdraw. Pressing forward, the French troops captured *Marokkanerwäldchen* [Moroccan Copse] and the situation along this sector if the front was becoming extremely precarious.

Local attacks and counter-attacks were inconclusive, casualties mounted on both sides and finally, by dint of accepting some loss of ground and bending back its left flank, Infantry Regiment 27 succeeded in closing the gap to Infantry Regiment 26 during the early hours of 20 June. The threat to the positions was thus removed, but in any case the impetus had gone out of the attack in this area too and, for the remainder of the month, the German defenders were able to improve their positions, with only minimal interference from the French artillery; there were certainly no more set piece attacks to deal with. Once again the regiment suffered a great many casualties. During the two weeks of June that Infantry Regiment 27 was in the line, one officer and 152 NCOs and men were killed and a further 345 wounded.

Although fighting continued sporadically into July, the main battle died away towards the end of June. There had been the possibility of a great operational success on 9 May, when the battle opened on a twenty five kilometre front, but tenacious defence had prevented the French army from exploiting its initial successes. The ensuing hard, attritional, struggle had worn down the German defence, but the French had suffered badly too. It is even possible that by striving constantly for local success, the French forfeited the opportunity to prepare and deliver a crushing blow on a wide front before the end of May. In the event, by the time such an operation was attempted in mid June, the opportunity had passed. Despite the weight of this attack, it came up against an alert defence that in several ways was better able to counter it than it had been five weeks previously.

Writing to General Joffre on 1 July 1915, General Foch made the point that, although the attack of 16 June had seemed to offer a greater chance of success than that of the previous month, 'in fact it had achieved a great deal less. The reasons for this can be explained easily: The enemy had piled up all their reserves [against it]; they had pulled together a powerful concentration of heavy artillery, which was liberally supplied with ammunition and they had exploited the terrain effectively.'[56]

Foch returned to this subject the following month:[57]

"In their usual energetic fashion, [the enemy] took all the necessary measures to parry and limit the consequences of the initial results:

- Nine divisions alerted as a result were deployed into the area between 9 and 18 May.
- New lines of defence were established to replace those we had captured . . .
- Above all, after 12 May, the heavy artillery was reinforced increasingly rapidly. After 18 May so many rapid-firing artillery pieces of all calibres were concentrated and supplied with an apparently inexhaustible quantity of ammunition that they were able to maintain intense fire all along the Tenth Army front.
- On 9 May we dominated the enemy artillery. After 20 May it dominated us and we never overcame that [problem].

"The consequences were as follows:

    – The work undertaken by our troops to consolidate the ground they had captured and to prepare the new attacks had to be completed under extremely precarious conditions and proved to be extremely costly . . . Despite all the care taken with the preparations for the new attack, they never reached the level achieved in the first case.

    – Everyone was of the opinion that the artillery preparation for 9 May was remarkably good, but many judged that of 16 June to be poor and insufficient . . . However 30,278 heavy shells were used in support of 9 May and 63,557 for 16 June . . .

    – Thanks to its reinforcement with heavy artillery, the enemy was able to put down a barrage of heavy calibre shells – frequently 210 mm – which lasted for several hours. This halted both our assaulting troops and the reinforcements which were trying to move up in support.[58]

    – It was not possible to achieve surprise twice over. Despite taking the precaution of trying to deceive the enemy through the use of sham attacks, one or two minutes after our infantry had launched their attacks, enemy defensive fire came down.

Hermann Stegemann, who chronicled the Great War in four volumes, summed up the spring battles in Artois succinctly and accurately.

"None of the fighting during this interim period of positional wafare could compare with the battles which raged around the Lorette Spur and the steep sides of Vimy Ridge, but even this battle, unparalleled in its extent and intensity, finally burnt out like an extinct volcano. The French had fought for the slopes of the Lorette Spur, the villages of Ablain – St Nazaire, Carency, La Targette, Neuville St Vaast and the trench system that bordered and linked these places, but they had not captured Givenchy-en-Gohelle, or the heights of La Folie, or Vimy, upon the possession of which victory depended." [59]

The latest operations in the Vimy area had cost the French Army 102,500 casualties, of whom 35,000 were killed.[60] True, it was now occupying forward positions which pressed closely against the lower slopes of Vimy Ridge, but the price paid had been appalling. In his Order of the Day of 23 July 1915 Crown Prince Rupprecht drew the final German line under the French spring offensive:

Crown Prince Rupprecht of Bavaria Sixth Army Commander [61]

"The battles around La Bassée and Arras have come to a temporary halt. The enemy has realised that his massed assaults are bound to be dashed to pieces against the iron wall of the Sixth Army. Since 9 May twelve British and twenty two French divisions, making use of massive quantities of ammunition, have attacked our vastly outnumbered troops. Major attacks on a broad front, varied by the most obstinately conducted fighting for individual localities [characterised the fighting]. The enemy's aim; namely, to bring about a deep penetration on a broad front and so turn the tide of the campaign in the west, was not achieved: they have lost the battle.

"I should like to thank all commanders and troops for their heroic courage and for the tough endurance they displayed throughout these ten difficult weeks. I am once more convinced that in all the arms and services, in every officer and man, there burns a spirit which will lead our people and our army on to ultimate victory. The Fatherland acknowledges with gratitude that which the army has achieved during the battle for La Bassée and Arras. Our time is not yet come. For now it is the army in the east which, thanks to the faithful steadfastness of our courageous troops in the west, has been able to thrust forward and, in its irresistible storm, cast the Russians to the ground. We must hold on in our current positions. It is entirely possible that the enemy are concentrating greater masses [of troops] with the aim of breaking through us. I know, however, that in that event the Sixth Army will stand to its arms once more and send the attackers home once more with bloody losses."

It was, of course, a considerable exaggeration to claim *tout court* that the Allies lost the battle. Sixteen square kilometres of terrain of tactical importance had been gained, which confronted the German army with a major operational problem. Whether the difficulties so posed were worth the cost in blood was for the Allies to decide and their generals were by now largely inured to the matter of high casualties. Of greater importance to them during the summer of 1915 was the realisation that in the Vimy area they had left the task only half complete.

Notes
1. Reichsarchiv: *Der Weltkrieg (Achter Band)* p 58
2. Freydorf: History Grenadier Regiment 109 p 232
3. From south to north the corps concerned were: XXI (Mask Ablain – St Nazaire, protect left flank and capture Souchez), XXXI (Mask western edges of Ablain – St Nazaire and Carency and assault from line Carency – La Targette towards Hill 119 (Pimple) and Hill 145 (exclusive)), XX (Assault from La Targette area to capture Hill 145, La Folie and Telegraph Hill) XVII (Assault from line Ecurie – Roclincourt to capture heights west of Farbus (excluding Telegraph Hill) to the railway bridge 400metres north of Bailleul Halt) and X (Assault from the line Roclincourt to the Arras – Bailleul road towards the line from the railway bridge to Point du Jour and protect right flank). See *Les Armées Francaises dans la Grande Guerre* Tome III p 34.
4. Bavarian Reserve Infantry Regiment 6 was transferred to the 10th Bavarian Infantry Division and Bavarian Reserve Infantry Regiment 13 became part of the 11th Bavarian Infantry Division, both regiments serving with distinction with these divisions; the 10th being primarily engaged on the Western Front and the 11th in the east.

5. Zahn: History Infantry Regiment 111 pp 119–120
6. Even though German accounts dismissed this penetration later as 'patrols and leading elements', it remains an outstanding achievement; it certainly rattled the defence at the time.
7. *Les Armées Francaises dans la Grande Guerre* Annex No. 1125 to Tome III
8. *Les Armées Francaises dans la Grande Guerre* Tome III p105. This is a harsh, but not totally unreasonable, judgement on the disastrous Battle of Aubers Ridge (9 May 1915) and the attacks at Festubert, which opened a week later. It is also interesting to note the difference in national perceptions about this period. After the total failure at Aubers Ridge, the British were actually quite proud of the fact that they had managed to switch the point of attack relatively quickly.
9. Dellmensingen: *Das Bayernbuch vom Weltkriege* pp 203 – 204
10. Zastrow: History Field Artillery Regiment 50 pp 99–101
11. Zastrow: History Field Artillery Regiment 50 p 102
12. Zahn: History Infantry Regiment 111 p 120
13. Freydorf: *op. cit.* pp 251- 261
14. Dellmensingen: *op.cit.* pp 205 – 206
15. *Hollerbüchsen* means something like 'Devils Rifles' or 'Hellish Guns.'
16. Demmler: History Bavarian Reserve Infantry Regiment 12 pp 110–116
17. Müller: History Reserve Infantry Regiment 99 p 58
18. *ibid.* pp 62 – 64
19. Falkenstein: History Infantry Regiment 93 pp 88 –91
20. Beumelburg: *Loretto* p 159
21. Guhr: History Infantry Regiment 157 p 54
22. *ibid.* p 55
23. *Schadenfreude* = to take pleasure from the discomfort of another.
24. Guhr: *op. cit.* p 56
25. Of these three officers, only Reserve Leutnant Strzibny has a known grave. He is buried in the German cemetery at Lens-Sallaumines Block 11 Grave 57.
26. Guhr: *op. cit.*pp 57–59
27. Schmidt: History Infantry Regiment 142 pp 57–58
28. Seiler: History Infantry Regiment 161 pp 13–14
29. *ibid.* pp 14–15
30. *ibid.* p 15
31. *ibid.* pp 15–16
32. This is a reference to one of the earliest examples of French battlefield retaliation to the use of gas by the German army at Ypres on 22 April 1915. The grenades involved would either have been of the *grenade suffocante* or Bertrand types. The former, which contained 160 g of ethylbromacetate, was procured in 1913 and the latter, which held a mere 25 g of chloracetone, was first introduced into service on 24 April 1915. See Jones *World War I Gas Warfare Tactics and Equipment* p 4.
33. History Infantry Regiment 160 pp 88–89
34. *ibid.* pp 89–90
35. At that time French machine guns fired a twenty five round strip of ammunition. The guns then had to be reloaded. It was not possible, therefore, to bring down continuous fire with these weapons.
36. History Infantry Regiment 114 pp182–183
37. *ibid.* p 187
38. *ibid* p 187

39. Kurt Männel was an outstanding soldier, who had been a confectioner in civilian life. By the time of his death near Hollebeke on 16 January 1918, he had risen to the rank of Vizefeldwebel and was the holder of the Iron Cross First and Second Class, the Duke of Saxony's Gallantry Award and the Service Medal with Swords. Männel has no known grave.

40. Schmidt-Oswald: History Infantry Regiment 153 p 393

41. Auenmüller: History Infantry Regiment 107 pp 116–117

42. Kriegsarchiv München HS 1992/5

43. Fromm: History Reserve Infantry Regiment 120 pp 28–29

44. Kriegsarchiv München HS 1992/5

45. History Infantry Regiment 160 pp 94–95

46. *Les Armées Francaises dans la Grande Guerre* Tome III pp 105–106

47. Kriegsarchiv München HS 1992/5. It should be noted that the projected move was an emergency measure, which was highly disadvantageous to the German defence. Placing the artillery largely to the east of Vimy Ridge caused difficulties of elevation and severely reduced the effective range of the field guns in particular.

48. Leutnants Josef Thom and Hermann Schulten were originally buried in Fresnes-lès-Montauban, but now lie close to one another in the German cemetery at Neuville St Vaast/Maison Blanche in Block 17 Graves 791 and 794 respectively.

49. Müller: *op. cit.* p 74

50. *ibid.* p 75

51. *ibid.* pp 75–76

52. Werner: History Infantry Regiment 27 p 114

53. Fließ: History Infantry Regiment 165 p 85

54. Werner: *op. cit.* p 114

55. Fließ: *op. cit.* p 86

56. *Les Armées Francaises dans la Grande Guerre* Tome III p106

57. *Les Armées Francaises dans la Grande Guerre* Annex No. 1125 to Tome III pp 500–501

58. There certainly was a powerful German response. Writing in his diary on 17 June, Crown Prince Rupprecht of Bavaria noted, 'Yesterday Army Group Lochow fired 100,000 shells, the greatest performance of the campaign. The enemy fired a great deal more, certainly three times as much. Day and night the windows ratted in Lille and there was so much noise that it was impossible to sleep.' Rupprecht: *Mein Kriegstagebuch,* Erster Band p 367

59. Stegemann: *Geschichte des Krieges, Dritter Band.* pp 235–236

60. *Les Armées Francaises dans la Grande Guerre* Tome III p101. German losses are harder to quantify, though they are almost certainly much lower. They were on the defensive and were heavily outnumbered throughout the battle. One assessment in Kriegsarchiv München HS 1992/10, puts the casualties suffered by the divisions most closely involved with the battle, *viz.* 1st and 5th Bavarian Reserve Divisions, 3rd Bavarian, 5th, 11th, 15th, 16th and 115th Infantry Divisions at something under 30,000, but not all the figures are taken from the divisional war diaries: those of 1st Bavarian Reserve Division, 3rd Bavarian Infantry Division, 15th and 115th are estimates, which could be too low.

61. Kriegsarchiv München HS 1992/10

CHAPTER THREE

The Battles of Autumn 1915

Although it is true that late September and a large part of the month of October 1915 saw especially heavy fighting in the Vimy area and it is convenient to consider these events as forming a distinct phase of operations, naturally there was no cessation of operations during the summer months. Apart from day to day incidents along the front, preparations for the renewal of the offensive were being observed by the German army from early August onwards. It did not take any great detective work to establish that the main objective of the French Tenth Army was to launch a major coordinated attack between Angres and Roclincourt, with the aim of seizing Vimy Ridge which, following the spring offensive, was now a mere 800 to 1200 metres in rear of the German front line positions.

Towards the end of August a major French redeployment was carried out. This led to a considerable reinforcement of Tenth Army when the French IX Corps, comprising the 17th, 18th and 152nd Divisions, arrived to take over positions on the right flank of Tenth Army. A territorial division (81st) arrived from Dunkirk to relieve 58th Division at the northern end of the Vimy front and enable the latter to go into army reserve. These additional forces, which were further augmented by the arrival of considerable quantities of heavy artillery, enabled Tenth Army to plan on launching its forthcoming attack with fourteen divisions and still maintain three divisions (130th, 58th and 154th) in reserve.[1] In response the German chain of command adjusted its dispositions and moved forward what artillery reserves were readily to hand. These did not amount to any especially significant quantity, although the opening of the preliminary bombardment, coupled with attacks by aircraft which bombed the stations at Douai, Somain, Wallers and Cambrai, gave the process further impetus.

Writing after the war, the commander of the German VI Corps provided a clear picture of the unfavourable position in which the defence found itself as the intelligence indicators began to multiply that a further major French offensive effort was rapidly approaching.

General der Infanterie Kurt von Pritzelwitz Commander VI Corps [2]

"I well remember how very concerned I was when, from the beginning of September, not a day went by without an increase in the French batteries which were drawn up opposite the corps in a half circle. By the middle of the month we were outnumbered in heavy artillery by four to one. Much the same was true of the main arm of battle, the infantry. Against the seven divisions, which were later joined by a Moroccan one and which were deployed along an eight kilometre front from Souchez to Roclincourt, the Silesian Corps could only muster seven regiments. Our aircraft, ranging far beyond the French front line, spotted numerous camps, which could only point to strong forces held back at second and third line. By means of intensive sapping the enemy trenches were advanced unceasingly closer and closer, until the jumping off points were extremely close.

"Anyone with eyes to see could not fail to draw the conclusion that the immediate future would see the development of an extremely serious situation. A major offensive aimed at a breakthrough was about to take place. With the weak forces at our disposal it was out of the question to attempt to disrupt or delay the multiplicity of measures being taken in preparation for a general offensive. The artillery, to which would have fallen the responsibility for this work, was already hard pressed; only by exerting a maximum effort could it even hold its own against the enemy superiority [in guns]. It was forced to move to a policy of nightly changes of position in order to prevent itself from being prematurely destroyed.

"With a force ratio like this, how would the decisive battle develop? Would we be able to withstand the shock of an attack launched by the enemy in overwhelming strength? Would the immensely powerful enemy pierce our lines and so endanger the entire German position? These were the questions which daily confronted each and every one of us. At the time we could not count on [the availability of] reserves. There were no reinforcements within sight. We were entirely on our own resources and there were no comforting answers to these difficult questions to be had. One thing alone was clear: the VI Corps would certainly do its duty in the face of the extremely heavy fighting which was to come.

"Already, well before 22 September, the artillery fire had increased to intense rates. Only by straining every sinew could our artillery maintain itself in order to be able to fulfil its main mission, which was to counter the enemy assault. For the infantry the nights were no longer long enough to enable them to make even emergency repairs to the immense destruction that the heavy shells had wrought on the trenches and obstacles. Meanwhile the numbers of casualties rose by the day. On 20 September a mighty concentration of fire by 160 French batteries crashed down with a violence which is beyond description. The entire terrain in and around the villages of Souchez, Givenchy, Vimy, Neuville and Thélus seemed to shake as though there was a massive earthquake. The earth itself seemed to be constantly on the move. The air above the ground was filled with a dense, impenetrable cloud of dirt, dust, smoke and poisonous gases. It hung in a great brown-black curtain, seemingly reaching up from the fields to the clouds themselves. The entire horizon and the land beneath it trembled under the dreadful thunder of the guns. Day and night, like a monstrous deep-throated shout, the continuous racket split the air."

The French army was determined this time to concentrate all its efforts in order to achieve the long-sought breakthrough in Artois. Immense quantities of ammunition were stockpiled, the new steel helmets were issued as a matter of priority and a complex fire plan fired by hundreds of guns was designed to facilitate the capture of the key terrain in a series of steps. The French plan envisaged that, 'The first step to be achieved by Tenth Army is the capture of the heights around Angres and Souchez by XXI Corps, Vimy Ridge by XXXIII, III, XII and XVII Corps and the line Beaurains–Blaireville Wood by XVII and IX Corps.'[3] To XXXIII Corps was entrusted the capture of Vimy Ridge from Hill 119 [The Pimple] to Hill 145 (Exclusive). Some idea of the confidence in the plan may be derived from the fact that the same Corps was given the subsequent objectives of Givenchy, Avion and Méricourt. It was similar story for III Corps, which was expected to capture Hill 145, La Folie and Bonval Woods then advance to secure Vimy and Acheville.[4] As the bombardment began to crash down and the front line troops undertook numerous preliminary operations, it remained to be seen if the French optimism was justified.

One of the first shocks occurred down near Roclincourt where the front line was held by regiments of 12th Infantry Division.

Reserve Hauptmann Gosna 9th Company Infantry Regiment 62 [5]

"During the night, I believe that it was 18/19 September 1915, I had only two sentries per platoon on duty on the front line trench. Towards 6.00 am I arranged for them to be relieved and for the ammunition stocks in the forward trenches to be replenished. I felt relaxed because no morning assault had taken place and I hoped to allow myself an hour in my dugout, which was located in the second trench of the First position. I had only been lying down for a few seconds when there was a violent explosion. The earth quaked and I was thrown from the bunk against the exit to the dugout. I did not lose consciousness and, despite the pain, I crawled quickly up towards the small hole which was all that remained of the entrance after it was partially blocked.

"I was confronted by a dreadful sight. I simply could not longer recognise the position to the front of my dugout. My head was numb after the collision with the wall of the exit, but the situation forced me to come to my senses rapidly. What follows describes what occurred in a period of approximately three minutes. The first enemy explosion had successfully blown up the front line trench in the centre of my company sector. The air was full of blackened lumps of earth and pieces of men who had been blown apart by the power of the explosion, which had, unfortunately, also set off our own charged mines. Memories of this awful incident will always remain vivid for the survivors. The explosion had also largely wrecked part of the second trench, killing many of the men who were accommodated there and destroying much of the underground workings. The dugout next to mine, which contained two sections, was buried.

"About one minute after the first explosion a second occurred in the left part of my sector and it also affected the right flank of our neighbours, the 10th Company commanded by my dearest comrade, Oberleutnant von Sodenstern. A few seconds later there was a third explosion on the right flank of my company sector. All three explosions were appallingly successful. Despite the ensuing confusion amongst the survivors and the fact that the front line trenches and its associated communications trenches no longer existed, every man attempted to take up a defensive position and hold on whilst trying to locate the nearest comrade. The shrieks and groans of the seriously wounded had a shattering effect on the nerves. Within a few moments my faithful Feldwebelleutnant Bronow and a number of survivors, disregarding a hail of enemy artillery and small arms fire, had forced their way over the top to me.

"This little band, well aware of the seriousness of the situation, calmly and determinedly set about defending to the last man our former position against a possible attack. In this time of immense shock, the value of close and well-practised comradeship-in-arms between leaders and subordinates was thoroughly underlined. Silently we hoped for powerful support from our neighbouring companies: 10th Company Infantry Regiment 62 to the left and 4th Company Infantry Regiment 63 from the far side of the road. As far as we could gauge, neither company seemed to have been much affected by the explosions. There were no linking trenches left, nor any telephone communications either. Because, for some unknown reason, the enemy did not immediately launch an attack, we set about the task of digging out the neighbouring dugout, in order to free any of the occupants who were still alive.

"In the meantime I made my way with two of my orderlies, moving in dashes from crater to crater, over to the left flank of the second trench in my sector and Brunow did the same to the right in order to check up on the situation and to find out how many survivors there were. Once we had dug out the unwounded, the wounded and the dead from collapsed dugouts and buried trenches, it transpired that I had lost about thirty men. Even though I was not present, work was going on through individual initiative everywhere. Throughout all the confusion, individuals kept appearing from the new craters and even the enemy trenches. They had been blown up into the air, but had survived by a miracle. Their condition was dreadful: jackets and trousers had been ripped off their bodies. They were suffering from shock and had blackened faces from the explosions. Despite the risks, we crawled towards one another and the severely wounded were dragged back into the deeper protection of our former second trench.

"These comrades were able to report that the enemy trench in this sector had apparently still not been reoccupied, but that there were still wounded and trapped men in our front line trench and in the mine craters. At that, Unteroffizier Berger distinguished himself through his courage, determination and energy. Racing forward with a few comrades equipped with spades, axes and hand grenades they saved all the remaining comrades who were still alive. I still have the image of him today as he, together with his comrades, all bathed in sweat, hauled back the wounded, who were bleeding heavily, through the heavily cratered terrain. The men he saved never forgot his performance; ever after and without exception they held the courageous Unteroffizier Berger in the highest regard."

The French were extremely slow to follow up, either because they had not appreciated how successful they had been or, possibly, because they feared retaliatory mines aimed at them. Believing that the entire company had been lost and the French army was occupying the positions, patrols from the battalion made their way forward later in the day and 9th Company was soon relieved. It had been a shattering experience for them; their morale was badly dented, but recovered somewhat after a period of rest in quarters at Neuvireuil. In the meantime Infantry Regiment 63 took steps to rectify the damage to their front line. This regiment maintained a pioneer company of about one hundred men under the command of Leutnant Zinnemann. Previously they had been employed mainly in support of engineer mining and sapping operations, but now the commander, Major von Weller, decided to hold it ready to be deployed forward to reinforce the front line troops. They had suffered significant losses transporting explosives forward and from harassing fire and were down to the strength of a weak platoon, but in the present circumstances every man counted.

Leutnant Zinnemann Pioneer Company Infantry Regiment 63 [6]

"The 23rd and 24th brought nothing but drum fire of the worst type. There could be no more doubt about it; a major French offensive could be launched at any moment. All possible reserves were called forward. I was given the task in the event of an enemy penetration of gathering together every available man who could be spared from the regimental staff and leading them forward, together my twenty remaining men, to occupy *Münchener Weg* [Munich Way] and to defend the flank to the front of Thélus . . . Then the day came which was to decide our fate. It was 25 September and it was raining. Despite this fact, one enemy air squadron after another appeared. Flying very low, they circled overhead and threw out bombs wherever a man showed himself. Even Thélus received the same treatment, but we saw it coming and retired to our cellar.

"It looked as though things were about to get serious, although we had been predicting the opening of an offensive for eight days by then. To our right we could see that things were getting very lively around the Lorette Spur. The continuous roar of guns could be heard, which could only mean that there was a battle in progress. It was 9.00 am when the concert began in our area. Thélus came in for treatment first, because the enemy assumed that that was where the reserves would be. Shells of the heaviest calibre crashed down amongst the ruins of the houses. One particularly heavy gun brought down fire in the immediate vicinity of our 'castle'. It was clear that if it landed a direct hit, we should all have had it. We prepared to move, but we also prepared ourselves mentally for the worst. Here, of course, we had no view of the battlefield; it was only possible to observe a short section of the main road through the village. It was certainly not out of the question that we might be surprised and captured!

"My men were all on permanent standby to intervene. I divided them into two main groups: trench patrol and street patrol, but I could not actually deploy them because I was under the direct orders of the commander. The result was that I could do nothing initially; I just sat there and got very bored. This was the first time that I had not been at the front during a battle. Instead I was located with the Regimental Commander. I climbed up to the observation post which had been set up in one room of the house. There were located the tripod binoculars of the battery which had been sent forward to us a short time earlier in the reinforcement role. Above our heads heavy shells roared to impact in the artillery positions along the La Folie Ridge. There was one booming salvo after another.

"Our artillery remained silent! . . . One enemy squadron observed our battery positions, a second was over Thélus, a third attacked targets along our approach routes and the fourth and fifth the positions from the main road forward. There were so many aircraft in the air that it was a wonder that they could find space to fly past one another. It was quite amazing! If we had wanted to shoot at them, it would have been difficult to decide where to start. It was not even possible to engage them with machine guns. There were few enough of them and we did not want to betray their positions early – otherwise their locations would have been destroyed by the artillery without delay. On the contrary they disappeared completely from view. An aircraft flying at 200 – 300 metres would otherwise have spotted them at once.

"At midday drum fire of unbelievable strength began coming down on the forward trenches. Once more I was at the tripod binoculars. I could clearly see each impact and its effect. Entire sections of ruined dugouts and, apparently, human bodies were flung through the air. The actual position was impossible to make out. There was just a constant series of fountains of earth thrown up and vague shapes, covered completely in brown and white haze. Dazzling yellow flashes stabbed at the ground and split the air. Clouds of shrapnel hung like white strips against the clouds. Through the misty haze, the low flying aircraft could be seen hanging in the air like vultures as they engaged ground targets. Along the horizon the captive balloons hung in rows from their cables.

"The air trembled, rumbled and thundered. With ears pricked and eyes straining through the chaos, we tried to detect some sort of indication that battle had been joined. It was an appalling spectacle! In the village shells still crashed down now and then and the occasional shrapnel round spat its lead balls against the crumbling walls of the nearby houses. I could hardly hear a thing; I was just trying to see when they were coming. My thoughts were with my dear comrades out forward. Who of them might still be alive? I thought, too, of the happy hours we had spent together. It all made me feel sad . . . I felt as though I was carrying out some sort of death watch. I climbed back down into the darkness of my cellar. Here we could only hear dull thuds and the endless rumbling of the impacts. The cellar shook. All of a sudden there was a terrible crash and a sound as though the walls were about to crash down. A direct hit had come into the house. Had I still been observing, it would have spelled the end of me. I hoped that we should be released from this mousetrap before it was too late. A second shell crashed into the courtyard, as did the next one. Then one hit the corner pillar of the ground floor wall, so the entire cellar rocked to and fro. We gathered in the entrance in case a direct hit collapsed the entire house. We had no wish to be buried alive in the rubble of Thélus. We were far more interested in settling up with that lot over there as far as possible! We were seized with cold fury. But against artillery fire the individual is helpless. He can only put his trust in fate."

As the time for the opening of the offensive drew closer, final preparations were made by the French troops. Rationing in that army was always a precarious matter, but every effort was made to ensure that the assaulting troops were provided with a good hot meal, that they had food to take over the top and that their water bottles were full (often with the rough red wine that was a staple of the French army at the time). The religious went to confession, tensions rose and some passed away the final hours in personal reflection or the committal of their innermost thoughts to paper.

Diary Entry of an anonymous French Officer 24 September 1915 [7]

"This evening we are entering the trenches. Tomorrow morning at about 6.00 am we shall launch our offensive. Our forces are enormous. Seventy six divisions are taking part, amongst them fifteen cavalry divisions. We have more than 3,000 guns, 350 of which are firing on our front. They have been firing for three days! Today there is a hell of a racket. They [the German guns] are answering us a little, but not in any strength.

"It is quite amazing! In less than twelve hours we shall be in the midst of a battle. Perhaps I shall already be a corpse! – or perhaps not. In just

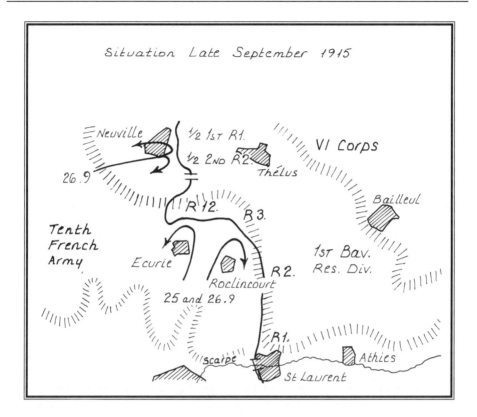

Situation Late September 1915

a few hours, many of those gathered here, smiling and full of life, will be dead. I have, perhaps, only eight or ten hours to live. Be that as it may. If it happens I shall be falling on the battlefield, fulfilling my duty at the head of my men. I put my trust in my guiding star. If I am lucky enough to come through, then my belief in the Cross will be confirmed. We are full of enthusiasm; the morale of the men is excellent. The push that we are launching will draw a line under everything. All our forces, all our wealth, have been laid on the line. If we succeed our land will be freed. If not, Paris is lost. We understand what is at stake and we shall gain the victory.

"I am fully prepared to give my life to save my country. I ask only one thing. If I am to die, let it be swift. I am ready. Of course I do not want to depart this life. I shall be leaving behind a mother to pray for, a father whom I love with all my heart, a life that promises to be happy and successful. But man is not master of his fate. I place my life in the hands of God. He will do what He knows to be right. I beg Him to protect and preserve me, so that I can once again fulfil my duty to my native land and embrace my mother once more. His will, not mine, be done! Long live France; to us the victory!

"I have just received a letter from Mama; the last before the battle. It touched me deeply and it made me cry a little! But Mama is so brave that I am convinced that I shall return and be able to embrace her once more. She gives me courage and moral strength. With thoughts of her, I shall lead my men. Long live Mama!"

After yet another grim night under severe bombardment and effectively with no sleep, the defenders were clustered in the entrances and stairwells of their dugouts as dawn broke. They were poised and ready to rush to man their positions as soon as the increasing activity in the French forward trenches was transformed into a mass attack – but nothing happened. The morning of 25 September dragged slowly by. Those who still had food and drink available to them shared out what they had. Equipment was checked and re-checked. Weapons were unwrapped from their protective cloths, cleaned and put away once more, near at hand and ready to be grabbed instantly. The bombardment increased to a frenzied intensity, continuing through midday and into the afternoon. Finally, just before 2.00 pm, the fire lifted. There was no mistaking the implication.

Reserve Leutnant Schubert 8th Company Infantry Regiment 63 [8]

"A dense, impenetrable cloud of dust and smoke hung over our lines. Our observers strained to see anything through the obscuration. Eyes were streaming through the effort to pierce the general murk which enveloped the entire area. Suddenly images began to emerge in amongst the clouds of smoke and dust: the enemy were closing in. A single shout, bawled down into the dugouts and the brave occupants were in their appointed places in moments. They came crawling out of the holes in the earth where they had endured for three days and three nights: crammed together, away from the sunlight, crouching next to one another in the stale, suffocating atmosphere and often with empty stomachs.

"Frequently it had proved to be impossible to maintain the regular supply of food and drink to the front line . . . but now nobody was thinking about hunger or thirst or the terrors and feats of endurance of the hours spent underground. Now everybody drew strength from the thought that the long awaited hour of reckoning with the enemy had arrived . . . eyes accustomed themselves swiftly to the bright daylight, as the *Feldgrauen* took cover on top of the shelled dugouts, on the remains of the parapet and parados of the flattened trench, or along the lips of the ploughed up craters. There they lay and poured death-dealing fire into the ranks of the assaulting Frenchmen."

Naturally all communication with the front had long since been severed. The intensity of the bombardment had made the movement of runners difficult, or even impossible. Commanders at all levels lacked information. It was clear that something major was taking place, but what? Near to the Regimental Headquarters of Infantry Regiment 63, which was responsible for the sector west of Thélus, a small reserve of assault pioneers was being held back at the direct disposal of its commander, Major von Weller.

Leutnant Zinnemann Pioneer Company Infantry Regiment 63 [9]

"At 2.15 pm it began to get calmer to the front. We, however, were still under extremely heavy fire. What could be happening at the front? I reported in [to the regimental commander] and said that I would go and try to see what was going on. Yes, came the reply. I was to go and reconnoitre the situation. Off I dashed, taking Gorzan and two other men with me; away from that dangerous cellar! We raced along the village street, but splinters and pieces of tile were whistling around our heads to such an extent that we deviated left through the gardens and towards the *Münchner Weg* [Munich Way]. In we jumped and pushed on forwards, towards where a hurricane was at full blast! The road had disappeared under a whirlwind of drum fire. It was impossible for anybody to move in either direction. We had to halt where we were, but we did have what was, potentially, a good viewpoint. All we could make out, however, was smoke and our red flares which, unfortunately, were going up along the front as far as the eye could see. This meant an attack on a frontage of at least ten kilometres.

"Because I could get no further forward, there was nothing for it but to turn back and report. The major was not very impressed with the paltry amount of information I had gathered, but he knew that it was not my fault. In the meantime a fragmentary report had arrived from 10th Company. According to this, Infantry Regiment 23 had been driven out of their defensive positions and 10th Company had deployed so as to cover the front in the direction of the alleged breakthrough. It was soon 4.00 pm and the fire began gradually to die away. A runner arrived from the front. Report from the forward battalion! The enemy had launched an attack, but had been partially beaten off. Casualties were very high. Oberarzt Dr Bauer and the Adjutant, our dear Oberleutnant Möbius, had been killed. The ammunition would only last until the following day. There was nothing to drink and medical teams were needed urgently. The motorised ambulance should be called forward; many men had been severely wounded . . . but other than that they would be able to hold on. What a man!

"We could just imagine him writing that with a smile on his face, 'Other than that we can hold on!' These brave Silesians were worth more than all the billons of the Americans. A little while later a small patrol led by an unteroffizier arrived bearing reports. The men were close to collapse with exhaustion. The unteroffizier handed over the grubby bundle of report forms from Major Pulst [Commanding Officer 1st Battalion Infantry Regiment 63], who had produced comprehensive details concerning the way the battle had developed from the point of view of the companies directly involved. He reported the situation as follows:

"French attacked along the entire front in dense waves at 2.15 pm. The front line trench was completely wrecked by drum fire. In consequence the French broke in successfully to sub-sectors f, e and g, then later into sections of *Hindenburg Weg* and *Eisener Kreuz Weg* [Hindenburg and Iron Cross Ways]. Towards 3.00 pm, the enemy attempted to capture Bastion 3. Attacking in deeply echeloned waves, the enemy launched forward but, at the cost of very heavy casualties, they were beaten off by 2nd and 11th Companies, together with a platoon of the Machine Gun Company. Leutnant Hansen and a small group of men are cut off in sub sector e. At 3.20 pm the enemy broke right through Infantry Regiment 23 and appeared to be attacking Thélus. There was no contact with Infantry Regiment 23. Some troops in Bastion 3 have been deployed to protect the right flank and are engaging advancing enemy troops. 8th Company has established contact with Bastion 4. Elements of 9th and 3rd Companies have established a blocking position in the southern section of *Eisener Kreuz Weg*. A report has just come in stating that to our left the position of Infantry Regiment 62 has also been lost. Infantry Regiment 63 has been surrounded Apparently Leutnant Hansen is still holding out in sub sector e. Certainly firing is still going on there. There is no report from sub-sector h. It seems that 4th Company has been lost. Further reports to follow.'

Major von Weller lost no time in passing on the new information back to Headquarters 12th Infantry Division, where similar reports of desperate fighting were arriving from all along the divisional frontage. It was clear that, despite the best efforts of the defence along this southern sector, the weight and ferocity of the French attacks had led to penetrations being made. The most serious appeared to be that into the Infantry Regiment 23 forward trench system. These had developed into potentially very dangerous attacks into the right flank of Infantry Regiment 63, so 12th Infantry Division ordered the preparation and conduct of a counter-attack the following night, aimed at restoring the original front line.

Leutnant Zinnemann Pioneer Company Infantry Regiment 63 [10]

"Together with his adjutant, the Regimental Commander studied the reports and marked up his map. Suddenly the telephone rang, 'Hallo, this is the command post of Infantry Regiment 63 . . . Hello . . . Good . . . Understood – Tonight then. Thank you.' The Commander had received a report from the command post of Infantry Regiment 23 that the regiment's First and Second Positions had been lost. It was planned to recapture the Second Position by means of a counter-attack that night. Could we also attack simultaneously from Bastions 3 and 4? As a result of this exchange the Major [von Weller] dictated an order, 'To Major Pulst [Commanding Officer 1st Battalion Infantry Regiment 63] Reports received. Thank the troops for their endurance. Contact with Infantry Regiment 23 reveals that the Second Line is to be recaptured tonight. I order, therefore, that Bastion 3 is to support this attack and make contact with Infantry Regiment 23. The same will apply to Bastion 4 and orders will be issued from here to that effect. Sub sector h is to be liberated. Reinforcements are being sent to the left flank and will be linking up with Infantry Regiment 62 and 1st Battalion Infantry Regiment 63. Orders have just arrived from [12th Infantry] Division that 7th Company Infantry Regiment 63 is to be subordinated to Infantry Regiment 23 and 5th and 8th Companies are to move to Bastion 4. 6th Company Infantry Regiment 63 is to remain in Thélus at divisional disposal. 12th Company Infantry Regiment 62 has been put under my command. As mentioned, I am going to deploy it on the left near Infantry Regiment 62, with its right flank on the road. 12th Company Infantry Regiment 62 is to make contact with Bastion 4. Good luck and victory!'

"The patrol led by the unteroffizier took the orders and raced off. In the meantime dusk was falling. Between 9.00 pm and 10.00 pm, a report arrived stating that Infantry Regiment 23 would not be attacking. Runners had to be despatched forward to Bastion 4 with a new situation report and instructions to relay it to Major Pulst. The regimental staff worked feverishly in the flickering candlelight. Oberleutnant Thomas, the regimental adjutant, and Leutnant Oertel, the orderly officer, were working flat out. The telephone to the rear was not working well; in fact it had to be repaired a few times. Links to the artillery were maintained by the leutnant allocated to us by Field Artillery Regiment 21, but he was not happy. Quite apart from losses of men, horses and guns, there was a lack of ammunition.

"After midnight a report arrived that our brave Upper Silesians had re-established contact with the men cut off in sub sector h. Leutnant Schnieber and his gallant 4th Company had gone into all-round defence and had held off all attacks. At 3.30 am there was to be an attack towards h, designed to eliminate all the French pockets of resistance between h and our second line. The telephone link was never stable. Our telephonists were at the end of their tether. Repair teams were out constantly, sometimes for hours at a time under fire . . . Then, of course, there was the misery of the battlefield. They were carried back in groundsheets. They were silent, only a few were moaning. A good thirty wounded were lying waiting for some sort of vehicle to take them away to the rear. About 2.00 am the long-awaited ambulances arrived, the motorised one was also there. It was loaded up first. The most serious cases on their stretchers were loaded into the interior of the modern vehicle and off it rattled. We could only hope that it arrived in the rear safely, because the road was constantly under heavy fire. The remaining wounded were divided amongst the other three vehicles and they set off too, moving with difficulty across the ploughed up terrain. For them the Battle of Arras was over, always provided that they arrived in hospital without further damage.

"I went down to the cellar, ate a meal prepared by the field kitchen and wrote a short letter home. I was not feeling particularly good; I was tired enough to drop and I fell asleep immediately on my double mattress. I was able to sleep for the hour before dawn, but then everything started up once more. It all began about 4.00 am. The enemy fired like men possessed. It never stopped. The village, too, came in for its share. The shells left unbelievably massive traces of their arrival right next to us. It seemed as though they were trying to reduce the already battered cellars to rubble and ashes. Towards midday red flares went up again at the front. A short while later our artillery opened up. We thought that all the guns had been destroyed, but they put down defensive fire so heavily that it seemed as though they had stolen the ammunition from the French.

"It was a pleasure to hear it. Well done the German artillery. Just keep firing like that! Everyone emerged from the cellars to take in the absorbing spectacle. To our front firing continued ceaselessly."

Whilst Zinnemann ate his meal and had a short rest, further forward a desperate, confused, close-quarter battle was being fought out in the dark.

Reserve Leutnant Schubert 8th Company Infantry Regiment 63 [11]

"3.30 am was the time at which the recapture of *Hindenburg-* and *Eisener Kreuz Weg* [Hindenburg and Iron Cross Ways] and the restoration of the link to 4th Company were to begin . . . It was a matter of wresting back from the enemy that which they had gained. Step by step we were to work our way forward to retake the remains of the trenches, wherever their possession was of use to us. A battle with hand grenades began. Grenades were the main weapon and a bitter and tough fight began: man against man. The old spirit of the 63rd was awakened amongst the ranks of the attackers. With loud shouts of *Hurra!* Offizierstellvertreter Beck and his men forced their way into a trench occupied by the enemy. Swinging coshes and spades they despatched numerous Frenchmen. Crater by crater, over walls of earth and timber barricades they were pushed backwards.

"Simultaneously a vicious grenade assault, commanded by Reserve Leutnant Zimmermann of 9th Company and comprising three sections of 9th Company and two of 6th Company, was launched from the barricade in *Eisener-Kreuz-Weg*. This attack regained a 150 metre section of trench for us. Following the success of these two operations, Leutnant

Zimmermann and Offizierstellvertreter Beck had the intention of re-establishing a direct link with the sector of 4th Company. The two of them crept up to and hurled themselves over an enemy barricade. At that precise moment shots rang out and Beck fell, shot through the head. Leutnant Zimmermann was reported missing and it later transpired that he had been captured. The recaptured trench was found to contain the bodies of fifteen French soldiers from Regiment 107. In addition masses of weapons, knapsacks and other equipment were discovered. The sections of trench were swiftly barricaded off in order to be ready to defend against enemy counter-attacks but, unfortunately, it was not possible to link up with 4th Company."

Back at Regimental Headquarters, Leutnant Zinnemann was not left for long to enjoy his rest period. Major von Weller, having received demands for situation reports from the divisional commander, needed to know, urgently, what was happening at the front.

Leutnant Zinnemann Pioneer Company Infantry Regiment 63 [12]

My Commander sent me forward. I was to go and see what I could discover. My two companions got ready. Each of us carried a carbine and two hand grenades. We had to get the job done. I was in the best of spirits: out into the open and away. The fresh air did us good and we were able to stretch our legs as we set off. Left and right of the road the houses were as full of holes as sieves. The road was dotted with new craters. No shells were falling on the village. Our target was the western exit of the village. From there it was possible to observe both the regimental sector and that of our neighbouring regiment. I arrived at the church in one piece. Massive shell craters, bigger than any we had ever seen before, had made the road completely impassable and we had to climb around the rims.

"This was not a place to linger. Haste was essential and we picked up our heels. Suddenly another of the monsters was on the way. We pressed ourselves against the wall. Blam! Crash! – and the fragments whirred and shrieked past us. We pushed on hurriedly. We had not reached the edge of the village when we met some soldiers coming the other way. 'The French have broken through!' How could they already have broken through? We had received no such report from our people. I took a close look at the men. They were not from our regiment but, rather, the one to our right! Ah, so that was the story! I took the men with me and hurried forward, meeting up with yet more battlefield stragglers. Gradually I had a small platoon of three sections and hoped to come across a small-scale scrap and be able to join in. It did not happen. A runner from the Regiment caught up with me, carrying an order that I was to return immediately. It was stated that the French had broken through and were surrounding Thélus!

"*Donnerwetter!* Had they captured our battalion? I thought that I might be commanding the only troops in the wreckage of Thélus and expected to come under attack at any moment. I ordered my party to move at ten metre intervals and brought up the rear with my two brave lads. We arrived at the church just as one of the heavy shells crashed down on the house of God. Instantly three men of the leading group fell to the ground screaming and the remainder disappeared into the nearest house. I rushed up and found that one man had been killed. The other two were still alive, but severely wounded. I bawled at the other men of this section and directed them to carry the wounded to the regimental command post. Taking the remainder of my men, I turned off the main street. I could hardly wander around the village as though nothing was happening! We pushed on through the garden of a house and jumped down into *Münchner Weg*. I wanted to find out once and for all what was happening. I looked down towards the main road. An enormous weight of fire was being brought down on the enemy, so there could be no Frenchmen there. I then looked towards the sector of our left hand neighbours, but could observe no Frenchmen there either. However, further to our front in a hollow from where the *Loën Graben*, which my company had dug, ran, I could clearly seem some sections of French soldiers through the telescope. They were easily distinguished by their pale blue coats and steel helmets. Since they had got so far forward, it could be fatal. I directed my men to man the communication trench and opened rapid rifle fire on them.

"Crack! Crack! Crack! Crack! We had been spotted and had come under machine gun fire. *Donnerwetter!* Had our front line really been lost? If that was the case, there would be no escape. There were no reserves available. The enemy would be able to advance to Oppy without hindrance and so gain six kilometres. I could weep! Our marvellous position! Our brave battalions! Where were they? In the meantime our rapid, well-aimed fire had forced the Frenchmen to withdraw into the shallow *Loën Graben* – in other words, I had succeeded in defending the south flank of Thélus in the nick of time. The enemy opened fire once more against our front line. What could that mean? Had our troops succeeded in holding their positions, despite being outflanked? How much longer could they hold on? – because they were surrounded and no ammunition, rations or water could be supplied to them.

"I could do nothing else but wait. I sent a runner back to the Regiment with my observations. He returned half an hour later, with a new mission for me. I was to secure the south of the village until evening. Troops from our right hand neighbours were located at the western entrance to the village and to the east some gunners, whose guns had been destroyed, were acting as infantry. The village was to be held at all costs! I stayed until evening, but the French did not appear. Firing was still going on to the front. That was a good sign, but it could hardly be expected that the troops would be able to hold out until morning. They had already been manning the trenches for three weeks without relief and to that must be added in factors such as the rain, the work, the strain and the violent fire which claimed so many victims. Night fell. A pause in the fighting forward began until, by 3.00 am, there was no more firing and everyone could breathe a sigh of relief.

"An order arrived for me. I was to go and replace Leutnant Luczny, Adjutant of 3rd Battalion. Luczny, who was a gunner, had been directed to go to Regimental Headquarters and act as Artillery Liaison Officer. His commander was deployed with his battalion not far from my present location and was occupying the remains of a cellar. I knew him. He was a calm man and I knew that it would be possible to have an excellent working relationship with him. His two companies were occupying the *Münchner Graben* and had the task of defending the southern approaches to the village. One company was close by, sheltering in the cellars of the houses. I checked to make certain that the area of the church had been kept free. The enemy was bringing down such heavy shells there that no cellar could have withstood them. The battalion Commander, Hauptmann Hofrichter, described to me how difficult it had been to reach the village. Accurate fire had been coming down on all the roads behind Oppy. It was impossible to traverse Willerval and they had had to deviate around it. The hills around Farbus were simply hellish and another deviation was necessary. Finally, after being on the march for six hours, they had reached the village in the evening. The enemy had fired so many shells and so much gas at our gun positions that they were totally enveloped in an impenetrable screen.

"Contrary to all expectations the night passed quietly. The first reports began arriving from the front. Enormous masses of the enemy had attacked the entire divisional sector. To the left of the Division where, apparently, the artillery preparation had been inadequate, they had enjoyed no success. Along our front they had also been repulsed, but there was still no contact with 4th Company. *Eiserner Kreuzweg* had been attacked. Leutnant Frömmert was seriously wounded, Leutnant Zimmerman was missing, believed killed and an offizierstellvertreter had been killed by a shot to the head. 6th and 9th Companies had attacked with bayonets and spades and had succeeded in a close-quarter battle in driving troops of the French 10th Regiment back to the Second Line. In our neighbour's sector the enemy had captured part of the Third Line and had broken through during the afternoon. That explained the individual Frenchmen whom I had seen by the *Loën Graben*. Our side had been successful and we were all pleased about it. What would morning bring? The same thing again, probably! Some prisoners were led past our houses. They were from the French 63rd Infantry Regiment.

What a coincidence! Our Pionier Battalion 6 also encountered Frenchman bearing the same number. That was really amazing."

Elsewhere, 26 September was day of utterly desperate fighting in the Infantry Regiment 51 sector. The previous day had already seen severe fighting in this area. The regiment had mown down the French attackers in their hundreds and captured eighty prisoners from the French Infantry Regiments 24, 28 and 74, but had been unable to prevent a small French pocket of resistance from being established on their left forward flank where they linked up with Grenadier Regiment 11. Overnight two companies of Fusilier Regiment 38 were rushed forward to take up a blocking positioning to the rear of the potential breakthrough and so prevent the risk from developing. A further attempt was made by 9th Company Infantry Regiment 51, under its commander, Landwehr Leutnant Reymann, to storm the French positions in the *Schloßgraben* and the La Folie Position. This was no easy task in the dark, but it was achieved, despite the loss of Reymann, who was leading courageously from the front.[13] Nevertheless the main pocket of resistance remained overnight and proved to be a weak point in the defence on 26 September.

During the very early morning a furious bombardment with mortars and artillery opened up on the Infantry Regiment 51 front. It was the preliminary to several different types of attack which persisted throughout the day. Efforts were made in the morning by the French to outflank 6th and 7th Companies on the left flank, but each time they were driven off. Some minor salients and projections in the line were under aimed fire from three sides and ground had to be given in order to avoid unnecessary casualties, which were still rising alarmingly as the day wore on. All the routes forward, with the exception of the *Transfeldgraben,* were being shelled constantly and that trench only seemed to escape the same treatment because it was not marked on the French trench maps at the time.

Attacks continued throughout the afternoon, with a particularly heavy one launched at 4.00 pm. The early ones had been beaten back, but this one was launched in great strength against a 300 metre wide sector held by 8th Company Infantry Regiment 51, which by now had been reduced to about forty men, some of whom were wounded. The survivors, most of whom were older men from the Landwehr, did their best, picking off large numbers of French infantrymen as they stormed forward, but they could not prevent some of them from getting into the forward positions where hand to hand of fighting of brutal savagery ensued. Wehrmann Paul Turek shot two Frenchmen dead and wounded a third then, having been shot through the head by a French officer with his revolver, used his last reserves of strength to smash the officer's skull with a hand grenade. He then fell down dead, next to the dying Frenchman.

Leutnant Zinnemann Adjutant 3rd Battalion Infantry Regiment 63 [14]

"Day dawned on 27 September. It was still raining and the trenches were full of mud, which was pleasant for neither side. Progress within them was slow. Punctually at 9.00 am French drum fire began to land.

It smashed down even more violently than on the previous day and Thélus came in for a large amount of it. The houses were simply swept away. It was impossible to move along the main road; piles of rafters and entire house fronts had collapsed into it. The Battalion remained on stand by. Towards midday the first of our red flares went up and we relayed the signals back to our artillery, which reacted instantly. The shells roared above our heads and across the flat ground to our front. The main road was under an extraordinary weight of fire. Almost none of the trees were still standing; they had been snapped off like match sticks.

"The attack ebbed and flowed. We stood idly by in the *Münchner Graben* [Munich Trench] and waited for the moment when we should have to intervene . . . At around midday a squadron of eight aircraft bombed Thélus with loud bangs and crashes. At long last the racket died down towards evening. Reports coming in spoke of a further attack all along the line. We lost Sector e, together with Leutnants Hansen and Scholz, who fell in hand to hand fighting. A number of troops had been cut off and captured. Only Sector h was holding out – for the third day! The French had made several attempts to capture it, but could not quite reach it. They occupied the large craters, but could make no more progress. They attempted to rally for an attack from there, but 4th Company had beaten them to a pulp with grenades and they did not even participate in the afternoon attack, which was in any case another French failure, with losses as high as during the previous assault.

"That night the Frenchman fired like mad men at the village. It was impossible to go out onto the road where one shell after another was landing. Towards morning the show was over. It was 28 September: quiet during the morning and only a few shells on the communication trenches in the afternoon. About 4.00 pm, violent drum fire suddenly came down once again. At that red flares went up and the assault flared up once more. Because the enemy had taken so little from us up to that point, they made an attempt now to achieve surprise. I was able to observe the fire exactly. Initially it came down exclusively on the front line for several minutes then it lifted directly onto the second line before lifting once more onto the road. It appeared as though the attacking Frenchmen were intended to follow this rolling barrage. The fire continued until night fell. From that time there was an uncanny silence. This was strange. Had they miscalculated the number of shells which would be required? It certainly appeared as though events were not playing out as intended. It was easy to imagine what effect this must be having on the senior French commanders! According to reports, the enemy left the trenches only along about half of the available frontage. There was also mention of the use by the French of snipers firing from their own trenches at men engaged in the close-quarter battle.

"The night was relatively quiet. We waited longingly for relief. The troops had spent too long in this position. For eight days they had received neither hot food nor hot drinks. For eight days they had been in the open and in the rain. Added to this was the fact that the daily losses weakened the troops considerably. A large number of commanders had been lost due to death, wounds or capture. There was a shortage of ammunition and essential equipment of all types. From every aspect we were no longer battleworthy; we needed to be withdrawn as soon as possible. The troops began to complain and these complaints were passed on to higher authority, but to no avail. There were hardly any reserves available on the Western Front. The Eastern Front had a greater need. We abandoned our hope of early relief.

"The first hopeful signs arrived on 29 September that our duties on this front were nearly at an end. As early as 3.00 am, companies of Bavarian Infantry Regiment 2 began arriving and relieving our forward companies, just as our 4th Company finally succeeded in breaking through to the recently recaptured *Eisener Kreuz Weg*. It was reduced to a small group of men under the heroic leadership of Leutnant Schnieber. For the time being we remained in Thélus as a reserve for the newly deployed troops. Around midday there was moderate artillery fire on *Münchner Weg,* as well as heavy shells which landed on Thélus. During the afternoon there was drum fire all along the sector. This lasted for between three and four hours. The enemy did not attack, but they wanted to wear us down and they fired desperately. It is possible that they intended to attack only using the artillery and, during the evening the show was over. It seemed as though the French were going to try something artistic during the night. That was always unpleasant, because it was impossible to tell where they had broken through and on which side we were outflanked.

"This time our batteries did not fall silent. They had been reinforced during the day and they fired with fresh intensity. This had a calming effect on us. We had quickly learned to derive pleasure from thoughts of the discomfiture of the enemy when our artillery was engaged in their pursuit. At 7.00 pm we were able to leave the cellars, which in some cases were almost collapsed. As it went dark we pulled back through a thin drizzle. We took this as a bonus because it freshened up our worn and dirty faces. After a seemingly endless march we arrived at Oppy, which was jam-packed with artillery and columns of vehicles. Our quarters had been occupied by newly-arrived troops. So there we were, back in Oppy but without as much as a wisp of straw on which to lay our heads, because fresh troops had taken our places while we had been fighting out in front. We tackled the matter energetically and room was found for our troops, who were desperately in need of rest. It was already light by the time that the last man had been accommodated. Then at last we could repair to one of the billets and throw ourselves down fully clothed on the hard tiled floor and fall asleep to rest our aching limbs."

Diary Entry of an Anonymous French Officer 28 September 1915 [15]

"The reason that I have written nothing since 24 September is that we have been reduced to a state of total indifference by the attack. My battalion has lost 1,300 men, twelve of them officers. There are only three of us left. We fear that there is about to be an enemy counter-attack and we are located in a very poor position. Our carefully prepared push has failed utterly. It is all over. To our right, where things have gone well, attempts are being made to salvage something out of the misfortune. That cannot disguise the fact that the first attacks did not reach the initial objectives. We were brought to a standstill at a bitterly high cost.

"The 103rd and 104th Infantry Regiments have refused to advance. My company has been reduced from 210 to thirty men. Things are much the same in the other regiments. I am utterly exhausted. We are being worn down by the fire of the guns. It is dreadful. We can hardly stay on our feet: and yet we must. The German troops are tremendous. I marvel and respect my opponents, because of their courage, because of their wonderful discipline and their attention to detail, even in the small things. Germany is extremely powerful and it got there through its own efforts. That is outstanding.

"Their most noble characteristics are extreme patience, endurance and perseverance, in order to achieve final success for the glory of their country. I cannot go into detail; it is forbidden."

For the time being the situation along the crucial sector forward of Vimy Ridge from La Folie Wood southwards was at least stable. Further north there was greater cause for concern. Earlier in the summer 123rd Infantry Division had taken over the northern end of the threatened sector from 8th Infantry Division. Infantry Regiment 178 took over the so-called *Hexenkessel* [Witches' Cauldron] in the north, whilst Infantry Regiment 182 assumed responsibility for the defence of Souchez. Both regiments were frequently engaged in close-quarter hand grenade battles, because the lines were very close in this area. The artillery battle was ceaseless, with the French continually bombarding the *Inselstellung* [Island Position], Givenchy itself and the *Gießlerhöhe,* whilst the German gunners retaliated against Notre Dame de Lorette, the *Franzosenkopf* [Frenchman's Head – a prominent salient] and *Marokkanerwäldchen* [Moroccan Copse], which had been lost during the spring battles. All this activity, however, could not disguise the fact the German positions were badly sited and poorly constructed.

The problems had been caused by the outcome of earlier fighting. The lines had solidified where particular battles had reached their high water mark and, despite endless work by the troops of 8th Infantry Division, nothing could overcome the fact that long lengths of the forward positions ran along the base of the Lorette Spur and so could be completely overlooked. Furthermore the positions formed a pronounced salient, vulnerable to flanking fire from the heights northwest of Neuville St Vaast, from which elevated locations much of the position was visible from the rear. Lack of depth ruled out simply withdrawing to fresh positions in rear and, which was worse, all the communications trenches leading forward to the three regimental sectors were channelled through the narrow valley of the Souchez River. In full view of observers from the Neuville direction, this meant that moving reserves of men and materiel forward was fraught with great danger.

To these geographical disadvantages must be added the fact that there was no continuous front line trench. Hardly anywhere did the First Position comprise two battle trenches linked by communication trenches. There were practically no safe dugouts, no effective wire obstacle and telephone cables ran forward only in the right hand sector. Most of these issues could have been addressed had there been a few weeks of calm before the storm. Not only was this not the case, but the quantities of artillery fire increased inexorably. By the time battle was joined there had been some improvements. For example, on the right where the fire was not so intense, temporary obstacles were placed, more dugouts constructed and, with the exception of the swamp to the southwest of Souchez, the front line did become continuous. All the remainder of the ceaseless labour had to be devoted to emergency repairs to the damage caused by the shelling.

The Saxon regiments of 123rd Infantry Division each operated a three day cycle of reliefs between their forward, support and reserve battalions (who were resting in Lens). This meant that the troops only had two nights rest in nine and conditions when they were forward were almost beyond human endurance. Nothing could move by day. The carrying forward of food and drink was almost impossible, even at night. Day and night were punctured by indirect fire, sniping and grenade fighting and the men of Infantry Regiment 182 manning the positions west of Souchez were up to their waists in water or crouching on small sandbag islands for seventy two hours at a time. Small wonder that the Division was badly worn down before battle was joined. Interrogation of a deserter revealed that the offensive was due to open at dawn on 25 September and all possible final preparations to meet it were made.

Reserves were moved forward and the sector commanders were ordered to pack their front line trenches with men. This was a high risk strategy, given the weight of the bombardment. Repeatedly in the literature of the Great War the defence speaks of unprecedented quantities of artillery fire. This was certainly the case prior to the September offensive, but it does seem that they had a case. When the main bombardment began on 20 September, prior to the ultimate increase to out and out drum fire, 7th Company Infantry Regiment 51, for example, located in the La Folie area, counted 330 shells, a quarter of them large calibre, landing on their sector – in five minutes![16]

On 24 September, artillery fire, increasing to drum fire, preceded several raids, launched by the British at Hulluch and Loos and the French at Souchez and Neuville St Vaast.[17] These were all driven off, but it was clear that the assault was imminent. Nevertheless, as day dawned on 25 September, everything was comparatively quiet along the Vimy front. Towards 7.00 am the sound of battle could be heard coming from away to the north and within two hours word reached the regiments from Corps Headquarters that the British had launched attacks astride the roads Vermelles – Hulluch and Béthune – Lens. By 10.00 am the news was of a critical situation, caused by the British capture of Loos and Hill 70. Immediately reserves were taken from 123rd Infantry Division and despatched to take part in counter-attacks. Meanwhile the defenders monitored the situation to their front with increasing concern. In the words of the Infantry Regiment 182 after action report:

> "At 12.45 reports arrived from the *Gießlerhöhe* that French soldiers in full assault order could be seen gathering in the *Franzosenkopf*. Simultaneously the enemy artillery fire increased to the heaviest drum fire imaginable. From 1.30 pm our own defensive artillery fire began coming down, having been called for by the Sector Commander. The entire Souchez Valley was shrouded in smoke dust. From there as far as Fosse 6, enemy sulphur gas shells were landing. The drum fire stopped slightly before then, at 2.00 pm, came the news that it appeared as though the front line had been overrun and that the enemy was already swarming beyond into the valley bottom. Despite the weight of machine gun fire we had put down, despite the heavy casualties we had caused the enemy, the successive dense attacking waves could be held no longer.
>
> "The few men in the forward position – there could be no question any more about 'trenches' – who had not fallen victim to the crushing drum fire, had almost all been wounded and captured. The only exception was the handful of men who, in small groups or individually, fought their way back through the valley of the Souchez River, making use of the stream bed [for cover]. Of the overrun troops of 3rd Battalion (the 9th Company with three officers and two platoons deployed forward), all were missing. Just to the north, in the Intermediate Position, six men of 10th Company under the courageous Gefreiter Quandt, held on to their trench until 2.00 pm, at which time a heavy concentration of sulphur gas shells[18] drove them back."[19]

The story was much the same throughout the Infantry Regiment 182 sector. Several local counter-attacks were launched, but even with the assistance of companies of Infantry Regiment 178 and Reserve Infantry Regiment 106, it was only possible roughly to stabilise the situation; the French remaining in possession of their gains.[20] On a day of hard infantry battle, there were still incidents which could raise a smile as they were told and re-told. During the afternoon of 25 September, for example, Gefreiter Marche of 2nd Company Fusilier Regiment 38, deployed near Souchez, displayed considerable presence of mind. He had been binding the wounds of a number of wounded defenders when he was suddenly approached by a group of French soldiers who demanded his surrender. Two of the Frenchmen were wounded and Marche greeted them in an open and friendly manner then set about bandaging their wounds in a most elaborate manner. This treatment so impressed the French group that they voluntarily picked up the German wounded and followed Marche along the trench, where they surrendered to other soldiers of 2nd Company![21]

On this first major day of battle there were also countless examples of brave conduct by individuals and groups of soldiers from both sides. At one critical moment in the battle, for example, the commander of 3rd Battalion Fusilier Regiment 38, whose command post was located close to Givenchy, had to pass a message back to regimental headquarters. All the approach routes, the communication trenches and Givenchy itself were under heavy fire from both high explosive and gas shells, whose stench filled the air. Despite all the fire, Fusilier Czogalla of 9th Company Fusilier Regiment 38 succeeded in traversing the smoking remains of Givenchy without being hit and delivering the message. He was told that he could wait where he was until the fire slackened but, after a short rest, he made his way back through the intense fire to deliver the reply to the Battalion command post. He was immediately awarded the Iron Cross Second Class for his bravery.[22] The same medal was given that day to another member of 9th Company – Fusilier Martinus, whose actions formed part of the 9th Company after action report:

> "The trenches were completely levelled and a large part of trench garrison was trapped beneath collapsed dugouts. Despite the fact that countless shells were landing in and around the trench, Fusilier Martinus worked tirelessly to release the trapped men, inspiring his comrades to help with the work. On several occasions during the day and regardless of the danger he carried wounded men back to the aid post through the wrecked communication trenches. As he was trying to rescue a badly wounded unteroffizier, who was buried, a shell exploded right next to him and he collapsed amongst a tangle of wrecked beams and falling sandbags. Recovering consciousness, he managed to free himself then, calmly, as though nothing had happened, he continued his rescue work. Thanks to his efforts he saved many of his comrades from certain and painful death."[23]

On Vimy Ridge itself, at about 1.30 pm on 25 September, the French bombardment lifted from the German front line. One of the observers from Field Artillery Regiment 6, who was deployed forward in *Foliegraben* and watched the initial assault unfold, wrote later:

Unteroffizier Hackenburg 3rd Battery Field Artillery Regiment 6 [24]

> "A little after 2.00 pm the French left their trenches shoulder to shoulder and disappeared into our forward positions. From the puffs of

smoke which began to appear a short time later, it was straightforward to conclude that battles with hand grenades were taking place. Reacting to flares fired upon the appearance of the French troops, our defensive fire came down and only a few individuals were able to follow the initial attacking line. After about fifteen minutes the German sentries had resumed their positions in the front line trench and were observing in the direction of the enemy trenches as though nothing had happened. For an hour the enemy artillery was almost silent. A few Frenchmen had penetrated between the first trenches and the *Reuß-Stellung* (Second Position). There they were picked off one by one from the *Transfeldgraben* and *Goebengraben*."

This was, however, not a typical outcome on a day when the initial French assault made some progress. Around La Folie Chateau, for example, there was a breakthrough between Grenadier Regiment 11 and Infantry Regiment 51. Luckily there was clear observation of these developments, so concentrated fire from 1st and 6th Batteries Field Artillery Regiment 6 and a hail of small arms fire from depth positions checked the progress of the attack. There was a minor crisis when the firing at intense rates almost exhausted the supplies on the gun positions, but 200 shells were rushed forward to 1st Battery from forward dumps in Vimy. The ammunition horses were too exhausted to haul supplies up to the steep slopes near La Folie, where 2nd Battery Field Artillery Regiment 6 had to save what little ammunition it had left in case it came under direct attack. Fortunately the situation was first stabilised, then resupply was possible overnight[25]

It is often easy to concentrate on the exploits of the infantry to the detriment of the artillery, but that would be to ignore the fact that cold-blooded courage under fire was required of the gunners too as they manned their guns, despite heavy counter-battery fire, and directed much-needed fire, regardless of the strain and the personal risk involved.

Kanonier Max Strehle 2nd Battery Field Artillery Regiment 245 [26]

"On 30 August our Division [123rd Infantry], to which Field Artillery Regiment 245 belonged, was called forward to the area of Lens. We had spent a long period of time at rest near Lille and were happy to move from the monotonous routine of life behind the lines. We knew quite well that a difficult time awaited us, because for a considerable time there had been feverish activity behind the French and British lines, which had been spotted by our determined airmen. Nevertheless we felt secure in the hands of our energetic and prudent officers: especially our own hauptmann. The early September days were generally quiet and we made good use of this time to develop our position, which was located in a series of gardens rising in terraces right by the western edge of the utterly wrecked village of Givenchy. Within the village itself or rather, in the cellars of the ruined buildings, we improvised such things as shell-proof dugouts for the officers and the remainder of the battalion, telephone exchanges, ammunition stores, aid posts and kitchens.

"On approximately 22 September the enemy began to bring down drum fire. They had achieved a superiority of three or four to one in guns of all calibres from the lightest to the heaviest. Initially, we let them get on with it and conserved our ammunition. Only when they paused for breath did we hurl across a few well-aimed concentrations. It was absolute hell. Stones and dust flew past our ears and poisonous gases made breathing difficult: at that time our gas masks had not reached their current state of development. Our batteries were constantly under fire from super-heavy calibre howitzers, whose fire was directed by low-flying enemy aircraft.

"This period of destructive fire lasted more than seventy hours. It completely flattened the forward trenches and the artillery observation posts. It was then that they launched their massed infantry attacks, but as they stormed forward, they were brought to a bloody standstill by our heroic defence and well-placed defensive fire. Further waves were driven forward and, when these began to hesitate, they were brought under fire by their own artillery.[27] Our battery was furthest forward and was able to bring down destructive fire on an enemy assembly trench to our right near Angres. The right flank was seriously threatened. The enemy infantry had already pushed forward 400 metres and threatened to encircle the whole of the *Gießlerhöhe*!

"However, without being seen by the nearby enemy infantry, we had hauled our right hand gun out of its concealed position and, firing from the open, under the calm direction of our beloved hauptmann, we sent shell after shell into the enemy assault trenches, where we could observe the appalling casualties they caused. There is no doubt that this action helped avert a catastrophe. When, later, our hauptmann's dugout was smashed, he moved into another from where he directed the fire of three batteries single handed. On 28 September, in accordance with the agreement between our officers, he should have been relieved of this extremely strenuous fire direction mission. He, however, stayed where he was, despite having held on for three days in this hell, saying 'I am not leaving my battery at such a difficult time!' That same afternoon his dugout was struck by a direct hit, bringing him a swift, painless death.

"He was faithful unto death! In the case of our Hauptmann Tankred Freyer of 2nd Battery Field Artillery Regiment 245 that statement was fully justified and his death upset every one of us very deeply. Every one who knew him and loved him, every last member of the battery, will never forget him! The following evening three of us went to recover his body in order to give it a decent burial. However, enemy infantry had closed up to within a few metres of the observation post and we were greeted by heavy rifle fire and grenades. Vizewachtmeister Wallbaum escaped unscathed, but my comrade Woidt was severely wounded and I could not help him back, being myself wounded in the hip and several places in the back. That same night our regiment was relieved and so it remained impossible to recover our dear fallen comrade.[28] May his name serve as a constant shining example of true comradeship and courage to our children and children's children! May the earth rest lightly on him!"

There can be no doubt that the defence faced a serious crisis in the early days of the renewed French offensive. The period 24 – 29 September, for example, saw the loss of several areas of tactical importance and cost the Saxon 123rd Infantry Division no fewer than twenty three officers and 595 other ranks killed, thirty five officers and 1029 other ranks wounded and thirty officers and 1,525 other ranks missing.[29] The survivors were exhausted, shaken and so worn down by the immense exertions of countering the initial French assaults that they were no longer in a fit state to continue to conduct the defence of this vital sector. Fortunately the Guard Corps had been withdrawn from the area northwest of Brest Litovsk a few days earlier and, moving west, was available, after the briefest of refits and receipt of reinforcements (which only brought rifle company strengths up to a maximum of 150 riflemen), to be rushed forward into the desperate battles around Vimy Ridge. No sooner did units arrive than they were thrown into the battle with little briefing and less preparation. It was an inauspicious start to this difficult tour of duty but, as always, the Guards rose to the challenge. The most threatened part of the line and by far the worst to attempt to defend was that around the *Gießlerhöhe,* where elements of Grenadier Guard Regiment 1 were deployed alongside Footguard Regiment 1.

Unteroffizier Schröder 5th Company Grenadier Guard Regiment 1 [30]

"We traversed Liévin and Angres, whose houses were completely in ruins. Stinking sulphurous fumes from heavy shells rose out of them. We soon entered a communications trench and there the company picked its way forward in single file. Each time a shell landed in the houses the men flinched and threw themselves down. They were recruits and this was the first time they had been in battle. We soon reached the front line. An unteroffizier of Infantry Regiment 27 pointed out the sentry positions and the dugouts for my section. Four of my men went on duty immediately; the remainder crawled into their dugouts, which measured a mere 1.5 m x 1.2 m x 1 m. A layer of planks covered the freezing cold and wet chalk soil. Rats were nesting behind the sections of tree trunks which acted as props; their scratching and squeaking went on all night. Sleep was out of the question. Outside was the constant roar of the guns and there could be an alarm at any moment, which meant rushing out to our alert positions, there to defend ourselves with rifles and grenades.

"These positions were a great deal different from our experience at

Bucquoy.[31] The endless shower of enemy shells and shrapnel on and behind the trenches got on our nerves. Furthermore, we were not able just to concern ourselves with war above ground. Underground the enemy also created uncertainty. Both we and the French drove tunnels forward and day and night listening posts were in action, checking for any sound of French mining operations. We too, in our dugouts, could clearly hear the sounds of the French working with spades and picks. Sometimes we thought that they were right beneath us. At nights we constructed saps forward from the front line trench and established listening posts there. The bodies of countless dead men lay between our lines and those of the French."

Major von Graese Commanding Officer 2nd Battalion Grenadier Guard Regiment 1 [32]

"Already during the first night I toured all the sectors. There was bad damage everywhere. The parapets were full of corpses and parts of corpses, as were the trenches themselves in places! Sub-sector Z2 was particularly dreadful. The enemy positions were mostly extremely close. In places their saps almost touched our trenches. It was a particularly unpleasant fact that entire stretches of the trench lines were under enfilade fire by enemy artillery. To the right they were threatened by the new British positions near Loos; to the left by the *Gießler Höhe* near Souchez, the western slopes of which were in French hands. Our left flank was under serious threat because Angres Copse, which had been devastated by shell fire and which was held by the Augusta Regiment [Grenadier Guard Regiment 4], was at constant risk of attack.

"The days from 1 to 4 October were utterly appalling. We cleared up corpses as best we could; burying them roughly in the heavy churned up soil. Work went on to improve the approach routes, which had almost all been wrecked by gun fire and to attempt to put the positions into some semblance of defensive order. All this took place under heavy fire, which tended to destroy repairs as soon as they had been completed. The consequence was heavy losses, especially in sub-sector Z2, which was occupied by 8th Company. They suffered six killed and twenty six seriously wounded. It was only possible to move these casualties, who included Leutnant von Portatius (suffering from burns to the face) and Reserve Leutnant Paul (shrapnel wounds), at night.

"Oberst von Stein visited the trenches whilst all this fire was coming down. His courageous calmness provided an outstanding example, as did the performance of the men, despite all the obstacles put in their way by the heavy chalk soil and the torrent of French fire. My dugout, known as 'The Limekiln', was renamed the 'Rats' Castle' by me. These stinking creatures scurried round the battlefield at night in masses as they gorged on the corpses. There was an excellent view from near the wireless station. The view at night was one of romance, punctuated as it was by the roar of the guns, their muzzle flashes and the flickering of flares. It was like an eerie, violent firework display".

Having carried out a difficult and dangerous relief in the line whilst under heavy fire, the forward sub-units of 2nd Battalion Grenadier Guard Regiment 2 found themselves clinging on to exceedingly exposed positions on the forward slopes of the *Gießlerhöhe*. By 11.00 am on 28 September the whole area was drenched with gas and subjected to an immense weight of drum fire as the French prepared to launch yet another attempt to seize control of this vital piece of terrain.

Reserve Leutnant Lottner 7th Company Grenadier Guard Regiment 2 [33]

"Angres itself was not actually under fire but, on the other hand, the deafening crashes, with their attendant columns of smoke, from the far side of the *Gießlerhöhe* showed that our 6th and 8th Companies were under heavy fire. The 6th Company was occupying the so-called *Hanggraben* [Slope Trench] which, as its name suggests, ran along the forward slope of the *Gießlerhöhe* facing the enemy. The 8th Company was to its right in the continuation of the line of the trench in the low ground. Rath [8th Company commander], who did not have room forward for all his men, had despatched half of them to the rear under Waechter. In the pitch black night, some of the men of 6th Company, having apparently been given the wrong information by the troops they had relieved, had occupied an old communication trench which led towards the enemy and so were presenting an exposed flank to them.

"Towards 3.00 pm the fire increased to one constant roar and remained like that until 6.00 pm. At that time Deutsch arrived, covered in mud, his face blackened with smoke and reported that he had had no choice but to evacuate the position in view of the intense fire. His men had simply melted away and the trench was totally ploughed up. He returned towards evening to the old position with nineteen men, all that he had been able up to that moment to muster from the 180 man strong company. More than sixty five men failed to reappear during the next few days. The enemy had attempted to launch an attack against the 8th Company frontage and had risen up out of their trenches. Well aimed small arms fire broke this attack up and they quickly disappeared back into cover. The 8th Company, whose position was not as exposed as that of the 6th, had suffered correspondingly less."

Yet again the defence seemed to be facing a major crisis. If nothing was done to counter the French advances, Givenchy itself would be at risk, the integrity of the entire defence would be in question and a major breakthrough, threatened for so long, would have become a reality. Reacting as fast as humanly possible, all remaining uncommitted troops of Grenadier Guard Regiment 2 were prepared and readied to launch a counter-attack in highly unfavourable circumstances.

Reserve Leutnant Lottner 7th Company Grenadier Guard Regiment 2 [34]

"Word having arrived that the enemy was in possession of the *Gießler Höhe* and that Givenchy was in danger, as soon as it went dark 5th and 7th Companies were alerted and despatched to the western exit of Givenchy. The heights were to be retaken by means of a counter-attack. Our attack orders were more or less as follows: *Advance in a skirmishing line until you meet the enemy then, with shouts of Hurra! and fixed bayonets, throw yourselves at them* . . . This was a difficult situation. We knew nothing of the terrain, the enemy or the junction points with our neighbours. It was pouring with rain and the night was pitch black. The fact that I had vivid memories of being shot in the stomach in a similar situation previously did not help to ensure my complete happiness, nor did the report, God be praised false, that Rath had been killed.

"Major von Bieberstein [Commanding Officer 2nd Battalion], whose command post had been set up in one of the cellars of the totally destroyed village, arranged for the junction point with the 1st Battalion to be located, as far as that was possible in the darkness. Then I remember the return of his tireless adjutant, Hildebrand, who had undertaken the task personally and who returned with the news that all the communication trenches leading forward were packed with the men of the 1st Battalion. Were we to add to the confusion? Finally it was established that the reports of the loss of the *Gießler Höhe* were incorrect. The whole business was over for me and I had some coffee and a meal from the field kitchen sheltering in the battalion command post . . .

"In the end we did not have to go seeking out the enemy with shouts of *Hurra!* But the 7th Company had to return at once to Angres to relieve 6th Company. I was ordered to occupy the *Gießler-Höhe-Graben* to the rear of 6th Company and to ensure that I linked up with 8th Company to the right and 1st Battalion to the left . . . We headed off in the deep narrow communication trench, which led from the crossroads in Angres via numerous acute changes of direction, forward to Souchez. All the time that it was in the chalk we were able, despite large quantities of thin grey mud which offered no firm footing and reached almost to the top of our boots and despite treacherous rifle-grabbing telephone wires, to pick our way forward with difficulty. Shuddering, we stepped on two corpses who had half sunk into the base of the trench, their clothing torn off by the passage of many feet.

"Soon, however, we were reduced to picking our way forward a step at a time. The leading group had arrived at the point where the trench was dug out of the mud. The occasional shell which crashed down very close made all the waiting very unpleasant. Finally our boots too were in the embrace of the clinging mud, forcing us to pull them up out of the mud by their straps with each step. I followed 8th Company until it had reached the place where its trenches forked off to the right, then I branched off left, so I that I should eventually link up with them on my right flank. In the trench, which became worse and worse and hard to distinguish, I came across two dead men of 6th Company and another who was seriously wounded. Soon I linked up with Deutsch and a few other men.

"In fact I had ended up in the 6th Company trench, when I was meant to be occupying a different one to the rear. Never mind, I had a junction point to the right as ordered. Now it was a matter of locating the 1st Battalion to the left. In the meantime I had to deploy the company, but where? The further on I pressed, accompanied by two recent arrivals, one of whom was named Herzwurm, the worse the picture grew. Totally flattened in places and half buried elsewhere, the trench threaded its way slightly uphill across the slope then, turning abruptly uphill over a sharp rise, disappeared into the chaos of a completely ploughed up plateau. A reconnaissance of this area in total darkness and in the rain was an immensely difficult undertaking.

"Slithering about and climbing on all fours, covered in clay from top to bottom, their hands and feet encased in lumps of clay, which found its way up their sleeves, tripping over their long coats, sweating and grumbling, the company inched its way forward. I deployed my left flank on the plateau. It was essential that they dug in quickly. This was far from easy. Each spade full of clay had to be scraped off the blades, but they went on digging. Some, who had no idea what the morning would bring, had to be forced not to be content with small holes only knee deep. Some of these had already wrapped themselves in their coats and had fallen asleep. I threw clods of clay at them or hit and kicked them awake. I shook one man violently to rouse him, only to discover that he was sleeping his last sleep. He was from 6th Company. Some men complained that, as they dug deeper, they kept hitting corpses and had to begin again in another place. It was soon obvious to me that to leave men here under heavy fire just meant useless sacrifice."

It was essential that the battered formations and units be relieved and elements of the Guard Corps continued to be fed forward for this purpose. Footguard Regiments 4 and 2 played a decisive role in bringing the advance in the La Folie area to a halt, then remained forward, assisted by surviving elements of 12th Infantry Division, to parry any further French attempts at assault in this area; whilst, to their north, between The Pimple and Hill 145, Footguard Regiments 1 and 3 in that order were involved in repelling the increasingly frantic attempts by the French troops to seize the crest of Vimy Ridge which was now so close as, seemingly, to be within their grasp. In incessant close-quarter fighting over the next few days the defence, buckling and yielding from time to time, nevertheless continued to hold firm but, inevitably, casualties were high. The company rifle strengths were in any case well below normal. There had not been sufficient time to complete the process of reinforcement. 10th Company Footguard Regiment 2, for example, went into battle on 28 September with only 120 men – one hundred short of their peacetime establishment. By 3 October, the close quarter fighting and, in particular, the extraordinary drum fire, had produced seventy five per cent casualties. Writing in the company war diary later, the Company Commander, Leutnant Hoyer, recorded his impressions of the effect of this fire and the associated bitter fighting:

"Already, during the night 1–2 October, the Company was gassed and everyone suffered from irritation of the mucous membranes. Early in the morning there was mortar fire and a hand grenade battle broke out in a nearby listening post. From 7.00 am the enemy fired mortars and gas all along our sector. This made our eyes stream and breathing was diffi-cult. Around midday drum fire began . . . soon to this was blended mortar fire, shelling with heavy artillery and rifle grenades. Hour by hour the fire became heavier. By 4.00 pm the trench had been flattened in many places and numerous dead and wounded lay strewn around. At about 6.00 pm the French launched an attack on the left flank but, with the assistance of 9th Company (Leutnant Eichler), which had suffered less, the attack was beaten off with heavy enemy losses.

"In the centre only a handful of men were left. They defended their position to the last, but were overwhelmed. At that the enemy occupied this section of trench and began to prepare it for defence. At that our artillery brought down high explosive and shrapnel fire on the trenches. The French were unable to hold on and they fell back. As the artillery fire slackened with the approach of night, the French launched forward once more in strength and were able to reoccupy the trench. It was impossible to launch a counter-attack with the company in its weakened state, so the French were able to develop the trench and establish blocks . . .

"During the night things became calmer, but from time to time mortar fire and battles with grenades or small arms broke out. At 3.00 am the 11th Company arrived in support and assisted in the repairs to the trenches. Not until morning were we gassed once more. At dawn 11th Company attempted to eject the enemy using grenades, but without artillery support this was unsuccessful. The boldest commander, Leutnant von Grodeck, was shot through the throat. 10th Company pulled back into the *Schwabentunnel* [Schwabian Tunnel] in reserve. The message did not reach some men on the extreme right flank and they remained on the position. From 12.30 to 1.30 pm, our artillery engaged the French pocket of resistance then a counter-attack with hand grenades began.

"From the left the 11th, now commanded by Offizierstellvertreter Wiseotte, pushed forward, whilst from the right the few remaining members of the 10th Company, were supported by 12th Company. Leutnant Bieger from 12th Company was killed, and Unteroffiziers Hallaß and Mecklenburg took the lead. The piles of corpses grew higher. Unteroffizier Hallaß, well known for his exploits at Swierczow, set off to link up with 11th Company, but to do this he had to run along a section of flattened trench. Shouting *Hurra!* his helmet bobbing about, this daring Unteroffizier fell, shot through the head."

The story was much the same for Footguard Regiment 1, whose 1st Battalion had been involved in a particularly heroic, if costly, counter-attack on 29 September which had ejected the French from their recently gained line in the *Prinz-Reuss-Stellung* near The Pimple and relieved some of the pressure on Footguard Regiment 3, whose sector this was. Despite the continuing violent reaction of the French troops, a 300 metre section of the front line had been regained and eight officers and 152 other ranks were captured.[35] The position was extraordinarily precarious, however, because French troops were still occupying positions to the left and right. Only a trickle of reinforcements – one platoon at a time – could be spared. Fire poured down on the Guards and losses continued to mount alarmingly. Eventually the position became untenable and had to be given up.

Leutnant von Werder 3rd Company Footguard Regiment 1 [36]

"30 September was a dreadful day. During the night a number of seriously wounded men, who had been lying out in the open, managed to crawl into the trenches. They moaned deliriously, calling for water, but there was none to be had. They were all fine young reinforcements, eighteen to twenty years old. They were wounded terribly and we had insufficient dressings. I myself bound up wounds which were so bad that I should never have believed that it was possible to suffer them and still be alive . . . We consoled ourselves with the thoughts of the evening and hopes that the relieving attack would succeed. At 10.00 pm I despatched a patrol with the report: 'Contact must be made with us tonight. All around the French are extremely active . . . both the fit troops and the wounded (about thirty) are suffering terribly from thirst. (I had noticed the previous day that the French were sapping vigorously forwards. My trench was already threatened from the rear by two advancing pincers, which were only one hundred metres apart and the French were doing everything possible to ensure that the gap was closed.)

"I received a reply to my report at 2.00 am. 'There are insufficient forces to guarantee that a link up will be achieved. By order of the

Regiment [Footguard Regiment 3], the company is to pull back tonight and to rally at the point from which the attack was launched. The troops manning the *La Folie-Stellung* have been warned about your withdrawal. The Best of Luck to you!' It was quite the worst thing that could have happened. My brave men had shed so much blood to capture the place and now we had to pull out. I summoned my platoon commanders. I looked up at the clear moonlit night. There were artillery and machine guns on three sides. How many casualties would there be? Who would succeed in passing through the gap?

"I decided to wait until 4.30 am, when morning mist would cover the moon. I directed that preparations for the move were to be conducted silently, that from time to time there was to be firing, that all the wounded were to be taken and that, when I fired one green rocket into the air as a signal, the entire company was to move off as one. Despite my orders, I knew full well that we should not be able to move all the wounded. My brave lads, many of them delirious, noticed our preparations and implored us [to take them too]. About 4.00 am I despatched a section with the walking wounded and four French officers; I wanted to see where the fire was fiercest. They came under particularly heavy fire from the left, so I decided to lead the company more to the right.

"At 4.45 am the moon was still shining mercilessly bright. The usual white wall on the horizon did not seem to want to appear. 'Pass the word! The Company will move off in ten minutes!' (As my section had pulled back I had noticed that the garrison of the *La Folie-Stellung* had joined in with the firing . . . so we also had to expect to be fired on by our own men) . . . I slung my carbine . . . 'Pass it on: Company move now!' We crawled away to the rear over the trenches, our hands and knees sinking in the mud. We moved from shell hole to shell hole, then risked running. Ping, ping, crack, crack, crack – shooting began from all sides. Everybody raced for the gap. I had previously designated the assembly point and said that it was every man for himself. A few shells crashed down. The small arms fire was very heavy; bullets cracked past our ears. Now and then there was a shout as men were hit and fell. 'Comrade! Comrade!' A few more dashes and our own trench, occupied by Footguard Regiment 3, was in front of us . . . through the obstacle, then we took a short pause. We were boiling hot and needed to get our breath back. Then we stepped off to our assembly point. 'Over here 3rd Company! Rally here!'

Naturally the French took this withdrawal as a sign of potential weakness and they were not long in seeking a way to exploit it.

Hauptmann Egon von Loebell 3rd Battalion Footguard Regiment 3 [37]

"In the early dawn I went forward with my adjutant to inspect the position in full detail. I met up with the courageous Bassewitz at the machine gun position where the *Hindenburg-Stellung* forked off from the *La Folie-Stellung*. He had been holding on in the front line for four days and nights without sleep, but he would not consider pulling back all the time that the situation remained so dangerous. The remnants of Company Werder, Footguard Regiment 1, had withdrawn during the night. It was obvious that the French would push forward into the abandoned position. I was at once convinced that the garrison of the *Hindenburggraben* was much too weak, but it was too late. Whilst I was still talking to Bassewitz, I could hear loud shouts coming from the former position of Company Werder.

"Bassewitz opined that it was the sound of Grenadier Regiment 10 recapturing the old position. I regarded it as the beginning of a French attack and so it proved. As soon as I spotted that it was an attack, I rushed back to the *Armierungsgraben,* roused the engineers who were sleeping there and led them forward with their hand grenades.[38] Reserve Leutnant Barella, a very keen officer of the Machine Gun Company, also rushed forward. In the meantime the following events had occurred: 10th and 9th Companies, who were located in the *Prinz-Reuß-Stellung,* had come under attack by strong French forces. Supported by Zander's Machine Gun Platoon, they had held on bravely. Unfortunately Landwehr Hauptmann Kraaz, commanding 9th Company, was shot through the head and killed, setting an excellent courageous example as he knelt on the parapet and fired at the enemy.[39]

"At the same time large numbers of French troops attacked out of the *Prinz-Reuß-Stellung* towards *Hindenburggraben.* They succeeded in overrunning the weak garrison and its machine gun[40] and then turned to attack 10th and 9th Companies from the rear. Vizefeldwebel Zander, proven in many a battle and skirmish, turned his machine guns to the rear and mowed down the Frenchmen in heaps. For the time being the danger was over here, but unfortunately Zander was wounded in the neck – though not mortally."

On 5.50 am 30 September a warning order from 21 Brigade arrived at the command post of Grenadier Regiment 10, which had been pulled back in reserve near Avion. During the previous night, a French attack had succeeded in driving a wedge between the sectors of Footguard Regiments 2 and 3 on the lower western slopes of Hill 145. Grenadier Regiment 10 was to move immediately into a holding area by the Avion – Vimy railway on the southeast edge of Avion, whilst the commander, Major von Ferentheil, went to receive orders at the headquarters of General von Friedburg. There the situation was explained to him. Apparently the enemy had launched an attack between *Armierungsgraben* and *Fischergraben* and had forced the left flank of Footguard Regiment 3 out of the La Folie Position. Footguard Regiment 2 was now deployed with its right flank just to the east of the La Folie Position. Both Grenadier Regiment 10 and Fusilier Regiment 38 were subordinated to 1 Guards Brigade.

Grenadier Regiment 10 was ordered to attack the enemy to the north of *Fischergraben* and to throw them back over the La Folie position and the communication trench which led from there to the *Prinz-Reuß-Stellung*. Having done this it was to establish and maintain contact with Footguard Regiment 3 in the *Prinz-Reuß-Stellung* and Footguard Regiment 2 in the La Folie Position. The counter-attack was mounted by the 1st and 2nd Battalions. They advanced on Hill 145, with the left flank of the 1st Battalion on the left anchored on Petit Vimy. To its left was the 2nd Battalion which, like the 1st, advanced on a 400 metre frontage. The commanding officer of 2nd Battalion, Hauptmann von Bültzingslöwen, was placed in overall command and he calmly set about arranging the battalions in their assembly area behind the start line.

Promptly at 10.00 am the attack began. The companies were arranged in waves at 150 metre spacing. The crest was reached without interference, then the waves descended on the surprised enemy troops. Unfortunately something went wrong with the artillery support. The moment of surprise passed and it was not possible to continue, initially, against the enemy positions. Nevertheless, part of the mission was accomplished. The gap between the Footguard Regiments was closed and the battalions dug in where they were. At 1.15 pm orders arrived from 1 Guards Brigade that the further advance had been cancelled; the adjoining attack had failed. At about 7.00pm the French renewed their assault, but were beaten back by Grenadier Regiment 10 with bloody casualties – thanks, at least in part, to outstanding fire support from Field Artillery Regiment 6. Under the energetic leadership of Hauptmann von Bültzingslöwen, by nightfall the two battalions had constructed a continuous trench at full depth and were beginning the construction of a second one to the rear. Once more the immediate crisis was over but the regiment had suffered casualties of ten killed (including Leutnants Stephan and Kretschmer) and forty one wounded.[41]

Amongst the Guards companies also ordered forward in support were those of 2nd Battalion Footguards Regiment 2, directed to advance on La Folie Wood.

Grenadier M Hoelscher 8th Company Footguard Regiment 2 [42]

> "The railway embankment bent away to the left and no longer afforded us any protection from the enemy artillery fire. 500 metres to our front we could make out a copse. In front of it was an empty meadow, completely devoid of cover. The company commander ordered us to deploy then, maintaining wide separation, to run across the meadow to the northern edge of the copse, where the company was to assemble. We had barely set foot on the meadow when the drum fire opened up once more. Heavy shells crashed down endlessly in our ranks, cloaking the entire meadow with smoke and dust. Dirt from the exploding shells was thrown up around our ears. We doubled across as fast as we could, arriving at the copse completely breathless.
>
> "As I was looking around for my comrades, I noticed that the company

commander, Hauptmann von Volkmann, was right next to me, so I was there when a Leutnant came racing over, bearing an order, 'The Company is to push forward to the western edge of the copse.' We had barely gone a few paces when a storm of small arms fire was opened on us. Because it was inconceivable that we should be fired on like that by our own side, there remained only one possibility; namely that the French had broken through the German front to our right and was seeking to roll it up. There was nothing for it but to throw ourselves to the ground and to crawl forward slowly. Anybody who attempted to rise to his feet was shot down instantly. The soft boggy ground meant that it was most unpleasant to crawl in. Nevertheless, in due course we finally arrived at the western edge of the copse.

"We remained lying there for some time. In the meantime it had become dark; the sun had disappeared long before and the moon rose slowly in the east. In the feeble moonlight I could only make out the terrain to my front with difficulty. Gradually, to my amazement, I made out a huge section of wall. It was some time before my eyes adjusted to the light then, as the moon rose higher in the sky, I realised that the ruined wall must have been part of a beautiful chateau.[43] The enemy guns, spewing fire, had done their destructive work well. There were only ruins to mark where this once-proud chateau had once stood. Now all that was left were the ghostly remains of the walls sticking up into the sky. The roof had long gone, as had the doors and windows.

"The interior was nothing but a heap of smoking ruins. The enemy artillery fire had died away and all was perfectly still. After days and nights of incessant drum fire, the silence was eerie. The silvery moonlight transformed the ground to our front into a fairy tale landscape. Lost in thought I lay on the sodden floor of the wood and stared at the chateau. Who might the owner of this chateau have been? Was he still living? Would the chateau be rebuilt after the war? I was thinking so deeply that it was a shock when I heard the order: 'Stand-by. 8th Company, close in!' I hoisted myself upright and went looking for my section. There were some dugouts to the left of the chateau. One was allocated to my section and we scrambled down into its wet earthy interior. There was still no rest, because one man from each section had to remain on guard. I was first on the roster so it was not until I was relieved an hour later that I could stretch out on the wet straw. I did not need a sleeping powder to send me to sleep."

By mid-October the Guard Corps had been in action continuously for over two weeks and the strain was beginning to tell. The attempt by the French to renew the offensive on 11 October after a further twenty four hour preliminary bombardment had withered away at the hands of the Guards and the Bavarians, but many of the defenders were close to collapse with the strain.

Major Graf von Stosch Commanding Officer 2nd Battalion Grenadier Guard Regiment 3 [44]

"The condition of the troops demands early relief. Some of the men have been deployed forward in battle for five days and all of them at least three days. During all that time they have not slept; artillery fire has been constant day and night. The few hours of relative quiet have had to be used to improve the positions. These offer no overhead cover; it has all been shot away or destroyed and there is a constant stream of casualties. The morale of the men is very low and the position is only being held by dint of moving them from place to place. The companies located in the gravel pits are also under continual artillery and heavy mortar fire. The edges of the gravel pit are so battered that all the dugouts have collapsed.

"Rationing leaves much to be desired. Many of the men are no longer able to keep down the cold food and this is weakening them. The worst feature of all, however, is the lack of suitable commanders. Hardly any officers are available for duty and, of those who are, some have suffered so badly from lack of sleep and being buried alive that they are no longer capable of setting a good example or devoting sufficient energy to their duties. The fighting strength of the companies is extremely low and there is a severe lack of junior leadership. For example, the 11th Company has been reduced to a small band of men, who lack any officers or NCOs. The demands being placed on the men exceed their ability to resist. In my opinion the men are no longer capable of offensive action.

"This is not caused by any lack of courage; rather it is due to utter exhaustion and overstrained nerves as a result of this tour of duty. I regard it as my duty to report these facts, which are the result of a careful examination of the condition of the companies either subordinated to me or in reserve."

Diary Entry of an anonymous French Officer 14 October 1915 [45]

"We have moved into the trenches for the winter. The offensive has been finally closed down. All in all it amounts to an admission of a general lack of ability. If we cannot break through the German lines with 3,000 guns and two million men, we shall never be able to break it. Bulgaria has come out against us. Greece has turned aside. It seems to be indifferent to our landings in Salonika, which is not promising. The Allies have no enthusiasm for it.

"Our expeditionary force comprises 500,000 men and it probably faces Greek hostility. We have forced ourselves on a neutral country! At the same time we shout about the German invasion of Belgium! We ought to keep quiet; we are just the same . . . If we were only to make a bit more use of lessons taught us by the Germans in the art of war, diplomacy, welfare arrangements and endurance it would do us much more good than trying to revile an opponent who in numerous ways is far superior to us.

"Today the German 105s [105 mm field howitzers] have blown some more of my men apart. There are still three days in the trenches to go."

By the time this last diary entry had been made, the severely weakened German defenders had completely broken the French second major attempt to secure Vimy Ridge which began on 11 October. Overall, since 25 September, the French losses had been less than half of what they had suffered during the spring offensive and the casualties on 11 October itself only amounted to a total of about 2,200 men, [46] but the problem was that no measurable progress was being made. Attacks were not being driven home with the élan for which the French were famous and, which was worse, the French chain of command began to fear that a powerful German counter-attack might catch them in unfavourable positions, which would be vulnerable to being overrun on a wide front. Whilst it is true that the German artillery reacted violently to the French attacks of mid-October, their infantry formations were in fact in no position to mount more than local actions. In truth both sides had fought each other to a temporary standstill, but the French blinked first. Already by the evening of 11 October, Commander Tenth Army, General d'Urbal, took the decision to suspend offensive operations and for his troops to consolidate their positions. [47] Perhaps he had a case. The final efforts by the remaining elements of the Guard Corps and the recently deployed regiments of 1st Bavarian Infantry Division, in particular, ensured that by 14 October the line had been restored more or less to where it had been prior to 11 October. At trench level, the change was noted immediately. Bavarian Infantry Regiment 2 noted that, 'The enemy seemed to be exhausted. During the next few days they remained relatively quiet, but we were extremely busy constructing defensible positions in the crater fields the drum fire had produced.'[48]

Neither the French chain of command, nor that of the German army, was content with the situation. Foch blamed the lack of success on insufficient artillery preparation, poor target selection, inaccurate engagements and a reticence to fire sufficiently large numbers of supporting concentrations during the fighting. Initially it was his intention to renew the offensive after a short delay, but it rapidly became clear that, after twenty days of hard fighting, d'Urbal's men were in no position to do so and, anyway, had no stomach for any such thing. Joffre, bowing to the inevitable, but officially blaming shrinking ammunition stockpiles, issued instructions on 14 October which suspended offensive operations in both Champagne and Artois.[49] Two days later d'Urbal issued his own orders to his corps commanders, stating that, 'due to the violence of their counter-attacks and the desperate defence they mounted, the enemy has demonstrated, at the cost of severe casualties, how far they are prepared to go to prevent our advance. The reinforcements they have had to direct to Artois, the numbers and quality of troops with which they have opposed us, indicate clearly that the efforts of Tenth Army have brought about a diversion, which will favour

Allied actions in other theatres of war' and announcing, 'that the period of active [operations] is over for Tenth Army.'[50] Bearing in mind that the intention had been to achieve a breakthrough, the dubiously asserted achievement of a diversion of resources was a dismal return for total losses amounting to 48,230 officers and other ranks.[51]

However, there was certainly disquiet on the German side. More ground had been lost and the defences had been squeezed ever closer to the crest of Vimy Ridge, to the point where the continuing viability of the positions was openly being questioned. Fought out, by 23 October the last of the formations of the Guard Corps had been withdrawn and had moved over to Second Army on the Somme. They had played a large part in the stabilisation of the situation but had not been able, for example, to recapture all of the lost ground around the *Gießlerhöhe* or Angres. The Army Commander, in a rather harsh judgement, blamed the speed with which the new recruits had had to be reinforced and also the overall attitude of troops returning to the Western Front after battles conducted in the east.

Crown Prince Rupprecht of Bavaria: Diary Entry 23 October 1915 [52]

"The final elements of the Guard Corps are moving today to Second Army. During its time with Sixth Army the Guards lost 117 officers and 7,327 other ranks. The fact that they did not achieve very much is due above all to deficiencies in the training of their reinforcement personnel and the haste with which it was conducted. It is said that one of the very few pre-war officers remarked most appositely to the officers of the troops who were relieving them that they were no longer the old Guards.

"It is regrettable that troops returning from the East often display a rather arrogant attitude. This manifests itself particularly sharply in the song *Im Osten kämpft das tapfere Heer, im Westen steht die Feuerwehr* [In the East the brave army is fighting; in the West the fire brigade is on standby]. This song caused an ugly brawl between the men of the I Bavarian Corps and troops who had returned from the east. The ensuing battle ended when the 'victorious army' was thrown out of the pub in question by the 'fire brigade'.

"Troops from the east always need some time to accustom themselves to the unusual demands of positional warfare in the west. A number of them also bring bad habits with them as well. They have accumulated far too many camp followers, they are extremely wasteful of materiel and they tend to neglect their accommodation, leaving it in a very bad state for the troops who have to follow them."

Once more the lines began to consolidate and, despite the atrocious conditions, recognisable positions, wired and designed to provide as much depth as possible, began to be created by dint of a ceaseless commitment of collective effort.

Vizefeldwebel Obrikat 4th Battery Guards Field Artillery Regiment 3 [53]

"The final days of October were marked by incessant heavy rain and extremely dense fog. Progressively the battle died away as a result and the batteries could begin, enthusiastically, to turn Vimy Ridge into a Garden of Eden; that is to say, they could further develop the positions. This task was not to the overwhelming pleasure of the gunners who said – and not without justification – that they would not themselves be in a position to enjoy the use of freshly prepared mined dugouts and beautifully arranged bunks. In the event they were quite correct. Suddenly, quite out of the blue and unexpectedly, the battery received the order during the night 27/28 October to change positions and to move to the location of, and relieve, 2nd Battery Guards Field Artillery Regiment 3, which was deployed south of Petit Vimy, along the road Lille-Arras, where the road to La Folie forked off."

"Moving along field tracks and muddy roads, where the guns sank up to their axles in the chalk slurry, we arrived at the designated area at 4.00 am. We were not used to being spoiled; we had certainly already experienced much during the battle for Vimy Ridge, but that which was offered to us a position came as a savage blow. The so-called position was located in a sunken road. The guns were placed on the western slope, together with the most basic shelter, comprising little more than pieces of roofing felt roughly fixed to the slope. To the rear the hollow was a bottomless stream of clinging mud. All the rain of the previous fortnight had flowed there and been blended with the clay by the nightly passage of ammunition wagons and field kitchens into a slurry of such consistency that it could only be traversed with the utmost care and at the cost of immense exertion.

"The handover passed smoothly, then the important thing was to disturb the enemy as little as possible during the next few days because it was planned to launch a limited attack designed to improve the infantry positions. Our 3rd Battalion had the task of supporting our Bavarian Infantry Regiment which was due to launch a surprise attack along the line *Artilleriegraben – 11er Weg* [Artillery Trench to 11th Way].[54] 30 October 1915 dawned. Everywhere it was deadly quiet. Carried on the wind from far away were the rattles and bangs of ammunition wagons and field kitchens returning home. Everybody was stood to. As always before such operations there was a slight air of excitement and tension was running high as we waited the signal to start. At 6.04 am the eerie silence was broken when, as though the jaws of hell had opened, a salvo from the heavy howitzers crashed down. For us it was an indication that we had to begin to bring down defensive fire; for the Bavarians it was the signal to launch the attack.

"For the first twenty minutes the battery fired at maximum rate at a defensive fire zone about 400 metres beyond the area being assaulted and then gradually reduced the intensity. Fire, with increasingly lengthy pauses, continued to come down until 9.00 am, when the guns gradually fell silent. We waited anxiously to see the outcome. We then heard that everything had gone smoothly for the attack, which had been conducted at the price of very light casualties. Meanwhile, unnoticed, the sun had risen, breaking through the thick cloud and casting its rays over the martyred, ploughed-up terrain. To our north, shining gold, were the ruins of the chapel of the dear Our Lady of Loretto.

"In the light of previous experience it was not to be expected that the French would tamely accept this setback, so increased alert was prescribed during the coming hours. Promptly, at 5.30 pm, a counter-attack was launched. This was countered vigorously by the battery and finally broke up in the face of German counter-actions. We were ordered to prepare a sudden concentration of fire against our sector at 6.00 am on 31 October, so the guns were all ready to fire when we received a signal, in the form of a red flare from a forward sentry. Heavy, sudden enemy drum fire on the trenches and approach routes made it clear that the French were trying once more to recapture the lost [positions]. Our immediate fire, combined with that of every other battery within range brought about the failure of all such attempts."

As autumn turned towards winter, the morale of the French troops in the Vimy area was at an extremely low ebb. There had been a trickle of desertions throughout the early part of the year. As early as 31 May a deserter, Mohamed ben Hamed of 4th Company 9th Algerian Tirailleur Regiment, told his interrogators that, 'The morale of the Colonial troops is bad; they are all embittered with the French'. [55] As may be seen from the diary entries quoted above, the bitter, fruitless, fighting had taken a severe toll on the French army. One of the consequences was an increase in desertions, including one extraordinary incident which occurred northeast of Ecurie on 16 and 18 November 1915. This came after several days of rain had turned the area into a swamp and the appalling conditions had led to an increase in incidents of fraternisation. [56] The French 78th Infantry Regiment had been in the line for several days, following a major parade, when General Bonfait, Commander of the French 23rd Division, exhorted the men not to let their courage and patience slip during the coming winter months, in order to be sure that they would be ready for the 'Final Blow', which was to occur in spring 1916.

Following a minor assault in the Ecurie area on 14 November, during which 3rd Company 78th Infantry Regiment suffered sixty casualties, disinclination to face another winter at the front led two men to desert. They shouted over their intentions in German then hurled themselves into a German advanced sap. As a result of their subsequent interrogation it was reported that:

"According to statements of the two men, only the fear of bad treatment by us is restraining many battle-weary Frenchman from desertion.

One of the deserters requested that we tie up a small white towel at the place where he had deserted. This was a signal to two of his comrades that their fear of maltreatment by us was unjustified. Once the towel had been secured in place during the night of 17/18 November as had been requested, the other two deserters, who had been waiting for the signal, came over to us. Their statements were in complete agreement with the other prisoners; namely, that in view of the state of morale over there, more men would desert as soon as they found the opportunity." [57]

Little information of either a tactical or background nature was obtained from these four but, as 1915 drew to a close, that was of less importance to the German chain of command than the clear evidence of very low morale which it indicated. The following December a postscript to the severe September battle was written, when a deserter from the French 107th Infantry Regiment, who had been taken prisoner to the north of Ecurie by troops of the 2nd Bavarian Infantry Division, was interrogated. The Intelligence Officer of IV Corps, von Mutzenbacher, reported:

"The prisoner described the attacks which were launched against the German army at the end of September along the line of the Lens-Arras road. 'At that time the French 63rd Infantry Regiment was deployed opposite a German regiment with the same number. The courage of the Germans came in for exceptional praise. It had proved to be impossible to capture prisoners. The few soldiers who were still alive and manning the trenches after the heavy bombardments put up a desperate defence. Not a single man would surrender. Later reserves stormed our 63rd Infantry Regiment and recaptured all the lost territory'. [58]

General von der Marwitz, commanding IV Corps, forwarded a copy of this report to 12th Division with a covering letter of his own:

"It gives me great pleasure to bring to the attention of the Regiment and its superiors this expression of recognition of its outstanding bravery by an enemy soldier." [59]

In accordance with its standard operating procedures, Sixth Army and all its subordinate formations spent considerable time and effort during late October and November collating and analysing the torrent of after-action reports, which had been produced by every level of command from company and battery upwards. This work was finally distilled into a closely printed twenty three page report entitled *The Autumn Battles of La Bassée and Arras from 25 September to 13 October 1915.* [60] The first half of the report comprises a clear and unemotional account of the battles waged against the French and British armies, but by far the most important and influential section is that which discusses in great detail the lessons learned. Subjects covered range from a debate concerning the balance of advantage between the use of forward and reverse slope positions, the fundamental importance of defence in depth, minor tactics, location and command and control of the artillery, ammunition stockpiles, the increasing role of the forward sub-sector battalion commanders (which later evolved into that group being given primacy of command in the tactical contact battle), to the best way of laying out wire obstacles and the minimum overhead cover required for dugouts.

These lessons were studied and applied throughout the Western Front. Time and again stress is laid in the German literature on their crucial importance for the future philosophy of defence and conduct of the battle. The fact that in the summer of 1916 British troops attacking on the Somme were confronted by German defenders who had been sheltering in mined dugouts with seven or eight metres of overhead cover, who were manning trenches too wide to jump and which were laid out with three separately wired trench lines in the First Position, was entirely due to the conscientious application of lessons bought at high cost in Artois the previous year. One of the ironies of Vimy Ridge is the fact that local geographical factors, lack of depth and diversion of effort to more pressing priorities elsewhere, meant that few of these lessons could be applied there.

Notes

1. Reichsarchiv: *Der Weltkrieg (Neunter Band)* p 42. By the time the preliminary bombardment began, General d'Urbal had at least 420 heavy guns at his disposal.
2. Burchardi: History Fusilier Regiment 38 pp 125–126
3. *Les Armées Françaises dans la Grande Guerre Tome III* p 341
4. *Les Armées Françaises dans la Grande Guerre Tome III* p 341
5. Reymann: History Infantry Regiment 62 pp 61–64
6. Kaiser: History Infantry Regiment 63 p 101
7. Kriegsarchiv München 1 Res Div Bd 44. These diary extracts and others which follow in this chapter were found on the battlefield in late October, translated and circulated by Intelligence Branch Sixth Army on 16 November 1915.
8. Kaiser: *op. cit.* p 98
9. *ibid.* pp 103 – 104
10. *ibid.* 104 – 105
11. *ibid.* pp 99–100
12. *ibid.* pp 105 – 108
13. Nollau: History Infantry Regiment 51 p 70
14. Kaiser: *op. cit.* pp 108 – 110
15. Kriegsarchiv München 1 Res Div Bd 44
16. Nollau: *op. cit.* p 67
17. Reichsarchiv: *Der Weltkrieg (Neunter Band)* pp 45–46
18. It seems certain that gas was fired in this area, but it is hard to be specific. The History of Reserve Infantry Regiment 106 (p33), for example, mentions shells containing picric acid, which is a normal ingredient of high explosive, in the same sentence as describing others as chemical filled. Doubtless gases of both types contributed to the poisonous atmosphere which hung low around Souchez that day.
19. Pache: History Infantry Regiment 182 pp 101–102
20. History Infantry Regiment 178 pp 55–56
21. Burchardi: *op. cit.* p 431
22. *ibid.* p 437
23. *ibid.* p 129
24. History Field Artillery Regiment 6 p 101

25. *ibid.* pp 101–102
26. Hottenroth: *Sachsen in großer Zeit Band I* pp 181–182
27. This statement is highly improbable. There were many rumours along these lines, but gunnery errors or misdirected fire were generally to blame.
28. In fact his body was recovered at some point. Hauptmann Tankred Freyer is buried in the German cemetery at Lens-Sallaumines Block 13, Grave 198.
29. Baumgarten-Crusius: *Sachsen in großer Zeit Band II* p238
30. Bose: History Grenadier Guard Regiment 1 p 228
31. This is a reference to the first tour of trench duty on the Western Front by the Guards in the autumn and winter of 1914–1915 when they occupied positions in the Hébuterne-Bucquoy area.
32. Bose: *op. cit.* pp 228–229
33. Rieben: History Grenadier Guard Regiment 2 pp 294–295
34. *ibid.* pp 296–297
35. Eitel Friedrich: History Footguard Regiment 1 p 129
36. *ibid.* pp 130–131
37. Loebell: *Mit dem 3. Garde-Regiment z.F. im Weltkriege 1914/18* pp 174–175
38. At that stage of the war throwing hand grenades was the province of the German engineers, who received special training in the subject.
39. Hauptmann Albert Kraaz, who was killed on 3 October 1915, is buried in the German cemetery at Billy Montigny Block 1 Grave 150.
40. It transpired later that the French, wearing the new helmets for the first time, were mistaken in the misty dawn for members of Footguard Regiment 1 withdrawing.
41. Schütz: History Grenadier Regiment 10 pp 98–99
42. Rieben: History Footguard Regiment 2 p 330
43. This a reference to La Folie Chateau, which was not totally wrecked until the battles of spring 1917.
44. Rosenberg-Lipinsky: History Grenadier Guard Regiment 3 pp 274–275
45. Kriegsarchiv München 1 Res Div Bd 44
46. *Les Armées Françaises dans la Grande Guerre Tome III* p 523
47. *ibid.* p 524
48. Staubwasser: History Bavarian Infantry Regiment 2 p28
49. *Les Armées Françaises dans la Grande Guerre Tome III* pp 526–527
50. *ibid.* p 528
51. *ibid.* p 540
52. Rupprecht: *Mein Kriegstagebuch. Erster Band* pp 399–400
53. Collenberg: History Guards Field Artillery Regiment 3 pp 187–188
54. 11er Weg = [Bavarian] Infantry Regiment 11 Way.
55. Kriegsarchiv München 1 Res. Div. Bd 45 (1)
56. According to the history of Bavarian Infantry Regiment 1 p28, long sections of trench had fallen in and the dugouts on both sides of No Man's Land were completely flooded. Neither side had any choice but to move about openly, even during daylight hours, and this quickly led to exchanges of bread, chocolate and cigarettes.
57. Kriegsarchiv München 1 Res. Div. Bd 45 (2)
58. Kaiser: *op. cit.* p 116
59. *ibid.* p 116
60. Kriegsarchiv München R.Komp Bd 200 A.O.K. 6 Ib Nr. 58385

CHAPTER FOUR

1916: Trench Warfare on Vimy Ridge

B y the end of 1915 French losses since the outbreak of the war had reached the staggering figure of 1,961,687, of whom 1,001,271 were killed or missing.[1] Although German losses were broadly similar (apart from having suffered a larger number wounded), the French army had always called up a far higher proportion of its available pool of manpower each year than the German army. As a result the French had no equivalent to the *Ersatzreserve*, which enabled the Germans to make good many of its early losses without having to rely solely on the call-up of succeeding year groups.[2] Various measures were undertaken by the French army to overcome the looming manpower crisis, but no amount of reorganisation or combing out could address the problem fully. It was essential that something was done, because in the closing months of 1915 the French intelligence services had tracked a steady augmentation of the number of German battalions on the Western Front.[3]

In addition to these difficulties, there was of course no unity of command on the Allied side so, in an effort to overcome the lack of a single point of direction, the second conference at Chantilly, which was held there on 6, 7 and 8 December, had as its main objective the need to produce a properly coordinated strategy for 1916. For some time the French had been pressing the British army to assume responsibility for a greater length of the front, but the British had manpower difficulties of their own as they attempted to build up their trained formations in France, whilst at the same time producing forces for other theatres. Negotiations continued into the new year but, in the event, the start of the Verdun offensive meant that the British had no choice but to accede to French demands for assistance so, from the middle of March 1916, the relief of the French Tenth Army having been completed, operations on the Vimy front became the responsibility of the British army.

At the turn of the year, however, these developments were still in the future; by January 1916 nothing had been settled. The dreadful winter weather which had marked the end of 1915 continued, making life miserable for both sides. The men of 17th Reserve Division, operating near to Souchez, were kept hard at work attempting to drain their waterlogged trenches by every means from the use of pumps to digging lengthy diversion trenches simply to disperse the water. Immense quantities of trench stores, including 15,000 metres of duckboarding, were placed by Reserve Infantry Regiment 76 alone during the first month of the year. Nevertheless, conditions were so bad that it was almost impossible for the front line soldiers to remain in their trenches and there was an unhealthy increase in the amount of fraternisation. Finally the regimental commander was forced, on 25 January 1916, to make his forward companies swap sectors in order to put a stop to it.[4] The amount of labour expended on the positions by 17th Reserve Division can perhaps best be judged by noting that, at different times, Reserve Jäger Battalion 9, 3rd Battalion Reserve Infantry Regiment 75, 2nd Battalion Reserve Infantry Regiment 86 and 2nd Company Reserve Infantry Regiment 86 were all pressed into service to labour in support of the forward sub-units of Reserve Infantry Regiment 76 and Infantry Regiment 163.[5] Despite all the effort, heavy rain and constant artillery and mortar fire combined to make progress extremely slow and painful.

Regardless of the appalling weather conditions, in order to increase the depth available to the defence and to distract attention away from German offensive preparations near Verdun, a series of minor attacks under the overall code name 'Rupprecht' was launched that month in the I Bavarian Reserve Corps area. A great deal of care was taken over the preparation for these limited scope operations. 1st Battalion Reserve Infantry Regiment 229 of 50th Reserve Division, for example, spent the days prior to the first of the assaults erecting dummy tented encampments and conducting simulated approach marches, in order to convey the impression to enemy aerial observers of a major build up in the area.[6] The first of these attacks was launched on 23 January by 2nd Bavarian Infantry Division, when a group of French trenches to the west of Thélus was captured. This was followed on 24 and 26 January by operations 'Rupprecht II' and 'Rupprecht III' mounted by 50th Reserve Division. Inevitably the fighting spilled over to the following day, the French having responded to the setbacks of 'Rupprecht III' by launching a series of hand grenade attacks during the night against the front of Reserve Infantry Regiment 230 of 50th Reserve Division in particular. At 3.00 am, French mortar fire came down heavily on the forward positions, followed at 5.40 am by further sharp grenade assaults against 5th and 6th Companies Reserve Infantry Regiment 230, which managed to beat them off. By 11.00 am drum fire was being brought down on the forward craters and, at 1.10 pm, it was necessary for the defenders to pull back.

Calling for volunteers, Leutnant Sprengel, commander of 5th Company, led forward Leutnants Seeger and Crusilla, together with twenty men and raced forward to reoccupy and hold the craters. The story of the day was later recounted in a letter home:

Leutnant Sprengel 5th Company Reserve Infantry Regiment 230 [7]

"At 7.30 we exploded our four mine galleries, each of which was charged with 350 *Zentner* [17.5 tonnes] of high explosive. The earth shook and we leapt up out of our second trench, crossing our first trench and occupying the French trenches and the craters. Right from the start I felt the hand of God on me. I arrived in Crater II ahead of everyone else; there was neither friend nor foe there. My platoon commander, Leutnant

M., joined me. I was ready to embrace him; I had not been left alone. However, in the explosive fumes, he took me for a Frenchman and fired a shot at me from five paces, which narrowly missed. At the time I just laughed at him and ticked him off for his poor marksmanship.

"It was then a matter of getting into the French second trench. It was occupied, but we soon ejected them through the use of grenades. A splendid gefreiter and a few men threw from above ground, whilst we stayed below in the trench and grenaded our way forward. The gefreiter was hit by a splinter from a shell fired by our artillery, which was bringing down defensive fire on the third trench. We linked up with 7th Company then we pushed on to the Intermediate Position, which seemed to be more or less empty. I pressed a Frenchman into service as a guide. He asked me again and again if I intended to slit his throat, but he was not much use. We spotted French steel helmets in the left hand sector of the Intermediate Position and brought down heavy fire in their direction. I now left two sections to consolidate the bridgehead, whilst I toured the new sector and went to report.

"It had all gone splendidly. We had been greeted by two machine guns, but had suffered few casualties. I had to take a firm grip of my men on several occasions. Instead of getting on with the development of the position, they were concentrating on the supplies of French red wine and the rations they had found. I was certain that we were going to be counter-attacked; they were not giving it a thought. In the meantime my two sections had returned from the Intermediate Position. They had failed to dig in and had had to withdraw in the face of French numerical superiority and a great shower of hand grenades. I sent at once for concertina barbed wire, so that we could establish an obstacle and bring the French to a halt fifty paces in front of the second trench.

"I had been wounded twice by fragments; once in the back and once in the leg. All seemed to be quiet, so I pulled back to Crater II. Everything was in order there and likewise in Crater III. Just as I arrived there, heavy mortar fire began falling on Crater IV and on the freshly dug communications trench running to the rear from Crater III. Once the fire died down a little, I thought once more about returning to Crater II but, hardly had I reached the exit, than there was a dreadful explosion in III. As the smoke cleared I counted ten dead. The remainder of the platoon, blood pouring from their mouths, swayed and staggered around help-lessly. I could not rally them and had to fetch reinforcements from the *Divisionsgraben*.

"Once again, as things calmed down, I returned to Crater II, where I discovered that five sections of 8th Company had arrived to reinforce the position. I was just deploying the men, when I heard cries for help from the right. The French had launched an attack with hand grenades. Taking a few volunteers, I was soon on the spot. It was not much of an affair, but by now the French artillery and mortars had zeroed in on Crater II. I set off for it, finding that another eight men had been killed and others were badly shaken and shell-shocked. I looked down into the hole which I had left not five minutes earlier. It was now filled with dead and wounded men and the groundsheet which I had stretched over it was peppered with holes from shrapnel balls. Gradually things calmed down and I went across to Crater III. I had my runner with me and I sent him across to Crater II and the second trench to its right where Leutnant Crusilla and three sections were located. They were to join me at once. It was getting dark and I was alone in the crater. The reinforcements were needed urgently. All I had near me were a few men snoring and my ruddy-complexioned batman, who was as calm as ever.

"Over from the Crater IV area came the sounds of another very heavy grenade battle. I was not long in doubt as to what was happening. The noises drew closer and suddenly the remainder of 6th Company leapt into my crater. There were barely twenty of them and I could not make them stay. A Gefreiter, whom I met later, told me that I had shouted at them. 'If your heart is beating inside you, Stay!' Three heeded my words and remained to hurl grenades at the French until our arms ached from the effort. The French pressed forward, much further than usual, until they were landing grenades in our crater – something they otherwise would never have achieved. A man standing on my right received one full in the face. The reinforcements arrived and everything quietened down. I spent the entire night sitting next to my friend S, who had deployed the remains of his company in my area. He was down to twenty men from 170."

Not to be outdone, 1st Bavarian Infantry Division was also involved further north in an attempt to improve the positions around the highly vulnerable Hill 145-Pimple sector. This operation was officially designated 'Rupprecht IV'.[8] The operation, which was planned to take place against the French Infantry Regiments 390 and 97 of the *Chasseurs Alpins* on 28 January, was to be preceded by a bombardment lasting several hours and the blowing of two mines – one on the left flank of the regimental sector and the other on the right. The initial assault was to be carried out by the 1st Battalion. Despite the relatively simple nature of the operation an enormous amount of planning and preparation was devoted to it. Observation and reconnaissance of the opposing positions were intensified, in order to ensure that all potential points of resistance had been noted in advance and, simultaneously, work began to develop jumping off trenches. Having sapped forward to within eighty to one hundred metres of the French lines, an assault trench, complete with dugouts, was constructed parallel to the French lines. Naturally the French could not miss observing the work and they did everything in their power to hinder it by means of small arms fire and artillery concentrations.

On 22 January the German batteries deployed in support of the attack began to range in on their targets. They and the batteries of neighbouring divisions which were to superimpose their fire on that of the organic batteries, were, concentrated into one overall artillery group for the duration of the operation. Initially the plan was that the bombardment, which was to begin at midday and the mines, which were to be blown at 4.00 pm, were to be followed by an assault by a single battalion. Generalleutnant Ritter von Schoch, the Divisional Commander, amended this on 26 January to, 'If the situation is favourable (enemy positions badly damaged, little resistance) Infantry Regiment 2 must be prepared to take advantage by seizing the front line enemy trenches from *Fischersappe*[9] to the *Transfeldsappe*[10]. In order to facilitate this, the crater forward of the *Transfeld* Gallery is to be occupied immediately after the explosion and a way is to be forced towards the north, in order to counter any troops advancing south from *Fischersappe.'* [11]

A reporter arrived at regimental headquarters prior to the attack, having been granted official permission to describe the events of the day

Dr. Max Osborn War Reporter [12]

"The task for the regiment was to recapture the enemy trenches on the western slopes of Vimy Ridge which had been lost prior to the arrival of 1st Bavarian Infantry Division. The operation was preceded by lengthy preparations. In two places on the flanks of the attack frontage, which was about 350 metres wide, significantly deep mine galleries had been driven forward by dint of much hard and painstaking work until they reached beneath the enemy trenches. Everything was ready. The mine chambers were charged and the engineers were at their posts. The artillery, firing from good covered positions and plentifully supplied with ammunition, was ready to support the infantry, upon whom everything depended. 28 January dawned. Suddenly, at midday, all hell broke loose. A ceaseless rain of German shells poured down on the enemy trenches; not only on the front line, but also on the depth positions and to cut off all the approach routes.

"Both light and heavy mortar bombs, some of them as heavy as fifty kilograms, were launched into the midst of the surprised Frenchmen. This went on for hours with no sort of pause or break. It was as though the German gunners were trying to demonstrate that they could bring down drum fire as well as either the French or the British. There was, however, one essential difference, as the Regimental Commander [Oberst Otto Staubwasser[13]] explained to me: 'On 10 and 11 October of the previous year, we had had to endure drum fire on exactly the same location for thirty hours. This was done without my men faltering in the least. God alone knows how they held on, but they did. That lot had had it after four hours.' Prisoners later explained, *Le bombardement était démoralisent* [The bombardment was demoralising]. They further reported that they had not been able to hold on in their trenches. Whilst the fire was still coming down, many attempted to move to the neighbouring sectors, or to desert. Others, including most of the officers, ran back to the trenches in the rear. [14]

"At exactly 4.00 pm and as suddenly as it had begun at midday, the firing ceased. It was as though an angry animal, which had been roaring and plunging for four hours, was silenced instantly by having its neck wrung. For a moment it was almost peacefully quiet on Vimy Ridge. All that could be heard was the sound of desultory shelling by the French batteries and the probing counter-battery fire of the German guns. But then there were fresh explosions as the underground mines went up to the left and right. The earth opened, flames and clouds of smoke, accompanied by great masses of earth were thrown skywards, before falling back down. In both places the French trenches disappeared, to be replaced by deep craters. At that the German infantry stormed forward as one. The 1st Battalion, commanded by Major Freiherr [Baron] von Imhof, attacked on the right. Oberleutnant Melber, officer commanding 1st Company, distinguishing himself in particular. On the left Battlegroup Zorn (5th and 7th Companies) led the assault.

"The companies climbed out of their trenches, threw themselves over the open ground, penetrated the wrecked wire obstacles and entered the enemy trenches. The French seemed to be transfixed. They did not fire at the assaulting troops. Instead they threw away their weapons, put up their hands and surrendered by complete sections. One of the Bavarians jumped into a sap head, grabbed the machine gun that was mounted there, leapt up onto the parapet and waved it shouting, *Da hamma das Kind von der Sappe I!* [Now we've got the brat from Sap 1!]. He then threw it down once again and charged on. Another eight enemy machine guns were also captured. Altogether the enemy position fell into our hands on almost a two kilometre front and 340 prisoners were captured. It was now essential to work with all speed to prepare the newly captured positions for defence. During this work, Leutnant Witte, one of the most energetic machine gun officers of the regiment, who had already been slightly wounded and, ignoring it, had carried on, was hit a second time – on this occasion fatally.[15] On hearing the news Oberarzt Dr. Mayr immediately rushed forward to the newly-captured front line trench to tend to him.

"In some places, however, the enemy continued to resist. There was hand-to-hand fighting. Some of the enemy behaved with great courage and disregard of death. One Frenchman was even lucky enough to be able to recover a machine gun from its built-in position, throw it over his shoulder and recover it to safety. Nevertheless, those who resisted were swiftly overcome and a great deal of materiel, ammunition, searchlights etc., was seized by the victors. The violence of the attack inspired our neighbours. Although their original task was simply to be prepared to repel any attempt by enemy in adjacent sectors to intervene, full of the offensive spirit, they stormed forward as well and quickly expanded the captured frontage to more than one and a half kilometres. Apart from one two hundred metre length, the captured territory extended back to the French second line.

"The infantry assault began at 4.00 pm and, by 4.08 pm we had captured everything that we had wanted to, was the way the regimental after action report described the events. Everything had been done in eight minutes; it had all gone like clockwork. Our casualties were light, but even so that means that a number of our courageous young men fell. Nevertheless the figures fade into insignificance compared with the losses the enemy suffered. It would not have been difficult to continue the advance. Momentum was on our side and the enemy would not have been able to do anything about it. However that was not in the commander's plan, which sought to achieve no more than an improvement in our positions. If the enemy were to have attacked once more, they would have found that we had the best possible defensive points in our possession. We really had a firm grip on Vimy Ridge, whereas we had previously been simply clinging on to the reverse slope. Now we had views over Neuville as far west as the next rise in the ground.

"The prisoners were in a pitiful state. They were treated with the greatest of care."

Even after making due allowance for the purple prose used by Osborn, it is clear that this was a successful attack: professionally mounted and vigorously conducted. As a result the lines had been advanced by an average of one hundred metres on a 1,700 metre front. Almost 340 prisoners, including one officer, had been captured, along with nine machine guns, two searchlights and large quantities of rifles and small arms ammunition. French casualties in killed and wounded were also high, especially from the effect of the two mines which, according to prisoner statements, came as a complete surprise. The aim had been achieved but, during what was for Bavarian Infantry Regiment 2 its first regimental-sized offensive operation since the end of the war of movement in autumn 1914, the casualties suffered were not light. The French artillery exacted a heavy price from the attackers during the night 28/29 January, when they were working to consolidate their gains. Altogether over the forty eight hour period of the operation the regiment suffered casualties of 370 killed and wounded: 200 of them in the 1st Battalion alone. [16]

Writing later, the Sixth Army Commander was unimpressed by the timing of these costly minor operations which, as conducted, were totally out of phase with operations down at Verdun.

Crown Prince Rupprecht of Bavaria Diary Entry 2 February 1916 [17]

"Request received today by telegraph from Army Group Crown Prince Wilhelm to launch diversionary attacks from 8 February, because the attack on Verdun is due to begin on 12 February. I really do not know how we shall be able to meet this requirement, or why it is that we were not informed in good time about the postponement of the offensive and why, despite our repeated submissions on the subject, we were ordered by the Army High Command to begin diversionary attacks during the last week of January? Now they and all the attendant sacrifices were in vain!"

One positive development which had emerged from the *Rupprecht* attacks was the proof they provided about the state of the French army in the Vimy area at the time. The experience of the German troops who encountered some French soldiers who had cast away their weapons and failed to put up serious resistance during the recent attacks was becoming quite widespread at the time. If French morale had been low at the end of 1915, the severe winter weather had certainly exacerbated the situation. In one four day period at the end of January, there were at least four instances of desertion from French Infantry Regiments 63, 97 and 405 in three separate cases on 19 January,[18] then large numbers of unwounded prisoners began to fall into German hands as a result of minor operations. For example, seventeen men from Infantry Regiment 226, 139 Brigade 79th Division, were captured between Neuville St Vaast and Petit Vimy on 26 January during Operation 'Rupprecht III'.[19] A further 82 prisoners from the same regiment were captured 800 metres northwest of Neuville St Vaast, just to the west of La Folie Wood, on 8 February[20] then, during the afternoon of 9 February, thirty nine men of various units of the French 47 Brigade were taken prisoner on and around the road Neuville St Vaast – Petit Vimy.

It was very evident from statements made by the deserters and prisoners that French morale was generally at a low ebb. The men who were captured on 9 February, for example, following a sharp bombardment and trench raid, were found sheltering in old mine craters and two saps. By the time the German raiders arrived they had already thrown down their weapons and were determined to offer no resistance. The solitary NCO present attempted to persuade the men to defend their position using boxes of hand grenades which were available, but they refused, saying that they were looking forward *au grand repos en Allemagne* [to having a good rest in Germany]. All the prisoners on 9 February commented about the speed and aggression of the German assault and the junior NCO remarked that there was no way in which the men of the French XII Corps could have launched anything similar. The chain of command noted this continuing evidence of poor French morale and field commanders were determined to exploit it in some way.

With February had come snow and frost which froze the ground and immediately improved conditions in the front line. Maximum opportunity was taken to work on the defences and to carry out a detailed reconnaissance of the exact line of the enemy positions in association with increased air reconnaissance. Based on the newly produced maps, it was decided that a further attempt was to be launched by the regiments of 17th Reserve Division to recapture the highest point of the *Gießlerhöhe* from the French. Strategically it was, of course, but one operation designed to distract attention from the opening of the offensive at Verdun, but in any case, locally, this 'Operation Hamburg' was urgently necessary because the crest overlooked the German-held positions in several directions and enemy observation from the Lorette Spur was already sufficiently problematic for the German defenders. Planning and preparation for the assault dominated life during mid-February. Large quantities of ammunition of all types were dumped forward, artillery pieces and mortars were ranged in as unobtrusively as possible, aid posts and casualty clearing stations were set up and troops were withdrawn behind the lines for intensive training and rehearsals.

The leading role in the attack, which was launched on a one thousand metre frontage, was played by sub-units of Infantry Regiment 163, reinforced by men of Reserve Infantry Regiment 76. In view of the fact that the objective was to recapture the crest line lost in late 1915, the distances to be covered in the initial assault were not great. In the area around what was later referred to as The Pimple, an advance of a mere 150 metres was necessary, whilst the men of 9th and 12th Companies Infantry Regiment 163 had a more difficult task, being required to assault uphill approximately 400 metres from the low ground of the *Kuhlsenke*, just north of Givenchy, before closing in on the enemy front line. One member of 6th Company Reserve Infantry Regiment 76 had a ringside seat as events unfolded during the early hours of 21 February.

Musketier Schulze 6th Company Reserve Infantry Regiment 76 [21]

"On the dot of 2.00 pm drum fire began coming down on the enemy positions. The hill was transformed into a sea of flames and thick black clouds swirled around over No Man's Land. The dreadful symphony of exploding shells and bursting shrapnel pots grew ever fiercer. All the guns were laid on the crest, pouring fire and iron on the ploughed up, battered ground whilst, all around, great columns of earth were thrown up into the sky in mad confusion. We were located back by the La Coulotte railway embankment, whose sides were pierced by deep, solid, mined dugouts. Nerves on edge, we followed the dreadful spectacle which was unfolding in front of our eyes. Now and then we dived for cover when an enemy shell landed in the reserve area by error.

"It seemed impossible that the fire could grow further in intensity, but it did and the flashes and explosions followed each other in a truly dizzying display. Behind us, as a result of all the muzzle flashes, we could make out the battery positions. The light crack of the field guns and howitzers blended with the duller roars of the heavy howitzers and 210 mm guns as they directed their fire forwards onto the hill which was totally cloaked with smoke and flames. The tension increased with each quarter of an hour. Could we do it? What would the cost in lives be?

"At 6.45 pm the attack was launched, but some minutes earlier our infantry had climbed out of their trenches and had overrun the first and second enemy trenches without any losses and without a shot being fired. The enemy had been totally pinned down by the iron hail of the artillery. Our infantry moved so fast that the artillery could not lift its fire onto depth targets fast enough. Green flares went up, 'Lift the fire; lift the fire further forward', they shrieked as the shells hammered down almost at the feet of the advancing infantry. New flares shot upwards, but they were noticeably further forward. Were they trying to advance for kilometres?

"One company had pushed on down into the valley as far as that dreadful place whose blood-soaked ruins went by the name of Souchez. There was no resistance, but they had to pull back. Their break in was too unexpected to be consolidated, so they returned, bringing with them seven officers, including a major and 300 other ranks and two heavy machine guns. The prisoners, all Frenchmen in their blue coats, came past us. They were visibly relieved at having escaped from the hellish fire. Evening had descended on the battlefield as the forward troops worked to reinforce the new positions and the enemy, which had apparently recovered from the shock, began to bring down a murderous rate of fire on all the approach routes and assembly areas. They seemed to be well acquainted with where they were located.

"Work continued. I believe that I shall never forget my journey forward as long as I live. My platoon had to carry coffee forward onto the position. Leutnant Grunewald led off, guided by a man from Infantry Regiment 163. I came next and was followed by the remainder of the platoon. Podzuk and I carried a large container of coffee suspended from a stout stick and so did all the other comrades who, arranged in pairs, were carrying more coffee containers. The old communication trenches had been badly damaged. Duckboards had been splintered by shells; some were tipped up or thrown partially out of the trenches and we were constantly under fire. It was as though every single gun on the other side was pouring its fire directly at this small group of men as they staggered forward, sweating profusely under the weight of the heavy coffee containers.

"Now and again a man went down, staggering and crying out when he was hit and the great coffee containers crashed to the ground. The whistling, cracking and roaring drowned out the cries of the wounded. All formation was lost. Some men fell out, others hung back, straggling. One or other pair suddenly had to dive for cover when the hail of death-dealing shrapnel balls rained down from above. Our guide from Infantry

Regiment 163 disappeared completely . . . We lost contact with our leutnant and suddenly we were in a trench, on our own and under fire. We pushed on trying to find the way forward and making use of the light from the succession of white flares, which were occasionally mixed with the green ones, to maintain direction.

"The state of the trench deteriorated constantly. There were wounded men lying groaning everywhere, whilst the dead stared with glassy eyes up at the night sky or the mud of the wrecked trenches. We pushed on past them; it was the living we had to help. Stretcher bearers staggered towards us carrying their groaning, bleeding loads in brown, muddy groundsheets. We pressed on, following the trench forward, on past the *Mergelgrube* where the wounded and dying had been collected. What scenes! It was the stuff of nightmares. The trench was now completely flattened. We climbed out and made our way across country. That was somewhat easier. We were surrounded by exploding shells, iron splinters and stray small arms fire – the bullets whizzing and whirring past us.

"From time to time flares shot up around our shadowy forms, lighting the battlefield as bright as day before everything sank back into the blackest night. Over us the stars shone calmly down on this dreadful scene. Then we recognised the old front line trenches. We must have now been on the final leg of our journey. We picked our way carefully over the remains of the barbed wire and the deep shell holes. Our artillery shells roared overhead, whilst all around us enemy shells crashed down, sending splinters hissing in all directions. We felt our strength ebbing away and our muscles giving up the unequal task, but we could not stay here in the open. We had to press on. The wooden pole dug into our shoulders like an iron bar; the heavy kettle suspended between us swung about like a great lead weight, becoming heavier with each step. But they needed coffee up at the front.

"It is amazing what strength even the weakest can summon up in situations like that. We could tell from the shells that were landing ever closer to us that we were nearing the front line trench, then we recognised from the remains of corrugated iron and the shape on the ground that we had arrived at a completely levelled trench. French rifles and equipment lay strewn around everywhere. This, the first French trench, was also littered with corpses, whose blood was soaking into the soil. Everywhere were tortured faces, torn apart and mutilated. We shuddered as the ice-cold hand of Death clapped us on the shoulder. We pressed on past the flickering images; we were not yet at our destination. The odd shriek could be heard, only to be drowned out by the crash of shells exploding and, in any case, we could not go seeking their origin. To keep our spirits up we shouted at one another, but the roar of the guns snatched our words away.

"Once more we were moving through the remains of barbed wire, its tentacles grabbing at our feet and tripping us. Our breath came in short gasps and we wheezed with the effort. Biting down hard on our lips we drew blood and the pain helped keep our minds clear of the mad imaginings that crowded in on us. Feelings of bitter anger rose within us. Gangs of men were labouring feverishly, their spades flying, to produce communication trenches to link the newly captured trenches to the rear. It was a matter of life and death to create a covered approach before the break of day lit up the ploughed up landscape once more. From the front came shouts, 'Over here! Over here!' Finally we slid down into a chest-high trench that was still being dug.

"Is this the front line trench of the 163rd?' we gasped. 'Yes.' 'Here is the coffee.' Then our strength drained away. It felt as though we were about to faint. A grey haze hung in front of our eyes. We still felt the terrible load, even though the great kettle had long since been taken away, so that the clay-covered figures could attack the contents. Slowly we regained an awareness of our surroundings. Dreadful images continued to tumble madly past us and cries of pain reached us from away in the distance. Our exhaustion protected us from the worst of the raw reality and allowed our heart rates to return to normal. We had arrived on the position of 1st Company. Reflected in their strained faces was all the tumult and anguish of the superhuman expenditure of energy, both physical and mental, of the past few hours. Ghostly figures moved around trembling and shaking. These were those whose nerves were not equal to the strain. Mingling with them, however, were men with laughing, unconcerned eyes and others with determined looks and set jaws.

"Everything was being conducted at breakneck speed and men dug for their lives, in order to ensure that they had cover and protection to meet the coming day. They greeted the wooden props and shuttering timber that carrying parties had brought forward even more warmly than food or drink. They grabbed everything available and called for more wood. Our container was empty. With one last look at the dreadful scenes of the night, we raced hurriedly back across the ploughed up terrain. Artillery fire came down with undiminished violence. We were indifferent to the impact of the shells. You might be hit, I might; the important thing was to get out of this witch's cauldron as fast as possible.

"In our haste we lost the line of the trench, found ourselves in the labyrinth of communication trenches and promptly discovered that we were lost. So began a frantic search, until we met some stretcher bearers who were transporting the wounded to the rear. We attached ourselves to them. Soaked to the skin, our clothes torn and gasping for breath, we arrived back at our dugout in the embankment as dawn broke. My body felt as heavy as lead as I sank down on a straw palliasse. Wild images flitted briefly through my mind until sheer exhaustion calmed my nerves and I was embraced by a deep dreamless sleep.''

In comparison with events before Verdun, this attack was a very minor affair. The German army was pleased with the result, but the French dismissed it subsequently in a very few words: 'On the Tenth Army front there was an assault on Givenchy Wood on 21 [February]. 800 – 900 metres of the French front line was captured, together with 300 – 400 metres of support trenches. Numbers of men from 130th Division were captured . . . Because they were about to be relieved by British troops no counter-action was taken, but mine warfare continued right up until 12 March between Neuville St Vaast and the Lille road.' [22]

By the third week of March the indicators that the British had taken over from the French on the Vimy sector began to multiply. In order to discover precisely which troops they were facing, a platoon of 3rd Company Bavarian Infantry Regiment 15 was poised to follow up the blowing of three mines at 3.00 am on 26 March north east of Ecurie.[23] Entering the enemy trenches, they quickly took prisoner a number of Scottish soldiers.[24] Their interrogation yielded, inevitably, in view of the numbers captured, a great deal of low-level intelligence, including the complete order of battle of 51st (Highland) Division, the name of the commanding officer and much more besides. It is clear that the shock of capture was quite marked. Up until the three mines exploded, killing or burying the majority of D Company 1/5th Battalion Gordon Highlanders, the unit had suffered very few casualties. Those captured stated that they had only survived because they were occupying an advanced section of trench to the front of the main position.

The newly-arrived British troops were much readier to conduct patrols and raids than had been their French predecessors. On 20 March, a small British patrol from the Northumberland Fusiliers made a concerted effort to break into the positions of 10th Company Reserve Infantry Regiment 84 of 18th Reserve Division, which was manning an exposed position near to Givenchy. The attempt, which was made at around 2.00 am, was spotted early by Reservist Wrange and Kriegsfreiwilliger Detken, who were manning a forward sap. The two men threw grenades and opened up with rapid rifle fire, killing two of the British soldiers; the remainder escaped. The advanced sap was immediately reinforced then, about thirty minutes later, the British made an effort to recover the bodies of the fallen, whilst maintaining lively rifle grenade fire on the forward sap. One of these grenades landed in the sap as a direct hit, slightly wounding Musketier Lück and Kriegsfreiwilliger Winnenberg and seriously wounding Ersatz-Reservist Albrecht.

There was a bright full moon throughout what remained of the night and this helped dissuade the British from further attempts to reach the bodies, though they continued to fire on the area to prevent the German troops from being able to obtain identifications. Throughout the following day sentries kept the area under constant observation in order to be able to forestall any daylight approach by the British. That evening the fire of two batteries was concentrated on the enemy trenches opposite the sap whilst the company commander, Leutnant Hardnow, assisted by Leutnant Bruhn, took up covering positions and Leutnant Berner and Kriegsfreiwilliger Butz of 10th Company crawled out beyond the wire to where one of the bodies lay. Ignoring enemy mortar fire and a hail of small arms fire, they tied a rope around the body and dragged it back to their wire obstacle, where the rope snapped and Leutnant Berner collapsed, totally exhausted by the effort.

Butz succeeded in helping Berner back into the trench then, joined by Leutnants Hardnow and Bruhn, managed to move a knife rest out of the way and haul in the body, despite the constant weight of fire which was coming down. A search of the corpse revealed that it was that of: *Capt. Adj. The Hon. SID Joisey 10 North D. Füs.* [sic = Captain and Adjutant The Hon. Sydney James Drever Joicey 10th Battalion Northumberland Fusiliers].[25] Joicey had been killed by rifle bullet, which had first ripped through a letter from his wife, which he had carried in the breast pocket of his tunic. This identification was regarded as highly significant by the German defenders, justifying all the effort which had gone into obtaining it.

In view of the outcome of this clash, the British lost no time in improving the wire obstacle in front of their lines. As a result, attempts made on 31 March by 5th Company and 28 April by 6th Company to obtain identifications were much less successful, as well as costing Bavarian Infantry Regiment 15 itself a number of casualties.[26] Nevertheless, on 28 April, during a raid, which also involved 2nd Battalion Bavarian Infantry Regiment 12,[27] Lance Corporal W Atkey from A Company 1/6th Battalion Seaforth Highlanders was captured. This was an ambitious operation. At 3.15 am six mines, involving twelve charges, weighing a total of 275 *Zentner* = 13,750 kg were detonated. Unfortunately the engineers had miscalculated. Large quantities of earth and chalk were flung back into the German front line, killing three of the raiding party who were sheltering there and injuring twenty others. Despite this setback, the five assault groups from 5th and 6th Companies Bavarian Infantry Regiment 12 hurled themselves forward as the German artillery opened up to seal off the area of the raid.

One of the groups, under Leutnant Momm, surprised five British soldiers, leaping at them with fixed bayonets. When these men reacted violently, wounding an Unteroffizier in the thumb, another raider threw a hand grenade which killed four of them; the fifth survived. Shells began to land near the patrol, so the commander gave the order to withdraw, taking the wounded Lance Corporal Atkey with them. None of the other four groups met the enemy and casualties were relatively high. In addition to the losses caused by the German mines going off, one man was missing, six were killed and nine were wounded. According to Atkey's interrogation report,[28] his unit was aware that mines were about to be set off along their front, but not exactly where. Apart from a few sentry posts, the remainder of the garrison had been pulled back into the second trench. He had been buried temporarily by the blast, then wounded by a hand grenade prior to his capture. In his statements to his interrogator, he confirmed most of the information obtained the previous month and provided some additional low-level intelligence. The regimental history of Bavarian Infantry Regiment 12 later claimed that Atkey's interrogation yielded important information. The report does not bear that out and the high casualties were certainly not justified by the results gained.

This operation rounded off a most successful month for the Sixth Army interrogators. In between the capture of the Gordon Highlanders and Lance Corporal Atkey, they were able to question Private AJ Belcher D Company 5th South Staffordshire Regiment, captured southeast of Neuville St Vaast on 3 April,[29] Private A Houlden A Company 1/4th Battalion Lincolnshire Regiment,[30] who was taken prisoner south of Souchez on 19 April, as well as a group of four men from A Company 11th Battalion Lancashire Fusiliers, captured just southeast of Souchez during the early hours of 26 April.[31] They also had the opportunity to talk to a deserter, Private William Holmes, a member of 6th (Service) Battalion King's Own Yorkshire Light Infantry, but they did not obtain much useful information from him. His interrogator felt that he was, 'mentally not quite normal' and he could not decide if his motivation for desertion was war-weariness or problems with his sergeant.[32]

By the beginning of May it was clear that resources were lacking for an attempt to be made on a large scale to launch an offensive in the Arras area in an attempt to divert attention from the fighting around Verdun, which was not going well; indeed, following discussions between General von Falkenhayn and the Commander of Sixth Army, Crown Prince Rupprecht of Bavaria, orders arrived that Sixth Army was to release I Bavarian Corps for operations around Verdun. It arrived there in time to be thrown into a critical situation around Fort Douaumont, but its loss was regarded as extremely serious by Crown Prince Rupprecht, who did not feel the move had been well handled.

Crown Prince Rupprecht of Bavaria Diary Entry 7 May 1916[33]

"On order of the Army High Command, Sixth Army now has to release I Bavarian Corps for service at Verdun. It is an extremely high quality corps, but is not suitable for immediate deployment to the Verdun area. It has been occupied constantly with the defensive battle since the autumn of 1914 and urgently requires rest, recuperation and training in offensive techniques. Had my opinion been sought, I should have recommended the Guards Reserve Corps. It is another very competent corps, which has already spent six months behind the lines at rest. VII Corps would have been another good choice. It had been out of the line for fourteen days and had already had the chance to practise its attack procedures.

"I cannot avoid noting my suspicion that considerations other than purely professional ones played a role in the decision of the High Command. I had three and a half Bavarian corps under my command which, for some gentlemen, was not a comfortable situation. I have never been able to establish why this is so, but I certainly remember last year, when the deployment of one Bavarian corps next to another seemed to make eminent sense, that my then chief of staff, Graf Lambsdorf, remonstrated with me. 'That would never do, that would amount to a Bavarian front!' "

Regardless of which troops remained to garrison the sector, it was, nevertheless, necessary to ensure that the Vimy front remained active, so plans for an operation with limited objectives to improve the positions on and around Hill 145 were speedily concluded. April had been a time of extremely active mining and counter-mining; the planned operation can be regarded, therefore, as an attempt to force home a temporary advantage and to consolidate a new front line designed to exploit the potential of all the craters which had blown during the past few weeks. It was to be the most ambitious operation in the area for the whole of 1916.

There was intensive patrol activity up and down the line. On 3 May, a reconnaissance by Vizefeldwebel Saß and Jäger Schönemann of 2nd Company Reserve Jäger Battalion 9, established that the old British front line on the lower slopes of Hill 145 had been abandoned and that masses of weapons and equipment were lying around everywhere. A follow-up operation two nights later confirmed this and twenty one rifles, a grenade launcher and some damaged machine guns were recovered. [34] The same day regiments of the Guards Reserve Corps arrived to relieve I Bavarian Corps and the German line up of troops who were to conduct Operation Schleswig Holstein was complete.[35]

It was certainly true that many of the Allied mine galleries which had been driven forward to attack the German front line had been intercepted and damaged or destroyed during the past few weeks and, although the German defenders had tended to rush to occupy the resulting craters and so inch their line forward, they were at a permanent disadvantage in this type of warfare. First the French and then the British miners were at a lower level than their German counterparts, so it was much easier for them to drive tunnels straight into the slopes all along the high ground from the *Gießler Höhe* down towards Roclincourt than it was for the German miners to react; they being forced to drive tunnels deeper to achieve the same result. In high tempo mining operations this was a major problem. It was also anticipated that the British response to earlier setbacks would be to increase the rate of working even further. The only solution, therefore, was to launch an attack designed to capture the trenches where the British mineshafts were located.

Down towards La Folie Farm, at the southern end of the 17th Reserve Division sector, seizure and development for defence of Craters IV and VIII by Reserve Jäger Battalion 9 had consolidated the left flank; whilst further north Infantry Regiment 163 and Reserve Infantry Regiment 86 had succeeded in advancing their lines forward sufficiently to capture two British mine entrances, but this

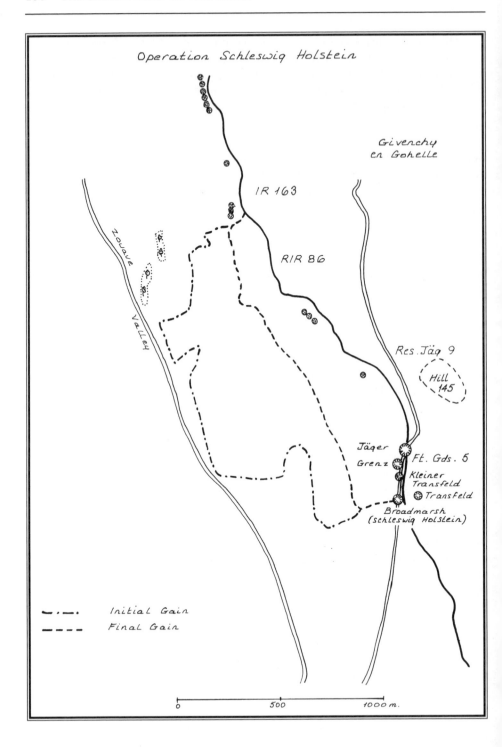

provided insufficient security. The plan was to attack in association with Footguard Regiment 5 of 3rd Guards Division to the south. There were to be seven companies in the leading wave and the intention was to advance the line by 400 metres on a 1,800 metre front. The decision made, it was followed by a frenzy of preparatory activity. In order to establish the precise location of trenches, dugouts and approach routes, there was a great increase of aerial photography, work by artillery observers and patrol operations.

Poor weather at the end of the first week in May, which was marked by cold, wind and rain, held back this work somewhat, but may have caused the British to lower their guard to some extent. Patrols reported constantly that the British front line appeared to be unoccupied in many places during the night. Finally, on 9 May, the operation order was issued, giving 'mid-May' as the timing for the attack. All the way down to company level every last detail of the operation was attended to, as preparations to cover all eventualities were completed. Some idea of the amount of work involved for what was a relatively minor affair may be derived from the statistic that 9,000 individual loads of ammunition and equipment had to be carried forward at night between 10 and 16 May. These included 3,000 rolls of concertina barbed wire, numerous temporary obstacles and kniferests, 175,000 sandbags, 2,400 spades and picks, 28,000 hand grenades, 14,700 flares and 2,600 pieces of shuttering timber.[36] This work did not go forward totally unmolested. At 9.00 pm on 13 May, the commander of 3rd Company Footguard Regiment 5 had just reported to his battalion commander that all was quiet, when there was sudden explosion, the situation changed rapidly and there was near-panic:

Oberleutnant Freiherr von Maltzau 3rd Company Footguard Regiment 5 [37]

"Suddenly heavy mortar and artillery fire began coming down on my company sector. A gefreiter reported that the alarm had been raised on the right. The sound of battle could be heard clearly. I rushed out of my dugout. Reserve Leutnant Astor came running up to me, shouting, 'The British are in our trench!' Another man with him bawled, 'Gas attack!' I fired a few flares calling for defensive fire and our artillery responded immediately. At that I ran towards the front line trench, revolver in my right hand and flare pistol in my left. I expected to bump into the British behind every traverse. To the right everyone was in his alert position. I ran to the left. A mortar bomb had landed in amongst a section and one dead man and two others who had been wounded, lay in the middle of the trench. As I swept past, one of them grabbed at my trench coat and screamed for help. I was not able to concern myself with him; I had more important matters to attend to. Up on the firing step stood two men, firing for all they were worth, despite having been wounded. They stayed at their posts. They were really great lads! Here everything was in order; there was no sign of the British.

"I ran on. Everywhere the sections were in their alert positions. On my left flank a line of British soldiers which had got forward during the firing had thrown grenades in response to a whistle signal. They had then taken cover in shell holes and attempted to crawl forward under our wire. For six to eight minutes they had thrown hand grenades at us until we were able to drive them away. No British soldiers had penetrated our wire obstacle, let alone got into our trenches. Meanwhile the exchanges of mortar and artillery fire continued and rifle grenades were fired on the left. This was supplemented by machine gun fire from the right flank. The 1st Company, which I had sent for, was not required so I sent it back. We remained stood-to throughout the night. There was a lot of work to be done. Small arms ammunition and hand grenades had to be replaced. In addition all the signal flares had been fired off. The dead and wounded had to be transported to the rear. Unfortunately there were lot of them. Those killed were: Gefreiters Brahm and Schirbel; Grenadiers Jähnen, Löwy, Möller and Schönwasser and fourteen men were wounded.[38] In addition one man had gone mad. He attempted to avoid a hand grenade and leapt out of his trench to move to the rear. It was case of out of the frying pan into the fire. He took refuge in a latrine where he was found amidst the hail of fire and out of his mind."

In parallel to the other preparations, artillery pieces and mortars were ranged in as unobtrusively as possible and further reinforcements arrived to boost the numbers of machine guns and trench mortars further. Some idea about the build up must have filtered through to the British because, although the old front line seemed to have been abandoned completely, work was going ahead to develop the support trench and additional rolls of barbed wire, together with other obstacles, were being laid all along the threatened sector. It was decided to make use of the old British trench as a jumping off point, so saps were driven forward towards it all along the attack sector. In the meantime the British began systematically to use their guns against the German positions in an attempt to disrupt the preliminaries. Observers in balloons directed the fire and the German positions began to suffer. Mining and counter-mining continued in the lead up to the assault, which was fixed for 18 May. A little later this was adjusted to 21 May to permit additional reconnaissance to take place and to complete the artillery preparations.

In addition to the entire Corps artillery, the attack frontage was due to be engaged by all the guns of IV Corps and the Guard Reserve Corps which were within range. Reinforced by an additional nine batteries of heavy howitzers, this meant that the fire plan would be undertaken by no fewer than eighty batteries: an immense weight of fire on a two kilometre frontage.[39] All the guns were ranged in by 17 May, there were further mine explosions then, on 19 May, after lengthy artillery fire, a British attack succeeded in wresting the Transfeld Crater on Hill 145 from the German defenders.[40] Final preparations were made on 20

May and during the night 20/21 May, all the assaulting forces moved into position. The artillery, having test fired their concentrations the previous day, began the bombardment at 5.30 pm. Gas shells were fired at the support and reserve areas behind the British front then, ten minutes later, the guns brought down fire for effect simultaneously. Sweeping the depth of the position from front to rear and back, all guns came down on the main position at exactly 6.00 pm.

Aerial observers in balloons and aircraft were in the air locating British battery positions, which were then engaged with counter-battery fire. Aircraft spotted twenty three batteries and the balloon crews a further sixty. The bombardment continued until 9.45 pm, with each four gun battery firing an average of 200 shells per hour. In reply the British fire was largely uncoordinated. There was little doubt that tactical surprise had been achieved. With most of the fire coming down on support and reserve trenches, together with approach routes, the remaining fire on the front line trench was lifted 150 metres at 9.45 pm and, one minute later, the assault began. On the frontage of Reserve Jäger Battalion 9, 1st and 4th Companies under Leutnants Schmeling and Trabandt respectively launched forward. Schmeling immediately fell wounded and his place was taken by Reserve Leutnant Schulz. Both companies encountered sharp resistance in the first British position, but it was short-lived.

Having overcome the first line of defence, there was much stiffer fight for the support trench, especially where the artillery fire had not been fully effective. In places the British troops barricaded sections of the trench and fought to the last. Some prisoners later explained that they fought in this manner because they had not expected that the attackers would take prisoners and feared that they would be killed whatever they did. On a day of high courage on both sides, Jäger Maaßen and Oberjäger Jürgensen earned great praise for capturing two machine guns in close quarter fighting. It was far from easy to maintain links to the regiments to the left and right, A special fighting patrol had to be despatched later to link up with Footguard Regiment 5 whilst, on the right, Reserve Infantry Regiment 86 had pushed forward so far that 4th Company Reserve Jäger Battalion 9 had to renew its assault and became bogged down with fighting for the depth positions to its front. Initially it was necessary to beat off several minor British counter-attacks but, during the night, the main effort by all companies was to develop the newly captured positions and to establish links to the rear.

The situation was much the same for the men of Footguard Regiment 5. Here Hauptmann Gutknecht, commanding officer 2nd Battalion, led his heavily rein-forced unit on a narrow front attack directed straight down to the low ground at the bottom of Hill 145. As the moment for the assault drew near, his men were packed, deeply echeloned, into every available piece of cover stretching back up Hill 145 from the Transfeld Crater area. One of the platoon commanders of 5th Company, which was in reserve, takes up the story.

Reserve Leutnant Krüger 5th Company Footguard Regiment 5 [41]

"The drum fire by our artillery and mortars began at 5.30 pm, increasing gradually to 9.45 pm. The earth trembled and shook slightly as a result of the explosions of the shells. We sat tightly wedged in our dugout, whilst our forward trenches were peppered with shell and mortar bomb splinters. There was a hellish roaring, howling, whistling, thundering and droning! The hands of the clocks crept forward. Our chatter died away, but jokes flew around, for we were only a few moments away from a fight for life or death. At 9.44 pm we poured out of our dugouts and raced towards our jumping-off point.

"9.45 pm! A severe shock shook the earth and a wave-like motion began beneath our feet. There was a great noise from deep down then, slowly, the earth in front of us began to heave upwards into what looked like a great mountain. Suddenly it burst open and great flames, crowned with a whitish-grey smoke cloud, leapt upwards. Gradually the smoke cleared and, like a shower of meteors, clods of clay and lumps of chalk rained down on us. It was a man-made earthquake! Gigantic! Dreadful to behold! Immediately after the production of the Schleswig-Holstein Crater [= Broadmarsh Crater], the assault waves of 8th and 5th Companies, together with their supporting engineers and machine gunners, rushed forward. Two assault groups from Basten's platoon and Heinig's section from Krüger's 5th Company platoon, reached the enemy side of the crater, together with twelve of the engineers.

"Its occupation was made difficult by a British machine gun located slightly further south. It engaged one of our machine guns and silenced it at once. The same fate befell the replacement machine gun and crew, who were hit as they hurried forward. Soon the machine gun commander, Unteroffizier Michel, was down to only a few men and it was not until the British machine gun was knocked out by one of our weapons firing from the central attack sector that the new crater was definitively occupied. The assaulting waves of Malcher's and Kuntzen's platoons from 8th Company were held up by the fire of a British machine gun, which suddenly popped up from the far side of the new Transfeld Crater. Kuntzen's platoon was shot down, almost to a man, but part of Malcher's platoon took the enemy behind the crater from a flank, whilst the sections of Vizefeldwebel Glade and Sergeant Böttcher attacked from the left and helped with the capture of the new Transfeld crater.

"Our magnificent men threw themselves into the battle with great daring. Together with the sections of Fiß and Wölk, I launched an attack between Schleswig-Holstein and Transfeld Craters in order to link up with the left flank of the 8th Company and also to close the wide gap between the 8th and Schleswig-Holstein Crater. In the process we came across Leutnant Kuntzen and many of the men of his platoon lying wounded in the open, then we stumbled into two men of Reserve Jäger Battalion 9 who had got lost. We were soon in contact with Malcher's platoon, however. A little later Vizefeldwebel Glade and Sergeant Böttcher, those two daringly irrepressible soldiers, both joined me after successfully completing their tasks. In order to press on with the work on the ploughed up chalk landscape, we also had to deploy Mellin's platoon from 5th Company.

"Oerter's platoon from 8th Company came forward to replace Kuntzen's destroyed platoon. This helped us to maintain the upper hand, despite the ensuing violent battle with hand grenades. By 10.15 pm contact had been made left and right with Reserve Jäger Battalion 9 and 5th Company. An attempt was made by Gefreiters Grosch and Wandt, together with Malcher's platoon, to push forward to the British third line but, caught in the concentrated fire of several British machine guns, almost all of them fell dead or wounded in an instant. Leaping into a British trench, Unteroffizier Rittershausen of 8th Company found two mine galleries and he cut all the cables, but the engineers with 5th Company, patrolling forward, were unable to locate any entrances . . . About one hour after the British trenches were occupied, Grenadier Wergen of 8th Company found another mine gallery leading off from a blind sap. Sixteen British soldiers had barricaded themselves in it, but they surrendered at the first demand.

"It was an appalling task to try to dig positions in this place and it demanded an immense expenditure of effort. The night was dark and the British hammered away with all calibres of weapons. This disturbance went on all night, so we had to alternate digging with fighting. This was especially the case on the 8th Company sector, where we formed a long human chain to pass thousands of hand grenades forward to where they were being thrown constantly. Explosions were continuous.[42] However, by dawn we had dug in over head height. The hardest task was to link up with the edge of the crater, because the British were throwing grenades into it from close range. The amount of earth thrown up meant that the rim of the crater was very high. As a result the hastily dug communication trenches were so shallow that in daylight it was necessary to crawl along them. Many a brave lad of my 5th Company was hit by flying lead here. The old British trenches contained many dead British soldiers and heaps of weapons and hand grenades, which we used to beat off British attacks."

From the early hours of 22 May, the situation in the newly captured front line, which overlooked Zouave Valley, remained extremely precarious. The German artillery fired frequent close defensive fire concentrations to support the hard-pressed front line defenders, who fought hard throughout the day to hold on to their gains. Heavy British artillery fire of all calibres was brought down on

Schleswig-Holstein Crater and the surrounding area between 7.00 am and 9.00 am, so that the German defenders were forced to thin out their defences and much of the construction work which had been achieved overnight was wrecked. To this bombardment was added fire from the direction of Neuville St Vaast and the Lorette Spur. It was as good as impossible to carry on digging and Leutnant Krüger's platoon lost so many men that it had to be replaced that evening by that of Leutnant Mellin. It was, however, not long before Krüger's men were back in the thick of the action. It was an extraordinary trial for them and costly too, as Krüger later recalled.

Reserve Leutnant Krüger 5th Company Footguard Regiment 5 [43]

"Because the position remained under heavy fire, during the day my sector was manned only by Sergeant Böttcher with twelve men. The new crater and the surrounding area had become hell on earth. The courageous Unteroffiziers Fiß and Handreack were buried alive and killed. They had attempted to take cover in a newly begun mine gallery, but a shell collapsed the entrance. Fiß lay outside, with a slight head wound, but he had been killed by blast, whereas Handreack was dug out by us and was found dead where he had been crouching. Unteroffizier Heinig had already fallen, mortally wounded in the back, during the initial occupation of the crater on 21 May. His body was subsequently thrown about by exploding shells, so it looked as though he was still alive, but we were unable to recover him from the crater until the evening of 22 May. [44]

"In addition to these three unteroffiziers, the blood of many other comrades was shed here. All the grenadiers had given of their best. If exhaustion and escape from the deafening racket caused them to nod over their spades or weapons, it took only a quick shout or their own feelings of personal responsibility to rouse them to further feats of superhuman effort. The following men distinguished themselves in particular during this battle: Gefreiters Kroll and Metzmacher; Grenadiers Bracht, Krolikowski, Mohrlang, Froitheim and Teschner – not forgetting the three unteroffiziers already mentioned. Many others did their duty to the last. Little Ketelsen, as he was known to all, a cheerful popular young soldier, was disembowelled by a direct hit by a dud shell. He died without previously losing consciousness. I look back with pride on all these men of 1st Platoon, 5th Company."

Crown Prince Rupprecht of Bavaria Diary Entry 22 May 1916 [45]

"During the night heavy artillery and mortar fire was brought down on the 18th Reserve Division. At 1.30 pm, 11.30 pm and at 4.35 am and 5.15 am enemy attacks were beaten off. There was heavy gun fire directed all night long against the front line, but this eased after 6.00 am. Yesterday evening enemy defensive artillery fire was only thin and the bursting point of the shrapnel shells was extraordinarily high; an observation that was also made during the last operation of II Bavarian Corps. Completely calm conditions facilitated the gassing of enemy observation posts and batteries on the Lorette Spur and in the valley of the Souchez river.

"By midday it was reported that yesterday's operation ran according to plan and that 220 prisoners altogether were conducted to the rear. Our airmen forced down enemy observation balloons just as the attack was beginning. In places the attack was pushed forward 700 metres beyond the final objective, which was the enemy third line trench. The artillery had to lengthen its range repeatedly in response to the firing of green flares. The British fought desperately. Generally speaking the only prisoners captured were those who had sought shelter in the dugouts. The morale of the prisoners is very low. The newly captured trenches can be enfiladed from Aix Noulette; the IV Corps artillery has been tasked with bringing down counter-battery fire against these flanking batteries.

"The Commander of IX Reserve Corps [General von Freytag-Loringhoven] is expecting a counter-attack this afternoon. As a result of the experiences from yesterday, he is of the opinion that it would be simple matter to break through the British front, provided that our army had two or three fresh corps in reserve. I share General von Boehn's view and I regret more than ever that the Army High Command did not choose, as I had wished, to concentrate its main spring offensive operations against the British north of the Somme and instead launched it against the strongest part of the Western Front around Verdun . . . "

As the Army Commander noted, one of the useful outcomes from Operation Schleswig Holstein, in addition to the advancement of the German front line, was the fact that a large number of prisoners were captured. Of the eight officers and 221 men involved, the great majority came from 140 and 141 Brigades of the British 47th Division, but fourteen men of 176 and 182 Tunnelling Companies Royal Engineers were also captured, as was a group of men of D Company 10th Battalion Cheshire Regiment from 7 Brigade, 25th Division. The German interrogators swiftly got to work on them and the result was a lengthy sequence of initial, main and supplementary interrogation reports and intelligence summaries. Examination of these reports provides an interesting insight into both the method of working of the interrogators and the intelligence staffs and the subjects which were of concern to them. It was clearly anticipated that there would be a good haul of prisoners, because in his initial report dated 23 May 1916, the head of intelligence at Sixth Army, Hauptmann Lübke, stated, 'The soldiers made a very good impression. (I saw them immediately after they were captured.) Only the nerves of the officers seemed to have been affected by the drum fire.' [46]

In other words, Lübke had gone forward to the prisoner holding cage and was able to make a swift assessment of the potential. Whilst the initial report concerned itself with matters of organisation, identity of commanders (which was complete in every detail for each unit and formation of 47th Division and also identified Sir Henry Wilson as Commander IV Corps and General [Sir Charles] Monro as First Army Commander) and minor tactical matters, of far greater importance to the German intelligence staffs was the material produced from the interrogation of the officers. Time was of the essence if maximum use was to be made of the shock of capture, so each officer was questioned individually as soon as possible. It is clear from the first of these 'officer reports' [47] that, firstly, improper pressure was not used against those captured and, secondly, that the interrogation team concentrated increasingly as time went on those most willing to speak to them.

The complete list of officers captured, in the sequence listed in the report, went as follows: Captain FM Davis C Company, 7th Battalion London Regiment, Second Lieutenant WV Brooks, D Company, 7th Battalion London Regiment, Captain GMB Portman, D Company, 8th Battalion London Regiment, Captain GN Clark, A Company, 8th Battalion London Regiment, Second Lieutenant CLE Wallace, D Company, 8th Battalion London Regiment, Second Lieutenant J Gurney, A Company, 8th Battalion London Regiment and Second Lieutenant EA Nowell[48] 19th Battalion London Regiment (attached to 8th Battalion London Regiment). Of these Brooks was noted as being, 'not well enough to be questioned, because of his wounds'. Captain Davis and Second Lieutenant Wallace refused to provide any other information of any kind apart from their ranks, names and units, but the other five provided background details on themselves and their experiences from arriving in France until the day of the attack. They then, collectively, provided the interrogators with the names of thirty five other officers, which enabled them to build up an almost complete order of battle of all key officer appointments in 140 Brigade.

Some tactical information was obtained at the same time, but during the next forty eight hours Gurney and Portman were re-interrogated, as was Brooks for the first time. Collectively they provided information on the methods of working of artillery forward observation officers, the numbers of machine guns available and how they were organised by the Machine Gun Corps. They then went on to describe dugout construction and the principles governing their placement, the routine in the line and the characteristics of a new type of trench mortar, including the organisation and subordination of the base plates. Having assisted their interrogators with precise definitions of military terms, such as 'Casualty Clearing Station', 'Strombus Horn' [used as a type of gas alarm] and 'Overhead Fire', the interrogation turned to political matters. It is clear that by now the sessions had developed into fairly free conversations, because opinions were ventured, in particular by Portman, on topics ranging from the causes of the war, the attitude of the British to the German people and their estimation of the value of the United States as an ally. [49]

Clearly encouraged by the information they had been able to glean, the same three officers and, in addition, Howell, were interviewed yet again. This time the subjects reported on were of a purely military nature, with information being proffered concerning training, equipment, clothing, divisional signs and ammunition supply. The size, composition and tasks of the engineers, especially tunnelling companies, were described and the numbering system in use was explained. The ensuing detailed report was rounded off by a description of entrenching battalions.[50] Encouraged by the result, the interrogators turned their attention to the specialists and the eleven men from 10th Battalion Cheshire Regiment (140 Brigade, 25th Division).

Three signallers attached to 8th Battalion London Regiment provided several useful pieces of information concerning signalling in general, improved security procedures and the characteristics of the new signal cable, which had been introduced to move away from 'earth return' systems, which were very susceptible to intercept. In order to clarify his points, one of the signallers helpfully provided his interrogators with two diagrams showing how the telephone network was laid out locally.[51] Less was obtained from the men of 10th Battalion Cheshire Regiment. There were no officers amongst them, so the intelligence generated was restricted mainly to the level of battalion and below. Nevertheless, between them these men provided a complete and accurate breakdown of the composition of 25th Division.[52] The processing of this mass of intelligence had kept the interrogation teams and the staffs busy for several days, but the various reports provided the chain of command with numerous valuable insights.

Local British counter-attacks having failed to restore the former positions and General Haig having specifically refused Lieutenant General Sir Henry Wilson, Commander of IV Corps, additional reinforcements or permission to launch a more ambitious counter-attack, due to the forthcoming demands of the Battle of the Somme, the two sides settled down and consolidated their new positions. Nevertheless minor operations continued throughout the coming weeks.

Offizierstellvertreter Hugo Gropp 2nd Company Reserve Infantry Regiment 76[53]

"Returning from leave in the Homeland during the night 29/30 May I found that my company was deployed on the Givenchy heights in an advanced position, which had been captured from the enemy by our courageous 163rd, during a daring attack launched on 21 May. Reserve Leutnant Hans Meyer handed over the company to me with the words. 'Things are pretty hot here. Not only are we subject to the usual artillery and mortar fire of different calibres, a lot of grenades – rifle and hand – are being used. Furthermore our engineers have discovered that the British are pushing forward mine galleries under our position. The Tommies are determined to get this trench back, so we must assume that we could be blown up and attacked at any moment.' I was soon to discover the accuracy of his observations and conclusions.

"That very same night British attacks began. At 12.45 am the garrison of the sap by Point 6 (a communications trench which ran towards the enemy position), which we had developed into an advanced sap, reported that they were under British attack. Making use of their old trench to creep forward a patrol, comprising twenty to twenty five men, was attempting to force their way into the advanced sap. It was only due to the alertness of the defenders – six men commanded by Unteroffizier Hachmöller – that the attack could be beaten off. Reserve Leutnant Pietzsker raced to the spot at the head of Unteroffizier Wetjen's section and drove off the enemy patrol with small arms fire and grenades before it could get into the sap. The enemy left one man dead and two seriously wounded behind, but the raid cost us two men killed also: Ersatz Reservists Wiencken[54] and Schirmeyer.

"The enemy repeated their attack at 2.00 am. The garrisons of Advanced Saps 25 and 25a, which had also been developed from old enemy communications trenches, reported simultaneously that British troops were creeping up on them. This time it was groups of ten to fifteen who were exploiting the cover of the old trenches. The garrisons of the saps succeeded in driving the enemy away with grenades and rifle fire. Half an hour later a formed up line of infantry closed up on the company position, reaching the rough line of the advanced saps and managing to enter Sap 25a. Vigorous and energetic counter-action by Reserve Vizefeldwebel Barfurth and the men of his platoon, who rushed to reinforce the threatened area, succeeded once more in forcing the enemy back.

"Both Vizefeldwebel Barfurth and the garrisons of the advanced saps had fought the enemy heroically at close quarters. Not one of our men took as much as a step backwards, even though the enemy considerably outnumbered them. As Vizefeldwebel Barfurth, who was seriously wounded when his leg was blown off, was being carried to me to report, I sought to console him, 'Keep your chin up Barfurth. It is going to be all right'. His reply was, 'Even if things do not go well, I depart with the great satisfaction of knowing that the British were not able to hold on to my sap!' That was the spirit of my 2nd Company, the spirit of our young Flanders soldiers of 1914 . . .

"Because the enemy had failed to enter our positions using surprise tactics, they then attempted it after thorough preparation. They moved forward heavy mortars and hammered our position ceaselessly, day and night with *Kugelminen* [Toffee Apples]. Fifteen bombs were counted in ten minutes, seventy in an hour and between 300 and 350 in one twenty four hour period. The trenches were flattened repeatedly; it made for an incredibly strenuous time for the company. We were all manning the trenches, from which we could see the huge mortar bombs flying through the air as they were launched from the British trenches. Even at night their burning fuses lit up their path. At a loud word of command, everyone had to run left or right and throw themselves down in the next traverse. That was the only way to avoid casualties, but so many of our brave comrades were, nevertheless, killed during those days. I think, in particular, of Reserve Leutnant Junge and Krankenträger Tiedemann, who died whilst trying to bind the wounds of helpless comrades who had fallen victim to the mortar fire and also those who were buried alive having retired to their shelters in order to get some sleep.

"In view of the unusual enemy activity the company stood-to throughout the night, every night. At 11.45 pm on 3 July, a violent explosion occurred exactly at Point 6 on the right flank of the company sub-sector. Twenty five to thirty metres of trench and its garrison, together with the men of Advanced Sap 6, were hurled into the air and a further section about twenty five metres long was flattened. Mine Galleries 13 and 14 were crushed. The resulting crater was ten to fifteen metres deep. Simultaneously with the explosion, enemy artillery and mortars opened up and the enemy attacked, meaning to occupy the crater and to roll up our trench either side of it. We called immediately for artillery fire which arrived promptly. Reserve Leutnant Pietzker and a group of volunteers ran across country and immediately occupied the northeast part of the crater. A little while later the company commander advanced similarly and took up positions on the southeast corner of the new crater. Two sections of 1st Company provided excellent support whilst this was being done.

"In the meantime, making use of the communications trench which led to Point 7, the enemy arrived on the western edge of the crater. All their efforts to push on further withered away at the hands of my brave 2nd Company. Whilst half of the company defended against the grenade assaults of the enemy, the other half worked to free trapped comrades and to prepare the crater and the remainder of the position for defence. Another difficult night went by. At dawn I could see over-fatigued faces everywhere. We were proud of the fact that our combined efforts had proved successful in preventing the enemy from stepping foot in our trenches and we thought, sadly, of our fallen comrades."

It was not only on the ground that the Vimy area was being contested. On 18 June a fierce air battle occurred between Vimy and nearby Sallaumines, where men of Reserve Infantry Regiment 76 were billeted during their rest period out of the line. There were numerous witnesses to the fierce dog fight.

Offizierstellvertreter Hugo Gropp 2nd Company Reserve Infantry Regiment 76[55]

"I have recently witnessed an immensely tragic incident. It was a dogfight directly above our billets in Sallaumines. There was nothing new about air battles around the area of Lens, but it was the first time that I had seen an aircraft crash. In fact not just one, but three aircraft came down within a few minutes of each other and each of the crash sites was in my immediate vicinity. It was time of tremendous tension. It happened between 9.00 pm and 10.00 pm. As far as I could make out the battle was between four large British biplanes and three small German Fokkers (monoplanes). It took the form of a wild encounter which ranged from high in the sky to just above our heads. The small, agile Fokkers swooped and dived trying to get behind their large opponents in what was a life and death struggle.

"All we could hear was the roar of the engines and the rattle of machine gun fire. The traffic on the roads stopped as all eyes were directed upwards expectantly. Suddenly one of the aircraft fell away from the fight. It was as though the pilot, having been hit by a bullet, had lost control of it. It hurtled from a great height towards the ground. I wanted to run towards it, but suddenly another was dropping out of the dogfight too. Whilst still high up an explosion tore it apart. The wings floated and tumbled towards the ground, whilst the fuselage, complete with engine, dived rapidly earthwards. For a moment I did not know which way to run. Then a British biplane glided down, whilst the pilot attempted, about 50 metres up, to regain control of it and get away.

"However he had a Fokker on his tail, so there was no escape. Giving up the attempt, he set the aircraft down in a field very close to where I was standing. It was a fine, proud-looking aircraft. Its pilot died shortly after landing, whilst his observer, who had a severe head wound, was immediately transported to hospital. I felt uneasy. A rumour was circulating that Immelmann had taken part in the battle. I moved swiftly to another crash site, filled with foreboding. A large number of soldiers were surrounding the aircraft, which had been reduced to a tangle of metal and wood. In amongst it, crushed beyond recognition, was a human body. The discovery of a *Pour le Mérite* [Blue Max] was a sad indication that our King of the Skies, Oberleutnant Immelmann, had fallen a victim of this dogfight.

"The very thought of this was too troubling to comprehend and I left the scene of the crash, deep in thought, not wanting to believe it was true. It was not until I read the Army Communiqué the following day that the shattering news was confirmed." [56]

The following six weeks were a period of relative quiet on Vimy Ridge. With the initial stages of the Battle of the Somme engaging the attention of the British to the south, they had no intention of stirring up trouble anywhere else along the front, whilst the defenders were content to take the opportunity of strengthening their defences further. However, mounting losses and the demands of the Somme fighting meant that forces had to be withdrawn from other parts of the Western Front to plug the gaps. It could only be a matter of time, therefore, before the current defenders of Vimy Ridge would be called on to carry out a tour of duty.

They had fought hard and successfully during the months they had spent in the area and their contribution was fully acknowledged in a special Sixth Army Order of the Day:

"Headquarters Sixth Army   20 July 1916

Army Order of the Day

On the occasion of its departure from the ranks of the formations which make up Sixth Army, I wish to express my heartiest thanks to – and fullest recognition of – the performance of IX Reserve Corps during the period in which it was subordinated to the Army. The Corps was pitched into the autumn battles of 1915 under the most difficult conditions and once more demonstrated its outstanding fighting spirit. Brilliant achievements, such as that of recapturing the hotly-contested *Gießler-Höhe* and the storming of the front line enemy positions on the slopes southwest of Givenchy en Gohelle, proved that the Corps has retained its irresistible offensive spirit. I am in no doubt that this spirit will prove itself equal to future tasks and I wish the Corps every success under its excellent, tried and tested commanders.

Signed: Rupprecht
Crown Prince of Bavaria" [57]

As part of the move of the headquarters and remaining formations of IX Reserve Corps to the fighting on the Somme at the end of the month, on 23 July units of 56th Infantry Division, which had been withdrawn from the Verdun area a few days earlier, began taking over the Vimy front from 3rd Guards Infantry Division. The left forward regiment, Fusilier Regiment 35, relieving Footguards Regiment 5, assumed responsibility for the critical sector between Hill 145 and La Folie Farm. It had been relatively quiet for some time, the previous occupants had done a great deal to improve the positions, or strengthen the wire obstacles. Nevertheless initial tours of inspection revealed numerous areas where the defences could be further improved. Meanwhile mining operations, which had left long lines of scars and interlocking craters all along the front, continued. The Fusiliers had only been in position for three days when they experienced their first mine blast. German sappers had laid and charged a mine forward of Sub-Sector *Fischer 4*, about 500 metres forward of La Folie Farm.

Reserve Leutnant Michaelsen Fusilier Regiment 35 [58]

"During the afternoon we were informed that at 3.00 am a crater would be blown on the left flank. 150 *Zentner* [7.5 tonnes] of explosive! My first thoughts were: 'The poor British'. An engineer told me that before they blew mines they would knock on the walls of the gallery. If the enemy heeded the warning they would be able to save themselves. Others were not so sympathetic and I do not believe that the British oppo-

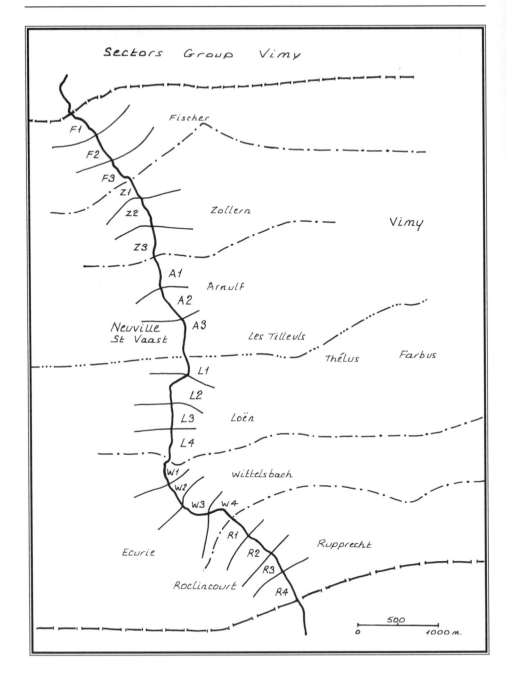

site would have shown any mercy. If it had not been for them, we should not still be fighting a war. During the evening an order of theirs sent over the telephone was intercepted. According to this the British intended to launch a gas attack that night, so we prepared ourselves.

"We manned the trenches, gas masks at the ready, from 10.00 pm to

2.00 am, but nothing happened. At that we went into our dugouts and lay down. Suddenly the Fähnrich dug me in the ribs. 'Did you not notice anything?' I looked at my watch; it was exactly 3.00 am. I had not felt the shock running through the earth, but the Fähnrich had certainly noted it. I then heard our artillery, which had opened up in an effort to hold the enemy in check if they attempted to launch an attack against the crater. For a few moments my thoughts went out to the British soldiers who had been blown up, then I fell asleep once more."

Despite this incident, it was a relatively quiet tour of duty, but British aircraft continually took advantage of the clear skies over Vimy Ridge to launch ground attacks on the defending troops. One such operation was attempted on 28 July, but it was intercepted.

Vizefeldwebel E Grosse Fusilier Regiment 35 [59]

"About twenty British [aircraft], recognisable from the markings beneath their wings, appeared at about 2,500 metres above Méricourt. Our anti-aircraft guns immediately fired a defensive barrage. The shells which exploded alongside, above and below these 'crates' produced balls of smoke which rapidly filled the clear skies with what looked like white cotton wool balls. The entire wing was plunged into confusion, with aircraft scattering in wild curves as they attempted to escape the curtain of fire. Now German fighter aircraft joined in, dog fighting with the British formation. Machine guns chattered and the anti-aircraft guns continued to fire.

"A short time later the defence began to be effective. A British aircraft shuddered, went into a spin, then side slipped away from the fight, pursued by one of our aircraft, firing constantly, which forced it down. The pilot of a second British aircraft attempted to land his burning aircraft, which was trailing a long streamer of smoke and flames. A third aircraft rocked violently and went into a vertical dive, throwing out its occupants. A fourth aircraft received a direct hit from the artillery. The petrol tank exploded, flames shot out and the aircraft was enveloped in black smoke. The enemy formation had been broken up and its aircraft scattered in all directions in the attempt to escape."

Back on Vimy Ridge the mining and counter-mining operations continued ceaselessly. Infantry Regiment 88, manning the right flank of the 56th Division sector on and around The Pimple forward of Givenchy, had a nerve-wracking time of it. This had been, in any case, an uncomfortable location ever since the French Army had recaptured the Lorette Spur. There were signs throughout the First Position and in the rear towards Givenchy warning, 'Danger, this place is overlooked from the Lorette Hill!'[60] It was the first time that the regiment had confronted the British army. Above ground, with both sides pre-occupied by the

Battle of the Somme, which was in full swing further south, there was not much activity. Sometimes hours went by without a shot being fired. This lack of activity had permitted grass to grow and flowers to push up in many places where the ground had been disturbed. Nevertheless the apparent tranquillity did not extend to the war underground. Beneath the ridge the engineers of both armies were still hard at work.

During the early days of August there was a distinct increase in activity. Shortly before midnight on 5 August, extremely heavy British artillery fire began landing on the left flank company of Infantry Regiment 88 and then, on the dot of midnight, a British camouflet was blown, crushing the German mine gallery 'Carlo'. At the time six engineers were working below in Carlo and only three of them could be saved. The explosion also damaged a part of the front line trench, but it was repairable. A British patrol, following up, was beaten back with hand grenades. It withdrew leaving two dead. Much the same fate was met by subsequent British probes that night. Having already detected that the British had pushed another gallery well forward under The Pimple between galleries 'Caspar' and 'Cäsar', the German engineers planned to respond to the destruction of Carlo with an explosion of their own. This occurred at 3.00 am on 7 August, causing a great deal of damage to both the British mine system as well as their forward trenches.

This pattern of activity continued until the middle of the month when, once again, the German engineers believed that another of their galleries, 'Goa', had been compromised. On 19 August they charged the completed mine chamber and blew the mine, which caused a considerable number of casualties. In the aftermath a wounded British sapper, half buried by the explosion, was recovered from a crater.

Reserve Leutnant Raßbach 12th Company Infantry Regiment 88 [61]

"About 12.30 am one of our sentry positions forward in the craters discovered a British soldier who had been knocked unconscious and thrown into the base of the crater. He called to his comrades for help, then when he noticed our sentry called out to him also. The sentry immediately reported this to me and I moved to the edge of the crater. At that the British shouted that they wished to recover their injured man. I informed them that [his recovery] would not be permitted unless we fetched him. These negotiations were broken off abruptly by firing which broke out on both sides. I called for Oberleutnant Schalloer to investigate the situation in person. An officer then appeared and it was agreed that two of our men and two of theirs would climb down into the crater and rescue the wounded man, who would be recovered by us.

"Removing all identifying marks from their uniforms, Oberleutnant Schalloer and Offizierstellvertreter Hahn went down into the crater and joined the British, who included one officer. Together they dug out the man, who was half buried. He was then lifted out of the crater on a stretcher by Oberlleutnant Schalloer, Offizierstellvertreter Hahn and Krankenträger Gefreiter Willmann and taken to the aid post. The British soldier was a corporal, with the letters R.E (Royal Engineers) on his epaulettes. [The British] mentioned that they had suffered eight men killed. Offizierstellvertreter Hahn observed that the entire British crater position had been destroyed."

On 23 August 23rd Reserve Division arrived from heavy fighting on the Somme around Monacu Farm and took over the front from near Angres to La Folie Wood, defending Vimy Ridge with three regiments in line. From north to south these were Reserve Grenadier Regiment 100, Reserve Infantry Regiment 101 and Reserve Infantry Regiment 102. To begin with Reserve Infantry Regiment 103 was retained near Douai as an army reserve. Opposing them were British regiments who had also arrived from the Somme. As a result there was little in the way of infantry operations, but activity levels in the air, below ground and with mortars and grenade launchers remained high. The artillery of both sides fired little; there seemed to be a tacit agreement to conserve ammunition, but sometimes at night there were exchanges of gun fire. From 28 August, Reserve Infantry Regiment 103 was introduced into the front line when the divisional sector was extended further north, but this was a short-lived measure. On 2 September it departed to become part of the new 211th Infantry Division.[62] There was disruption to other regiments of 23rd Reserve Division at the time because of the formation of the new Infantry Regiment 392. Reserve Infantry Regiment 100 had to give up 2nd Company complete, plus one platoon (seventy grenadiers) from 7th Company,[63] Reserve Infantry Regiment 101 lost its 8th Company to provide the nucleus for the new 1st Battalion[64] and Reserve Infantry Regiment 102 also gave up its 7th Company.[65]

When these manpower losses, which were only gradually made up by the arrival of drafts (some of them of doubtful quality), is coupled to the fact that each regiment also had to find large permanent work parties to labour for the engineers, it is easy to see why the summer of 1916 was relatively quiet on Vimy Ridge. The emphasis here is on the word 'relatively'. Within the under strength rifle companies the demands of routine in the line nevertheless fell particularly heavily; whilst patrolling and small-scale raids, such as the one on 9 October led by Reserve Leutnant Schräger of the Divisional Assault Troop on an advanced sap, which led to the capture of prisoners from the British 25th Division, also took a toll.[66] When, eventually, 23rd Reserve Division was relieved in mid October, Reserve Infantry Regiment 101 noted that, 'The ceaseless mine warfare and exchanges of artillery fire which, together with mortar fire did so much damage, the strenuous and time-consuming daily struggles to repair damaged trenches, coupled with the constant danger of being blown up at any moment by underground mine blasts, meant that the battalions in the line suffered a great deal and were very worn down. Higher authority had to be made aware of this.'[67]

Having defended Vimy Ridge successfully, if unspectacularly, ever since they were relieved on the Somme almost two months earlier, by mid-October the regiments of 23rd Reserve Division prepared to hand over to 6th Bavarian Reserve Division. The formal handover between Grenadier Reserve Infantry Regiment 100 and Bavarian Reserve Infantry Regiment 16 took place on 18 October when a hand over/take over certificate prepared by the Saxons was signed by the two commanders. The certificate includes a complete description of the situation within Sector *Fischer* [i.e. the Hill 145 area] during the days leading up to the arrival of the Canadians from the battles around Courcelette ands so provides a useful summary of the state of the defences as the final winter when the German army was still in possession of Vimy Ridge approached. 'Sector *Fischer* is in a defensible condition and is linked firmly to Sector *Döberitz* on the right and Sector *Arnulf* on the left . . . It is characterised by craters forward of, or comprising, the front line trenches, which are in defensible condition. A Second Position exists, but is generally little developed. The approach trench for Sub-Sectors *Fischer I* and *Fischer II* is *Fischergang;* that for *Fischer III and Fischer IV* is *Staubwassergang*[68] . . . The garrison can only be accommodated in the First Position, where the dugouts have three and a half to six metres of overhead cover . . . Mine galleries lead off from each Sub-Sector. Some are still being worked . . . The distance between the two [opposing] positions varies between thirty and 180 metres. The front line and saps are held by sentry posts only . . . [Enemy] artillery fire is generally light and mostly restricted to engagement of the rear areas by light and medium calibre weapons. Recently Sub-Sector *F I* has been engaged by large calibre weapons from the area of the Lorette Spur. There has been no patrol activity in recent days. The last occasion was against Sub-Sector *F IV* on 14 October. The heavy engagement of Sub-Sector *F I* leads to the suspicion that a raid is being planned against it . . . There have been no recent mine explosions, but one point in Sub-Sector *F I* is believed to be at risk.'[69] The report concluded with a description of German offensive activities and drew attention to the most urgent outstanding work on the positions. With the withdrawal of 23rd Reserve Division, the troops which were to oppose the newly arriving Canadians on Vimy Ridge, until the arrival in the area of the Prussian 79th Reserve Division at the beginning of March 1917, were almost complete.

In October 1916, 6th Bavarian Reserve Division still comprised four regiments. For the next four months it occupied the line from Angres in the north to La Folie Wood in the south, with Sectors *Mecklenburg,*[70] *Burg, Döberitz and Fischer* the responsibility of Bavarian Reserve Infantry Regiments 21, 20, 17 and 16 respectively. The Ridge to the south was garrisoned initially by the regiments of the Prussian 12th Reserve Division but, as the winter went by, the situation changed several times with the formation of 16th Bavarian Division in January 1917 and the deployment of 79th Reserve Division. These major moves, coupled with regimental reliefs in the line and moves from one sector to another, made for a complicated situation, which must have been difficult for Canadian intelligence staffs to keep abreast of, despite identifications obtained during raids and patrols. The one constant throughout was the fact that I Bavarian Reserve Corps, also referred to as 'Group Vimy', had command responsibility from Angres in the north to the Scarpe in the south.

Bavarian Reserve Infantry Regiment 17, arriving on and around The Pimple, hoped and believed that they were in for a rest cure after a desperately hard tour of duty near Eaucourt l'Abbaye and Le Sars on the Somme. Naturally the intensity of operations was much lower, but the endless hard labour to maintain the positions during the bad winter weather and the attrition caused by mortar and artillery fire, together with raiding, patrolling and mine warfare, meant that their losses cumulatively during the four month period amounted to 120 killed, almost 400 wounded and forty missing.[71] This is easily explained. Once the Canadian troops were in position and had begun to recover from the mauling they had received on the Somme, they adopted an extremely aggressive posture. There was an immediate upsurge in patrolling and raiding all along the Vimy front. On the slopes of The Pimple this was not restricted to operations at night. Foggy days were also exploited by Canadian units and there were numerous sharp close-quarter battles as a result.[72] The Bavarians were not even left alone on Christmas Day. Luckily for Bavarian Reserve Infantry Regiment 21, a sharp-eyed patrol commander, Infanterist Bohnhuber of 4th Company, spotted during the night 24/25 December that gaps had been cut in the Allied wire opposite the *Gießler Höhe* so, when a violent bombardment by batteries from previously unused positions was followed by assaults at 4.00 am, then again during the evening of 25 December, a fully alerted defence was able to defeat all the attacks, but at the cost of ruined Christmas celebrations and casualties of four killed, twenty five wounded and six missing. The regiment was not best pleased.[73]

Increased offensive activity by both sides meant, naturally, additional opportunities for prisoners to be taken and information to be extracted from them. In November and December there were several occasions when the German defenders took Canadian soldiers prisoner. On 16 November, for example, a member of a Canadian patrol found himself temporarily blinded by the intense light of a flare when he was extremely close to the forward trenches of Reserve Infantry Regiment 38. The other members of his patrol escaped into the night, but he could not see where he was going and blundered into a snatch team, who took him prisoner. He provided the defenders with one of the first identifications, being a member of an (unnamed) unit of the 3rd Canadian Division.[74] Some of the resulting interrogation reports concerning these prisoners survive. The first two such incidents, during the nights 28/29 November and 14/15 December, both took place northeast of Neuville St Vaast in exactly the same circumstances. German patrols operating forward in No Man's Land surrounded the men, who were manning an advance sap, approximately one hundred metres in front of the Canadian lines, surprised the occupants and overpowered them. Such are the similarities that the incidents may have happened in exactly the same sap. The first patrol captured four men of C Company 58th Canadian Battalion of 9 Brigade, 3rd Canadian Division and the second two men from A Company, 49th Canadian Battalion, 7 Brigade, 3rd Canadian Division. The third capture of this type took place by chance, during the night 23/24 December, when a three man reconnaissance patrol from 46th Canadian Battalion, 10 Brigade 4th Canadian Division led by a lieutenant, was launched forward into No Man's Land 'south east of Souchez'[75] after a German patrol had been driven away from the Canadian wire. Their movements were detected near the German wire and a pre-arranged drill was put in place to surround and snatch them.

Naturally all the prisoners were subject to interrogation. Examination of their interrogation reports shows clearly what subjects were of interest to the intelligence staff at that time. Apart from the usual questions concerning identification of officers within the chain of command, orders of battle and location of units and formations, the information on which most importance was placed related to losses incurred during the battles around Courcelette on the Somme and the subsequent arrival of reinforcements. From this they gleaned that in the case of the 58th Battalion, 'During the final attack, of 900 men of 58th Battalion, only about 150 returned.' [76] For its part the 49th Battalion, '. . . had very severe casualties on the Somme. [It] lost approximately 500 men during the assaults on Courcelette.' [77] The picture was much the same for the 46th Battalion, which 'lost about 50% of its strength on the Somme, but is now once more up to strength (approximately 1,000 men)'. It had, 'received between 300 and 400 reinforcements, all of them men with between five and ten months of training in Canada and a further two months in England.' [78]

The interrogators also wanted to know about any preparations for a major attack, but none of those captured had any such knowledge. One man from the 46th Battalion even ventured the opinion that the allocation of this sector was to provide them with a type of rest after the Somme fighting, which must have sounded familiar. The German army had been using the area for the same reason for the past five months. The other main point of interest concerned the build up of the Canadian Army, with particular reference to the 5th Canadian Division in England and if there were plans for a 6th Canadian Division.[79] Some information was obtained concerning the 5th Division and collectively the prisoners provided their captors with the fact that the Canadian Battalions with the highest numbers were 215th (30 November), 246th (15 December) and 275th (24 December). All the prisoners reported that morale was good and one of them explained that the tough outdoor upbringing of the majority of the Canadian volunteer soldiers made them better able to master the prevailing conditions than their British counterparts. All this information and the mass of minor detail which was also obtained was of great use to Sixth Army which, confronted by Canadian troops for the first time, was anxious to build up the intelligence picture with the least possible delay.

In a further development of the policy applied to the 23rd Reserve Division four months earlier and due to a combination of the manpower losses at Verdun and on the Somme beginning to bite, coupled with the need to expand the number of divisions in the German army, the High Command issued a directive in early December which affected every part of the army.

Crown Prince Rupprecht of Bavaria Diary Entry 9 December 1916 [80]

> "Each battalion has to release one hundred fit, battle-hardened men, including Iron Cross holders and similar. They are to be sent back to the homeland for allocation to new formations in order to stiffen them. In return each battalion will receive one hundred men, fit only for static duties, to carry out supporting functions."

The measure was unpopular, both with units concerned and the men directed to transfer. Nevertheless it had to be done. It represents, perhaps, the first realisation that the war was not going Germany's way and, with the Canadian forces opposing them becoming increasingly assertive and its greatest trial on Vimy Ridge yet to come, it was an inauspicious end to the year for its defenders. In November the first reports began to arrive from agents and other sources that a British offensive was being planned between La Bassée and Arras and although the chain of command dismissed the idea based on their local observations, nevertheless from early December increased attention began to be placed on the possibility of an assault on Vimy Ridge.[81] From the turn of the year this risk jostled for first position with an attack against the Messines Ridge in all intelligence summaries and assessments.

It was not only within the army that signs of strains were showing. On 12 December Germany made its so-called *Friedensangebot* [Offer of Peace] to the Allies. Crown Prince Ruprecht noted immediately in his diary, 'It is to be hoped that this matter has been clarified with at least one or the other of the enemy powers; otherwise the risk is that it will be interpreted by our opponents as a sign of weakness, which will boost their hopes of victory.'[82] That was a moderate response to Bethmann-Hollweg's initiative. The majority of the senior military leaders treated the whole idea with complete contempt. In the event the terms were so completely unacceptable that the Allies had no hesitation in dismissing the offer out of hand, at once and in the strongest terms. This was not before the initiative had been trumpeted far and wide, however, including in a special Order of the Day to the troops, signed by the Kaiser himself. The information reached the men of Reserve Infantry Regiment 38, occupying Sector *Loën,* forward of Thélus, that same day and was the cause of considerable discussion within the regiment. The following day it was the subject of a private letter home from a member of the regiment.

> "As surprised as I was yesterday when we were informed by the Army Order about the Offer of Peace, I was really delighted about it. Initially the general reaction to the surprise was not one of pleasure. The obvious thought which stood in the way of happiness was of the apparent pointlessness of such an offer and the hue and cry it would cause; that it was a sign of German weakness and our need for peace. Still, the more I think about it and turn it over in my mind, the more certain I am that for us and for the whole of humanity it represents an immeasurably great

service. The facts speak too loud to permit the accusation to be thrown at us that we simply have to sue for peace; but it is certainly true that it proves that sense still prevails in the world and that enough blood has already been spilt. The first move had to be made by one of the two warring parties and I find it good that it has come from us. In my considered opinion, the moment chosen is far from unfavourable. I believe, notwithstanding all the bluster of the leaders of the Entente, that the seeds which have been sown will in many instances fall on fertile soil.

The peoples of all lands long for peace, perhaps least of all in England, but those who govern that country will find it increasingly difficult now to keep the hands of their people to the plough in pursuit of their utopian war-prolonging aims. It is possible, probable even, that at first our offer will be refused haughtily, but it will continue to work away. In the light of new successes, with which we can certainly reckon, it will expose more and more the madness and irresponsibility of those who hold power within the Entente and so lead to peace. It is now riskier than ever to predict that we could just as easily move swiftly to a ceasefire and genuine peace, as it is to suggest that the war will continue raging more dreadful than before. But the service of the Kaiser and his advisers to humanity is that they, before the world, quite openly and unreservedly, have stretched out the hand of peace. Simultaneously, our government has knocked the weapons out of the hands of those of our own people who assert that those who govern us and those who supply our war materiel have a vested interest in prolonging the war. Should peace not come, then every German can see that it is not our fault if the war continues and it should be clear to all bar the Social Democrats that such ideas are based on nonsense. So out of the situation may arise a new unity – provided, that is, that the Ultras, with their idiotic war aims, do not ruin everything! How can any man of common sense think in terms, for example, of the annexation of the whole of Belgium!"[83]

What is interesting about this letter, with all its humbug and wishful thinking, is that it mirrors completely the false appreciation made by the German government of the national characteristics of the Allies and their solidarity; not to mention their underestimation of Allied determination – precisely because so much blood and treasure had already been sacrificed – to bring hostilities to a decisive conclusion regardless of the cost. The war would go on. For the men manning the water and mud-filled trenches along the desolate expanse of Vimy Ridge, that was bleak prospect.

Notes

1. *Les Armées Françaises dans la Grande Guerre Tome III* p 602
2. The *Ersatzreserve* comprised men who were in every way fit and suitable for military service, but were not required for service in the active army. Instead they

carried out four periods of military training spread over a twelve year period before transferring to the *Landsturm*.

3. *Les Armées Françaises dans la Grande Guerre Tome III* p 645 Between 15 November and 5 December the numbers increased from 1,231 to 1,254.
4. Gropp: *Hanseaten im Kampf* pp 115 – 116
5. Ritter: History Infantry Regiment 163 p 91
6. Wiederich: History Reserve Infantry Regiment 229 p 44
7. Niebelschutz: History Reserve Infantry Regiment 230 pp 67–68
8. Kriegsarchiv München HS 1962 p 4
9. Later this trench became known as *Fischer Gang*.
10. Later this became known as *Transfeld Weg*.
11. Kriegsarchiv München HS 1962 pp 8–9
12. Staubwasser: History Bavarian Infantry Regiment 2 pp 76–79
13. *Staubwasser Weg*, the major communication trench in what became Sector *Zollern*, was named after him.
14. This is an implausible suggestion. Evidently Osborn was no stranger to the use of artistic licence.
15. Reserve Leutnant Heinrich Witte was evacuated to a field hospital, but succumbed to his wounds on 8 February 1916. He is buried in the German cemetery at Billy-Montigny Block 5 Grave 105.
16. Kriegsarchiv München HS 1962 p 17
17. Kronprinz Rupprecht *Mein Kriegstagebuch Erster Band* p 422
18. Kriegsarchiv München AOK 6 Bd 433 N.O. A.O.K. 6 B. Nr. 4048 22.1.1916; N.O. A.O.K. 6 B. Nr. 4058 22.1.1916; 1 Res Division Bd 45 N.O. IV., I. Bayer. u. IX, Res. K. 22. Januar 1916
19. Kriegsarchiv München 1 Reserve Division Bd 45 N.O. A.O.K. 6 B. Nr. 4118 31.1.1916
20. Kriegsarchiv München AOK 6 Bd 433 N.O. A.O.K. 6 B. Nr. 4202 9.2.1916
21. Gropp: *Hanseaten im Kampf* pp 117 – 121
22. *Les Armées Françaises dans la Grande Guerre Tome IV 1er Volume* p 504–505
23. Haupt: History Bavarian Infantry Regiment 15 p 39
24. According to the interrogation report (Kriegsarchiv München 1 Res. Div. Bd 45:NO A.O.K. 6 B. No 4476 28.3.1916), fourteen men (one sergeant, one corporal and ten private soldiers) were captured. Three of them were wounded.
25. Speck: History Reserve Infantry Regiment 84 p 50. Captain Joicey, son of the first Baron Joicey, is buried in Grave IV F 1 of Liévin Communal Cemetery Extension.
26. Haupt: History Bavarian Infantry Regiment 15 pp 39–40
27. History Bavarian Infantry Regiment 12 pp 76–77
28. Kriegsarchiv München AOK 6 Bd 433: NO A.O.K. 6 B. No 4677 29.4.1916
29. Kriegsarchiv München AOK 6 Bd 433: NO A.O.K. 6 B. No 4533 6.4.1916
30. Kriegsarchiv München 1 Res. Div. Bd 45: NO A.O.K. 6 B. No 4630 21.4.1916
31. Kriegsarchiv München AOK 6 Bd 433: NO A.O.K. 6 B. No 4667 28.4.1916
32. Kriegsarchiv München Pi Btl 17 Bd 9 General-Kdo I. Bayer. Res. Corps K. H. Qu. 18.4.1916
33. Kronprinz Rupprecht *Mein Kriegstagebuch Erster Band* pp 455 – 460. It is certainly the case that Crown Prince Rupprecht's misgivings were not widely shared. Post war the Official History confined itself to the remark, 'Although the army had to relinquish five divisions in May and June, receiving only four in return, in mid June it still possessed relatively strong forces . . .' See *Der Weltkrieg Zehnter Band* p 272.

34. Karitzky: History Reserve Jäger Battalion 9 pp 42–43
35. It is probable that this code word was selected because the regiments of 17th Reserve Division were raised in the north of Germany. Infantry Regiment 163, for example, actually had 'Schleswig Holstein' as part of its title.
36. Karitzky: History Reserve Jäger Battalion 9 pp 44
37. Stosch: History Footguard Regiment 5 p 245
38. The fallen are buried in scattered locations in the German cemetery at Neuville St Vaast/Maison Blanche. Grenadier [*sic.*] Georg Brahm lies in Block 8 Grave 167, Grenadier [*sic*] Paul Schirbel in Block 9 Grave 583, Grenadier Bernhard Jähnen in Block 8 Grave 133, Grenadier Julius Löwy in Block 8 Grave 181, Grenadier Moritz Möller in Block 8 Grave 169 and Grenadier Albert Schönwasser in Block 9 Grave 563.
39. The British Official History *France and Belgium 1916 Sir Douglas Haig's Command to the 1st July: Battle of the Somme* pp 224 – 225 ascribes this to the fact that General von Freytag-Loringhoven, at that time Deputy Chief of the General Staff at Supreme Headquarters under Falkenhayn, had been granted temporary leave of absence to gain command experience at the front and was commander of both IX Reserve Corps and 17th Reserve Division for the operation. The implication being that he had particular influence at Supreme Headquarters and was able to arrange for a disproportionate amount of artillery support. This explanation is improbable. Even a limited operation of this magnitude would have been cleared through Sixth Army to Supreme Headquarters and large quantities of resources would have been allocated to support it as a matter of course in order to ensure success. For example, a similar operation, code named *Strandfest,* was approved in July 1917 to reduce the Allied bridgehead east of the River Yser on the Belgian Coast. That operation, also involving a single division on a similar frontage and expected to be completed in under one hour, was allocated seventy three additional batteries of field guns, light and heavy howitzers. These were supplemented by further super-heavy weapons and three railway guns. The guns were supplied with 300,000 shells and the operation was originally due to have naval gunfire in support. See Sheldon *The German Army at Passchendaele* pp 34–39.
40. Two craters bore the name Transfeld. They are both close together on the western slopes of Hill 145 within the grounds of the Vimy Memorial. Because the German accounts speak of the loss of, 'the small Transfeld Crater', it is possible that this crater was actually the one known as Neuer Transfeld, which is still visible about thirty metres northwest of Broadmarsh (Schleswig Holstein) Crater.
41. Stosch: History Footguard Regiment 5 pp 248 – 250
42. It was during this battle with hand grenades that Lieutenant RBB Jones, 8th Battalion Loyal North Lancashire Regiment, was awarded the Victoria Cross for his inspirational gallantry in holding back the German advance until the supply of hand grenades ran out and he himself was shot through the head and killed instantly.
43. Stosch: History Footguard Regiment 5 pp 250–251
44. Unteroffiziers Gustav Fiß, Wilhelm Hardreack and Bernhard Heinig are buried in the German cemetery at Neuville St Vaast/Maison Blanche in Block 8 Grave 233, Block 9 Grave 666 and Block 8 Grave 227 respectively.
45. Kronprinz Rupprecht *Mein Kriegstagebuch Erster Band* pp 469–470
46. Kriegsarchiv München 1 Reserve Division Bd 45 NO AOK 6 B No. 4860 23.5.1916
47. Kriegsarchiv München 1 Reserve Division Bd 45 NOAOK 6 B No. 4870 25.5.1916

48. In a later report this officer's name is given as Howell, which seems more probable.
49. Kriegsarchiv München 1 Reserve Division Bd 45 NO AOK 6 B No. 4884 25.5.1916 It is interesting to note that all three officers were scathing in their criticism of the Wilson government and the President himself. Portman was quoted as saying that, 'Wilson as President and Head of State was the most laughable figure in history'. Both the American army and its fleet were described as, 'a joke' and there was more in a similar vein.
50. Kriegsarchiv München 1 Reserve Division Bd 45 NO AOK 6 B No. 4909 29.5.1916
51. Kriegsarchiv München 1 Reserve Division Bd 45 NO AOK 6 B No. 4892 26.5.1916
52. Kriegsarchiv München 1 Reserve Division Bd 45 NOAOK 6 B No. 4879 25.5.1916)
53. Gropp: *Hanseaten im Kampf* pp 123–125
54. Ersatzreservist Ludwig Wiencken is buried in the German cemetery at Lens-Sallaumines Block 7 Grave 410
55. Gropp: *Hanseaten im Kampf* pp 127–128
56. Immelmann, following pre-war service as a cadet, returned to the German army in 1914 and was trained as a pilot during the winter of 1914 – 1915. His early service was unspectacular, but the arrival in the German inventory of the Fokker *Eindekker*, which featured a revolutionary machine gun firing forward through the propeller (originally a French invention), provided him with the chance to become one of the first fighter aces of the war. By the end of 1915, with five kills to his credit, he was being referred to by the German press as *Der Adler von Lille* [The Eagle of Lille]. Awarded the Pour le Mérite on 12 January 1916, the same day as Oswald Boelcke, who was to die in a mid-air collision over Pozières in October 1916, Immelmann went on to score at least fifteen victories before his death. His name is famous in aviation circles because of the aerobatic 'Immelmann Turn', a roll off the top, which enables an aeroplane to reverse direction swiftly, albeit at the cost of reduced forward speed. In fact, it is believed that this manoeuvre has nothing to do with Immelmann. As practised by him, it apparently comprised a near – vertical diving attack, followed by a zooming climb to a wingover, which enabled him to attack his target in a fresh dive and so achieve surprise. The exact circumstances of his death in the dogfight with the FE–2bs of 25 Squadron RFC are unclear. Some sources blamed friendly anti-aircraft fire, but this is unlikely. The History of the Guards Reserve Infantry Regiment Nr. 64 (p 86) supports this theory, but states that his crash occurred as an isolated incident later that evening: 'Just before darkness fell, another Fokker arrived from Douai and cruised above our lines. We thought that it must be our Immelmann once again. Tensely, many men followed his every movement through telescopes. Everything was calm; now and then a shell was fired. Suddenly something terrible happened. The aircraft split in two; probably hit by a shell splinter. For a moment both sections hung in the air then they fell vertically to earth. The occupant was completely smashed up by the crash. He was recognised as Immelmann from his Pour le Mérite.' Despite this account, the probability is that he was either shot down by a British aircraft, or his forward-firing machine gun was not properly synchronised and he shot off his own propeller. Either way, his loss was keenly felt. Immelmann is buried in his home city of Dresden.
57. Karitzky: History Reserve Jäger Battalion 9 pp 54
58. History Fusilier Regiment 35 pp 173–174
59. History Fusilier Regiment 35 p 174
60. History Infantry Regiment 88 p 268

61. History Infantry Regiment 88 p 272
62. Poland: History Reserve Infantry Regiment 103 pp 72–74
63. Martin: History Grenadier Reserve Regiment 100 p 67
64. Klitzsch: History Reserve Infantry Regiment 101 p 72
65. Trümper-Bödemann: History Reserve Infantry Regiment 102 p 91
66. Baumgarten-Crusius: *Sachsen in Großer Zeit Band III* p 90
67. Klitzsch: History Reserve Infantry Regiment 101 p 74
68. Sub Sector *Fischer IV* subsequently became part of Sector *Zollern* when the boundaries were adjusted. *Staubwassergang* is more generally known as *Staubwasser Weg*.
69. Kriegsarchiv München Reserve Infantry Regiment 16 18.10.16
70. Somewhat confusingly, the name of this sector was altered from *Mecklenburg* to *Schwerin* in early 1917, presumably as part of the reorganisation of the front when additional reinforcements were placed in the front line
71. Großman: History Bavarian Reserve Infantry Regiment 17 p 66
72. Großman: History Bavarian Reserve Infantry Regiment 17 p 67
73. Braun: History Bavarian Reserve Infantry Regiment 21 p 61
74. Hasselbach: History Reserve Infantry Regiment 38 p 158
75. The expression, 'southeast of Souchez', generally refers to the area of The Pimple.
76. Kriegsarchiv München AOK 6 Bd 433: NO A.O.K. 6 B. Nr. 7400 30.11.16
77. Kriegsarchiv München AOK 6 Bd 433: NO A.O.K. 6 B. Nr. 7616 15.12.16
78. Kriegsarchiv München AOK 6 Bd 433: NO A.O.K. 6 B. Nr. 7757 24.12.16
79. In fact the 5th Canadian Division never saw active service in France. It was broken up later and its manpower used to reinforce 1st – 4th Canadian Divisions. A 6th Canadian Division was never formed at all.
80. Kronprinz Rupprecht *Mein Kriegstagebuch Zweiter Band* p 67
81. *Der Weltkrieg 1914–1918 Elfter Band* p 176
82. Kronprinz Rupprecht *Mein Kriegstagebuch Zweiter Band* p 69
83. Hasselbach: History Reserve Infantry Regiment 38 pp 159–160

Notre Dame de Lorette Before the War.

Vimy Colliery Winter 1914 – 1915 in use as a Command Post.

The Ruins of Notre Dame de Lorette March 1915.

Gun Position on the
Lorette Spur March 1915.

Captured French Trench Lorette Spur
3 March 1915 *(Lambrecht Collection)*.

Battlefield Cemetery Schlammulde
Lorette Spur.

Carency May 1915.

Forward Trench and Mined Dugout Labyrinth
Spring 1915.

French Aid Post in the Ruins of Notre Dame de
Lorette May 1915

French Prisoners captured 9 May 1915.

Souchez Centre Summer 1915.

Souchez and the Lower Slopes of the
Lorette Spur Summer 1915.

Street Scene Neuville St Vaast May 1915.

La Folie Chateau Summer 1915.

Trench Periscope in use
Neuville St Vaast May 1915.

A Pile of Dud Shells La Folie
September 1915.

Men of Infantry Regiment 62
Roclincourt September 1915.

Battalion Command Post Infantry
Regiment 51dug into the Railway
Embankment Vimy September 191⁵

Pumping out a Forward Trench near the
Fünf Wege Kreuz Winter 1915/1916.

Trudl Mine Crater Operation Rupprecht I
January 1916.

The Battle with the Mud Gießler Höhe
February 1916.

Trenches Captured during Operation Hamburg, Gießler Höhe March 1916.

British Dead hung up on the Barbed Wire May 1916.

60 metre Crater VIII at La
e prepared for Defence
1916.

Miners Entering a Gallery The Pimple
Spring 1916.

A Miner Dumping Spoil La Folie 1916.

A Fokker F III of the Type flown by Oberleutnar
Max Immelmann.

Oberleutnant Max Immelmann,
taken shortly before his death.

The Tangled Wreckage of Immelmann's Aircraf
Sallaumines 18 June 1916 *(Lambrecht Collection)*.

Ruined Church at Vimy Summer 1916.

admarsh Crater Summer 1916.

Aid Post Givenchy Autumn 191[...]

Aftermath of a British Mine La Folie Summer 1916.

...pers of the Bavarian Pionier Regiment operating a Lanz Mortar .

...nier Dohl near Fischerweg January 1917.
...binson Collection)

Pionier Frese leaves Broadmarsh Crater
January 1917. *(Robinson Collection)*

The Pimple and Gießler Höhe from Givenchy March 1917.

Leutnant Olaf Grieben Reserve Pionier Battalion 19 Hill 145 January 1917. *(Robinson Collection)*

Thélus Late March 1917.

us under Bombardment April 1917.

eavy Shell exploding in Vimy Village April 1917.

Hill 145 from the air March 1917. *(Lambrecht Collection)*

210 mm Howitzer Crew in Action Vimy April 1917.

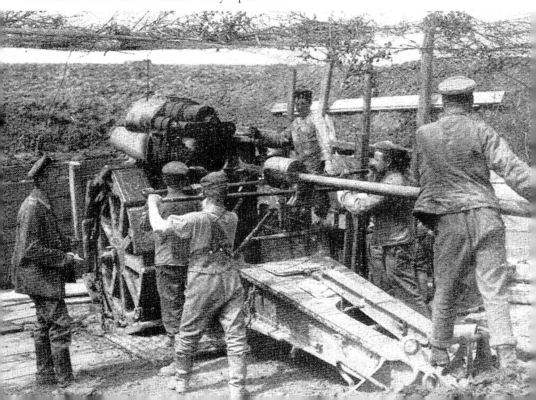

CHAPTER FIVE

Mining BeneathVimy Ridge

The early stalemate along the Western Front took both sides to the conflict by surprise. Suddenly their war of movement had become entirely static and they were ill-equipped, both in terms of doctrine and equipment, to deal with the new challenges of positional warfare. Sapping and mining had a long history in all European armies, but even so the need to attempt to break static defensive lines by mining beneath them and blowing them up with hidden explosives meant that old techniques had to be re-learned rapidly and under pressure on the battlefield. Much had to be improvised because, although, for example, mining was recognised as one of the responsibilities of the engineers in the Bavarian army, it was merely one of fourteen main tasks[1] and rarely practised. Not only that, but there were simply too few army engineers to cope with all the work thrust on them by trench warfare. The situation was the same for the Allies. On 23 January 1916, for example, of the seventy one prisoners from the French 23rd Division, XII Corps, captured after the German engineers had blown a large crater to the north of Roclincourt and the follow up attack had taken a section of French trench, six were from the French 6th Engineer Regiment. Their interrogation report confirmed information obtained during questioning of French engineers on 27 February and 30 November 1915.[2]

The men stated that their company had been created by drawing men from all the regiments of 23rd Division. They were mostly older men and consideration had been given to their civilian trades: apart from coal miners, who were very numerous in all armies in 1914, carpenters, builders and labourers were preferred. Other companies in the regiment were genuine engineers and although they carried out most of the mining work which required specialist skills, their expertise was also passed on to this *companie auxiliaire* [auxiliary company], as shown by the ability of the prisoners to describe their mining techniques and listening procedures in detail. Similar stories were told when men of the Royal Engineers began to fall into German hands, once the La Bassée – Arras sector had been taken over in early 1916. Men of 170 Mining Company Royal Engineers, captured near Hohenzollern Redoubt on 18 and 20 March 1916, informed their captors that they had received no special training and that they had been recruited directly out of the coal mines to fill up the ranks of the tunnelling companies.[3]

This was confirmed later that same year in May when men from 170, 176 and 180 Tunnelling Companies R.E. were captured, some near Vermelles[4] and others as a consequence of Operation *Schleswig Holstein* on Vimy Ridge, as described in Chapter 4.[5] From these interrogations came the information that although the miners had indeed arrived direct from the mines in the United Kingdom, they had spent between eight and fourteen days at Chatham where they had been clothed and equipped, taught to salute and to march and given a short home leave before taking up their tunnelling duties. For its part, the German army also improvised in much the same way. On 7 April 1916, for example, the Commander of I Bavarian Corps, General der Infanterie Ritter von Xylander, signed an order directing the formation of a 'Mining Company No. 3'.[6] A mere four days were allowed for the process, something made possible only due to the fact that the unit was to be formed entirely from within the resources of the Corps.

> "I Bavarian Corps is to establish a mining company. The company will be entitled 'Mining Company No. 3'.[7] It will be subordinated to 2nd Infantry Division . . . In order to fill out the ranks the following personnel are to be provided:
>
> "1st and 2nd Infantry Divisions are each to find: one Leutnant (to be a junior officer, commissioned after 7 January 1914); nine unteroffiziers; ten gefreiters and ninety one private soldiers. One of the gefreiters and one of the private soldiers must be a cyclist and, in addition, 1st Infantry Division is to produce one armourer and 2nd Infantry Division one feldwebel.
>
> "Commander Engineers is to furnish: one engineer officer as commander; two engineer officers or offizierstellvertreters as platoon commanders and the following engineer-trained non-commissioned ranks: one vizefeldwebel; three unteroffiziers; four gefreiters; sixteen sappers and one medical unteroffizier.
>
> "Commander Supply, Corps Senior Medical Officer and Corps Paymaster are to produce one supply officer and nine supply-trained other ranks, one medical officer and one pay clerk [respectively] . . .
>
> "Both officers and other ranks may be drawn from any arm or service, but only those who have already been involved in mine warfare and are sufficiently experience are to be put forward. Miners are preferred. The filling of the officer appointments is to be regarded as a temporary measure. They will be reported by Corps Headquarters to [Sixth] Army, with a request for confirmation . . . "

From first to last, therefore, the mining duties were carried out mainly by men who were miners in civilian life, but almost all of whom were novices at military mining and its peculiar demands. What follows is not an attempt at a comprehensive treatment of German mining under Vimy Ridge. That would take a book in itself. Instead, the aim is provide a flavour of a style of warfare which, although practised all along the Western Front wherever the conditions were suitable, was conducted with a rare intensity in this sector.

Already by early 1915 the entire Vimy front between Angres in the north and St Laurent Blangy in the south had been split between the various engineer and mining companies. The first mines were exploded on the Western Front in late 1914 and thereafter the pace of events picked up very swiftly. Bavarian

Reserve Engineer Company 1, profiting from the close proximity of the opposing lines in its sector to the south of Thélus, had already blown twenty mines by the end of March 1915. It followed this performance with a further twenty four in April alone. Three mines were blown on 7 and again on 17 April then, on 25 April, four were blown in one single day.[8] These were mostly shallow mine galleries, of no great length, but generally dug forward to a fork where two passages led forward to separate mine chambers. By 6 May 1915 the company was working simultaneously on twenty six galleries, with an average length of between twenty five and thirty metres.[9] It was an extraordinary rate of work in the chalk of the Vimy area. More galleries were added during May and, by the end of that month, there had been a further eleven mine blasts, some of them involving a large amount of explosives.[10]

Elsewhere at this time, in the northern part of the I Bavarian Reserve Corps sector, the men of 4th Company Engineer Battalion 19 were working actively or listening in twenty seven galleries and the men of 4th Company Engineer Regiment 2 were covering no fewer than forty three galleries.[11] At times the French were blowing craters from galleries eight to ten metres deep and fifteen to twenty metres in diameter, which indicated the use of significantly large charges, but other mines were much smaller, as was the case for the German engineers, who frequently resorted to charges of two hundred kilograms or less – especially in the case of counter-mining or when camouflets were used.[12] For a complete month from mid-May 1915 the spring battles for Vimy Ridge were in full swing, but it is apparent that the work of the miners continued almost uninterrupted, apart from cases where French advances overran the entrances to working galleries. Naturally the pressure of the fighting meant that mining had to compete with numerous other engineer tasks as far as the allocation of resources was concerned. Nevertheless, with reports from the listening stations that, in places, French miners had penetrated beneath German galleries, sub-units, such as 2nd Company Bavarian Engineer Regiment 19, subordinated to 1st Bavarian Reserve Division, were directed, on 17 May, by Commander Engineers at I Bavarian Reserve Corps, to give absolute priority to preparing the appropriate galleries for firing and to destroy the French works.[13]

By mid October 1915 the main autumn battles for Vimy Ridge had died down, but the intensity of mining, which continued unabated right through the summer, barely slackened. Tit-for-tat explosions occurred up and down the line, with a flurry of activity to the southwest of Thélus during the second half of the month. Reserve Leutnant Knorr, commander 2nd Company Bavarian Engineer Regiment, reported that, having just taken over the sector, he had discovered that the French were actively driving galleries forward and that they were very close to the German lines. Knorr immediately ordered the digging of a defensive gallery. This was driven at great speed. On 18 October twenty five sections of timbering were installed; on 19 October this had risen to thirty four at seven metres depth and the following day the figure placed had reached forty three. In a clear illustration of the risks of allowing the other side to steal an advantage underground, it was too little, too late. On 21 October the French blew two mines and followed up by forcing their way into the German front line trench. The attempted assault was, in fact, not as successful as it might have been. The 2nd Company war diary subsequently recorded:

> "Due to the dash of the mining team (Unteroffizier Schaller and Pioniers Jahreis, Keck and Krauser), together with the infantry, they were ejected and six prisoners were taken. Our mine was not damaged and was driven forward to the forty ninth set of supports. There was heavy mortar fire throughout the day. These included mortar bombs with five fins, weighing an estimated eighty kilograms." [14]

As a result of this French action, on 22 October Generalleutnant von Hartz, Commander of Bavarian 2nd Infantry Division, ordered that no fewer than twelve mine galleries were to be prepared to be blown. All other engineer work was to be suspended temporarily. Leutnant Knorr's men were split into three shifts, each working nine hour stints, to allow for handover, whilst maintaining the tempo of mining operations. Within two days the mines were prepared, but left at a high state of readiness. This was slightly unfortunate, because the French engineers blew three mines along the Arras – Lille road on 26 October which wrecked three of the German galleries. In the ensuing battle German troops occupied two of the craters and the French the third.

Unteroffizier Geiger 2nd Company Bavarian Pionier Regiment [15]

"I was in charge of Mining Teams 1 and 2, which were working in Galleries 1 and 2, which led off from the *Offizier-Sappe* [Officers' Sap]. Gallery 1 was being worked by Pioniers Johannes Stumpf, Eichhorn and Benker. I was in Gallery 2, together with Pioniers Dietz, Dippel and Fischer. At approximately 4.10 pm I heard a loud explosion, which buried the entrance to Gallery 2. I immediately began shifting the masses of earth blocking the entrance and attempted to open an air hole. The work was very strenuous and I, like the other two [*sic.*] engineers, was close to suffocation before we finally succeeded in piercing a way through the plug of earth. Two hours had flown by since the explosions. I got the others to enlarge the hole carefully then listened to see if anyone was nearby. I could hear French being spoken and, as I inched my way up higher, I could see six Frenchmen in front of me. I could also hear shells landing very close by.

"Because all our weapons were buried, I decided to wait until it was completely dark. In the meantime I had the hole enlarged so that we could crawl out. I observed the Frenchmen and when I saw four of them go over to a wounded man to attend to him, I said to the three engineers, 'I'll leap across and overpower the two Frenchmen. You follow me. We want to get back to our own lines at all costs.'

"I crawled out, knocked the two French men to the ground and successfully made it to the next shell hole. Behind me I could hear shouts of *Allemands!* [Germans!]. Because the three engineers did not come, I assume that the four Frenchmen had come rushing up and had over-powered them. There were French corpses in my shell hole. Once everything quietened down I crawled up to the edge of the crater then raced for our lines, which I reached safely. Pioniers Stumpf, Eichhorn[16] and Benker in Gallery 1 were probably dead, because the French crater was only two metres from the gallery. Certainly I could see no sign of this gallery."

This minor incident had cost the engineers three killed and three missing. The following day work continued on ten galleries then, on 29 October, two more galleries were charged, with 860 and 600 kilograms of explosive respectively. That evening ten NCOs and 139 infantrymen arrived to act as labourers. On 30 October the two galleries were blown. The firing circuit failed in one case, but it was believed at the time that a nearby French gallery had been crushed by the explosion of the second mine. On this occasion neither side occupied the resulting crater and, as the month ended, the injection of infantry manpower enabled work to go ahead in no fewer than seventeen galleries.

If October had seen frantic activity on this small sector of the front, the pace of events in November, far from slackening, increased further. Its entire fighting strength – four officers and 242 other ranks – moved onto a punishing routine of twelve hour shifts, working actively on seventeen galleries. There was a terrify-ing incident on 2 November.

Reserve Leutnant Knorr 2nd Company Bavarian Pionier Regiment [17]

"At 11.00 am the enemy broke through into Gallery 12. Surprised, they raced back to the entrance of their tunnel and brought down rifle fire along it. At that, we enlarged the opening and occupied it with two sentries until we had placed a charge. Meanwhile it appeared that the enemy had tried to blow some sort of charge, because the sentries felt a sharp increase in air pressure, accompanied by a flash, which knocked them down. They were dragged unconscious out of the gallery. A combi-nation of this incident and an infantry relief in the line delayed the charging of the gallery until the following day."

Despite this narrow escape, this gallery, which had been completed in only nine days, was loaded with any explosive which was to hand. As an indication of the pressure under which the mining and counter-mining was being conducted, the charge when finally placed and tamped, comprised two hundred kilograms of safety explosive, together with two boxes of standard army explosive and an earth mortar bomb, which were set off with a time fuze. Improvised or not, the charge had the desired effect and, as soon as the fumes cleared, a branching gallery –

12a – was begun. On 4 November the firing circuit in the gallery which had failed to work on 30 October was repaired and a French tunnel, having been detected extremely close to one point of this 'Gallery 6', was wrecked by the camouflet effect of the 600 kilogram charge which exploded correctly at the second attempt.

The following day a further French tunnel was detected about to break into Gallery 4a; the German miners placed an earth mortar bomb against the wall and blew it, bringing enemy mining to a temporary standstill. In retaliation, a French camouflet went off on 9 November, causing minor damage to Gallery 4a and, on 10 November, a further French mine was fired, but to no effect. On 14 November Bavarian Infantry Regiment 3 launched a raid in an attempt to capture the entrances to some of the French galleries. This was unsuccessful, but instead attracted a deluge of French heavy mortar fire on 15 November which wrecked Galleries 13b and 13c. Work immediately began on two additional galleries. By 19 November the opposing teams of miners had worked to within two metres of one another near the French lines. With both sides aware of each other, work was suspended and an uneasy truce prevailed. With a start being made on 24 November on yet more galleries, the company was now working no fewer than twenty simultaneously. The sector was the most active on the Vimy front at the time. It was felt to be too great a responsibility for the relatively inexperienced Knorr (whose heroics during these difficult days was fully recognised by the regimental commander) and Hauptmann Düll, a highly experienced mining engineer from 52nd Infantry Division, arrived to take over.

In fact Knorr handed over a favourable underground tactical situation to Düll. The latter carried out a detailed examination of all the possibilities and decided to launch an attack from Offensive Mine *Dora*[18], which was intended to wreck French attempts to sap around the 30 October and 4 November craters. This gallery was thirty six metres long and had been driven at a depth of eight metres. For speed the French troops had been pushing forward a shallow sap very rapidly. The noise of digging could be clearly heard overhead, so Düll took the decision to charge *Dora* as swiftly, but as silently, as possible. With the utmost care, 820 kilograms was placed in position and all was set for a coordinated attack on 27 November.

Hauptmann Düll 2nd Company Bavarian Pionier Regiment [19]

"Following agreement with Bavarian Infantry Regiment 3, the intention was to blow Gallery *Dora*, with the aim of destroying the French branching sap which was heading for the craters from 30 October and 4 November just beyond the point where it forked, to capture the entire sap and to wreck any mine galleries leading off from it. The aim was achieved completely. When the mine exploded eight French soldiers were catapulted into the air and the moans of the wounded could be heard coming from the crater. Both wounded and unwounded French soldiers made their way into our position. So far eleven prisoners have been taken.

"The branching sap is in our possession and has been turned around against the enemy. It is currently not possible to say if any galleries lead off from it, because the greater part of the sap was buried by the debris from the explosion. During the assault on the French sap and the subsequent battle with hand grenades, the following members of the company distinguished themselves: Offizerstellvertreter Heil, Unteroffizier Oberhofer, Pioniers Spindler and Mederer. Engineer casualties were: Offizerstellvertreter Heil, severely wounded in the neck, Unteroffizier Oberhofer slight wound to one arm and Pionier Bachmann slightly wounded by grenade fragments."

A special Bavarian 2nd Infantry Division Order of the Day was signed by Generalleutnant von Hartz on 28 November:

"At 4.00 pm on 27 November a French branching sap and, with it, an extremely unpleasant mine system, located on the right flank of Bavarian Infantry Regiment 3, was destroyed by an explosion. Following the explosion men of 9th and 12th Companies Infantry Regiment 162, together with some engineers from 2nd Company Bavarian Engineer Regiment, launched an attack in broad daylight against French troops holding the western edges of two craters located to the south of the new crater. They threw the French back, occupied the trench and have established a link with the eastern edge of the new crater.

"I am extremely pleased about this daring operation and wish to express my fullest recognition of all participants, especially the miners and their infantry support teams."[20]

Over a five week period, therefore, 2nd Company Bavarian Engineer Regiment had reacted decisively to the work of the French miners, who had had a useful start. A counter-mine system had swiftly been improvised and between 20 October and 30 November twenty mine galleries, one of them forty six metres long, had been driven forward. Four French explosions meant that slight damage had been caused to the German network at one point, but the German miners had carried out four successful explosions in response. It was no mean achievement.

In one of the clearest indications of the pace of events underground and the importance attached by both sides to offensive and defensive mining, on 8 October 1915, one year after the arrival of the German army on Vimy Ridge, the General der Pioniere [Commander Engineers] at Sixth Army tasked his engineer commanders at each corps headquarters to produce a paper listing the main lessons learned from months of intensive mine warfare. The chief engineer at I Bavarian Corps passed on the tasking to his divisions, then compiled a comprehensive report, which was forwarded to Army Headquarters on 24 October 1915.

Experiences in Mine Warfare [21]

Within the I Bavarian Corps sector the following technical experience has been gained:

1. Entrance to the Mine Gallery.

It has proved to be advantageous, always to construct a chamber at the entrance to the gallery. This chamber has to provide protection against artillery engagements and space for tools, equipment, sandbags, rescue equipment and prepared charges, as well as the teams responsible for the removal of spoil. It has often proved to be best to drive forward from an already existing mined dugout with two to three metres of overhead cover. This brings with it the additional advantage that the entrance of the actual mine gallery can be located four to five metres deeper than would otherwise be the case. However, even when no suitable dugout is available, it is advisable, unless haste is of the utmost importance, to begin by digging steps downwards from a trench, as though for the construction of a mined dugout. This provides the necessary overhead protection from artillery fire and the chamber may be dug retrospectively as work progresses on the gallery. It is, in fact, best not to locate the chamber off the battle trench but instead, if time is short, to dig a blind sap[22] *forward* and start work there. If plenty of time is available, it is recommended to place the chamber in a trench *behind* the firing line.

Both methods mean that the removal of spoil does not interfere with normal traffic in the battle trench. The entrance forward of the front line has the advantage that time is saved mining but, because of its obvious location, it tends to attract more mortar and artillery fire. Placement of the entrance in a mined dugout means, naturally, that the best way to proceed is to dig an inclined gallery. This, however, has disadvantages. Depth is gained only gradually and the removal of spoil is rendered more difficult. Gaining depth by means of shafts, apart from the fact that forward progress is slowed, has the particular disadvantage that ventilation of the mine after an explosion has occurred in the gallery occurs significantly more slowly. The use of shafts is only advisable if enemy miners have already been detected in the vicinity and it is essential to dig rapidly beneath the enemy gallery.

2. Depth of the Mined Galleries.

The normal depth at which galleries should be driven forward has been shown to be twelve to fifteen metres. In general the depth of the galleries has been dictated by the prevailing conditions of water and the going. When mine warfare is continued over a prolonged period, there is a mutual tendency to strive to go as deep into the rock as possible. Recently depths of twenty to twenty five metres have been the rule.

3. Casing

When galleries are being driven forward, only the larger casings have proved themselves (0.80 x 1.20 metres). Timbering of smaller dimensions makes work difficult after only a short period of time. The air gets so bad that progress becomes very slow. In the clay and chalk conditions, such as those which obtain in the I Bavarian Corps sector, it has proved possible in many places to work without timbering at all. Here the use of the French gallery profile is especially recommended. Although the amount of spoil to be removed is very similar to that generated by the use of our larger casings, the work is significantly easier, because the miner can work whilst standing upright. Because the working conditions are more comfortable and removal of spoil is simpler, it is possible to push the gallery forward rapidly. The French gallery design is used throughout the Corps area . . .

4. Driving Galleries

Thus far, in places where the enemy trenches were within one hundred metres of our positions and if we intended either to blow them up or to prevent an enemy mining attack, we have driven galleries directly towards the enemy positions. In these instances, it has proved necessary to drive forward simultaneously several mine galleries, whose separation is dependent on the geological conditions, so as to be able to counter an enemy mining attack. The driving of a *single* gallery, provided that it contains branch tunnels, has certainly proved itself whenever it has been necessary to blow up the enemy positions in one particular place, but the method is disadvantageous if countering an enemy mine attack becomes necessary. The best defence against offensive mining is to dig a cross gallery, linking the individual drives. The disadvantage of this cross gallery is that it requires a great deal of work and so interferes with the best defence against enemy mining; namely to attack first . . .

It is also disadvantageous to drive a gallery towards the enemy position at right angles, because after the enemy fire trench is blown up, the enemy artillery immediately engages that part of our trenches directly opposite the explosion and so brings down fire on the equipment chamber. On the basis of this experience and examination of enemy mine galleries which have been discovered, it is recommended to drive the galleries towards the enemy position at a more acute angle. This method has the advantage that it provides inherent protection, without the great amount of work which the creation of a lateral gallery demands. The advantage of improved ventilation can be achieved through the crossing of the galleries; furthermore these angled galleries permit offensive mining at any time against any point of the enemy lines.

5. Ventilation

The old manual rotary blowers have proved to be unusable. The noise immediately attracts artillery fire. The noise is not only clearly audible on the position, it is also carried forward along the ventilation pipes and can be heard loudly at the head of the gallery. Good, however, are the new silent, belt-driven rotary pumps, as are the box pumps, but they cannot be used over long distances. The electrical suction pump has proved to be best of all. The extractors are very effective, but are dependent on the availability of good safety cables and a secure place for the generator. The installation of the ventilation pipes must be synchronised with the driving of the gallery. They must also fit together tightly. If not, excessive noise is created by the hissing of the air, too much of which escapes. The ventilation pipes must be bent away from the mine entrance otherwise the bad, exhausted, air is re-circulated. Cross galleries improve the ventilation considerably. If the same team of diggers is left in one position for an extended period this work tends to become possible. One [mining] company has trialled ventilation by means of drilling air holes five to ten centimetres in diameter up to the surface. These have proved to be very good, but may only be produced if the depth of the workings is not too deep (approximately six metres). If a lightweight drilling rig was available this would ease the process. These boreholes may not be placed at the face. Instead they must be located at least ten metres to the rear and be directed to the rear. At night, if work is to continue, they must be blocked up firmly, in order to prevent the escape of noise or the slightest glimmer of light. If ventilation is needed, then work must be suspended during that time.

6. *Lighting*

Naked acetylene lights may not be used, because they turn the air bad so quickly that it is impossible to remain in the gallery. Bicycle lamps are good, but lots of jets must be available, because they have to be cleaned or exchanged regularly. 'Beagid' safety lamps are good, but large amounts of special fuel has to be available for them. Candles will only burn in short galleries. In galleries longer than seventy metres candles either give only very poor light or are ruled out completely. Electric torches are excellent. However, lots of batteries are needed, each of which last about two hours. Even better would be larger electric lamps with lead acid or larger dry batteries carried in a separate battery pouch. Electric light produced by generators is best of all. Its main advantage is the fact that electric lights, when lit, do not deplete the oxygen, which is of the utmost important for the teams working in the galleries. During the loading of mines only pocket torches are suitable for use.

7. *Tools*

[Standard] mining tools have proved to be satisfactory, but the miners' truck cannot be used. The best method is to extract spoil in sandbags, or on two-man carrying frames, such as the French use. Drill lengths need to be restricted to between fifty centimetres and one metre in length, in order that they may employed in all directions in the galleries. Wooden shafts of hammers must not exceed eighty centimetres in length.

8. *Silent Working*

Above all, silent working requires changes in the footwear worn by the teams working in the gallery. Shoes made of straw or felt have proved to be effective and the same applies to the use of gym shoes or oversocks on boots. In an emergency, it is sufficient to wrap sandbags around the boots. Straw has to be laid along the floor of the gallery. This in turn has to be covered with a fine layer of earth to prevent the straw from rustling. In clay the face must be worked with a pointed tool and picks should not be used. If supporting timbers are used, there must be no hammering. The miners soon learn how to press the timbers and wedges silently into place. In limestone or chalk, sound is transmitted further than in clay or loam. In limestone every sound may be detected at a distance of twenty five to thirty metres. In clay it is possible for galleries to approach to within five to six metres of each other undetected.

9. Listening

It is best to listen with the unaided ear to the sounds of enemy mining. In that way, experienced personnel can judge how close the enemy miners are working. Listening using microphones is intended to establish if working is taking place and, if so, where. Their use is most appropriate in mine systems which are not being worked and are serving a purely defensive purpose. From the listening post, double cables of exactly the same length must be run forward to the microphones. If a listening pause is ordered then the engineer duty officer must ensure that all work, including that of the infantry in their dugouts, ceases within a two hundred metre radius. Specially experienced miners must be trained for listening duty because, with much practice, they will be able to establish the distance to enemy miners with fair accuracy.

10. Dispersal Trenches

In order to disperse the spoil which has to be removed from the galleries and if there are not suitable places such as disused dugouts or gravel pits on hand, trenches and saps need to be dug to the rear, so that they can be filled up gradually. Obvious heaps and, in particular, the raising of parapets, may not occur under any circumstances.

11. Rescue Equipment

The smoke-proof equipment is too clumsy for use in timbered galleries. The individual is encumbered and the length of the hose is too short. The oxygen equipment has proved to be useful, but can only be used by trained personnel. Teams of rescue engineers must always be available and may not be used for any other duty. The miniature Dräger escape equipment is a handy size and has proved itself excellent for rescue purposes. For use in mines it would be helpful if it came with a safety helmet instead of the simple nose clip. Training on the use of the equipment must be continuous and the sets must be carefully and frequently checked.

12. Charging

The use of powder[23] for explosions has the advantage that the effect is more extensive, but carries with it the disadvantage that charging takes longer. The copper powder containers are very heavy and difficult to transport along timbered galleries. Reloading the powder into sandbags takes a long time and increases the risks during charging. In addition the use of powder leads to such deterioration in air quality that men have been rendered unconscious by it. Furthermore, after an explosion using powder the gases take noticeably longer to clear from the gallery. Safety explosive have much higher detonation velocities, so their effect is not so extensive as is the case with the use of powder. On the other hand loading and tamping is much simpler.

In order to increase the likelihood of successful initiation, two separate electrical circuits are laid, in order that the failure of one may be replaced immediately by the other. In order to avoid mistakes, one circuit is simply laid through the tamping and only connected if the other one should fail. It is a principle that a single detonator may never be used. Firing circuits which are expected to be laid and kept in position for long periods are best protected in metal tubes against the risk of being cut by artillery fire.

13. Safety of the Working Miners

In order to provide the miners with personal protection in the event of them being surprised they must be equipped with pistols. In order not to hinder their work, these must be secured with a short leather strap. In case a mine has to be fired in an emergency and a message has to be passed rapidly to miners working at the end of what are frequently long galleries, to withdraw to a safe area, the installation of alarm bells is recommended.

14. General

Most mine warfare takes place where the positions are within one hundred metres of each other. The aim is either to destroy the enemy positions through mine explosions, or to thwart the offensive mining of the enemy. In extended positions it is generally the case that the only possible way of forcing the enemy miners to concentrate their entire efforts against us and so prevent them from launching attacks on other parts of our line, is to mine ceaselessly beneath places in the line which jut out forwards. If our galleries are laid out defensively, increased security can be achieved, because the enemy cannot close up on our positions without coming up against one of our galleries. However these local security measures must not be allowed to inhibit our will to attack and such measures should only be taken where no offensive mining is planned.

If enemy miners make their presence felt, then all means must be employed to drive the enemy miners away from us. For example, the enemy must be forced by our offensive mines to blow his prematurely. If, on the other hand, the enemy miners manage to pass unhindered through the defensive mine system towards our position there is a danger that our engineers will be pressed back against our lines, from where the risk of the explosion of camouflets will make our advance from our defensive mine system extremely difficult. Along the remaining, less threatened parts of our front, listening posts must be pushed right forward to improve security. These areas must also be developed into a network of mines as soon as manpower is available, in order to provide the basis for a renewal of offensive mining at these points . . .

So much for the practicalities distilled over many months from hard experience. One of the young engineer officers employed under Vimy Ridge left a somewhat more vivid account of the way he and his fellow engineers learned these same lessons in practice.

Reserve Leutnant Otto Riebieke 2nd Company Engineer Regiment 28 [24]

"War underground is numbered amongst the most terrible types of fighting which occurred during the World War. There are few who can really imagine what took place in the bowels of the earth when the Army communiqué contained the terse words, 'We have blown a mine'. It was in fact the most monstrous style of warfare imaginable and was conducted by a few men in narrow, airless galleries filled with chalk or clay dust who, at the cost of endless demands on their nerves, gave it all their strength and energy. This was the domain of the sappers; men of steel, both physically and mentally. It was utterly different from the experience of those who confronted the enemy under starry skies or in broad daylight. In the war underground there was no light, no fresh air and no visibility. But the enemy was close, often so very close that he could be heard speaking or even priming his charges, which he might blow at any moment . . . or even in a couple of seconds.

"But he cannot be allowed to, he shall not! So, during every moment of grace, during every single, terrible minute when he might be blown sky high the engineer worked and grafted to get his blow in first. In a mined dug out deep beneath Vimy Ridge I once saw a rough sketch, carved swiftly in the chalk. It was of a dark mine, out of whose cracks and crevices, death in all its forms grinned grimly, but within which a miner worked away calmly. His lined face betrayed his recognition of the constant danger, but his haughty look told of his disdain. The heading where his pick was at work bore the word, 'Regardless'. That was the mettle of the miners who were engaged hour after hour in a battle against men and explosives deep down and far from daylight.

"It was necessary to be well informed to know where the engineers were conducting their war. Nothing special betrayed the way into their underground galleries. They just looked like the entrances to normal mined dug outs. The huge quantities of spoil, the white chalk, or the yellow clay, which were removed from the earth at night, were carefully buried in shell craters and thus put out of sight. Barely a light coloured stone or heap of spoil remained which could not be explained away. The miners closed on the enemy armed with picks, spades, chisels and drilling machines. The spoil was carted away in sandbags or miners trucks and day and night the mines swallowed props and casing timber which had to be brought forward from far to the rear. The entrance to the underground labyrinth opened out from one or other of the forward trenches into a steeply descending gallery or shaft. There, deeper than a house, was the workplace of the sappers, who climbed in and out using ladders.

"They had been working for weeks on this particular shaft. Shifts went on day and night, their picks sinking into the tough clay or striking the hard masses of stone . . . .and then the time came to drive towards the enemy. How far away were they? The question remained unspoken. Tak, tak, went the short-shafted picks as they slowly drove their horizontal gallery towards the enemy. The air became sticky and low on oxygen. The miners' lamps would barely stay alight and their lungs could hardly breathe. 'The air pump must be installed!' reported the corporal in charge of the shift. A technical team installed it in chamber by the entrance, whilst others fitted up a generator to provide electric light. It was a quiet machine, whose humming was nevertheless silenced, because enemy miners were at work too.

"Great masses of stone resisted the picks. They were removed using liquid air. A layer of granite barred the way, but it was overcome with electrically powered drills. Water flooded into the workings. Pumps were installed and the work continued. The heat underground became insufferable. The miners took their jackets off and soon they stood bare-chested like the journeymen of Vulcan in the depths of this dreadful battle. The air became thinner and thinner; the length of the galleries was too great for the air pumps. Oxygen cylinders were installed . . . and the work continued. The miners worked ceaselessly. Only during 'Listening Watches' did they lay their tools aside and eavesdrop, lying stretched out on the ground to try to determine where the others, those from over the other side, the enemy, were. Had they themselves been spotted? It was possible, but they certainly would not be allowed to gain an advantage on us. The most sensitive types of listening apparatus revealed where the enemy was lurking. They were beneath us. Right then, we had to go lower and, once again, we sank a shaft deeper into the bowels of the earth. Deeper and still deeper went the work of the miners and once more we drove our gallery in the direction of the enemy.

"But what was that? The enemy had stopped hammering! Just now and again they knocked on the stony wall. They were trying to trick us! Between the hammer blows, the scraping and scratching, could be heard the sound of muffled footfalls, grinding and tapping. They were installing a charge; they were trying to blow us up! Where could his gallery be? There: two or three metres to the right of us and a little higher. The heads of the galleries had been driven perhaps ten to fifteen metres past one another. 'This is where he is going to blow!' whispered the engineer officer, who crept around quietly and applied his listening device to the wall. A red marker was stuck in the wall. That was the point. That was where he was piling his explosives. Still? Yes! He had only just begun. The characteristic noise of the placing of the lowest level of explosives could be heard.

"Action! The sappers wrapped rags around their nailed boots and laid straw mats on the floor of the gallery. Hammering continued at the face. The enemy could not be allowed to discover that we knew about the charging of his gallery. He had to believe that our work was continuing. In the meantime, we set about charging as well. The explosives were passed forward from hand to hand through the long gallery. The infantry lent a hand; they knew what was at stake. Forward the packages piled up. How far had the enemy progressed? The officer listened repeatedly. He was stacking more slowly. Silently the shadows of the miners stood out on the phosphorescent walls, as they passed the explosives from hand to hand. *Zentner* [fifty kilograms] by *Zentner* the charge was built up. They cared nothing for their own lives. It was the enemy that they were after and to achieve that no words were needed, just actions.

"The air pumps hissed as they pushed out air at the highest pressure possible. At the head of the gallery, the miners hammered away at the wall to deceive the enemy. That was the only sound that could be heard in the gallery, despite the frantic work. The engineer officer tipped off his sergeant. 'They are quiet' – a hundred thoughts raced through their heads. What were they up to? Were they ready? Were they going to blow – right then? Then, taking all of us and our explosives with them? Their faces were serious, motionless. They urged the miners on. They were engaged in a life and death race. Faster and faster they flung the packages of explosive forward. Had the enemy drum fire begun? That would be a sign that their explosion was imminent. From outside, came the reply. 'No!' From forward came the report that the charge was complete. Detonators were inserted into the explosives and the firing cable was rolled out along the gallery to the firing point in a nearby dug out.

"Tamp it!' Filled sand bags were passed forward. Hundreds of them were piled up around the explosives. At the work face, the miners continued to hammer away at the wall in a deceptive rhythm. The engineer officer nodded. Everything fell silent. The whirring motors were switched off. During these seconds, even the beating of hearts could be heard. The sergeant crouched next to the engineer officer who was lying on the floor. 'What is happening?' – 'They are working!' They were working once more! The whisper passed the length of the gallery, the motors started up again. Hammering on the wall continued and the work went on. Metre by metre the tamping was built up. 'Clear out!' One by one the men emerged from the entrance to the mine and disappeared into the night. The officer tested the firing circuit: 'Everything is in order!' Neighbouring dug outs were warned. The infantry pulled back.

"Outside dawn was breaking. The first of the larks awoke and rose up into the sky from the coarse grass. Suddenly the ground heaved. A dull thud rolled across the morning landscape . . . deep below the earth the miners had won a victory! The enemy were crushed, the gallery they had charged to attack us was destroyed. But these camouflets were not the objective of mine warfare. Those were just the battle between outposts; defensive fights in the great underground struggle. Branching repeatedly, the galleries were driven forward against the enemy. They sought to get beneath their lines and to blow up their main strong points. The enemy attempted the same thing and often both sides spent months pushing out networks of galleries just to defend the positions of their own infantry. At various depths and in widely differing geological layers these defensive galleries probed forward, acting as feelers for the main body of the army and detecting the enemy galleries in order to destroy them in time.

"Hand to hand battles also occurred. This dreadful fighting took place far from daylight when suddenly the thin walls which separated the opposing galleries were broken through. Then there would be a bursting of hand grenades and explosive charges which snuffed out the light and there, in the dark, far below the infantry trenches, men fought one another hand to hand with daggers, pistols and coshes in the most appalling battles on earth. Some of the heroic deeds of the miners were well known. Sometimes the enemy got the upper hand and they blew themselves and their tunnels up in order to avoid the risk of the enemy gaining access to the rear of their infantry. Tragedies of which we shall never know anything were played out also in the deep recesses of the earth. So beneath the earth an extraordinary burrowing warfare developed. A more unnatural and nerve-wracking style of war fighting can barely be imagined. But this was no mere mechanical struggle, instead it demanded mental commitment if it was to enjoy defensive victories and moreover if offensive operations were to be conducted successfully. The way from starting chamber to the enemy position demanded the sacrificial commitment of men, materiel and effort. Frequently the intended objective could not be achieved, or only if the purpose was modified totally.

"At long last the work and struggle by day and night, after months of labour and despite all counter efforts would be successful and the mine had penetrated beneath the enemy position. The sappers sat forty, fifty or even seventy metres beneath the enemy. Then it was a matter of bringing in sufficient explosives to ensure that the huge weight of earth above would be thrown up in one blast. To achieve this it was necessary to bring forward thousands of kilograms of explosives in their individual packages the entire length of the gallery, which might be two hundred metres long. This could

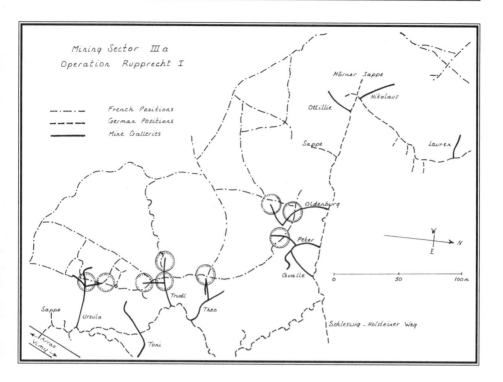

be the work of many days, because the gallery had to be blocked back a long way in order to ensure that the explosion was properly tamped. Then the big moment would arrive. In the dug outs, the assault troops primed their hand grenades. Machine guns were brought up from below. Howitzers, like grotesque giraffes, stared up at the rising moon. The black muzzles of the batteries lay in wait to bring fire down on the enemy positions. Officers manned all the observation equipment. Telephonists listened intently and battlefield runners stood by.

"The hands of the clock moved to the appointed second. The engineer officer twisted the small switch of his firing device and, with a thunderous crash, which vibrated throughout the positions, enormous quantities of earth and rocks were projected skywards. The air was filled with the roar from a hundred guns, from machine guns and mortars, from a thousand rifles and hand grenades. Then at the same instant, through the dust which darkened the sky, through the smoke and gases of the explosion, the assault force raced forward to occupy the steaming hot forward edge of the crater.

'We blew a mine', the Army communiqué would state briefly."

As has been mentioned in the previous chapter, January 1916 saw the start of the series of 'Rupprecht' limited scope attacks, each of which was more or less successful. What was not stressed, however, was the extent to which their effective execution depended on the contribution of the engineers and miners. Already outlined are the emergency measures and counter-mining activities of 2nd Company Bavarian Pionier Regiment in the improvised 'minefield' to the southwest of Thélus. December was a relatively quiet time on this particular sector, but the work previously achieved and the number of galleries driven forward by the company had the potential to be incorporated into future offensive operations. So it was that when the planners of 2nd Bavarian Infantry Division were drawing up a selection of possible locations for 'Rupprecht I', it was decided to exploit the potential of the newly created minefield and to launch the attack near to Thélus. 2nd Field Engineer Company of I Bavarian Corps took over the sector at the beginning of January and their war diary indicates how efficiently and swiftly the miners could operate when they had the initiative.[25]

"The Company assumed responsibility for the minefield in Sector IIIa on 5 January 1916. Its initial intention was to ignore the existing galleries, which had been dug at five to six metres depth and, instead, to create five deep galleries, beginning at the entrances to Galleries Dora, Irma, Lina, Oldenburg and Tom and driving them forward offensively against the enemy positions. Initial work (creation of gallery entrances of high profile, with fifteen steps and equipment chambers measuring 2 x 2 x 1.8 metres) was almost finished when, on 9 January 1916, orders arrived stating that the galleries in the left half of Sector IIIa were to be used in an operation against the so-called *Halbmondstellung* [Half Moon Position] and were to be ready for blowing by the end of January. On 11 January the date for readiness was moved to 20 January.

"Following comprehensive examination and survey of our own position and the galleries in question, which had been prepared by 2nd Company [Bavarian] Engineer Regiment, it transpired that Galleries *Oldenburg, Peter, Theo, Trudl* and *Ursula* could be used to achieve the intended aim. To place the mine chambers directly beneath the critical points of the enemy positions would, however, require the digging of a total of ninety metres of branching galleries and the working of five new headings. By forcing the pace, the galleries had been lengthened sufficiently by 17 January.[26] Thanks to energetic work by the officers responsible for the mine field and the exemplary cooperation of all the other ranks involved, charging with a total of approximately 120 *Zentner* [120 x 50 kilograms = six tonnes] of high explosives and subsequent tamping was achieved so swiftly that, by 20 January, all the mines were ready to be blown.

"During the day prior to the operation it was established by the team checking the firing circuits that that in Gallery *Ursula* was defective. On receipt of this information, the duty engineer officer, Leutnant Meyer, immediately set all available manpower to work in an attempt to rectify the problem. Having removed all of its tamping and the forward charge itself, it transpired that the cabling in both the left hand branch and the one leading to the mine straight ahead lacked continuity. Because there was insufficient time to replace and re-tamp these two mines, they were abandoned and only the mines in the right hand branch and at the junction of the branches were retained.

"It is possible that the explanation for the sudden fault may lie in the fact that when the heavy howitzers were ranging in during the morning of 22 January the shock of a shell landing nearby crushed the cables. We are convinced that it was not caused by the enemy either removing the charge or cutting the cables because French prisoners captured later during the attack stated that despite the high speed [and inevitably noisy] construction of the mine galleries and the extensive operation to charge and tamp the mines, none of these preparations was noticed by the enemy: despite the fact that the mines had been laid directly beneath the enemy trenches and that we could hear the enemy moving about and working in the trench above our heads. The firing circuits for *Oldenburg* and *Peter* were combined, as were those for *Trudl* and *Theo,* but that for *Ursula* was separate. The charges were blown from three different positions, with one exploder used in each location."

The company commander and his platoon commanders later summarised the day of the attack from the engineer perspective as follows:

Hauptmann Bracker 2nd Field Engineer Company [27]

"The company provided three parties [for the operation]:
1. To accompany the assault force: two officers (Leutnant Müller and Reserve Leutnant Albert), six unteroffiziers and 42 sappers.
2. To blow the mines: one officer (Reserve Leutnant Meyer), four unteroffiziers and two sappers.
3. To operate the earth mortars: one unteroffizier and twelve sappers. Command of the earth mortars was undertaken by the officer in charge of initiating the mines.[28]

"The assaulting sappers were directed towards the tips of the saps which were to be captured. Reserve Leutnant Albert commanded the sappers in the area of 10th Company and Leutnant Müller those in the 11th Company sector. The effect of our explosions was such that, unfortunately, a large number (sixteen) of the sappers who were due to take part in the assault were eliminated, injured, at the outset. With the exception of one man, killed by a blow, the injuries were generally slight: crushing, bruising and sprains. Ignoring the violent effect of the mines, which must have been due to the shallowness of the mine chambers, the remaining sappers hurled themselves forward courageously behind their officers in order to fulfil their tasks. Together with the infantry they succeeded in seizing and holding the places to which they had been directed.

"This led in turn to sharp battles with hand grenades, during which Leutnant Müller distinguished himself, beating off two French grenade attacks, which were directed against the barricaded *Richard* Sap. Reserve Leutnant Albert, who advanced along the sap on the extreme right of the attack frontage, was wounded in the shoulder, hand, thigh and lower leg by an enemy hand grenade. As a result, at 8.15 am, he was forced to withdraw, but not until he had given the necessary orders for the blocking of the captured saps and supply of trench stores. His task had proven to be particularly difficult because the trench layout in his sector was in many ways different from what had been established during the reconnaissance. Reserve Leutnant Meyer immediately took over the gap left by the departure of Leutnant Albert, taking over the technical direction of the blocking of the saps and development of the defences of the position in the 10th Company area . . .

"Leutnant Müller also carried out a useful service by instructing the infantry in the enemy trenches on the use of the hand grenades which were found in huge quantities on the position, thus enabling the potential of this captured ammunition to be exploited fully. The gallery which was discovered in the left sector of the new position had been dug as an inclined gallery. The two man listening post located inside was captured personally by Leutnant Müller. A second listening post, said by the prisoners to have been occupied by four men at the moment of the explosions, seems to have been totally buried and no trace of the entrance could be found anywhere.

"The two earth mortar sections, each equipped with two weapons, were dug in on the right flank of the attack frontage behind the *Hörnersappe* and on the left flank behind the so-called Old Trench. Twenty seven rounds were fired in support of the attack and the remainder of the total allocation of forty two rounds was reserved, in accordance with orders, ready to deal with an enemy counter-attack . . . Company losses amounted to one unteroffizier and two sappers killed. One officer and sixteen sappers were wounded or injured."

Leutnant Albert 2nd Field Engineer Company [29]

"In accordance with the battalion order, the three sections of engineers (three unteroffiziers and nineteen sappers) allocated to me were distributed within the infantry dugouts near to the entrances to Galleries *Theo* and *Oldenburg* during the evening of 22 January. At 5.15 am on 23 January, I reported to the company commander of 10th Company Bavarian Infantry Regiment 15, after which I went along the positions once more and directed the distribution of hand grenades. The infantry being ready, we completed our preparations by 6.15 am. The mines were detonated at 7.20 am. Some individuals immediately became casualties as a result of the quantities of earth and barbed wire thrown into the air. Rödler's section in particular was affected and it was half an hour before Rödler himself could be dug out from where he was buried. As soon as the pillars of earth had fallen back to the ground, we launched forward.

"For a brief moment the assault group was wedged together in the French *Preussensappe* [Prussian Sap]. This confusion was caused by the devastation following the explosions and the darkness caused by all the dust, reinforced by large quantities of powder smoke. An additional problem was that we found not one trench leading forward but five. I split up my men once more, sending one group up each trench and pushed forward with Unteroffizier Moser's section along a sap leading half right. Here we bumped up against the enemy. We pushed them back in a hand grenade battle, until we reached the appointed place where we began work on a trench barricade. The French threw hand grenades in an attempt to prevent us from carrying out the work. During this time I was wounded, as were some of my men. Because it was not completely clear where we were, the supply of hand grenades faltered. As I was pulling back, I directed some infantrymen to maintain the link forwards and to ensure that the hand grenades which I had demanded were moved to where they were needed."

Leutnant Meyer 2nd Field Engineer Company [30]

"The preparations for the attack were complete by 1.00 am on 23 January. At midday on 22 January it was reported that the mine system *Ursula* was not usable. The mine at the crossroads was immediately dismantled and it was established that the two forward mines – *Ursula III* and another which had been placed right at the tip of the *Ursula* gallery – were not functioning. The two mines were isolated from the rest of the system and abandoned because there was insufficient time to investigate the cause of the failure further. Tamping was completed at 1.00 am on 23 January.

"The following personnel were allocated to the firing points:

Gallery *Oldenburg:* Unteroffizier Ammerling and Gefreiter Matthes (three charges).

Galleries *Theo* and *Trudl:* Unteroffiziers Walter and Schmid (four charges).

Gallery *Ursula:* Unteroffizier Lettle and Gefreiter Birzle (two charges).

"The firing circuits were checked hourly – at 6.00 am for the final time. At 7.00 am the cables were connected to the exploders and, in accordance with the orders, the mines were blown at 7.20 am. The effect of the mines was quite extraordinary. The galleries were five to six metres below ground, but the craters, which were all located on or behind the enemy positions, were from eight to ten metres deep and twenty to twenty five metres in diameter.

"The earth mortars which had been allocated to me were dug in as follows:

Two weapons in the right hand extension of Sap 4 behind the *Hörnerspitze*. From here fire could be brought down on the enemy posisions to the right of the *Hörnerspitze*.

Two weapons immediately behind Gallery *Ursula*. These weapons were placed so as to be able to fire onto the crater field to the left [west] of the Lille – Arras road.

At the start of the attack and in accordance with orders, the two sections fired thirteen and fourteen bombs respectively. Seven rounds per fire position were kept in reserve in case of an enemy counter-attack.

"Shortly after the successful blowing of the mines, I moved up to the front line trench, so as to orientate myself. The infantrymen were already beginning to prepare the craters for defence by digging firing steps beneath the rims. In order to provide protection to the rear as well, I had this work stopped and directed that new positions were to be dug in front of the craters and that advantage was to be taken of the fog to place hasty wire obstacles. Having been informed about the activities of Leutnant Albert, I moved over to the right flank by the *Bayernsappe* [Bavarian Sap], where I arranged for four communication trenches leading towards the enemy to be blocked and for the barriers to be protected by barbed wire. It was possible to traverse the position from right to left under cover so, once an initial barbed wire obstacle, comprising two rows of concertina wire, was in position, the engineer work was complete for the time being. I went to the battalion command post on *Lübecker-Weg* [Lübeck Way] to provide a report about the captured position and its development . . . and at 4.00 pm I was relieved by Leutnant Kling."

Leutnant Müller 2nd Field Engineer Company [31]

"Of the engineers allocated to me for the operation, one unteroffizier and twelve sappers were under my direct command and located in the forward trench near to Gallery *Ursula*. Two unteroffiziers and nine sappers were in position next to *Trudl*. My task was to capture Sap *Richard;* my second section was to barricade *Konrad.* The explosions had a surprisingly violent effect and, although we were thirty metres away, we were buried in a massive downpour of lumps of clay, which filled half the trench. As a result, five men of my group were knocked out immediately. Nevertheless the remainder assaulted with great daring, though the advance was impeded considerably by the darkness and dense powder smoke. Changes to the landscape made orientation a near impossibility; only the cries of a few half-buried Frenchmen indicated the correct direction to us. Part of the wire obstacle was buried; the remainder was piled up high, which also made the advance difficult.

"On arrival in the enemy trenches, all the assault groups were bunched up tightly, because everybody had lost their sense of direction. The trench itself was half full of debris from the explosions and offered little in the way of protection. Here we suffered our first casualties when we came under machine gun fire from our half right. If the assault force had not been as strong as it was, the attack would have stalled at this point. Some men pushed along a trench, where they bumped into French defenders and were forced back, having taken casualties. Hand grenades were then used to drive the enemy back out of the trench, which later became known as *Qualle*. A combination of exploding grenades and artillery defensive fire produced so much smoke that it was impossible to see more than five metres.

"At the next trench junction we met up with Leutnant Knabe, who had advanced through *Ottilie* and *Paula*. We carried on another twenty five metres in *Richard* and began to build our barricade. To begin with we continued to be pestered by the French throwing grenades, but by dint of throwing concentrations of grenades at five to fifteen minute intervals, we kept them out of throwing range. At 9.00 am the French, suddenly and with much shouting, launched an attack. The first three were brought down with rifle fire; the remainder were kept at bay with showers of hand grenades. Thirty minutes later, the enemy launched a grenade attack along *Richard.* The leading man was felled by a rifle shot and the remainder gave up, amidst a torrent of grenades.

"The French contented themselves with what they had done and, given outstanding assistance by the fog, we were able to get on with the construction of wire obstacles and trench barricades. By the time the fog lifted at 11.00 am, two rows of concertina wire had been erected from *Martha* to *Siegfried.* [32] In view of the fact that there was no more engineer work left, I withdrew my men and handed over the position to 3 Platoon, 11th Company. At 11.30 I conducted a complete inspection of the newly won position, checking it, in particular, for mine galleries and firing wires. I found an inclined gallery in *Oswald* where I rounded up two French miners. The gallery was being used as a listening post and was only nine metres in length.

"During assaults on enemy trenches of this type, the following techniques have proved themselves: Two men armed with rifles should lead, followed immediately by a skilled grenade thrower. Men following up should be armed with large quantities of hand grenades. Dugouts and blind sections of trenches should have grenades thrown into them before being followed up immediately, though dugouts should be cleared by moppers up. It is extremely advantageous to train men in the use of French hand grenades. There are always hundreds of them lying around and they are very effective. In the [newly captured] position, I instructed all present on the use of French grenades. The supply of trench stores went very quickly and smoothly, so the position was in a completely defensible state by 11.00 am."

The detonation of mines played an important part in the initial stages of all the 'Rupprecht' Operations and that was particularly the case for 'Rupprecht III', which was conducted by the regiments of 50th Reserve Division on 26 January. The division had been manning a sector north of Les Tilleuls [= modern Le Vert Tilleul, west of Thélus]. The regiments had been in the line since late 1915 and were already closely involved with the underground war; Reserve Infantry Regiment 230, for example, having formed a 'Tunnel Construction Company', commanded by Leutnant Hartmann, at the end of December.[33] The task of this company was to develop further work which the Bavarians had previously carried out on the *Prinz Arnulf* Tunnel. This feature, together with a second one, the *Völker* Tunnel in the south of Sector *Arnulf,* were designed to provide covered routes forward to the front line, as well as large-scale protection for headquarters and resting personnel, their equipment and ammunition.

Full advantage was taken of the relatively dry conditions during the first half of January to continue to drive Galleries I, II, III and IV, upon which the miners worked ceaselessly by day and night. The completion of the galleries, which had been begun earlier by the Bavarians, approached. They had been driven forward from the divisional front line trenches towards the enemy until they were right under the French battle trenches. The galleries culminated in mine chambers which, in this case, were especially large. They were charged with powdered explosive and, such was their size, they contained 'several hundred *Zentner*'[34] of explosives. At that time these were unprecedented quantities and their effect was expected to be considerable. There were one or two minor alarms, caused by concern that the French engineers might have picked up the sounds of the German miners at work, but these proved to be false and gradually the mines were fully charged, tamped and ready to be used.

In the meantime the assault troops were pulled out of the line and sent to practise the assault on the French mine and trench system on a training area between Acheville and Fresnoy. As the day for the attack approached the troops were trained to a high pitch, but there were still many unanswered questions. What would be the approximate size of the craters? How were they to be assaulted and then defended? What effect would the rocky debris from the mine craters have? Should the assault force be stationed forward in the front line trenches or be withdrawn further to the rear? What was the best time of day for the assault? Reserve Infantry Regiment 230 had to make most of the decisions itself, because explosions of these dimensions had never occurred before and

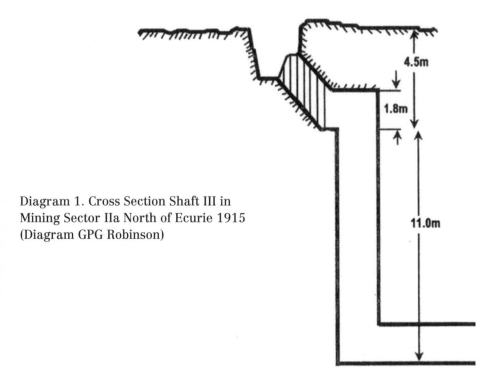

Diagram 1. Cross Section Shaft III in
Mining Sector IIa North of Ecurie 1915
(Diagram GPG Robinson)

there was no experience upon which to draw. Finally it was decided that the
attack would be launched at 7.30 am on 26 January and, in the case of Reserve
Infantry Regiment 230, its 3rd Battalion moved forward from Fresnoy during the
night of 25/26 January, so as to be ready for the assault.

The French clearly had their suspicions about what might happen along this
part of the Vimy front, because mortar fire was incessant during the hours
leading up to the attack. Nevertheless, by 6.50 am, all the forward battalions of
50th Reserve Division reported that they were in position and, promptly at 7.30
am, as planned, the four great mines were blown. The most southerly mine was
first to be detonated, followed at short intervals by the other three. As soon as
the rocks and clods of chalky earth (which turned out to be much less of a
problem than anticipated) had fallen to the ground, the attack was launched. One
of the members of 11th Company later described what happened:[35]

> "The company spent 25 January 1916 in Fresnoy. Each man was
> aware of what was about to happen to us, because mines were due to be
> detonated on 26 January. Nobody stood around moping or with anxious
> faces. The regimental band played at midday and everyone enjoyed not
> only the music, but also the dancing of an elderly Frenchwoman, who
> was so inspired by the sound of the music to appear as though she was
> harking back to her time as a prima ballerina. During the afternoon we

had the opportunity to send our thoughts home and many of us took the opportunity to write a last letter . . .

"We were all in good spirits when we moved towards the position at about 1.00 am. It was a clear, starry night and all was still over the wide expanse of the plain to our front. We waded through the filth and the mud of the 'Road of Death' which led down to Arras, until the sheer difficulty of the approach route reduced even the most vocal to silence. Silently the column advanced in single file, each man lost in thought about the past and his home, homeland, wife and child. Ever closer we drew to the bare, bleak crest of Vimy Ridge and ever more clearly could we watch the bright rise and slow, majestic falling away and fading of the signal flares which, for the observer, provided a mirror image of the life of man. But this was not time for idle thoughts. Now the call of military duty demanded a man's full commitment. He must be calm and collected.

"Our company was in support during the explosions and the following assault so, finally, after a great deal of hard work, we took up our positions in the second trench. Once more there was time for reflection as it gradually became light and each man occupied himself with the anxious question, 'What does the day hold for me?' I believe that many a comrade made his peace with God and prayed hard with all his heart. So there we stood in the early hours of 26 January 1916, leaning against the damp wall of the trench, man by man, our gas masks ready on our chests and we waited tensely for the explosions. Suddenly there was an order from the company commander. In a hurry he rushed around from man to man, 'Open your mouth!' Everyone stood there, mouths gaping. The odd nervous one ducked down while others strained to see in all directions through the morning mist. Still more stood there in silence, staring forwards.

"Everywhere the tension was acute as we waited, feverishly, for the violent crash which everybody knew was about to happen. Suddenly the word raced along the line of men who stood there with fixed stares and their mouths forced even wider open, 'Stand by!' and, almost immediately a noise began, down in the deepest of depths – a violent, dull underground roaring. The earth heaved and shook and a pillar of fire roared up into the sky. With great rattling and crashing sounds the debris dropped back to earth. The morning fog dispersed and the tension was broken by the shouts of *Hurra!* of the assaulting troops mingling with the notes of the buglers blowing 'Advance at the double!'

"Four massive craters had been blown and occupied by us. However, under the concentrated mortar and artillery fire, it was necessary a short time later to withdraw from Crater 4. At that, we in support were moved further forward. It was a ghastly move through mud-filled trenches under heavy artillery fire, as we climbed over the bodies of our fallen and wounded comrades. The drive for self-preservation did not, however, leave us with much opportunity to express our sympathy and we simply had to plough through the corpses. As evening approached on 26 January, we received orders to retake the lost crater. We knew only too well what a difficult task we had been given, but we soon found ourselves lined up in a wrecked trench, up to our knees in mud, our bayonets fixed and our teeth chattering.

"The moon cast a pale, ghostly light on the ploughed up ground and the mysterious deep, water-filled, shell holes. In the distance a machine gun fired the odd burst, but otherwise all was quiet. To the left we could hear the dull report of exploding mortar bombs and fiery trails, arcing through the sky, pointed the way that Death had taken. Over there the high lip of the crater, bathed in the silvery-white moonlight, beckoned to us and bid us come. 'Stand by!' – the word was passed swiftly from mouth to mouth down the line of soldiers. Hand grenades were clasped tightly and rifles were held in an iron grip. The peep of a whistle sounded shrill in the still of the night and there was a confused rush as, with jaws clenched, everyone launched themselves forward.

"But the Frenchmen had been lying in wait. Mortar bombs crashed down all round, machine guns chattered and hand grenades barred our way to the crater. Shouts of anger and pain filled the air, but it was no good, we had to pull back. We found ourselves, much reduced, huddled in a sap. Now and again a further attempt was made, but it was all in vain. Filled with bitterness, we attempted to recover our dead and wounded but, even in that endeavour, we had very little success. Many of our dear comrades had to lie where they had fallen – and over all this the moon cast a silver light on friend and foe, cold and heartless.

"We passed the following day in the mud and water of the front line trench . . . Finally we were relieved and the company pulled back into the *Schwaben Tunnel* [located 1,500 metres north of Le Vert Tilleul]. It was a hard road back, through the pitch black night and the flattened trenches. Many a man was trapped up to his hips in the mud, but helping hands pulled them free and we plodded our way to the rear and rest . . . "

With all this activity along the Vimy front, by early 1916 there were so many mine galleries prepared between Angres and the Maison Blanche area south of Roclincourt that finding sufficient number of trained men to listen for the sound of enemy in the inactive galleries was proving to be extremely difficult. I Bavarian Corps turned to technology to provide a solution and, on 14 February, Major Georg Vogl wrote a report[36] concerning the experiences gained in the Corps area to Commander Engineers at Sixth Army. It is quite evident from what he wrote that, initially, pressure of events forced the German army to rush into service, without trialling and quite indiscriminately, any piece of equipment which might conceivably be of use.

"Listening equipment provides a good means of ensuring surveillance of defensive mine galleries, in which work had been suspended, either temporarily or for a protracted period. The main advantage is that is possible for one man, operating from a single listening station, to monitor up to ten galleries. If such equipment is lacking, it means that each individual gallery must be provided with a man on listening watch. A further advantage is the fact that the working conditions for the listeners can be improved, due to the fact that the equipment may be operated from the open air or from a good dugout.

"Of the electrical listening equipment available, the *Edelmann* listening device has won most popular acclaim. One disadvantage of this equipment and other similar types is the fact that they are far too sensitive. If trenches and galleries are both in chalk the equipment will record all small arms shots or artillery firing in the same way as the noise of mining. This can often lead to dangerous errors. If the enemy opposite is particularly active, then the equipment simply cannot be used.

"In all mine systems where work is being carried out, especially where the presence of enemy miners has already been established, all experienced engineer companies withdraw the listening equipment and establish posts which rely on the unaided human ear in the galleries. In these cases the listening equipment is ineffective. It indicates the presence of mining noise, but not its strength or direction. Mechanical aids such as the *Phonodoskop* made by Bazzi-Binanchi or listening trumpets, on the other hand, have no value. The practised ear can make out as much without them. In chalk it is so difficult to conceal the sound of mining that even an untrained observer can give a fairly accurate estimate of strength and direction without resort to any type of aid.

"Where mine warfare is being conducted actively, electric listening devices have been used for the following purposes:
- To continue to carry out surveillance in galleries where an enemy explosion is expected, but where we do not wish to risk a human observer.
- In cases where our galleries are charged, so as to establish when the enemy miners are working and so bring about a successful explosion.

It is possible to obtain false readings from sensitive equipment, however, which means that the desired aim cannot always be achieved. In addition the microphones are really far too expensive to employ in this manner, because in both these instances they are lost [once charges are blown].

"It would seem feasible, therefore, to make reductions in the previous allocation of these items of equipment. The usefulness of the current generous allocation is not in proportion to the attendant costs. There is a general view, also proposed here, that only one type, namely the

Edelmann equipment, should be retained. The remainder can be withdrawn completely from service. At present there is only one area within
the I Bavarian Corps sector where there is a complete [dormant] mine
system. Underground work is going on everywhere else."

Vogl's final sentence was nothing less than the truth as mining and counter
mining flared along the front. Operation *Schleswig Holstein* has been discussed
elsewhere, but in many respects it was simply a further development of a long-
running struggle for dominance at the foot of Hill 145. Hauptmann Erich
Karitzky, writing after the war in the history of Reserve Jäger Battalion 9,
provided a vivid account of the days which preceded the operation; designed to
wrest the initiative away from the British tunnelling companies:[37]

"From the middle of [April] there was considerable turmoil in the
positions. Mining preparations were well advanced on both sides.
Listening posts and mine galleries were now very close to one another.
The first blasts occurred in neighbouring sectors. On 16 April the British
blew a mine under Bavarian Infantry Regiment 24 then, on 18 April, the
Bavarians retaliated at the *Transfeld* Crater. On 19 April the British set
off a mine to our right in the Reserve Infantry Regiment 86 sector. On 20
April there were two tit for tat blasts by the Bavarians and a further one
on 24 April. On each occasion there was the usual fight for the crater
and heavy artillery fire from both sides, which spilled over into our area.
What a pleasant neighbourhood![38]

"In Gallery 12 in our sector the sound of enemy mining was detected
on 25 April. Reacting swiftly, a forty *Zentner* [40 x 50kg = two tonnes]
camouflet was blown in the right hand branch at 1.00 pm. This set off a
British charge, which was apparently located right next to it so, instead
of a camouflet, a crater forty metres in diameter and ten metres deep
(Crater IV) was created. Thanks to the daring actions of Reserve
Leutnant Schmeling, commander of 1st Company, the crater was seized
and preparation for defence began. Reserve Leutnant Schulz and twenty
four Jägers rushed across from Sap 2 to the crater, occupied the threatened western lip and defended it in a battle with hand grenades.

"During the day work began on preparing the edge of the crater for
defence and that night, despite two further attacks with hand grenades
by the British, it was protected by a barbed wire obstacle. In that way
we secured the crater as an advanced post sixty metres in front of our
positions. The subsequent report commended especially Reserve
Leutnant von Schmeling, Reserve Leutnant Schulz, Vizefeldwebel
Bartelsen, Gefreiter Landsmann and Jägers Blunk, Scheuermann,
Wedekind, Wolff, Ebet, Vorrath and Knoop. The following morning, the
26th, there was a further explosion in the Reserve Infantry Regiment 86
sector, which provoked another violent exchange of artillery fire all
along the line. The explosions continued when another mine was

detonated away to our right near *Fünfwegekreuz* [Five-Way Junction, located on The Pimple] which was held by Infantry Regiment 163.[39] At that moment they were conducting a relief in the line, which was made extremely difficult because of the weight of artillery fire coming down on the positions and the rear area. This fire continued on 27 April . . .

"On 28 April, Gallery 12 in our sector was finally ready to be blown. It had been charged with 120 *Zentner* [120 x 50 kilograms = six tonnes] of explosive. Simultaneously the Bavarians were to blow a nearby gallery containing fifty *Zentner* [two and a half tonnes]. At 8.30 pm we blew Crater VIII, located only eighteen metres from Crater IV which had been produced on 25 April. It was fifty two metres in diameter and eleven metres deep. The Bavarian crater was thirty two metres in diameter and eight metres deep. Immediately after the explosions, artillery fire poured down on the sector. Despite the fire, Leutnant Nielsen and his riflemen rushed to the western edge of the crater and threw back the enemy, who had arrived simultaneously, with hand grenades and held the position until reinforcements arrived. Our machine guns played a not un-important role in ensuring that we held on to the crater.

"After about two hours the artillery fire reduced somewhat and for the remainder of night the place was a hive of activity as the crater was prepared for defence, making use of copious quantities of trench stores carried forward by the companies in support. By morning the new Crater VIII and Crater IV had been linked via Sap 3 to the previous front line trench. The morning was quiet, but heavy fire for effect came down on the entire battalion position during the afternoon, with the craters being given special attention . . . All the trenches suffered badly, in particular the route forward to the craters and the approach routes from the rear. At 8.00 pm it was necessary for a platoon of 3rd Company to take over the craters. The 15th Company had been weakened by all the casualties it had suffered. Later this duty was taken on by two officers (Reserve Leutnants Kasper and Sengstacke) and five sections of 2nd Company.

"During the night the destructive fire of the enemy was interspersed with three attacks using hand grenades, but all were beaten off. The artillery fire continued to be heavy all night . . . Total losses during these days of fighting for the craters amounted to twenty killed and seventy nine wounded. From 30 April to 5 May things were relatively quiet. The enemy artillery concentrated on the rear areas, which was fortunate; at the front much maintenance and improvement of the positions was required. Examination of enemy corpses revealed that we had been opposed during the past few days by the Worcestershire-Regiment [*sic*. 3rd Battalion Worcestershire Regiment, 7 Brigade, 25th Division]."

During spring and early summer 1916, 17th Reserve Division was occupying the front from the *Gießler Höhe* down towards La Folie Wood. At that time a great deal of mining was going on around The Pimple in particular. During the weeks before they moved south to the Somme their members had time to get to know the engineers and the mining teams and to develop considerable admiration for their courage, skill and determination.

Offizierstellvertreter Hugo Gropp Reserve Infantry Regiment 76 [40]

"In this position we saw for the first time with our own eyes the underground work of our engineer comrades: the explosions, the preparations for them and the mining operations deep beneath the earth. We gaped at the huge craters on and in front of our positions and gained a vivid impression of the appalling nature of this style of warfare. We ourselves experienced mine blasts, together with the battles with hand grenades and the artillery barrages which came down when we had to rush forward and occupy the rims of the craters after successful explosions. We developed and maintained the friendliest of relationships with our engineers and stood by to assist them in their heavy labours. Like many of you we practised our first aid on them when they emerged from their galleries exhausted by their labours or, overcome by poisonous fumes, had to be carried out to the open air. We followed the progress of their workings and those of the enemy with the greatest of interest; jointly evaluating the results obtained by the listening posts. Hardly a day passed without an explosion or the crushing of an enemy gallery underground. We even felt the explosions of the particularly large charges ten kilometres behind the lines in our billets in Sallaumines.

"It is night —-Ping! A rifle shot. Ping! Ping! Ping!, another two, three or four. Crumpf! Crumpf! – hand grenades. Rattattattatt! – a machine gun joins in, hammering hard against the stony parapet of the trench. One man is wounded, but that is all. Forward in the sap head they have been duelling: six metres from one another; exactly six metres. How many men have carried out sentry duty there? One hundred? Two hundred? Five hundred? A thousand? Nobody knows, but each one of those thousand pairs of eyes had estimated this six metres. On one occasion a pole was pushed forward through the confusion of barbed wire and slowly and carefully they checked the distance with great exactness. Now at the head of the sap a notice has been placed: *Enemy – six metres!*

"One man wounded – nothing else.' 'Is it slight?' 'Head wound.' 'Hey sapper, how's it going down in the gallery?' 'We are going to finish off that sniper tonight, Herr Leutnant!' 'Well done sapper. Good evening.' In the pump house, five metres beneath the earth, breathe the lungs of the gallery. They push the stale air up the eight steps out of the dugout, wheezing asthmatically. Two men turn the handle of the suction pump so that they have air down below, so that their lights can burn, so that they can live and fight down there, twenty five metres deeper down in the white chalk. Up the many steps the miners carefully carry the loosened spoil, the stones, the earth and the chalk up from the depths. How much work is behind them? – weeks and months of it.

"They have mined and extracted the spoil ceaselessly, working their way down into the earth then forwards in a straight line. They have listened to see how far away those over there were and calculated that they could be blown up tomorrow, today, this hour or this very minute and clenched their fists in anger as the enemy crushed their gallery. Thirty metres from them the walls were crumpled like paper, but they mined around the wrecked gallery and have finally reached their objective. They have done their calculations and reckon that they are now under the second enemy trench. They have been carrying explosives forward since last night, throughout the day and now again tonight. In the gallery, where it is so narrow that two men can only pass one another with difficulty, tallow candles gutter in the thick atmosphere. The build up of nitrogen affects them, the light they give barely shines fifty centimetres and every time a shell lands overhead the lights go out.

"The miners hardly exchange a word. Their work is conducted in an utterly profound silence. They pass the explosives forward from hand to hand. In parallel galleries listening teams maintain security. Above them the enemy sniper still looses off his shots, whilst below the enemy miners hammer at the chalk. Two engineers remain by a wall of sandbag tamping, whilst a third listens to the enemy through the chalk. He lies flat out on the floor of the gallery and presses his ear down firmly on the clay. Pink . . . pink . . . pink, hammers the enemy. They are trying to steal a march on us; wanting to blow us up. Can they already have prepared their mine chamber? Are they carrying the explosives forward? No. Pink . . . pink . . . pink they continue to hammer, whilst their nailed boots crunch into the chalk. We first discovered them thirty three nights ago. Since then we have been working against one another.

"Psst, comrade! Whispers one to another. In order to remain silent as we walk, we have wrapped sandbags around our feet. Only the glimmers of the candles, which hang in the air like balloons, pierce the gloom. 'Can you hear the Tommies talking? One is complaining loudly, whilst other speak in murmurs.' 'Yes I can hear them. It looks as though their work is finished . . . they are departing, one of them scraping his spade behind him. We need to report this, because we want to get them.' 'Psst keep quiet!'- 'Listen, their relief has arrived. They are greeting one another . . . now they are picking at the chalk once more. Let's get them. Is the charging complete?' 'Nearly. It is being tamped now.' 'Is it a large charge?' 'Bigger than anything used so far in the war.'

"The moon rides above the position, glowing a reddish yellow from the horizon and casting an uncertain light over the position. A few shots are exchanged. Sentries are relieved for the third time. Midnight approaches. Nothing appears to be abnormal. The engineer leutnant looks at his watch – five minutes to go! Everything is ready and the artillery has reported all guns laid. The artillery lies in wait; its barrels pointed at the third enemy trench. At each gun position the gunners busy themselves with piles of ammunition. Four minutes to go. The firing circuits are checked and are in order. The entire sector is being observed through tripod binoculars. Infantrymen prepare their grenades for throwing. Three minutes to go. Two minutes to go! The machine guns are ready to open fire. The mortars stare up at the moon like prehistoric monsters watching its track through the sky. One minute to go – then! Telephonists are poised at their apparatus, battle orderlies and runners wait. Still thirty seconds to go!

"Suddenly the engineer officer twists the little knob. Bursting, heaving, bending, breaking, cracking, thundering, heaving: immense quantities of earth are launched skywards towards the moon. The position shudders as though there has been an earthquake, a catastrophe. It is as if everything has been upended; turned on its head. The air shrieks itself hot; filled with the thunder of a hundred guns and the racket caused by machine guns, grenade launchers, rifle shots and grenades exploding. Fragments whir and hum in all directions . . . from the other side come giant mortar bombs and crashing shells, but the enemy are shooting blind and not at individual targets as we are. Yes, the enemy is shooting blind out of anger, because we have ripped away part of his very being: a three hundred metre section of his lines, taken together with a great many soldiers, dugouts, materiel and weapons; taken because we pinned them down in their trenches, because our assault troops manned the still-hot and smoking rim of the crater and threw grenades at him, because we were firmly emplaced in the middle of their position. We got there first, so it was anger, anger! The mine crater has been blown and held as directed! Five words appear in the Army Communiqué: 'We exploded a mine successfully.'"

Further to the south and having taken over from 1st Bavarian Infantry Division, the regiments of 4th Guards Infantry Division assumed responsibility for the front northwest of Thélus. It was the first experience of the area for the men of Reserve Infantry Regiment 93 and they found that it took some acclimatisation. They, too, became involved in the construction of protective tunnels leading forward in this vulnerable area. They found the work in the chalk hard, but commented that a well-organised company working hard and efficiently could place up to 250 supports during a five day period. The work on the tunnels was a routine matter. Far less easy to come to terms with was the fact that, 'the main characteristic and least pleasant feature on Vimy Ridge were the mine explosions'.[41] Recalling his time on the Ridge, one of its members later wrote:

"I recollect the eerie feeling we had when we were down in our dugouts and could hear, coming from deep down in the earth, the tapping of the British who were opposite us. It was on the morning after the British had launched the previous evening a violent but unsuccessful attack against a IX Corps unit to our right. At daybreak I was manning the head of a sap, about forty metres from the British lines. This sap had been pushed forward about ten metres to the front of our trench. Up until a few days previously this had been the location of a machine gun, which engaged targets in the area and brought down fire on the enemy rear area in a manner which they had probably found unpleasant. The machine gun had been withdrawn, because a listening post had established the fact that the British were setting about blowing up the sap.

"At night in our dugout, when everything was still, we could clearly hear the British picking at the rock. Once the machine gun was withdrawn we were highly indignant that we were expected to continue to man a sentry post in this sap continuously every night, despite the fact that it could be blown up at any moment. The engineers, who were working their way forward to the British from the same sap told us, nevertheless, that things were not so serious; it would take the Tommies at least another three days to mine under the sap and blow it up. In any case it would not come to that, because they would deploy a camouflet against the British first . . .

"Naturally the British had also detected the sound of our engineers working, so it was a question of who would blow first. Frequently the engineers would spend days at a time listening in their narrow galleries, so that they could time their explosions for when they heard the sound of the British working. Equally it was often the case that the enemy penetrated unnoticed beneath our positions and blew them up. That always caused serious casualties. For the infantry occupying adjacent positions it was then essential to occupy the resulting crater immediately before the British could get there. Disputed occupation of these craters always led to extended battles with hand grenades.

"During the morning when I was on sentry duty in the sap, the engineers and their supporting platoon of grenadiers were hard at work. I questioned one of these comrades, who was collecting sandbags full of spoil from the gallery and carrying them to the rear where they were being used to develop a trench, how far away the British were now. That was, incidentally, the worried question that all comrades who came forward to relieve us always asked first. The engineer said that he could not say for sure, but that the British were still working and so long as that continued to be the case they could not blow a mine. 'How far have you got up to now?' He said that they were more or less beneath the British, that they would bring forward dynamite tonight and should they detect sounds of the British, they would crush them.

"Thank heavens', I said. This was a view shared by my comrades when I crawled back into our dugout as it became light. The sap was unmanned during the day. I lay on my bunk and pulled a groundsheet over my head. This place was full of an unusually large number of rats. They were big and clumsy, these rats. You could almost stamp on their heads. They ate everything. It was even said that men had been eaten by them when they were asleep. It was far from uncommon for them to run over a ground-sheet while the occupant was asleep. They had good places to hide in the chalk soil behind the timbering. I had just fallen asleep, possibly I had had half an hour, when I was woken by a terrible detonation. Above my head two thick beams cracked and sagged, allowing chalk to fall down on the groundsheet and rifles, which had been hanging on the wall, clattered to the ground.

"We sat up and looked around with pale, anxious faces. Mine explosions were nothing new here, but never before had one gone off so close to us. 'Everybody out! Out!' came the shouts from above. Shuddering, we felt for our rifles and crawled out. 'Everyone to his stand-to position!' ordered the Feldwebel. Just as I was approaching my sentry position near the sap, somebody shouted to me that some comrades were buried. The man to whom I had been speaking earlier lay in the sap by the buried entrance to the crushed gallery, his face bloody. He did not seem to be badly hurt, but had been cut on the head by a piece of flying chalk. He said that they had been deceived by the British, who had simply been pretending to work, even though they had apparently had a completely prepared charge ready.

"As a result the Tommies were in front of them and had crushed their gallery, leaving two men buried inside. This latter point was confirmed later in a thoroughly gruesome manner. Whilst one of the engineers who had been working furthest forward was apparently killed instantly, the other was trapped by his legs, which were gripped tight by the collapsed chalk walls on either side. We could hear the moans and groans of this unfortunate man. The rescue was extremely difficult. Only one man at a time could crawl into the gallery and almost four metres had to be cleared before the man could be reached. Three engineers relieved one another, an hour at a time. They finally reached and freed their comrade, but he had to have both legs amputated and he died later.[42]

One bad experience cannot, of course, be taken as entirely typical of this period which, as far as Vimy Ridge was concerned, was dominated by mine warfare. One of the other regiments of 4th Guards Infantry Division manned the La Folie sector for several weeks, prior to its move south to the Somme in late July.

Reserve Leutnant Krüger 5th Company Footguard Regiment 5 [43]

"In order not to be surprised by enemy mine explosions, listening pauses were observed daily. With the exception of those on sentry duty, everyone else had to remain in the dugouts and stay as silent as mice. Our own miners stopped work too at these times. Everybody had to report any observations. Quite often we heard hammering underground and the sound of pick on chalk. That meant that the British were still mining, so there was no danger. If, however, everything was quiet, or if the sounds of objects being slid were heard (movement forward of boxes of explosive) then it was time for countermeasures to be taken at once.

"In general our engineers would then fire a weak charge which crushed the enemy's gallery. This would not produce a crater. That usually meant weeks more work for the Tommies before their gallery was ready to be blown. This was nerve-wracking form of warfare! We had the feeling that we had the advantage over our opponents on Vimy Ridge in this black art. Despite the destruction of the woodland, the endless explosions and all the shooting, La Folie Wood still had a deer in it. We never pursued it. It seemed as though this most beautiful, and most tender of all the game animals was a messenger from God."

Later that year, towards the end of June, men of Reserve Infantry Regiment 76 returning to the line after a period in reserve, found themselves caught up in the continuing underground battle for domination of The Pimple. It came as rude shock to men who were hoping that their return would be to a quiet sector.

Offizierstellvertreter Hugo Gropp Reserve Infantry Regiment 76 [44]

"We occupied an uncomfortable position high up on Vimy Ridge, where we were vulnerable to mortars of all calibres and flanking fire from the direction of Loos, not to mention the risk of being blown up by mines placed fifty metres down[45] . . . I accompanied my predecessor around the platoon trenches. Everything was as it should be. 'What's the mining situation like?' 'Everything is quiet. The engineers have not noticed any activity by the Tommies.' That, at least, was a comfort. We were not going to be attacked from below. Feeling calm I sought out my dugout, from which one of our mine galleries led off. An icy wind blew out of it, enough to chill a man to the bone. Thick blankets and a groundsheet had been draped over it to separate the entrance from the dugout . . .

"I had just begun to make myself comfortable on my bed, when a platoon runner rushed in, stumbling in his haste. 'The British are here!' 'Where?' 'Down in a gallery.' 'You must be mad. Where are they exactly?' 'Down below in the gallery. I wanted to see how far it had been driven forward below and I could hear them very clearly.' Damn and blast it! This was a right kettle of fish! My predecessor had only just finished explaining that would be as comfortable here as we would be in Lünzmann's Oyster Bar[46] and now it turned out that the Tommies were already beneath us. 'Are you sure you have not made a mistake?' 'No, no, absolutely not.' There was nothing else for it. I had to go below and check for myself. Removing anything which might catch on the timbering and picking up my revolver, I went down the mineshaft. It was necessary to crawl because these shafts measured only sixty by eighty centimetres and each of the frames was set twenty five to thirty centimetres lower than the previous one.

"I scrabbled rapidly backwards down the first hundred steps, but then I had to be more careful. I now turned to face forwards. If that lot really had broken in, how would it be if I approached them like a crab? I shone my torch around. There was nothing to be seen or heard. I was enveloped in profound silence. I could almost hear my own heart beating. I pushed on. The air became cold and heavy and it was in any case already difficult to make progress along this stooping-height tunnel. There was still no end in sight of the gallery, but it was at least not quite so steep. Once more I checked around; once more I could detect nothing. There was nothing but the eerie silence of being far from any living being. It was a vile feeling. I should have liked nothing more than to have turned around got away from that place.

"I pushed on further. Finally I reached the end of the gallery. I listened with all might my might, but nothing could be heard. Could the geophones have picked up my movement? Minute after minute went by. Nothing could be heard and yet there must have been some truth in it. The lad could not have been wrong to that extent. Still all was quiet – the awful stillness pressed in on me – It would be preferable to be wallowing in the thickest mud imaginable in an open trench, rather than to be here, utterly alone fifty metres below ground. I suddenly thought to myself, 'Could the Tommies have already charged their mine and be ready to blow it?' It was certainly the right time; they often used the twilight for the purpose. 'Good God; not that! – To meet a lonely death fifty metres below ground?[47] No, not that!' I scrambled back up as fast as I could, hoping against hope that the Tommies would not blow before I was outside once more. Having returned safely things did not seem so bad and I noticed that I was much calmer.

"Leutnant Meyer was every bit as surprised as I had been. The two of us crawled back down the shaft. That was much more pleasant. Quietly we slid down and, sure enough, we could now hear the enemy making a noise above us. It sounded as though heavy objects were being pushed along. That was enough for us: out we went. They had obviously worked out our working times and listening watches and were making use of the periods in between. Leutnant Meyer went immediately to report to the *K.T.K.*[48] A camouflet was to be exploded at once in the gallery. The support battalion and the engineer officer were alerted. Every man in the supporting company had to carry a box of explosives forward and each of them had to make two or three trips forward from the engineer depot in order to transport all the boxes, which had to be moved carefully and quietly so that the Tommies would not notice anything. Within the shaft work went forward at a feverish pace. A man sat on every third step and passed the boxes of explosives forward. The ventilation system was on, in order to supply the men with fresh air. Who was in the lead – us, or the Tommies?

"Ceaselessly box after box was passed forward. It was already afternoon by the time the last of them had made its way down. It was high time that the sandbags were sent down as well, so that tamping could take place. Quick, quick, quick, the mine was due to be blown at 6.00 pm. By 5.30 pm the work was complete, including the firing circuit. Dripping with sweat, the men pulled out; their duty done. Now it was down to us. The sentries in the vicinity of the gallery were withdrawn and the position evacuated over a one hundred metre stretch. The machine guns were ready to fire, the hand grenades were placed ready to be grabbed and final instructions were given. The dance could now begin.

"6.00 pm. The first shells hissed overhead as they crashed down on the enemy trenches. A shock! The earth rocked, was heaved upwards violently, swayed about then was thrown clear of the surrounding earth. Standing upright I watched a pillar of earth being shot into the air, then all of us who were near the entrance to the gallery were on our backs, knocked down by the shock, as though struck by lightning. Then, just as if a hurricane had struck, everything which had been hanging on the walls of the dugout – gas masks, belts of ammunition, coats and personal equipment – was hurled out of the dugout, as though it had been shot out of a pistol. Luckily nobody was standing directly in front of the entrance; he would have been torn apart.

"As quickly as it had appeared, the ghost disappeared once more. The explosive gases had heaved the earth upwards, but then opened a way into the gallery and vented near to where we were standing. We scrambled to our feet and helped to re-establish the correct manning of the company position. The explosion had not created a new crater. This was fortunate, because it meant that we did not have to fight for possession of it. Of course there was a price to pay. The Tommies wanted revenge and were soon pounding our position with mortar fire and all calibres of artillery. Soon everything disappeared under fire and smoke. 'Look out! Look out!' Machine guns were chattering away wildly, raking the positions and the area in between. We pressed ourselves hard in against the side of the trench, seeking some protection from the mass of iron fragments and clods of earth that were flying around. Shells burst ceaselessly with nerve-wracking crashes. It was no use, however, we had to hold where we were. Our own artillery joined in strongly. It was a tense situation, but, equally we had shown the Tommies a thing or two."

The German engineers might well have scored a success on this occasion, but they were not the only ones capable of delivering unpleasant surprises. Gropp, once more:[49]

"On 3 July the Company was manning the front line trenches and receiving the constant greetings of the enemy artillery. Boom – crash! Boom – crash! It went on all day long, broken only by pauses of differing lengths. That evening the air was filled with a howling, roaring sound, like that of Woden's wild warriors. Countless steel greetings poured down from the enemy. Boom – crash! The clock showed 11.45 pm when, suddenly, something weird and dreadful happened. The earth rocked. On the right flank of our sector the ground writhed in wild anguish. A yellowish-black cloud rose into the sky, whilst all around clods of earth mixed with pieces of timber and metal, rained down over a wide area. The earth had received a gaping wound.

"Where once our sap head had been located, a crater now yawned, sixty metres wide and twenty metres deep. Some members of the garrison of the sap were flung into the air, others were buried. Twenty metres of trench were levelled and two mine galleries were buried, together with the engineers who were working in them. Two sections of our men were also buried by falling debris. We were all filled with paralyzing horror, but the moment demanded action. 'Volunteers!' bawled the voice of Leutnant Pietzker, 'Follow me!' Together with his brave little band, he raced for the northeast lip of the crater which had just been formed. A little later he was followed in the same way by Leutnant Morgenroth, whilst sections from 1st Company rushed over to assist. They arrived in the nick of time.

"The enemy had occupied the western edge of the crater immediately after the explosion. Ready to do battle, the opponents were lined up, barely eighty metres apart. Back in the trench gallant work was being carried out, in an attempt to save living beings from death by suffocation. Unfortunately our efforts were in vain. At 1.50 am British hand grenades were thrown and their artillery resumed its destructive work. The enemy then attacked our right flank and the left flank of the 2nd Company. Our infantry immediately produced its own defensive fire, as large numbers of hand grenades were thrown at the attackers. The machine gunners joined in, creating a hail of iron of their own. The enemy had to fall back, but our casualties were very heavy that night: fifteen killed and ten wounded."[50]

Mining and counter-mining continued all along the Vimy front right through the autumn of 1916 and the early months of 1917. Even after 79th Reserve Division arrived at the beginning of March and thoughts on both sides were turning more to the forthcoming battle, work continued, especially around The Pimple and in the vicinity of Hill 145. One of the engineer officers involved was eighteen year old Reserve Leutnant Olaf Grieben who, in a series of letters written in the late 1980s, provided a great deal of information about German mining during that period.

Reserve Leutnant Olaf Grieben 9th Company Reserve Engineer Battalion 19[51]

"The three mining platoons rotated the duties, each platoon spending twenty four hours at a time on the position. They would, for example, leave their billets at 6.00 pm, carry out mining tasks from 8.00 pm one day until 8.00 pm the next, then return to billets arriving at 10.00 pm. On the other hand the duty engineer officer spent three days continuously forward. His duties were to maintain liaison with the infantry battalion commander of the sector and to divide the remainder of his time between supervision of mining and listening watch.

"In consequence he was constantly on the move, by day as well as night. This involved moving above cover because the trenches were in a state of collapse and the going was extremely difficult. Decision making was difficult, especially when reports from the listening parties indicated that there was a risk of a British mine explosion. This meant that, as a precaution, the infantry had to be moved out of the danger area, which in turn carried the risk that the British [*sic*] would spot what was happening and rush to capture the unoccupied position. It was only when I was older that I came to realise what responsibility I had borne, aged only eighteen and a half.

" . . . On 27 January 1917, the Kaiser's birthday, there were special rations and everyone was in good spirits. I was down in Gallery 23, discussing listening reports. There was a constant increase in the sound of battle (artillery and mortar fire). Suddenly a voice bawled down into the gallery, 'Herr Leutnant, the Tommies are in the trench!' This was followed by a thumping sound coming down the stairs and I leapt back. But what was bumping down from step to step was not the man who had shouted; instead it was a British demolition charge, probably with a delay fuze. It rolled down the horizontal gallery and came to rest in full view of the entrance chamber to the gallery. Every one of us down in the dugout was filled with horror. If it had detonated, our lives would all have been snuffed out. But it did not; it was a dud. All of us rushed out of the other entrance! Not a shot was fired. The man who had shouted lay there, his skull smashed in by a British [*sic*] trench cosh . . . "

At the beginning of January, Headquarters VI Reserve Corps produced a comprehensive situation report relating to the frontages of 6th Bavarian

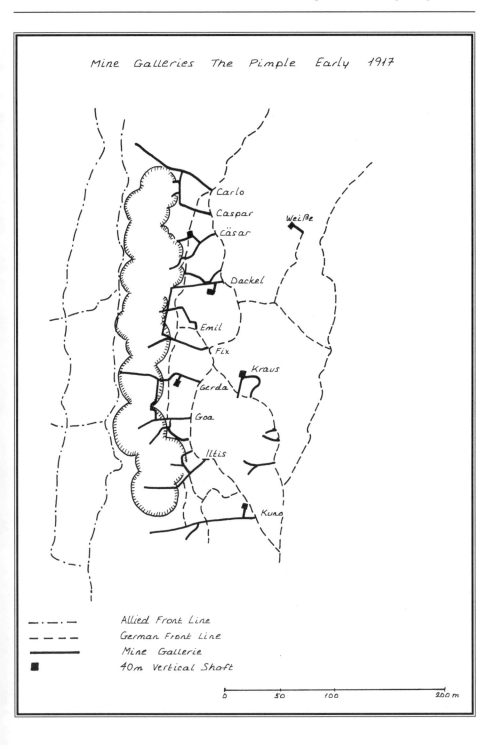

Mine Galleries The Pimple Early 1917

Carlo
Caspar
Cäsar
Weiße
Dackel
Emil
Fix
Kraus
Gerda
Goa
Iltis
Kuno

_ . _ . _   Allied Front Line
_ _ _ _   German Front Line
_____   Mine Gallerie
■   40m Vertical Shaft

0   50   100   200 m

Reserve Division, then responsible for Sectors *Burg, Döberitz* and *Fischer* and that of 12th Reserve Division whose formations were manning Sectors *Arnulf, Loën* and *Wittelsbach.* This report[52] contained information relating to mining, which provides a useful description of where the priorities for the Allies lay at this time.

> "Mine warfare plays very significant role in the sector [of 6th Bavarian Reserve Division]. Throughout the sector the mine systems are very extensive, but the most important sector is *Döberitz.* Whereas the pace of activity is general moderate in *Burg* and from Sub-Sector *F2* south, in *Döberitz* mine warfare is conducted at an extremely rapid pace. It is the enemy's clear intention to throw us back off the hill [The Pimple]. It is essential that the initiative is seized back from the enemy by deploying a strong force of miners in this sector.
>
> "A serious error has been made, in that the majority of shafts have been driven forward from the front line trench of the First Position. This means that the entrances are constantly being damaged by enemy mortar fire and the work is suffering considerably as well. An improvement in the situation can only be achieved slowly by starting new gallery entrances from the second trench, or even further to the rear . . . [53]
>
> "It must be assumed that the enemy have a mine system all along the entire position [opposite 12th Reserve Division]. Although not the slightest noise had been detected there [last summer] for two to three months, it does appear that the enemy have been driving forwards since the beginning of September against *Arnulf* North and *Loën.* Just recently the sound of mining has been detected opposite Sub-Sectors *L2* and *L3.* On two occasions in December there were mine blasts in Sector *Arnulf,* but this in itself does not amount to genuine mine warfare. Correspondingly we reduced our mining activity in the area, so that we restricted ourselves to maintaining listening stations in the galleries beneath Sectors *Loën* and *Wittelsbach* and only continued active mining in Sector *Arnulf.*"

Throughout the remainder of January and the first half of February German engineers continued to pick up the sound of Allied mining near The Pimple. Despite the pace of work, which meant that miners were always in short supply, it was decided to take counter-action in this sector. It is clear that Allied work was well advanced because, on 19 February, they exploded a mine in Sector *Döberitz 3.* 16th Bavarian Infantry Division immediately issued an order:

> "The enemy attacked Sector *Döberitz* yesterday morning, apparently in conjunction with the simultaneous firing of a mine. They were driven off . . . 9th Infantry Brigade is to ensure that a [new] continuous line of defence is established. The enemy are to be prevented from establishing themselves in and in front of the new crater . . . " [54]

A subsequent decision was for offensive mines to be fired in Sub-Sector *Döberitz 4*. Work went ahead to prepare a group of galleries for this purpose, but the task was competing for manpower with a long list of priorities and, according to the 16th Bavarian Infantry Division Weekly Report for 8 – 15 March 1917, 'The loading of the mine galleries in *D4* is only proceeding slowly, because the dreadful condition of the ground is making the move forward of the necessary explosives extremely difficult.'[55]

A great deal of noisy activity in Sector *Zollern*, held by Reserve Infantry Regiment 262, was detected near to Broadmarsh/*Schleswig Holstein* Crater and, therefore, very close to the German Galleries 37 and 39, during the nights 5/6 and 7/8 March in particular.[56] During the coming days the area was kept under close observation and, as a result, the 79th Reserve Division Situation Report for 10 March 1917 reported, 'The pile of chalk at Blue Point 58 (5911) gets bigger by the day. It is quite obvious that mine galleries are being driven forward from that direction against our Galleries 37 and 38. The sounds of enemy mining can be heard clearly from the neighbouring galleries . . .'[57] The following day, it was reported that, 'work took place again on the piles of chalk in Sectors *Fischer 2* and *Zollern 2'*, [58] then, on 13 March, reporting on the events of the previous day, this was expanded: 'There appear to be entrances to the enemy mining system at Blue Points 94 and 95 [*Fischer 1*], 108 [*Fischer 2*], 34/35 [*Fischer 3*] and 42 [*Zollern*]. Every day the piles of sandbags and heaps of chalk grow. Repeated concentrations of fire by our artillery have only led to pauses in the work . . .'[59]

During the next few days accounts of raiding and patrolling dominated the daily Situation Reports, but the perceived developing risk, especially to Sector *Zollern*, was taken extremely seriously and plans were made by the German miners to take pre-emptive action in this critical sector. In the meantime harassing fire with artillery and mortars was maintained against the suspected entrances to the enemy galleries. Finally, the Commander Engineers at Headquarters I Bavarian Reserve Corps decided that the risk to the German front line in Sector *Zollern* was so great that there was to be offensive action in Mining Sector 1. Galleries 35, 36, 37 and 38 were to be charged and blown. The intention was to use 700 *Zentner* [700 x 50 kilograms = 35 tonnes] of explosive. This was one of the largest explosions of its type ever, certainly on the German side of the lines, up until that moment of the war.[60]

Reserve Infantry Regiment 262, commanded by Major Freiherr von Rotenhan, was involved in producing the labour required to move this mass of explosive. Its regimental history later recalled:

> "During the night 22/23 March, charging of the four mine galleries was completed and the explosion took place at 4.10 am. Everything went according to plan. Our own lines were barely touched and the rim of the easternmost crater, which was approximately four metres high, was occupied by us. The explosion took place in front of the 5th Company Sector, which at the time was being commanded temporarily by Reserve

Leutnant Mauer. The company was deployed on the right [northern] flank of the regiment *(Zollern I)*. Altogether four craters were produced. Unfortuantely, during this operation two of our comrades – Unteroffizier Gürtler and Grenadier Bartel – were shot through the head and killed by British [*sic.*] snipers. With the death of Unteroffizier Gürtler, a secondary school teacher by profession, 5th Company lost a man whose exemplary soldierly bearing and unshakeable calmness meant that he would never be forgotten. The extent of the explosion, during which Engineer (Mining) Company 293 distinguished itself greatly, was underlined by the fact that during the previous nights a relay team of 400 men from 1st Battalion Reserve Infantry Regiment 262 brought up a total of nearly 150 *Zentner* to the front line."[61]

In actual fact what the Germans had probably detected was the work of the Allied miners putting the finishing touches to offensive mines, designed to be blown at the start of the main assault on Vimy Ridge. In the event, the ground was so badly torn up on the lower slopes of Hill 145 by the 23 March blasts that, taken together with countless other craters from the previous eighteen months, the plan to blow additional mines in support of the Canadian infantry on 9 April in this particular area was scrapped, although routes down into the Longfellow crater were produced when 172nd Tunnelling Company blew three mobile charges. Traversing the terrain was already a major problem, without adding to it. Other large preliminary mines were blown by the British engineers just before the assault did take place, including one massive one in the south of the regimental area, near the boundary with Sector *Arnulf*.

Following closely on the heels of the *Zollern* mine blasts, work was completed on the major offensive mining attack planned to counter Allied mining efforts against The Pimple. It is small wonder that charging the galleries had been such a long drawn out affair, because no less than forty five tonnes of explosive was used. The gaping craters that were such a feature of this area for many years were, however, the result of earlier explosions. This attack had a different objective. In his report of 28 March 1917,[62] the Mining Commander at 16th Bavarian Infantry Division described the ultimate success of this difficult operation:

> "Sector *Döberitz*: Enemy mining activity in this area was once again intense. It appeared as if the enemy had spotted the charging work in Sub-Sector *D4* and had been attempting, by means of the hasty production of a mine chamber, to gain an advantage over us. During a short period of time the sound of fifty shot holes being fired was detected under our lines between Mine Galleries 18 and 19.[63] Our response was to accelerate the preparations for the blowing of the mines, the date of which was moved forward twenty four hours. At 5.30 am on 26 March, Mine Galleries 18, 19, 20, 20(I), 21 and 22, charged collectively with 45,000 kilograms [of explosives] were blown. The explosions worked perfectly. No craters were produced, but the shockwaves penetrated right down to

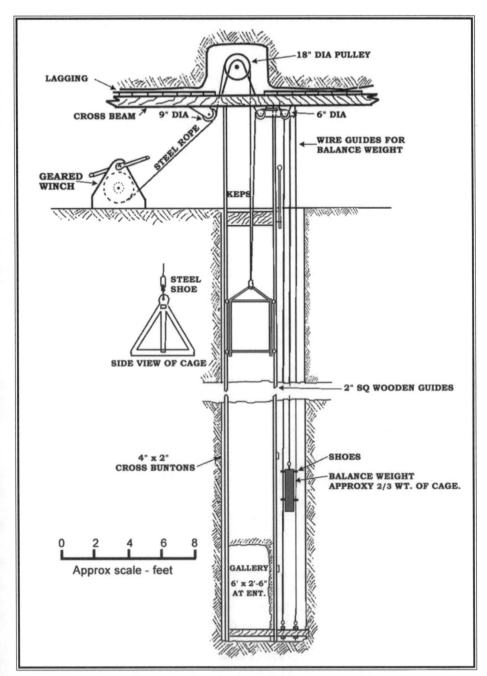

Diagram 2. Typical German Winching Arrangement during Shaft Construction
(Diagram GPG Robinson)

the water table, so the enemy, who were working rather deeper than we were, could not fail to have been affected.

"The galleries where the explosions had occurred were tested for gas that evening. This established the fact that the upper parts of those galleries which survived intact are reusable. It may be presumed that this series of explosions has rendered impossible further use of this particular mine system, even if major clearance work is undertaken."

Although this attack was the major event in *Döberitz* towards the end of March 1917, it was not the only engineering project in that sector at the time. The Engineer Commander continues:

"In the Sector of 3rd Company Engineer Regiment 20, the enemy has been hard at work and has approached to within eight metres of Mine Gallery 3a. Because the enemy were expected to close in here, Mine Gallery 3a had been charged previously with 125 *Zentner* [125 x 50 kilograms = 6.25 tonnes] of explosive. This was blown at 8.40 am on 25 March. Here, too, there was no crater but, because this was a very strong charge, it may certainly be assumed that it crushed the workings of the enemy. During the days following the explosions no further enemy mining activity has been detected."

It is, perhaps, indicative of the stress placed on mining that during March 1917, 16th Bavarian Infantry Division still had no fewer than six mining companies operating along the front in Sectors *Schwerin, Ansbach, Burg* and *Döberitz,* though it is true that *Schwerin*, together with 1st Company Engineer Battalion 20, was handed over complete to 80th Reserve Division on 26 March in association with the final deployment of divisions in the Vimy area ahead of the forthcoming defensive battle. It is interesting to examine the Weekly Report for 22–28 March 1917 by the Commander Mining of 16th Bavarian Infantry Division,[64] because it is indicative of the amount of underground work still being carried out at this time all along the Vimy front. The company sectors were distributed south along the divisional front as far as the northern approach to Hill 145.

"In the sector of 1st Company Engineer Regiment 20 a listening watch was maintained in all galleries up to 24 March. No sound of enemy mining was detected. On 24 and 25 March, Sub-Sectors *S[chwerin] 1, 2 and 3* were handed over to Bavarian Mining Company 4. 2nd Company Engineer Regiment 20 assumed responsibility for Sub-Sectors *B[urg] 1* and *B2*, whilst retaining its previous sector . . . 1st Company Engineer Regiment 20 took over the previous sector of Bavarian Mining Company 4 and continued the existing work patterns . . .

"In the sector of 2nd Company Engineer Regiment 20 the following week was carried out:
  – Gallery *Axel*: de-watering
  – Galleries *Bello e, B3* and *B4* were all driven forward, in addition to

clearance work on blockages to the blind sap leading to the entrances and de-watering.
- Gallery *Weisse a* was also driven forward. Its blocked blind sap was also cleared and de-watering took place.

The ladders in all vertical shafts were tested and, if necessary, re-secured.

"The following work was carried out in the following galleries of Bavarian Mining Company 4 [located in Sector *Döberitz*]:
- Gallery *Gerda b* was driven forward
- In Gallery *Goa*, work continued to link it into the associated crater in front of the position.
- In Gallery *Kuno,* clearance work took place and a ventilation system was installed.
- Gallery *Kurt* was driven forward.
- Clearance work took place in Gallery *1*.

Listeners in the vertical shaft of *Gerda* detected enemy miners who were working twenty to twenty five metres half right . . . On 24 and 25 March the sector was handed over to 1st Company Engineer Regiment 20 and Mining Company 4 moved to Sector *Schwerin*.

"In the sector of 3rd Company Engineer Regiment 20 work took place at the following points:
- Gallery *3*. Mine Chamber 3a was charged and tamped.
- Galleries *Otto a, b* and *c* were driven forward and work took place to clear entrance a, which was blocked.
- Gallery *Konrad a* was driven forward and track was laid to facilitate the movement forward of explosives.

Listening watch in this sector revealed the following information:
- Gallery *2c* Enemy mining was detected fifteen metres distant, half right on 22 March.
- Gallery *3a* On 22 and 23 March, enemy miners were heard working left and half left at about eight to ten metres distance.
- Gallery *3b* The sound of enemy mining was detected ten metres to the right on 22, 23 and 24 March.
- Gallery *3c* To the left of the vertical shaft, enemy miners were heard working fifteen to twenty metres away on 22 and 23 March.
- Gallery *4a* Enemy mining was detected at an unknown distance half right from the tamped charge
- Gallery *4b* The sound of enemy miners was heard at an unknown distance half left.
- Gallery *5b* Half left of the fork in the gallery enemy knocking could be heard at a distance of eighteen to twenty metres.
- *5d* Half left of the main gallery, enemy knocking or hammering was heard at a distance of between twenty and twenty four metres on 23 and 24 March.

- Gallery *6a* On 23 and 24 March enemy knocking could be heard half
left at a distance of between twenty and twenty four metres.

"Work was carried out as follows in the sector of 4th Company
Engineer Regiment 20:
- Gallery *12* The entrance has been collapsed completely by enemy
fire. Clearance work is in progress.
- Gallery *13 L* This was driven forward. Steps and a hand rail have
been installed and the windlass has been removed. The passage
would otherwise have been too narrow in the event that it needed
to be charged. The ventilation system has been completed.
- Galleries *14 L* and *R* were driven forward and the linking gallery
reinforced with wood.
- Gallery *Fritz b* was driven forward. A hand rail and steps have been
installed and the ventilation system has been completed.
- Gallery *Paul b* was driven forward. A hand rail and steps have been
installed.

"In 4th Company Engineer Regiment 20 sector, all six galleries in the
front line were charged and tamped. At 5.30 am 26 March all the mine
chambers were exploded simultaneously. The explosions were apparently effective."

What is notable here is not so much the detail but the fact that all this work,
some of it only of apparent use in the long term, was carried out, despite the fact
that the bombardment in support of the attack on Vimy Ridge had already begun
on 20 March. Not only were the German mining companies able to carry out
maintenance and listening in their galleries but, as has been noted, during this
final week of March they also detonated two massive series of explosions in
Sectors *Döberitz* and *Zollern*. It is important to emphasise the scale of the
German mining effort, even during the final weeks of their occupation of Vimy
Ridge when there were many other demands on their engineering resources,
because it is not uncommon to come across the assertion that once the Royal
Engineers had become established in the area, the German miners were contin-
ually bested.

The facts do not support this interpretation. The opposing efforts to achieve
dominance or to obtain local tactical advantages had certainly left the entire front
from Angres, through the *Gießler Höhe*, The Pimple, Hill 145, La Folie, Thélus,
Ecurie and Roclincourt to St Laurent Blangy, pockmarked with countless craters,
the production of which had absorbed the total efforts of thousands of miners
and their labourers. As a result, soldiers manning the front line and advanced
saps during this time, lived with constant psychological pressure and the fear of
being blown up. However the question must be posed: did this vast outpouring
of effort, this massive investment in the war underground, lead to a decisive
advantage for either side? Elsewhere on the Western Front, it most certainly did;

the use of mines at Messines the following June was undoubtedly decisive but, here at Vimy, the lines moved hardly at all.

Nevertheless, by early 1916, the German miners had gained a clear underground lead over their French counterparts. The British mining companies managed first to check this offensive, then to counter it and to develop systems which prevented the Germans from turning their favourable situation into one of distinct tactical advantage. The very fact that Operation *Schleswig Holstein* was launched at the end of May 1916 is proof of the effectiveness of the work. In addition, it can be argued that the production of the many subways to facilitate the move forward of the Canadian Corps during the night 8/9 April 1917 was of the first importance, though this work was an adjunct to British mining operations and not their *raison d'être,* just as was the case for the German engineers, who produced the *Schwaben, Prinz Arnulf, Völker* and other tunnels, in order to provide covered approaches to the front.

In the final analysis, the lasting thought created and sustained by the legacy of craters along the front line: many of them now filled in, but the surviving examples green, shallower than before and softened by time, is the devotion to duty and heroism of the men of both sides involved in mining and counter-mining on Vimy Ridge. Working in appalling conditions and at constant risk of their health and their lives, they gave their all, elevating their craft to levels rarely reached on other sectors of the Western Front. Their courage and skill was seldom equalled and never surpassed.

Wer ist mächtiger als der Tod?
Wer da lachen kann, wenn er droht!
Und wer, wenn die Erde bebt, kann stehn?
Wer nicht fürchtet unterzugehn!

Who is mightier than Death?
He who simply mocks its threat!
Who stands fast when the earth quakes and heaves?
He who cares not if this life he leaves!

Friedrich Rückert[65]

Notes
1. Lehmann: History K.B. Pionier Regiment p 17
2. Kriegsarchiv München 1 Res. Div. Bd 45 N.O. A.O.K. 6 B. Nr. 4079 26.1.16
3. Kriegsarchiv München AOK 6 Bd 433 N.O. A.O.K. 6 B. Nr. 4459 22.3.16
4. Kriegsarchiv München AOK 6 Bd 433 N.O. A.O.K. 6 B. Nr. 4792 13. Mai 1916
5. Kriegsarchiv München 1. Res. Div. Bd 45 N.O. A.O.K. 6 B. Nr. 4884 25.V.1916
6. Kriegsarchiv München Pi. Btl. 1 Bd 5 I.B.A.K. No. 5459 7.4.1916
7. Eventually a total of four mining companies were raised in this way.
8. Kriegsarchiv München R. Pi. Kp. 1 Bd 2 *Spreng-Trichter*
9. Kriegsarchiv München R. Pi. Kp. 1 Bd 1 *Kriegstagebuch*

10. Kriegsarchiv München R. Pi. Kp. 1 Bd 2 *Spreng-Trichter*
11. Kriegsarchiv München Pi. Btl. 17 Bd 6 . Kommandeur der Pioniere I.B.R.K. 6.5.15
12. A camouflet is a sub-surface charge which is designed to be contained within the earth and not break surface. One common use of relatively small charges was to place and tamp them in close proximity to an enemy mine gallery. These were intended, when exploded, to crush or collapse the opponent's underground workings.
13. Kriegsarchiv München Pi. Btl. 17 Bd 6 . Kommandeur der Pioniere I.B.R.K. 17.5.15
14. Lehmann: History K.B. Pionier Regiment p 263
15. Lehmann: History K.B. Pionier Regiment p 264
16. The body of Pionier Georg Eichhorn was recovered later. He is buried in the German cemetery at St Laurent Blangy in the *Kamaradengrab*.
17. Lehmann: History K.B. Pionier Regiment p 274
18. *Dora* was located in the northern section of Sector *Wittelsbach*, approximately 1,500 metres southwest of Thélus
19. Lehmann: History K.B. Pionier Regiment p 276
20. Lehmann: History K.B. Pionier Regiment p 276
21. Kriegsarchiv München Pi Btl 1 Bd 4 No. 2271 Kommandeur der Pioniere I.B.A.K. 24.10.15
22. A blind sap comprises a section of trench dug out from an existing trench, usually at right angles to it and designed to fulfil a particular purpose. It was not otherwise connected to the trench system. Apart from being used to place mortar pits or the start of mine galleries, one of the most common uses was as an advanced post, forward of the front line and intended to prevent patrols or raiding parties from making surprise attacks on the main position.
23. The use of the term 'powder' in this context should not be taken to mean black powder (i.e. gunpowder). The German engineers had access to powdered explosives, such as *Westfalite*, *Donarit* and *Glückauf*, all of which were had similar heaving properties as Ammonal. *Glückauf* was an explosive of the Grisoutite type, containing ammonium nitrate and vegetable meal, to which, depending on the formulation, any of the following could be added: sugar, resin, fatty oil, potassium nitrate, ammonium oxalate, copper ammonium nitrate or sodium chloride. It had been used previously in potash mining. *Donarit* was the trade name of another Grisoutite type. It was made by Carbonite of Hamburg. The usual mixture was ammonium nitrate (eighty parts), TNT (twelve parts), rye flour (four parts) and nitroglycerine (four parts). *Westfalite* was fabricated in both the United Kingdom and Germany and used for coal mining, or more general blasting. The German type was formulated in many different ways, but originally was made by milling ammonium nitrate with an alcoholic solution of gum lace.
24. *Unsere Pioniere im Weltkrieg* pp 63–68
25. Kriegsarchiv München 2. Feld-Pion.-Komp. I B.A.K. Beilage 34a 24.1.1916
26. Time was frequently saved on occasions like this by making use of the redundant parts of the galleries for stacking spoil.
27. Kriegsarchiv München 2. Feld-Pion.-Komp. I B.A.K. Beilage 34a 24.1.1916
28. In the German army at the time heavy howitzers were known as 'mortars'. In order to make it clear that this type of mortar was altogether lighter, dug into a static position and manned, not by the artillery, but usually by engineers at this stage of the war, they were referred to generically as *Erdmörser* [earth mortars]. They launched large mortar bombs relatively short distances.

29. Kriegsarchiv München 2. Feld-Pion.-Komp. I B.A.K. Beilage 34a 24.1.1916
30. Kriegsarchiv München 2. Feld-Pion.-Komp. I B.A.K. Beilage 34a 24.1.1916
31. Kriegsarchiv München 2. Feld-Pion.-Komp. I B.A.K. Beilage 34a 24.1.1916
32. Trench names beginning with letters in sequence, in this case apparently from *Konrad* to *Siegfried*, are indicative of names allocated prior to the operation to the trenches and saps in the area to be captured. This facilitated the giving of orders and passage of information.
33. Niebelschütz: History Reserve Infantry Regiment 230 p 59
34. Niebelschütz: History Reserve Infantry Regiment 230 p 60
35. Niebelschütz: History Reserve Infantry Regiment 230 pp 63 – 66
36. Kriegsarchiv München Pi. Btl. 1 Bd 5 Kommandeur der Pioniere I. B.A.K. 14.2.1916
37. Karitzky: History Reserve Jäger Battalion 9 pp 41 – 42
38. During this exchange of mine blasts, the British miners were from 182nd Tunnelling Company RE. The German blow on 18 April killed four British sappers and destroyed thirty three metres of gallery. Retaliating on 20 April, the British blew a camouflet weighing about 550 kilograms, which damaged the German mine system and may have exploded a pre-positioned mine. Subsequent German blasts damaged two more British headings and the bombardment on 24 April also damaged a British mine gallery entrance and the trench leading to it.
39. This mine, blown at 8.00 pm German time, caused considerable damage to the workings and equipment of 176th Tunnelling Company RE. It could have been worse. Listeners detected German activity and a critical section of trench was evacuated. The company commander, Major G Momber RE, reported later that he was certain that the lives of at least thirty infantrymen had been saved and three other men who had been buried were dug out alive by one of the sappers.
40. Gropp: History Reserve Infantry Regiment 76 pp 129–132
41. Sievers: History Reserve Infantry Regiment 93 p 122
42. Sievers: History Reserve Infantry Regiment 93 pp 122–124
43. Stosch: History Footguard Regiment 5 p 244
44. Gropp: History Reserve Infantry Regiment 76 pp 136–140
45. Gropp's estimate of depth is highly improbable. Although the record shows that mines beginning at the base of shafts were driven forty or more metres below the ground, inclined galleries were shallower. It is much more likely that these workings were approximately twenty five to thirty metres down.
46. Lünzmann's was a well-known Hamburg eating establishment.
47. Comment has already been made that this depth is most improbable. Nevertheless to be alone in a tiny passage twenty five to thirty metres below ground would have been quite sufficient in the circumstances to induce feelings of claustrophobia and fear.
48. K.T.K = *Kampftruppenkommandeur* [Commander of the Forward Troops]. This was the title given to the battalion commander of the forward battalion of a regiment, who was in command of all troops in a particular sector, regardless of their unit affiliation.
49. Gropp: History Reserve Infantry Regiment 76 pp 133–134
50. This operation was the work of 176th Tunnelling Company RE. The British version of events tallies exactly with the German one. At 10.45 pm British time (11.45 German time) two charges of 4,000 and 2,725 kilograms were blown simultaneously, which explains why the ensuing crater was so large. There was

German attempt at retaliation the following night when a camouflet was blown but, according to the records it, 'did little damage'.

51. Robinson Collection: Personal communication Olaf Grieben 15.1.1989
52. Kriegsarchiv München I Reserve Korps Bd 147 (10.1.1917)
53. It is interesting to note that this elementary error was still being made eighteen months after Commander Engineers at I Bavarian Corps had laid out the options clearly. Either the passage of information was less than ideal or something had gone awry with the approval of plans and subsequent inspections.
54. Kriegsarchiv München 11 I.R. Bd 16 (20 Februar 1917)
55. Kriegsarchiv München 16th Infantry Division Bd 4 : 54 (15 März 1917)
56. Kriegsarchiv München 1. Res Division Bd 20 : 173 (7.3.1917) and 235 (10.3.1917)
57. Kriegsarchiv München 1. Res Division Bd 20 : 257 (11.3.1917) It is interesting to note that the British Inspector of Mines in a report written in late April 1917 admitted that British spoil disposal was a weak point in their mining technique. 'Disposal of Spoil. The enemy pays strict attention to this. No cases of large visible dumps are reported; it is extremely probable that this is one reason why his rate of progress underground is so much slower than ours – for unless large working-parties were provided, the mining shifts would have to clear the bags. In this respect the German work compares very favourably with ours, for as a rule the site of our underground work is betrayed by enormous accumulations of spoil.'
58. Kriegsarchiv München 1. Res Division Bd 20 : 277 (12.3.1917)
59. Kriegsarchiv München 1. Res Division Bd 20 : 299 (13.3.1917)
60. The blowing of these four mines produced what was later given the name the 'Longfellow Crater' by the Allies. The craters are located (and may still be seen) between Broadmarsh Crater and the Visitor Centre of the Canadian National Memorial, Vimy. See *The Battle for Vimy Ridge 1917* Jack Sheldon and Nigel Cave pp 218–219. The main aim seems to have been to disrupt British mines. In fact the nearest galleries were those dug to attack the Broadmarsh Crater and the Durand Mine. Apart from slight roof fall, neither was affected. The explosions did, however, destroy a 'Wombat' drilling chamber at the end of Black Watch Tunnel, causing it to be abandoned.
61. Fischer: History Reserve Infantry Regiment 262 p 107
62. Kriegsarchiv München 16th Infantry Division Bd 4 : 94 (28.3. [17])
63. Prior to the assault on 9 April 1917, several subways were driven forward under the slopes of The Pimple, without any concern about the noise this produced. It is probable that this work was the source of the sounds heard by the German listening team and what they were actually witnessing was the construction of one or more of Coburg, Gobron, Blue Bull or Vincent subways.
64. Kriegsarchiv München 16th Infantry Division Bd 4 : 95 (28.3. [17])
65. The quotation is from *Der Rätsel der Elfen* [The Riddle of the Elves] by Friedrich Rückert (1788–1866), who wrote under the pseudonym Freimund Raimar. Rückert was a prolific poet with mastery of many different forms of verse and an outstanding self-taught orientalist.

CHAPTER SIX

1917: The Build Up to the Assault on Vimy Ridge

On 3 January 1917, the Intelligence Branch at Sixth Army issued a secret internal memorandum on a distribution list restricted to the Commander, Chief of Staff and the Heads of the Operational and Logistic Branches:

"The Military Attaché in Stockholm despatched a telegram on 2 January 1917 stating that a pro-German Swede had written from London that British soldiers have been informed that an offensive is planned for the new year. To that end troops and stockpiles of ammunition are being positioned around Arras." [1]

The report was only one of many such which were received and processed by the intelligence staffs in the higher headquarter around that time. It was already perfectly clear that a major Allied offensive was in the offing, but not where it would be launched so, two days later, the Operations Branch issued down to corps and divisional headquarters an extract of an assessment made (presumably) by the Army High Command relating to possible options open to the Allies:[2]

"Top Secret! To be handled by officers only!

Subject – Offensive Options for the Entente.

The following extract from a Top Secret report is intended to be seen only by those on the distribution list. There is to be no further written distribution – not even in the form of extracts.

At the same time the relevant [headquarters] are, on the basis of this extract, to ensure that all necessary steps are taken to ensure that measures taken by the enemy on the Army front are recognised in time and reported. This applies especially to [signs of] systematic preparations for the offensive, establishment of exact information concerning the enemy order of battle and deployment, the introduction of fresh enemy formations or the retention behind the front of formations withdrawn from it.

Extract

"Reports relating to the forthcoming offensives – almost every sector of the Western Front has been mentioned in this context – probably owe their origin to the fact that the French and the British are preparing the entire length of their fronts for the assault. Examination of press reports indicates that it is the intention of the enemy to conceal the location of their main thrusts until the last minute so that the spring offensive may be launched with surprise. Once more the region of the Somme has been under consideration. Further, priority for the French will be Champagne and for the British the sector Arras – Lille. If political considerations are of overriding importance then the French might launch a main offensive in Lorraine, with a subsidiary one in Alsace, whilst the British could chose Belgian territory (Messines Ridge and the coast).

"The systematic preparation of the entire front means that it will not be as easy to determine the attack sectors in good time, as it was prior to the offensives of autumn 1915 and before the Battle of the Somme, for example. Many of the indicators of previous attacks, such as the construction of new battery positions, or the move forward and development of infantry trenches will be lacking and it is always possible to range in the artillery in an unobtrusive manner. More than before it is going to be important to establish the pattern of deployment along the enemy front and to detect when fresh enemy formations have been placed in position (in some circumstances these may only be deployed for short periods for the purpose of orientation). Above all every effort must be made and all sources exploited (statements by prisoners of war; information from letters and agents) to determine the location of formations held back out of the line. Their movement forward in large numbers will be one of the primary indicators that an attack is imminent. Aerial reconnaissance to spot the establishment of new camps or increased traffic will also provide clues as to where concentrations are occurring behind the lines.

"There are numerous mentions in the foreign press that there will be constant thrusts, i.e. local attacks with limited objectives, to keep the German army occupied and to prevent its reserves from being rested. Such attacks can be expected at any time, anywhere along the line . . . Nothing specific can yet be said regarding the timing of the great offensive of 1917. Above all it will depend upon when the preparations are complete. This will include the transportation to France of at least some of the second line Territorial Divisions, currently stationed in England and the formation of fresh French formations using coloured Frenchmen. The involvement of General Nivelle is a guarantee that the attack will only be launched after the most careful preparations, down to the smallest detail, have been completed. As a result there is no possibility that the French-British army will be ready to attack before 1 March.

"The choice of start date will be dependent on the weather and the general situation; especially the situation in the south and southeast. The assessment of the situation and the options open to Germany will also play a role. The offensive would only be long delayed after 1 March if the intention was that Russia should be involved."

Attack is universally regarded as the best form of defence so, at the turn of the year, the planners at Army Group Crown Prince Rupprecht were directed to draft an options paper: *Proposal for Operations in the French Theatre of Operations in Spring 1917.*[3] This was signed by the Chief of Staff, General der Infanterie Hermann von Kuhl, on 15 January. After reviewing the numbers of Allied troops located in France, together with anticipated future reinforcements, the paper outlined the possible offensive options open to the Allies in 1917. Although the planners concluded that it was, at that stage, impossible to predict where the attacks might occur, an assault on Vimy Ridge was certainly included as a possibility. The paper then went on to consider what pre-emptive actions were open to the German army in general and the Army Group in particular.

An offensive, designed to lead to a breakthrough, was briefly considered then discounted; the means were lacking and the risk of failure, with consequent irreplaceable losses, too high. Attacks with limited objectives were then considered. The short list included the Loos salient, an attack astride the Somme, an assault by Seventh Army between the Oise-Aisne Canal and Berry au Bac and an attack on Arras. It was considered that although an Arras offensive would have a morale value if it was achieved, any thoughts of pressing forward to retake the Lorette Spur would be impossible and that anyway it would take two months to prepare and require a minimum of eight divisions and 150 heavy artillery batteries in support.

Doubt was cast on the ability of the German army to create sufficient fighting power to make even these limited objectives feasible in the near term. There was also the particular risk that if divisions were used up in the assault, the Army Group would be ill-placed to counter likely enemy attacks as and when they were mounted. The paper finally concluded that,

> "There is nothing else for it, but to prepare for the anticipated attacks and to ensure that the troops are as well prepared as possible to counter them. Despite the difficulty in accepting the fact, despite the beneficial effect on the morale of our men, any thought of conducting even limited attacks must be renounced. It is essential that we win the 1917 campaign, which we shall do if we succeed through defensive battles in holding on to what we currently have.
>
> "Small-scale operations, such as those conducted by First Army at Bouchavesnes and Second Army near La Maisonette, which can either be mounted from within our own resources, or with very limited reinforcement, must be launched wherever and whenever possible, in order to raise the spirits of the troops."

There the matter rested at the strategic and operational levels for the time being. Along Vimy Ridge the pattern of low-level skirmishing continued throughout January and into February then, on 12 February, an extraordinary incident occurred somewhere around the La Folie area, when a deserter from C Company Royal Canadian Regiment succeeded in slipping away from his own lines and making himself known to men of Reserve Infantry Regiment 23 from 12th Reserve Division. It was almost their last act at the end of a three month tour of duty in the

Vimy area, because the regiments of 1st Bavarian Reserve Division took over the sector two days later. The man's real name was Otto Ludwig Dörr. He was nineteen years old at the time and had been born in Frankfurt am Main, where his father had worked as the driver of a hackney carriage. Dörr was interrogated on at least three occasions, cooperating fully with his questioners on each occasion.

When he was questioned at Headquarters VI Reserve Corps,[4] he provided the information that he and his parents left for Saskatchewan in 1906, where his father bought a parcel of land and took up farming. Later he and his brother also worked on the farm. Three years after they arrived in Canada the family became naturalised, but never forgot their German roots. Immediately after the outbreak of the war, Dörr decided that he wished to fight for Germany, but the only way he could think of achieving it was to join the Canadian army. Without mentioning anything to his father, he enlisted in Saskatoon in April 1916 under a false name and was posted to the 97th Battalion. According to his Sixth Army interrogator,[5] after training in Toronto and Aldershot, Nova Scotia, he left Canada with his Battalion on 17 September 1916, on board HMT Olympic,[6] which also transported the 100th, 107th, 108th and 144th Battalions, together with a battery of field guns to England.

After a few weeks in England, he left for France on 21 October 1916 with a draft of 152 trained men of 97th Battalion, who were sent to join the Royal Canadian Regiment. He then spent some weeks in France undergoing advanced training and being issued with additional clothing and equipment, before joining the Royal Canadian Regiment in mid-December 1916. On his arrival he was employed as a

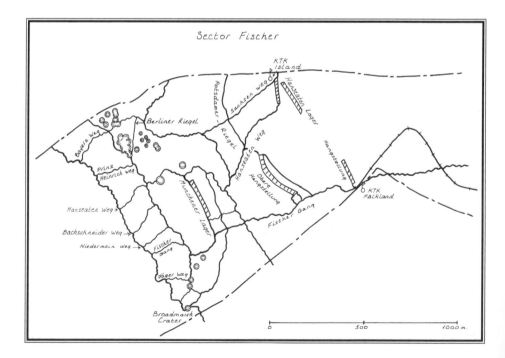

stretcher bearer, even though he had not received relevant training. Once he was sent into the trenches he constantly sought an opportunity to desert. This finally occurred during the morning of 11 February [*sic*][7] when he found himself unobserved near to a crater. He moved from the lip of the crater to a sap, which led towards the German lines. Nearing them he came under fire, but took cover in a shell hole until the firing stopped. He then shouted to the German troops to indicate his intentions and entered the German trenches.

Unsurprisingly, Dörr provided the Germans with a great deal of background information on a wide range of topics. At a later stage he was interviewed at length (about British protective gas equipment on one occasion),[8] but initially it was of more use to his interrogators to know about the whereabouts of the various Canadian formations, locations of mine galleries and ammunition and stores dumps. All of this was forthcoming, as were these forecasts:

> "Because recently a great deal of ammunition has been dumped behind this front and new guns have been moved into position, there is much talk amongst the troops of a major Canadian attack against Vimy Ridge."[9]

> "A more-or-less strong British offensive is predicted for the early part of the year. It is expected to be a dreadful clash (infernal hell [*sic*]). For the Canadians, Vimy Ridge, north of Neuville St Vaast, has been selected as the objective for attack. The prisoner claims to have observed a constant build up of artillery. He does not believe, however, that the attack will begin before the middle of March."[10]

On 13 February a large scale raid was launched by 4th Canadian Division against The Pimple in Sector *Döberitz*. Commanded by Lieutenant Colonel Davies, Commanding Officer of 44th Battalion and with the assistance of men of 176th Tunnelling Company RE, the aim of this operation was to capture prisoners and materiel from the German positions. Manning this sector at the time was Bavarian Infantry Regiment 11 of the newly formed 16th Bavarian Infantry Division, with four companies forward, divided between the first and second trenches of the First Position and with access to good quality deep mined dugouts. The regimental history describes the operation in rather guarded terms:[11]

> "Suddenly, during the early morning of 13 February, heavy artillery and mortar fire started coming down along the full length of Vimy Ridge then, at 5.15 am, the enemy attacked the two right hand companies in Sector *Döberitz* in three strong waves. They succeeded in penetrating the forward positions in several places but, after a lengthy battle with many casualties, they were driven out once more."

Because of the high number of Canadian casualties, the raid cannot be regarded as particularly successful, despite the fact that the Canadians claimed that they had captured fifty two prisoners and inflicted a further 160 casualties. It is difficult to understand how they were able to arrive at that figure, but they were, in fact, very close to the truth. Responding to a very terse and coldly worded tasking by 9 Bavarian Brigade Commander, Generalmajor Großmann – [12]

"Subject: Operation on 13 February.

I require a sketch map which clearly indicates the following items:
– Where did the enemy assault groups force their way in? Which routes did they probably use? What are the places where enemy dead were found?
– Which dugouts were crushed or buried by the <u>bombardment</u>?
– Which dugouts were damaged by having hand grenades or incendiary devices thrown into them?
– In which of the destroyed dugouts are there still the bodies of men who were buried? Approximate total?"

- Bavarian Infantry Regiment 11 reported that their casualties had been forty four killed (including Oberleutnant Breher and Reserve Leutnant Reuter[13]), 110 wounded (including Vizefeldwebel and Offizierstellvertreter Brehm) and fifty two missing

In addition to the casualties they had caused, the Canadians believed that they had destroyed forty one dugouts and five mine galleries. During the course of the operation, a sergeant from 44th Battalion was taken prisoner, together with four severely wounded men from 46th and 50th Battalions.[14] Fortunately, examination of the sergeant's lengthy interrogation report[15] permits a somewhat clearer picture to be drawn of how this major raid, which involved one officer and eighty men from each of 44th, 46th, 47th and 50th Battalions, was planned and conducted. There had been one complete rehearsal in open country near Bouvigny the previous day by all involved in this ambitious operation. During the night 12/13 February they had moved forward into trenches which had been held by men of 46th and 50th Battalions for the previous twenty four hours and launched their attack after a pause of fifteen minutes, advancing directly behind the barrage through gaps in the wire which had been prepared previously.

At precisely 4.00 am (Allied time) the British artillery opened up. This was the signal for the start of the raid . . . Each battalion group had about twenty riflemen. The remainder were made up of bombers, carriers and stretcher bearers. Fire support was provided by two Lewis gun teams in No Man's Land. Even before the attackers reached the first German trench defensive artillery fire was brought down, causing casualties to mount. As the raiders reached the first German trench, their artillery fire was lifted onto the second trench. In the opinion of the sergeant only a few men had been able to get forward to the second trench, even though the orders had been to advance at all costs as far as the German third trench.

The entire operation was scheduled to last only thirty minutes. The lack of complete success was put down by the sergeant to, 'Insufficient preparation. All the participants stormed forward blindly, without having a clear idea about their tasks.' He also felt that, 'the Germans must have been ready for the attack because [their] artillery fire came down like lightning'. The routes back to the Canadian trenches were marked with white tape to simplify the withdrawal, but there was no designated signal for the start of it. The Canadian intelligence staffs undoubtedly obtained much useful information from the interrogation of the German prisoners, but the advantage was not simply to one side. Once again, the report by the German interrogators had yielded a great deal of low-level intelligence and further confirmation that, 'There was much talk of the start of the major Spring Offensive not being far off.'

Despite the high cost of this raid – admittedly to both sides – there was no let up in the pattern of raiding and patrolling, especially along the front between the *Gießler Höhe* and the La Folie Sector. There was another sharp raid directed against Bavarian Infantry Regiment 11 on The Pimple on 16 February. Once more this was preceded by heavy artillery fire along the length of the frontage of 16th Bavarian Infantry Division which began coming down at 4.00 am. Bavarian Infantry Regiment 14, which had barely been touched by the 13 February raid, commented that this time they were not attacked either and attributed this, possibly, to the speed with which their artillery brought down defensive fire to their front.[16] Regardless of the truth, which was probably that their sector was not actually included in the plan for the raid, it is obvious that constant activity like this was bound to increase the watchfulness of their defenders, who must have taken every possible measure to ensure that their guns and all other means of defence were maintained at the highest state of alert at all times. Not only that, but the state of the ground, during this part of February when a sudden thaw made it almost impossible to traverse the terrain quietly or swiftly, all played in to the hands of the defence.

Regardless of the difficulties, the Canadian 4th Division pressed on with its plans, all the time being observed as closely as possible by the watchful defenders. VI Reserve Corps reported on 22 February:[17]

> "No major new battle positions have been observed between 15 and 22 February. Forward of Sector *Fischer* and the right flank of *Arnulf* the number of enemy mortars has been increased and a white band, some 1,200 metres long, together with five white boards at intervals of 150 – 200 metres have been observed in the enemy's wire obstacle. This could indicate a forthcoming operation against the *Fischer – Arnulf* Sector.[18] In isolated locations some minor sandbag work has been seen, but there are no further indications of a gas attack. Nevertheless this remains a risk in Sector *Wittelsbach*. Mining is still continuing in Sectors *Magdeburg, Döberitz* and *Fischer* . . . "

The corps was certainly correct concerning mining in *Döberitz,* because there were yet more operations, which involved the use of mines, against The Pimple on 19 February. The following day they were the subject of an order by 16th Bavarian Infantry Division, which was signed by the Divisional Commander, Generalmajor Ritter von Möhl.[19]

"Yesterday morning the enemy attacked Sector *Döberitz*, apparently in conjunction with a mine explosion. They were beaten off. During a later attack on Sub-Sector *Döberitz 1* at 6.30 pm, the enemy managed to break into a section of trench before being ejected once more, having left behind large quantities of ammunition, grenades and prepared explosive charges. The artillery worked extremely closely with the infantry during the countering of these raids. I wish to express my appreciation of this, as well as the work of the engineers.

"Everything possible is being done to improve the situation in Sector *Döberitz*. Replacements have been demanded and requests have been made for increased holdings of mortar and artillery ammunition. In a short time the sector of Bavarian Infantry Regiment 11, which is most affected, will be reduced in width. Until then we must hold on as before. 9 [Bavarian] Infantry Brigade is to ensure that a continuous defensive line is re-established. The enemy are to be prevented from establishing themselves in and behind the newly created crater. In addition, until 79th Reserve Division arrives to assume control of Sector *Fischer*, the linkage between Sub-Sectors *Fischer 1* and *Döberitz 4* is to be established so securely that the enemy are prevented from achieving penetrations there."

Despite the fact that the Canadian had been conducting a vigorous policy of offensive patrolling and raiding the length of Vimy Ridge for some weeks at this point, it was the events of mid-February that brought about the first clear-cut example of the effect of all this pressure on the hard-pressed defenders of the key terrain around The Pimple. The memorandum despatched by Oberstleutnant Carl, commander of Bavarian Infantry Regiment 11, to his Brigade Commander, Generalmajor Großmann, on 20 February[20] usefully summarises the concerns of the defenders at this time and provides an accurate description of the accrued losses to date during this costly tour of duty.

"Between 12 and 19 February, the infantry garrison of Sector *Döberitz* has suffered the following casualties: Killed seventy nine; Wounded 217: Total 296. Most of these casualties have been caused by artillery and mortar fire and some by hand grenades during the four major enemy raids on 13, 16 and 19 February (morning and evening). There is no reason to assume that the casualty rate is going to reduce during the foreseeable future.

"The Forward Battalion (2nd Battalion Bavarian Infantry Regiment 11) is occupying the four company Sub-Sectors *Döberitz 1 – 4*. Backing it up is the Support Battalion (1st Battalion Bavarian Infantry Regiment 11). Because of the casualties this battalion suffered when it was Forward Battalion between 12 and 18 February, it only has 259 riflemen still in the line. This weakened strength is sufficient for the fulfilment of its task of maintaining the security of its positions, but is barely so for its task of transporting rations up to the Forward Battalion and definitely not for any necessary counter-stroke or to provide work parties required for the maintenance and improvement of the positions.

"3rd Battalion Bavarian Infantry Regiment 11, which is currently resting, provided more than one third of its strength to reinforce the Forward Battalion between 13 and 18 February. As a result, it cannot be immediately moved back into the front line; otherwise there will be nowhere near sufficient numbers of battle-ready troops available to relieve the Forward Battalion. If enemy attacks against Sector *Döberitz* continue, 2nd Battalion Bavarian Infantry Regiment 11, the Forward Battalion, is going to suffer further severe casualties (losses during the enemy attacks on 19 February: fourteen killed and forty nine wounded).

"It must be assumed, therefore, that the 2nd Battalion, which cannot be reinforced by the current Support Battalion, will not be able to complete its full tour of seven days as Forward Battalion, as is presently envisaged; it will have to be withdrawn into support much sooner. If the 3rd Battalion is to relieve the 2nd Battalion in the front line, the latter, despite its weakened state, will have to move into support. When that happens, the 1st Battalion, which is more than 250 men under strength, will be at rest but, without considerable reinforcement, will not be strong enough to be deployed [subsequently] as Forward Battalion in Sector *Döberitz*.

"Because Bavarian Infantry Regiment 11 is already more than 900 men below strength, because the requested reinforcements are neither likely to arrive during the next ten days, nor to be in the required numbers, I am bringing the particular circumstances of the situation in Sector *Döberitz* to the attention of the chain of command. In my opinion it will be insufficient to reduce its width by a single company sub-sector; rather I consider reduction by two company sub-sectors to be essential."

Analysis of all this raiding gradually began to be factored into the weekly assessments further up the chain of command:

Sixth Army Appreciation of the Situation 24 February 1917 [21]

"[There are] further signs of strong troop concentrations west and southwest of Arras . . . There have been twenty three enemy raids . . . most of them against the Army's right flank but, above all, east of Souchez, where there were three repetitions . . . [Enemy] artillery engaged systematically positions on the Army right flank. This included concentrated fire from many frontal and flanking batteries against Vimy Ridge from Givenchy to Roclincourt . . .

"General Impression. Signs are increasing concerning a forthcoming attack . . . but the strong impression is that nothing is planned to the south of Armentièrers; on the other hand an attack against Vimy Ridge is, as before, [assessed to be] probable."

This point of view was obviously shared at Headquarters Army Group, as evidenced by a diary entry of the commander at the end of February.

Crown Prince Rupprecht of Bavaria: Diary Entry 27 February 1917 [22]

"It does not appear that there is the threat of an immediate attack against the Wijtschate Salient [Messines Ridge]. Proof that no attack is to be expected in the area to the south of Armentières is the deployment there of the inexperienced British 57th Division. Our positions on Vimy Ridge have been so damaged by enemy shells and even more by the effect of the weather that they are ripe for attack. Hardly anywhere is the front line protected by a wire obstacle and it is impossible any more to speak in terms of continuous trenches. Nothing much can be done about this until the beginning of the dry time of year. There is a lack of indicators to suggest that an enemy attack is in the offing, despite the fact that enemy reinforcements have been detected either side of Arras."

During the early morning of 1 March, 4th Canadian Division mounted a very large scale raid designed to locate and destroy German mine galleries from Sector *Zollern* to Sector *Döberitz*, with the main weight of the attack falling on the newly arrived Reserve Infantry Regiment 261 of the Prussian 79th Reserve Division, which was deployed in Sector *Fischer* forward of Hill 145. No fewer than 1,700 men of 11 and 12 Canadian Brigades were involved and, attacking from north to south, were the 73rd, 72nd, 75th and 54th Battalions. The Canadians advanced in waves, the first of which was intended to occupy the front line trench and hold it until succeeding waves had passed through, penetrated into the depths of the German First position and returned; their mission accomplished. So much for the theory: in practice everything went wrong. The attempted use of gas was unsuccessful and the infantry tactics failed against the German defenders, who brought down artillery and mortar fire against the advancing Canadians, driving the rest off with small arms fire and determined local counter-attacks. The Canadians had fallen in dense masses and the attack petered out in front of the barbed wire obstacle. A renewal of the attack at 6.00 am suffered the same fate.

Leutnant Hoppe and Vizefeldwebel Hentschel of 4th Company and Gefreiter Königstein and Signaller Soch of 2nd Company Reserve Infantry Regiment 261, in particular, distinguished themselves during the defeat of this raid. [23] There were German casualties of course, but this was a Canadian disaster. At the end of the operation, hundreds of the participants were dead, wounded or missing and the men of the 4th Division had little or nothing to show for their sacrifice. The following day the commander of Reserve Infantry Regiment 261 offered the Canadians a short ceasefire so that they could recover their dead. Writing about the incident later, he recalled:

Oberst Wilhelm von Goerne, Reserve Infantry Regiment 261 [24]

"On 1 March 1917 took place the great Canadian raid against Vimy Ridge, where Reserve Infantry Regiment 261 had taken up positions just the day previously. This large scale attack, which was renewed several times during the night, was beaten off completely by 2nd, 4th, 9th and 11th Companies which were holding the front line. Not one single enemy soldier got into our trenches. Only the English [*sic*] Major Lucas was hanging on the barbed wire obstacle; otherwise none of the enemy dead could be seen from the trenches. [25] According to the statements of our men, the enemy must have suffered significant casualties. Because I wanted to convince myself of the existence of these allegedly enormous casualties, I went forward of the barbed wire under cover of the fog on the morning of 2nd March from the trenches of 9th Company. I was accompanied by Hauptmann von Koppelow, commander of the 12th Company. Here, hard up against the barbed wire, we came across the dead Canadians, who were indeed very numerous. In fact all the shell holes were filled with the dead. When we were approximately in the centre of No Man's Land, where we could just make out the outlines of the enemy trenches, a shot rang out from there. Hauptmann von Koppelow raised his stick and shouted towards the English [*sic*] trenches that they should cut out that stupid firing. I said, 'Call out to them that the chap should come over here.'

"I should here explain: Until he became a Fahnenjunker [Officer Cadet], Hauptmann von Koppelow had grown up in England. His mother was English. Whenever he spoke German, his English accent was very marked. He also looked very much like an Englishman; to such an extent that, on several occasions, persons behind the front with nothing better to do wanted to arrest him. Initially there was no response to Hauptmann von Koppelow's shouts. Finally a steel helmet and, gradually, a head appeared. Apparently the chap did not trust our peaceful intentions, but in the end he came forward. We asked him where his battalion or regimental commander might be and said that he was to tell him that he should come and meet us. It was still rather foggy, so that although they were only sixty metres away, we could barely make out the enemy trenches. Nobody fired, because Hauptmann von Koppelow had shouted out once more in his perfect English that nobody was to be so stupid as to shoot.

"After about ten minutes an English [*sic*] major arrived, accompanied by two runners armed with rifles. We saluted each other in silence. I opened the conversation, drawing attention to the many dead and pointing out that here and there amongst them there could well be wounded. If he was agreeable, we could negotiate a means of recovering the fallen. He agreed. In the meantime visibility had become clearer and curious faces were to be seen everywhere looking out from the trenches.

We both called several men to us and gave instructions that the word was to be passed along the trenches that there was to be no firing. In addition both sides telephoned higher authority to request permission, which was granted. The artillery was also instructed not to open fire.

"Meanwhile additional officers and runners had arrived from both sides. I had sent for Oberleutnant von Trotha, Oberleutnant Zickner,[26] Rittmeister von Schwerin and several others. Oberleutnants von Trotha and Zickner in particular spoke good English. By now about ten Canadians and ten members of the 261st were standing next to one another. We agreed that a line, to which we would carry the dead, should be drawn in the middle. Here they would be received by the enemy. Assault ladders, which had been intended for use during the raid and which were lying everywhere in profusion, were used to mark the line. Neither party was to cross this line and there was to be no fraternisation. Now the work began. Our men carried the dead on assault ladders to the centre and from there they were taken by the Canadians back to their own trenches. The whole of No Man's Land soon resembled an ant hill as, across the entire regimental front, men hurried to and fro with [these improvised] stretchers.

"We officers stood together with the Canadians on one spot, all of us with pistols on our belts. There was no opportunity for either side to examine the opposing positions. A fleeting glance at the other positions was the most that could have been achieved. Eventually I offered the Canadian officers a cigarette. They all lit up, with the exception of the Canadian major, who put his cigarette away. I asked him why he was not smoking it and he explained that he wanted to keep it as a souvenir. I asked him if he would like another one to smoke and offered him one, which he lit. A conversation never got going. There was really no point in asking anything, because nobody could have given an answer.

"By 2.00 pm about 600–800 dead men had been carried over.[27] We then decided to call a halt for the day, so that it would be possible this same day to transport the dead further to the rear and agreed, having synchronised watches and decided on agreed signals, to resume work the following day at 8.00 am provided that our superiors were in agreement. We further agreed that there would be no firing before 6.00 pm in order to facilitate the move to the rear of the fallen, but that after that the war would continue in the usual manner.

"We went our separate ways at 2.00 pm and even shook hands. Shortly after we had parted, an English [sic] officer of the divisional staff appeared at our trench. He was there to pass on the particular thanks of the divisional commander and to state that the gesture would be reciprocated if a similar situation arose in future. I must state that the Canadians, by their upright military bearing and their behaviour, made an outstanding impression on us. They could almost have been from the 261st!

"Rittmeister von Schwerin had made use of the opportunity to verify the fields of fire of his machine guns and to adjust some of them. Unfortunately it was not possible to continue with the recovery operation the following day. Our superiors were in agreement, but our Bavarian neighbours, having initially agreed, withdrew their assent. All members of the 261st who were present for this remarkable episode, the like of which never occurred on any other occasion during the war, will certainly often have pleasant memories of it."

The Commander of I Bavarian Reserve Corps, General der Infanterie Karl Ritter von Fasbender, was extremely pleased with the performance of the Prussian troops who had only been under his command for twenty four hours and he lost no time in publishing a special Order of the Day on 2 March[28]:

Corps Order of the Day

"During the beating off of the British [*sic*] attack, which was launched during the early hours of 1 March 1917 by three battalions[29] against Sectors *Döberitz, Fischer* and *Zollern,* Regiments 261 and 262 performed brilliantly.

"Almost everywhere the enemy assault withered away in front of our shot-up obstacle, thanks to the small arms fire of the defenders and the timely and swift production of defensive fire by the artillery and mortars. Where the British [*sic*] succeeded temporarily in forcing a way into our trenches, they were ejected by the daring assault troop of 4th Company Reserve Infantry Regiment 261, who engaged them in bitter hand to hand fighting.

"The enemy suffered bloody losses; 160 dead British [*sic*] soldiers lie in front of our positions. Eleven prisoners and one machine gun were captured. Despite their overwhelming superiority the enemy did not succeed in taking one single prisoner.[30]

"I am delighted to be able, in the first days they have been under my command, to congratulate the courageous Regiments 261 and 262 for their marvellous success.

Signed: von Fasbender"

The raid of 1 March was such an utter *débâcle* and the casualties were so high that it is possible that it was the most costly failure of its type of the entire war on the Western Front. The story soon spread (and persists to this day) that somehow the defenders must have had advance information and set a trap which was sprung when the assault began. The eighteen NCOs and men of the Canadian 72nd and 75th Battalions who were captured during the operation definitely thought so. The Head of Intelligence at Sixth Army, Hauptmann Tettenborn, who signed their interrogation report, stated: 'The prisoners can only explain the total failure of the attack by claiming that the Germans must have been informed about the intended operation in advance and lured the attackers into a trap'.[31] There is almost certainly no truth in the suggestion.

There is no mention of any such thing in any of the histories of the regiments of 79th Reserve Division or 16th Bavarian Infantry Division, nor in the monograph *Die 79. Reserve-Division in der Schlacht auf der Vimy-Höhe / April 1917* [79th Reserve Division in the Battle of Vimy Ridge April 1917] by Generalleutnant Alfred Dieterich, who was the Brigade Commander at the time. Indeed, Dieterich states, 'Hardly had the 79th Reserve Division taken up its new positions than, on 1 March, the Canadian Division opposite attempted to capture Vimy Ridge by means of a surprise thrust with strong forces'.[32] In addition, the War Diary of I Bavarian Reserve Corps for 1 March 1917 includes the following entry:[33]

> "6.00 am. The enemy, who have apparently observed the relief of 16th Bavarian Infantry Division by 79th Reserve Division during the past few days, attacked with four battalions at 6.00 am after heavy artillery and mortar preparatory fire (which included gas shells). Whilst the attack could be beaten back in Sectors *Zollern* North (Reserve Infantry Regiment 262), *Fischer 2* and *Fischer 3*, the enemy did force a way into *Fischer 1*. A counterstroke by Reserve Infantry Regiment 261 drove them off once more, capturing eleven prisoners and one machine gun . . . Our casualties amounted to twenty four killed, with no missing. The bloody enemy casualties appear, however, to be very considerable. The performance of the two regiments must be assessed as all the greater because the enemy thrust was driven home in great strength against trenches which had only just been taken over, were largely collapsed and were located in a position that was a sea of mud, which made forward movement difficult . . . "

In fact, out of the large quantities of surviving primary documentation relating to events on and around Vimy Ridge in 1917, the only slight hint that something of the kind was being planned is contained in the interrogation report, dated 27 February 1917, of a sergeant from 'M Company 3rd Battalion Special Brigade RE'.[34]

This man, who is not named, told his interrogator a complete cock and bull story concerning the manner of his capture. He claimed that he was engaged in work, such as construction of temporary camps or roads behind the lines and that he and a companion decided, on their own initiative, to visit the front line to the west of Vimy during the evening of 25 February. Despite being unfamiliar with the ground they attempted to reach the front line, but it had been destroyed by German mortar fire. They lost their way and ended up blundering into the German positions, where his companion was killed and he was captured.

In fact M Company was one of three Special Companies RE (F, M and N), responsible for the delivery on Vimy Ridge of cloud gas from cylinders, so the likelihood is that the sergeant was engaged either in a reconnaissance concerning the future location of cylinders, or was actually involved in their placement at the time of capture. It appears that his story, implausible though it was, was accepted by the Germans and the important paragraph in his interrogation report is the one which states:

"The prisoner maintains that shortly before he was captured he heard from a friend that, according to a rumour, an attack will take place during the night of 26 or 27 February in the sector of 4th Canadian Division. He does not know if it will be a large scale operation or a 'raid' [original inverted commas]. He heard this rumour from only <u>one</u> [original emphasis] of his friends."

It is not completely clear if a telephoned warning had already been passed on to the forward troops, though it probably had been – that was the usual procedure. However it is certain from examination of the mass of surviving source material that no contingency plan was made, nor were there any special arrangements in place to meet the 4th Division raid. Furthermore the insertion of 79th Reserve Division into the Vimy Front, with all its attendant disruption such as radical changes to boundaries and artillery defensive fire zones, to name but two important factors, was barely complete when the raid was launched. It is militarily inconceivable that these changes would have been made at that precise moment if there had been foreknowledge on the German side.

It is far more likely that the operation failed because it was too large and unwieldy, was poorly prepared and badly executed. The use of gas seems, for example, to have been particularly incompetently handled. Despite the fact that the raid was postponed to await a favourable wind, when phosgene and chlorine were eventually released it seems to have been Canadian soldiers who were poisoned. Some of the Germans were completely unaware that any cylinder gas had been used. The Daily Situation Report of Reserve Infantry Regiment 261 for 1 March stated,

"From 3.00 am there was heavy artillery and mortar fire along the whole of the divisional sector and also the adjoining Sector *Döberitz* of 16th Bavarian Infantry Division.[35] The enemy fired a lot of gas, but there was no cloud gas attack. The gas alarm was raised promptly and only four men were slightly affected by it." [36]

Somewhat strangely, the eighteen prisoners (ten from 72nd Battalion 12 Canadian Brigade and eight from 75th Battalion 11 Canadian Brigade), who provided a great deal of intelligence to their interrogators subsequently, mentioned the fact that they had been told that the attack would be preceded by a release of gas, but that none of them had seen any cylinders installed in their trenches and that, furthermore, none of them had been masked up at any time during the raid.

If the use of gas was a fiasco, the German defenders were not impressed either with the tactics employed by the raiders:

"About 5.30 am [*sic*]", stated the Reserve Infantry Regiment 261 Situation Report for 1 March, the British [*sic*] launched an attack on a three battalion front all along Sectors *Döberitz – Fischer – Zollern*. In the lead were six companies armed with Lewis guns. Strong patrols closed in the front of *Zollern 2* and *3*, creeping and rushing forward. Elsewhere the enemy made use of tactics which have been obsolete since the 1915 battles in Champagne; that is to say they advanced in dense waves in quick succession. There were four such waves on the right flank of *Fischer 4*. Columns, two to three men wide, were also used, exploiting old trenches in No Man's Land to the greatest extent possible.

"Because the attack was spotted in time, it was possible to occupy the trenches correctly, to bring down artillery and mortar defensive fire and to mount the machine guns in their firing positions. [As a result] along almost the entire length of the divisional frontage the attack was brought to a standstill, with extremely heavy casualties, in front of the remains of our obstacle. Only on the extreme right flank did the enemy succeed in breaking into a part of Sector *Döberitz* on a one hundred metre front at about 6.00 am. An assault group from 4th Company Reserve Infantry Regiment 261 under Vizefeldwebel Henschel succeed in ejecting them within half an hour, British [*sic*] dead and wounded, eight prisoners and one machine gun fell into our hands in this area . . . "

The execution of the raid clearly did not go to plan, but there were also deficiencies in the preparations.

"There had been no rehearsals for the operation", stated the prisoners. "Instead, during a recent six day period at rest, the participants had simply had the German positions explained to them [on a model] which had the layout marked with small flags. Whilst the battalions were at rest, use was made of sketches so that the NCOs could be given more detailed briefings about the front to be attacked." [37]

From the approximately 1,700 Canadian raiders, no fewer than 687 – including two battalion commanders – became casualties.[38] German casualties were much lighter, but not insignificant. From 6th and 7th Companies Reserve Infantry Regiment 262, for example, ten men were killed, one man died later of his wounds and an unknown number were wounded and Reserve Infantry Regiment 261, which bore the brunt of the raid, reported, 'One officer killed, one offizierstellvertreter slightly wounded; twenty four men killed, thirteen seriously wounded; fifteen slightly wounded, one buried alive and four slightly affected by gas'.[39] In all, including estimated casualties from 16th Bavarian Infantry Division, there were probably about 120 German casualties in all.

The death of Leutnant Lieser of 12th Company was a blow to Reserve Infantry Regiment 261. He was the first of the officers of that regiment to be killed on the Western Front.[40] Writing after the war in the Regimental Newsletter, one of his former comrades described how he met his death.

Signaller Arthur Lauch 12th Company Reserve Infantry Regiment 261 [41]

"At the end of February 1917, the Fusilier [3rd] Battalion moved into position on Vimy Ridge for the first time. 12th Company occupied the so-called Second Trench, which was located close behind the front line. At that time the courageous and much-loved Leutnant Lieser was deputising for its normal commander, Hauptmann von Koppelow. The dugout in which Leutnant Lieser passed the last night of February with his batman, three runners and we three signallers was located about fifty metres behind the 12th Company line and was a large former British dugout with two entrances and wide steps. The entrances, which now faced in the direction of the enemy, were very unfavourably placed for us . . .

"28 February drew to a close. It was cold and rainy, just as it had been for the past few days. A pitch black night descended. As it went dark there was the usual activity in the muddy, shelled-ploughed terrain: ration carriers and carrying parties began their work. Often they got lost for hours in this desolate area and, not infrequently, stumbled around for hours; all this amidst constant artillery and mortar fire, as well as the crack of machine gun fire. The best means of orientation in this darkness was when flares went up; that provided us with some idea of direction and distance to be travelled. This particular night a runner and I were detailed to fetch cooked food, cold rations and the mail. It was not until just before 10.00 pm that we arrived back at our dugout.

"Frequent stumbles and the need to take cover were the reasons why the food containers were often only half full when they were brought up to our comrades manning the forward positions. After the meal, two of the signallers went out to trace a fault. That was no small thing in this darkness and difficult terrain, but they succeeded in re-establishing the link to the KTK [*Kampftruppenkommandeur* = Commander of the Forward Troops]. Towards midnight, everyone less one signaller, who kept watch in the light of a candle by the telephone, settled down for a rest. Leutnant Lieser and his batman occupied one end of the dugout, which was six to eight metres long. The three runners and three signallers were at the other end. At both ends at least twenty steep steps led up to the open air.

"Towards 4.00 am, violent artillery and mortar fire started coming down on our sector. We all leapt up. Leutnant Lieser shouted to us, 'Everybody stand by!' Two runners had to move at once to the platoon commanders. We signallers donned our steel helmets and armed ourselves with hand grenades. At that moment, barely three minutes after the drum fire began, there was an appalling crash. The candles went out and the dugout rocked in complete darkness. Masses of earth came down the steps. A heavy shell had come down in our entrance, which was facing the Tommies. We quickly lit the candles and Leutnant Lieser shouted to us, 'Meinschin, check if the other entrance is usable!'

"Our comrade Meinschin went over to the entrance, returned and said, 'Herr Leutnant, the staircase is buried almost to the bottom!' That same instant he collapsed silently to the ground. I was standing right next to

Meinschin and was just about to ask him what the problem was, when I too fainted. I did not regain consciousness fully until fourteen hours later in the field hospital at Hénin-Liétard. I had not the slightest idea what happened during that time. It was not until I was discharged from hospital that I found out what had occurred. On the basis of what I was told, I shall outline the course of events. Signaller Meinschin and I collapsed almost simultaneously. Signaller Pietzshke, who was a few paces from us, saw what happened and called out to Leutnant Lieser. Both naturally assumed that there was a danger of gas, both put on their gas masks, moved to look at us, but they also collapsed.

"In Lieser's corner of the dugout were his batman and the other signaller. By the light of a candle they saw what had happened and rushed up out of the second entrance to fetch a medical orderly. The drum fire continued to hammer down. The batman and runner had only been out of the entrance for a few seconds when another shell landed, levelling the ground and burying the second entrance. It was certainly a most unusual situation for a large dugout with massive entrances to be buried in a few moments. After a comparatively short, but very violent, bombardment the enemy attacked in dense masses and was beaten off with huge losses. However, the Canadians were so angered that they launched another sharp attack at daybreak. This was also defeated short of our front line. This bold defeat of a mass attack was one of the best things [Hauptmann] von Knobelsdorff's battalion ever achieved.

"As soon as things calmed down in the early morning, the rescue work began on the buried dugout of the company commander. A number of engineers and other comrades from 12th Company, under the command of the courageous Leutnant Loddig, who had come forward from von der Knesebeck's company, worked feverishly to free us. An opening was made after several hours of work. Courageously, Sanitätsunteroffizier Bock squeezed through the small opening and, with a strenuous effort, brought us up to daylight. Unfortunately there was no sign of life from Leutnant Lieser or Signaller Pietzschke.[42] Meinschin was still breathing shallowly; I a little more strongly, but giving off severe rattling sounds in the windpipe . . .

"When I first came to at the aid post by the coalmine in Vimy, I was amazed to find myself surrounded by wounded men. That evening in the hospital at Hénin-Liétard I was able to collect my thoughts. I could think back clearly to the explosion of the shell and Meinschin collapsing. After that I could remember nothing. The faithful Meinschin died in the bed next to me on 5 March, without regaining consciousness. After a little less than three weeks, I returned to 12th Company in its bivouac at Rouvroy and discovered everything outlined above. The poisoning was caused by carbon monoxide from the shell which blew in the first entrance. Gas masks were ineffective against it. I could hardly credit my miraculous escape. Leutnant Lieser was the first officer of our regiment to be lowered to his final rest on the Western Front. Deeply moved, I stood by the freshly dug graves of Leutnant Lieser and the other good comrades from 1 March in the Heroes' Cemetery in Rouvroy one bleak wintry day.

Und wer den Tod im heil'gen Kampfe fand
Ruht auch im fremder Erde im Vaterland"[43]

Sixth Army Appreciation of the Situation 3 March 1917 [44]

"[There has been] a further increase in the number of batteries firing along the sector Lens – Roclincourt . . . and an increase in raids and patrols. Thirty six operations, eleven of them large, have occurred. The greatest amount of activity was east of Armentières and, strongest of all east of Souchez . . . The artillery mainly engaged our positions with concentrations up to drum fire, in support of operations . . . but guns were ranged in on routes to the east of Vimy Ridge.

"General Impression. There are no further signs on the Army's right flank of preparations for attack . . . Against Vimy Ridge attacks to capture local positions west of Givenchy, or even the entire ridge, are possible. Reinforcements received to date are insufficient to guarantee security in the event of a surprise attack. More howitzers and manpower are needed, all the more so because the positions are in bad condition. There are still no signs that a major attempt at a breakthrough is planned."

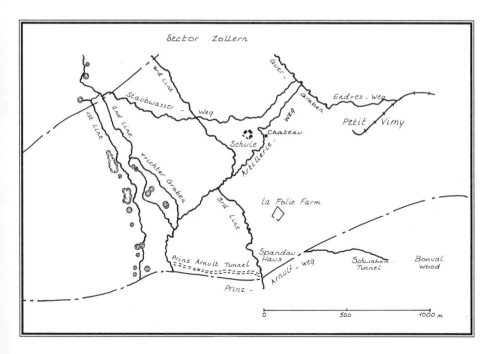

Sixth Army Appreciation of the Situation 10 March 1917 [45]

"[The presence of] 1st and 4th Canadian Divisions has been confirmed, as has that of 51st [Highland] and 34th Divisions near Roclincourt . . . It cannot be ruled out that the enemy has increased the density of the troops in the front line. It is highly probable that the number of enemy divisions in and behind the front near Arras has increased overall . . . Evaluation of [aerial] photographs taken during the snow has indicated concentrations of manned and, therefore, usable, batteries massed against Vimy Ridge . . . There has been intense air activity during the past three days . . . Enemy aircraft are very numerous, with up to thirty operating simultaneously above a single corps . . . *Jagdstaffel* 11 [Richthofen's Fighter Squadron] has been markedly superior to the enemy, shooting down aircraft on 4, 5 and 6 March without loss and a further nine enemy aircraft on 9 March, but our own inferiority in army support aircraft is very noticeable . . .

"General Impression. . . . There are no additional attack indicators for an assault on Vimy Ridge, but the new observations concerning enemy artillery positions confirm the possibility of [such an operation] once more.

The pressure of the seemingly never-ending series of raids by the Canadians against Vimy Ridge during the weeks leading up to mid-March were by now becoming a cause for concern at Headquarters Sixth Army. Following representations from VI Reserve Corps, Generalobest Freiherr Ludwig von Falkenhausen, Sixth Army Commander, wrote to Army Group Crown Prince Rupprecht on 14 March[46] seeking clearance to plan and launch a pre-emptive Operation, code named Munich:

"The repeated British [*sic*] operations opposite Givenchy-en-Gohelle have proved once more how desirable it would be if our positions on the crest there were of greater depth. The various operations during the winter and spring of 1916 did of course result in some ground being gained but, even at the time, Army Headquarters regarded the amount involved as insufficient and intended to gain more terrain to the front in this sector. Events elsewhere in the Western Theatre of Operations prevented this intention from being carried out.

"It has recently been established that the enemy is mining actively in this area. Seizure of his front line trenches would gain us control over his mine galleries. Such an operation would provide us with the following advantages:

1 It would improve our observation over No Man's Land and so would make it much more difficult for the enemy to assemble troops for a surprise attack there.
2 Artillery observation would be fundamentally improved.
3 The increased depth of our positions would mean far higher casual-

ties for the enemy if they wished to attempt to capture the most important parts of our lines.

4 At one fell swoop the enemy would be put at a disadvantage in the underground mining battle.

Finally, an operation like this would have a very beneficial effect on the morale of our troops – especially in the current situation. I give my warmest support, therefore, to the intention of Headquarters VI Reserve Corps to launch an attack during the last week of March to capture the [relevant] enemy trenches . . . and request the allocation of those forces which the Army cannot provide from its own resources . . . "

In his consideration of these proposals, the Army Group Commander had some reservations, which he recorded the following day.

Crown Prince Rupprecht of Bavaria: Diary Entry 15 March 1917 [47]

"Sixth Army is advocating an operation planned by the 16th Bavarian Infantry Division for the end of March. In order to mount the operation, which is to take place on and to the south of the *Gießler Höhe,* reinforcement by one regiment (which will not be used in the actual attack) has been requested. I harboured some doubts about whether it would actually be advantageous to attempt to advance beyond the first enemy trenches and directed Sixth Army to investigate if we could [instead] dig in on the forward slope above the enemy position.

"Nevertheless, I approved the operation, which aims to strengthen our positions in a particularly vulnerable point and should show the enemy that we are not content just to resign ourselves to passive defence."

The Army Group Commander returned to this subject five days later:

Crown Prince Rupprecht of Bavaria: Diary Entry 15 March 1917 [48]

"With regard to the operation of 16th Bavarian Division on the *Gießler Höhe* (Codename Munich), which the Army High Command has recently approved, Sixth Army is now having second thoughts. The current position on the plateau around the *Gießler Höhe* is already overlooked from the Lorette Spur and the same will apply if the lines are advanced to the forward slope in front of the enemy's front line. This will make it very difficult to push forward communication trenches and to maintain them in a passable condition despite all the enemy artillery fire. Resort will have to be made to tunnels. Despite [these difficulties] I regard the Operation as justified, because it will upset the enemy's plans if they intend to launch an attack on Vimy Ridge."

Operation Munich was intended to capture the northern section of Zouave Valley in particular. Had it been conducted and had it been successful, it would certainly have affected at least the four most northerly subways, tunnelled to facilitate the move forward of the Canadian troops during the night 8/9 April but, as will be seen, circumstances prevented its launch. Nevertheless, approval having been granted, the German chain of command and planning staffs treated the question of its preparation with the utmost seriousness. It was no mere paper exercise. The Operation Plan went through several different versions, with amendments or replacement orders being produced as circumstances altered. Sometimes this was due to changes in forward deployment or alterations in the width of regimental sectors between the *Gießler Höhe* and Hill 145; at other times postponement of the operation or cancellation after a faltering start was the cause. The final version[49] was issued by 9 Bavarian Brigade on 4 April to coincide with the further division of this part of the front into Sectors *Burg* (Bavarian Reserve Infantry Regiment 21), *Ansbach* (Bavarian Infantry Regiment 14) and *Döberitz* (much reduced in width and held by Bavarian Infantry Regiment 11).

The production of the 4 April order, which replaced that of 26 March, is clear proof that, right up until the end, there was a firm intention to carry the battle to the Canadians.[50] Each change involved an enormous amount of extra work for the infantry and artillery staffs, not to mention the allocation of additional resources and their movement forward. Given the pressure of events this would not have been undertaken on a whim or with the vague hope that something of the sort could be mounted. The artillerymen, in particular, were keen to see an improvement in their situation. At the northern end of the Bavarian 16th Infantry Division sector a combination of mining, counter-mining and minor battles for the ensuing craters meant that around The Pimple the German front line ran partly along the crest and partly behind it.

As a result the observers had no worthwhile view forward over much of this critical sector. It was possible to see some parts of the enemy rear area from the front line trench up on the *Gießler Höhe*, but this provided only a partial solution. Communications between the observers and the gun positions were essential, but could only be guaranteed on calm days between major actions – and not always then. It was obvious to all that, as soon as battle was joined, or a major bombardment began, all communications would fail; at precisely the moment they were most needed. With the front line further forward, the observers could be positioned in rear of the forward positions and thus be far better placed to influence the battle. As a result the divisional mission, which highlighted this issue, remained unchanged throughout each variant of the plan during the following three weeks:[51]

> "On X Day the division will launch an attack forward from Sectors *Burg South* and *Döberitz* [In the 4 April version, this becomes Sectors *Ansbach* and *Döberitz*[52]]. Purpose: To gain an improved defensive position, which will permit us observation over No Man's Land, will ease artillery observation and retention of the *Gießler Höhe* and remove the danger of mining . . ."

The preliminary remarks in the version of the Operation Order issued by 9 Bavarian Brigade make interesting reading[53]

> "Maintenance of secrecy is the precondition for success. Telephone conversations concerning the operation are completely forbidden forward of Brigade and Artillery Group level and the greatest caution is to be exercised in rearward communications as far as the timings are concerned.
>
> "Phase 1 of the operation is based on the enemy being surprised. It is essential that surprise is achieved. Every man is to be made aware of this. Holding on to the newly-won positions is going to place enormous demands on the troops; but they must be equal to these demands; otherwise the casualties which will necessarily be incurred will have been suffered in vain.
>
> "All preparations for the attack are to be made without their purpose being revealed. Those involved are only to be given information concerning the operation that is essential to them . . . The attack will take place on X Day at Time T.[54]"

Armed with the information contained in the order, the formations, units and detachments of 16th Bavarian Infantry Division set about preparing for their role in the forthcoming operation. Elsewhere on the Vimy front the normal pattern of operations were continued. A few days later, for example, following a raid conducted by units of the British 152 Brigade, 51st (Highland) Division 'northeast of Roclincourt', two wounded men of 8th Battalion Argyll and Sutherland Highlanders were captured. They explained to their interrogators that the operation had only local significance. The aim had been to capture prisoners and to destroy dugouts. 'The real offensive is expected to be launched in three to four weeks.'[55]

By mid-March a series of intelligence reports and appreciations of the situation concerning the increasing likelihood of a major attack aimed at capturing Vimy Ridge had been channelled up the chain of command, so a conference attended by First Quartermaster General Ludendorff was convened at the Headquarters of I Bavarian Reserve Corps in Douai on 18 March. In attendance were numerous senior staff officers, who had travelled with Ludendorff, as well as the chiefs of staff of Army Group Crown Prince Rupprecht (General der Infanterie Hermann von Kuhl) and Sixth Army (Generalmajor Karl Freiherr von Nagel zu Aichberg). Following the usual preliminaries, the conference opened with a briefing by the Corps Commander, General der Infanterie Karl Ritter von Fasbender. The confirmatory notes, prepared the previous day for Ludendorff and used by Fasbender as the basis for his presentation, provide an illuminating summary of German concerns and priorities as the decisive moment approached.[56]

The briefing opened with a statement concerning the 'Tactical and Operational Significance of Vimy Ridge', which concluded, 'If Vimy Ridge were to be in the hands of the enemy, the position of VI Reserve Corps around Lens and XII Reserve

Corps on and around the Scarpe would become untenable in the long run.'
Fasbender then turned his attention to the geography of his positions. This is
particularly interesting, because the assessment was made prior to the battle
and is in sharp contrast to the frequently repeated assertion in Allied accounts
that the Vimy position was as good as impregnable and viewed as such by the
German defenders. Nothing could be further from the truth and German
commanders were extremely concerned about the implications of its inherent
weaknesses:

> "Geographical Setting of our Position. Unfavourable. Total lack of
> depth. Initial enemy success [would be] extraordinarily difficult to rectify.
> The enemy cannot be allowed to achieve an initial success here. The
> adverse location of our positions is not neutralised by the physical devel-
> opment of the defences. The state of the defences is bad (influence of
> weather and the effect of fire, coupled with insufficient manpower avail-
> able to predecessors [in this sector]).
>
> "Above all there is no deployment in depth on the position, nor are the
> [existing positions] properly linked up. It is precisely at those points where
> the positions are geographically the weakest (on the northern flank) that
> their physical state is worst (mostly shot away)."

The briefing then moved on to outline the deficiencies which needed to be recti-
fied urgently:

> "The weaknesses of the geography of our position and its defences can
> only be balanced out by the quantity and quality of the defensive forces
> and defensive materiel [original emphasis] made available. The infantry
> is sufficiently strong and high enough quality to beat off the initial assault.
> The number of machine guns must be increased because, in the current
> situation, they provide the backbone of the defence.[57]

Corps artillery assets were then summarised: 'Field Artillery – Twenty one
batteries plus sixteen 90 mm guns (average defensive fire zone widths: 79th
Reserve Division 330 metres; 1st Bavarian Reserve Division 380 metres). Fourteen
and a half batteries of heavy guns, six of which are obsolescent. No [original
emphasis] modern heavy howitzers.' As far as their deployment and reinforcement requirements were concerned, 'The enemy has located almost every single
battery position (captured pilots' maps) and has ranged in accurately on them.
Considerable losses are to be feared. Three batteries are required immediately to
replace defensive fire batteries which have been knocked out. Reinforcement of
the heavy artillery by about three heavy howitzers and one 100 mm gun battery
is needed to facilitate counter-battery fire.'

The Corps Commander had some reservations about air assets, but felt that
German technical superiority was sufficient to balance out the Allied numerical
advantage unless the sortie rate was intensified considerably. He concluded by
providing his assessment of the situation and the expected date for the assault:

"Corps Headquarters assesses that there will be a strong British assault across the entire corps frontage. This conviction is founded on the following points:

– The significance of Vimy Ridge in the case of an enemy offensive launched at the tip of the *Siegfriedstellung* [Hindenburg Line] south of the Scarpe which, in view of the overall situation, seems likely – indicators of its preparation are multiplying.

– The appearance of rested, high quality, divisions (34th, 51st [Highland] and 3rd Canadian north of the Scarpe).

– Certain special indicators: notes found on a British pilot shot down over Vimy and the statements of prisoners from 3rd Canadian Division.

"The current posture of the enemy opposite the Corps front does not support any suggestion that a major offensive is imminent, although the numerous enemy raids might, in themselves, suggest the opposite. In addition, the fact that these operations cause the smashing of one part after another of our positions means that they do serve to prepare the way for a major assault. During the past week fifty enemy batteries have been located. Of these fifteen are medium and five heavy. The generally bad weather has made it impossible to determine the exact number of enemy batteries. The enemy artillery has ranged in on almost all [of our] batteries, all significant parts of the position and the rear communications.

"It is improbable [that the attack will take place] whilst the ground is so sodden. If it begins to dry out an enemy offensive could open at any time."

The subsequent discussions were summarised in the Corps War Diary by the Chief of Staff, Major Ritter von Lenz:[58]

"The First Quartermaster General associated himself with the broad thrust of the briefing which he was given. It is probable that 80th Reserve Division will be placed at the disposal of Sixth Army. The General [von Fasbender] requested that in no circumstances should the current sector boundaries be torn apart again. The most useful thing would be reinforcements in the form of infantry working parties. The requested batteries would probably be forthcoming, but probably would be employed initially in support of Operation Munich to be conducted by 16th Bavarian Infantry Division.[59]

"A second air detachment is fairly certain to be deployed [to the area]. Ammunition to permit the heavy batteries to range in can always be authorised. Divisional commanders were to pay particular attention to the repair and maintenance of the heavy batteries and to their training. If the newly arrived Machine Gun Sharp Shooter Detachment 28 was not in a fit state to be used, steps would be taken to replace it by another detachment currently training in Rocroy. The detachment was not to be broken up amongst the regiments.

"There was almost universal agreement concerning the assessment of the situation between the Army High Command, the Army Group, Sixth Army and Corps headquarters, though there was tendency for the first two named to regard the expected offensive against the flank of the Hindenburg Line and Vimy Ridge as having local, rather than broad, operational significance."[60]

Back at trench level the pattern of patrols and raids continued with undiminished intensity. These caused damage and casualties all along the I Bavarian Reserve Corps front, but also yielded a constant trickle of prisoners, who each contributed towards the development of a comprehensive intelligence picture. These individuals were not only captured during Canadian raids. The Canadians may have been responsible for the more ambitious operations, but the German regiments all operated an active patrolling policy. 'By means of numerous, nightly patrols, we observed the enemy positions in detail', recorded the historian of Reserve Infantry Regiment 263. 'It became clear that, sooner or later, we should have to reckon on a large scale enemy offensive' and that thought was encapsulated in an order by the regimental commander:[61]

> "Our senior commanders have made it clear that we shall shortly have to conduct a major defensive action from our current positions. I require all battalion and company commanders to make the seriousness of the situation crystal clear to their subordinates and to encourage and inspire them to put their entire energy into the fastest possible development of the positions. They must work to the very limit of human capacity. Only if that occurs, only then, can we be certain that we shall prevail in the event of an attack."

In the case of Reserve Infantry Regiment 262, Unteroffizier Gronau of 11th Company clashed with six Canadians in an advanced sap on 8 March. Two days later, Unteroffizier Gansen, 1st Company, carried out a solo patrol to investigate if craters to the front of his sub-sector were unoccupied. 12 March saw two patrols being mounted by Unteroffizier Taschner and two men of 8th Company and a nine man patrol launched forward from 2nd Company under the command of Gefreiter Wigger.[62] These small scale patrols were mainly designed to gather information but, simultaneously, planning was continuing for a much more ambitious operation. During the early morning of 15 March, 43rd Battalion, 9 Brigade, 3rd Canadian Division was raided by a party from 1st Battalion Reserve Infantry Regiment 262: seventy nine men strong, led by Leutnant Heuser and mounted with the express intention of snatching one or more prisoners.

Preceded by a powerful, if brief, barrage fired by artillery and mortars, the raiders, divided into two groups, broke into the Canadian front line near La Folie Farm. Once in the forward trench, the raiders cleared along it in both directions causing damage and becoming involved, especially in the case of the more southerly group, in a bitterly fought close-quarter battle. Having snatched two prisoners successfully, the raiders did not linger, but withdrew rapidly to their own lines. The Germans believed that the Canadians had suffered some five casualties in addition to the loss of the prisoners. They themselves had five men wounded. For his part in this successful operation, Leutnant Heuser was awarded the Iron Cross First Class.

It transpired later that one of the prisoners was a Serbian immigrant. Both men were interrogated in detail, the report appearing the following day and revealing several interesting items of intelligence.[63] In addition to the usual low-level background information, the location of various headquarters and a detailed breakdown of the whereabouts and projected moves of 2nd, 3rd and 4th Canadian Divisions was given and the two men revealed that, 'During the forthcoming spring offensive, the Canadians have been earmarked for Vimy Ridge. According to a rumour this will take place when the weather conditions are dryer.' Also of significance to the German intelligence officers was the snippet of information that during its last period out of the line,

> "The 43rd Infantry Battalion practised attacks on a trench system in the area of Auchel, which corresponded exactly with the German trenches opposite [their current position]. During these exercises the men were directed to study the layout of these trenches carefully, 'because it might be of some use to you in the near future'."

The German intelligence officers were not slow in drawing the appropriate conclusions from this document and others which came their way at this time. Not that the defenders were aware of it, but the complex artillery and mortar preparation of the battlefield had begun on 20 March. There had been a considerable amount of shelling throughout the previous weeks, but the defenders, especially those manning places which were to be the foci of the forthcoming assault, were quick to pick up on the increase in fire. 'There was rather heavy artillery fire on [Sectors] *Fischer*, *Zollern* and *Arnulf*, reported 79th Reserve Division on 21 March,[64] 'and about 700 shells came down as harassing fire on the rear areas. The observation post of 7th Battery Field Artillery Regiment 63 received numerous heavy shells. There was moderate mortar fire on *Arnulf* and *Zollern*. Ten mortar bombs, several of them heavy, landed on *Fischer*. In the *Münchener Lager* [Munich Position] one round threw up a crater three metres deep and six metres wide.'

By the following day, despite the fact that during the morning 800 shells hit the positions and 1,000 more (followed by another 550 in the afternoon) harassed the rear areas, 79th Reserve Division was reporting that 'Enemy artillery fire was still heavy, though perhaps not as heavy as it had been for the past few days. The ammunition was extremely variable in quality. Of the rounds fired at *Prinz Arnulf Weg* [Prince Arnulf Way] and the Third Line in Sector *Arnulf*, sixty to seventy per cent were duds.'[65] This pattern of shelling, with occasional responses from the German artillery, then continued for a further week.

From the end of March the British massed the divisions of their Third and Fourth Armies opposite the German Sixth Army either side of Arras. With its main effort on the left flank, their aim was to break through between Souchez and Quéant via Vimy Ridge and along the banks of the Scarpe towards Cambrai. Simultaneously thousands of guns and mortars opened up destructive fire at the German front opposite, aided by numerous squadrons of aircraft. This fire soon put anything experienced on the Somme in the shade. A great deal more ammunition fired – according to some estimates about twice as much ammunition was fired during the first week at Vimy as during the bombardment prior to the Battle of the Somme, whilst during the second week the figure was six times as much – and, furthermore, the length of front to be bombarded was considerably shorter. Soon all the positions north and south of the Scarpe were shattered and the German batteries were drenched repeatedly with gas.

The heaviest weight of fire was directed against the ridge between Givenchy and Farbus. Whilst it was possible during the first days of the artillery battle to establish the approximate weight of British artillery fire (most days 12,000 – 15,000 shells rained down on the positions of the 79th Reserve Division), later such was the intensity of the fighting that further attempts to count the quantities fired became impossible. Although initially the greatest weight of fire came down on Sector *Fischer*, later it switched, with even greater intensity, to Sector *Arnulf*. From the end of March built up areas and roads a long way behind the lines also

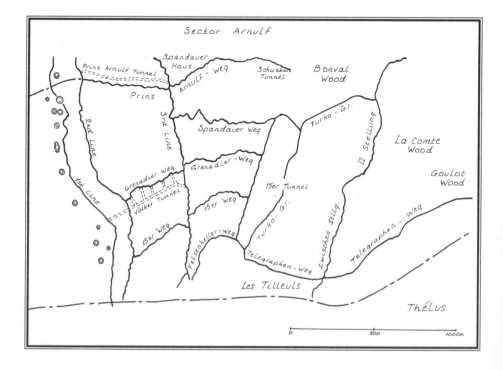

suffered from British artillery fire. After several of the French inhabitants had been killed in this way, the local population was moved out of the endangered villages to the rear. The launch site of the observation balloon at Acheville was frequently a target for the British guns.

With the opening of the bombardment General der Infanterie Karl Ritter von Fasbender, Commander I Bavarian Reserve Corps, issued a directive to his three divisions: 79th Reserve Division, 1st Bavarian Reserve Division and 14th Bavarian Infantry Division. This was designed to ensure that the forthcoming defensive battle would be prepared for and fought in a coordinated way, in accordance with a Corps concept for battle.[66]

"Subject: Preparations for the Defensive Battle

1. In view of the extent of the work necessary on the positions, it is especially important that, within the context of an all-embracing plan, efforts are concentrated on those places which will be tactically the most important in the defensive battle. All other [work] is ruthlessly to be set aside in favour of priority places. The divisions have the necessary oversight. They must ensure that they exert decisive influence on the type and extent of the work on the positions. This must be done on the basis of a division-wide work plan which covers all the individual sectors and lays down precise tasks. The necessary materiel and manpower is then to be provided at the relevant times and places. [The plans must be drawn up] so as to ensure that regimental and divisional boundaries are not treated as dividing walls against tactical cooperation. It is essential that care is taken with the placement of machine guns, so that their mutually supporting fire can be brought to bear from a flank.

2. It is anticipated that, with the exception of the *Siegfried-Ecke* [Siegfried Corner] to the south of the Scarpe, the British attack will be directed all along the front from the Souchez River to the Scarpe. Within this front the enemy is likely to launch particularly heavy attacks against several localities. Points will be selected for major break-ins where the enemy considers that they offer the best chances for the continuation of the attack in order to achieve the overall aim. The places which the enemy has singled out for damage by means of artillery and mortar fire or raids provide a starting point in this respect. At Verdun and on the Somme the enemy concentrated their attacks against sector boundaries. In view of this, particular attention would seem to be appropriate in the following places:
   - The divisional boundary to the right [north] of 79th Reserve Division.
   - The positions in the Second Line either side of the junction of *Fischergang* and *Staubwasserweg* [Fischer Alley and Staubwasser Way].

- The positions in the Second Line either side of the junction of *Prinz Arnulf Tunnel* and *Prinz Arnulf Weg*.
- The positions in the Second Line either side of the junction of *Grenadierweg* [Grenadier Way] and the *Völkertunnel.*
- The positions either side of the road Neuville St Vaast – Thélus (Divisional boundary!).
- The positions in the First line either side of the forward limit of *Grävenitzweg.*
- Positions either side of the track between Roclincourt and Thélus.

3. In addition every effort is to be made, by means of the closest possible observation of enemy digging operations and the placement of their destructive fire, to clarify further the assessment of probable enemy main break-in points.

4. Special measures are to be taken at the probable enemy main break-in points to ensure that any enemy attack can be beaten off or nipped in the bud, or that any enemy who have managed to break in can be prevented from expanding their foothold and can be rapidly ejected by means of a counter-stroke. This can be achieved by:
   - <u>Prepared defences</u>. (Constant improvement of the smashed trenches and obstacles; placement of stop lines and obstacles at right angles to the front; company dumps of wire obstacles that can be laid rapidly)
   - <u>Deployment of the garrison</u>. (Distribution of machine guns, light mortars and grenade launchers)
   - <u>Increases in destructive and defensive fire</u>. (Due consideration having been given to the [risk of] loss of our guns)
   - <u>Artillery Planning</u>. (Designed to engage enemy forces and armoured vehicles which have broken in). The guns of the close support battery are in themselves insufficient for this purpose.

5. *These passive preparatory measures alone are insufficient.*[67] Enemy batteries should already be being engaged systematically whenever suitable opportunities present themselves. The necessary ammunition for this is ready and available. All necessary steps are to be taken in order to ensure that the means are available to fire gas as soon as the enemy preparations for the attack commence. We must adapt our response to the gradual transition to battle. This means that we must make it difficult for the enemy to prepare for battle by engaging with planned, heavy, destructive fire their observation points, mortar base plates and approach routes.

In both respects we must do considerably more than has been done so far. More precisely, we must ensure that the medium mortars and, wherever they can be deployed successfully, the heavy howitzers are better exploited and so deliver destructive fire.

6. There is to be:
  - sharpest attention to detail, in order to ensure that enemy attack plans are discovered in good time.
  - carefully planned and controlled, but ceaseless, digging efforts, in order to maintain and improve the tactically most important parts of our positions.
  - systematic engagement of the enemy artillery and destruction of all installations, which are particularly valuable to the enemy as they complete their attack preparations.

Signed: von Fasbender

Upon receipt of this directive, the divisions which made up Group Vimy were quick to issue their own orders. On 28 March, for example, Generalmajor Freiherr von Pechmann, Commander 1st Bavarian Reserve Division, signed off an order relating to the development of the defences in his sector:[68]

"In order to strengthen the divisional northern flank a sack-like defensive layout is needed. To that end a wire obstacle is to be constructed from *Felsenkellerweg* [Rock Cellar Way] to *Bukaresterweg* [Bucharest Way] in order to constrain and channel any enemy who break in astride the Neuville – Thélus road. 79th Reserve Division will continue the work from that point. In order to prevent Sector *Wittelsbach* from being cut off from the southwest and south, an obstacle is to be constructed along the line *Landwehrweg – Wittelsbacherweg* as far as the *Zwischenstellung* [Intermediate Position].

"Both these stop lines are to be constructed using continuous wire obstacles and the trenches named are to be prepared for use as battle positions. Working parties for these projects from the Third Line to the rear will be found by the Pioneers of 4th Company Infantry Regiment 86. Forward of that point manpower of the regiments and their supporting engineers are to be used. The development of these strong stop lines as far back as the Second Position is to be driven forward vigorously. As soon as reasonably usable posts have been constructed, they are to be manned by machine guns and close support infantry is to be provided. From now on, some forces are to be deployed in the Second Position in all three sectors so as to ensure that it is securely held. With these measures, we shall be approaching our aim of ensuring that we achieve the interlinked latticework defensive system, which will give the Sector particular strength."

Generalleutnant von Bacmeister, commanding 79th Reserve Division also issued an assessment on 30 March, indicating very clearly that he, too, was under no illusions concerning the timescale and nature of the approaching offensive. This document was later captured, translated and studied by the Canadians.[69]

" . . . North of Arras the British will be forced, according to the nature of the ground, to deliver a joint attack on the long narrow Vimy Ridge, the possession of which gives them possession of the high ground in this vicinity and would also be a safeguard against German attacks on the British left flank near Arras. Opposed to the division are Canadian troops. The 3rd Canadian Division on the right flank of the division came in to the line about the middle of March. Recent identifications place the 2nd Canadian on the left flank.[70] The extreme flanks of the Canadian Corps have closed in towards the centre, so that it now occupies a smaller front than it did a few weeks ago. The Corps is now echeloned in depth and this formation points to operations on a large scale.

"... [Although] there are no signs of an immediate attack, it is very certain that the Canadians are planning an attack on a large scale in the immediate future and both flanks of the division can be considered as the chief points where the attack will be pressed home. The statement of a prisoner captured early today that the attack was to take place between 20 March and 6 April confirms the above.

Signed: von Bacmeister"

Although both Group Vimy and its forward divisions were increasingly convinced that an assault on Vimy Ridge could not be long delayed and were taking all appropriate precautions, the overall situation was still far less clear-cut as far as the Army Group Commander was concerned.

Crown Prince Rupprecht of Bavaria: Diary Entry 26 March 1917 [71]

"Sixth Army has written in its weekly report for 24 March: The reinforcement of the enemy artillery, which has been observed since the end of February, has been confirmed further ... The reason for the massing of enemy forces either side of Arras is still not completely clear. Possibly the enemy fears an attack and, therefore, has only deployed some of the available divisions in the front line. Whatever the explanation, the deployment is not normal for a major offensive. Because the possession of Vimy Ridge would be of far greater significance than the gaining of ground around Arras, it would seem, despite the greater concentration of force near the latter, that an attack on Vimy Ridge is the more probable. Nevertheless, both possibilities must be borne in mind."

On 26 March, the first attempt to launch Operation Munich began. As indicated at the I Bavarian Reserve Corps conference of 18 March, artillery reinforcements were moved forward to bolster the guns of 16th Bavarian Infantry Division, which were already under enough pressure trying to respond to the increasing weight of enemy fire, without having to fire the Munich preliminary bombardment as well. This was no easy task. The main priority for the Allied artillery was against the frontage of 79th Reserve Division and the southern part of 16th Bavarian Infantry Division, the German sound ranging troops had identified an increase of one third in the number of batteries firing on this front within the past two weeks so, in addition to the plans for Munich, the artillery staffs were working flat out to amend their other defensive fire plans simultaneously.

Nevertheless the gunners had to respond to a decision to attempt Operation Munich on 29 March and on 26 March destructive fire began to be brought down on the area to be assaulted. This continued through 27 March then, on 28 March, Bavarian Infantry Regiment 11 conducted a major rehearsal for the attack in a specially marked out area behind the lines. All was ready but, at 7.45 am on 29 March, 16th Bavarian Infantry Division issued an order: 'Munich postponed, due to bad weather. The effect achieved [so far] by artillery and mortar fire is to be maintained by means of the continuing use of harassing fire by the artillery, mortars, machine guns and grenade launchers.'[72] Perhaps it was just as well. That evening a telephone intercept team noted a conversation which made it clear that the Canadians were expecting an attack that night. Operational security had not been as tight as had been wished; possibly the bombardment betrayed the plan.

During the evening of 29 March Reserve Infantry Regiment 263 captured four men of the Canadian 31st Battalion, 6 Brigade, 2nd Canadian Division during a raid launched astride the Neuville-Thélus road in sector *Arnulf 3*. The aim had been to take German prisoners but, instead, the capture of these men provided the Germans with some much-needed valuable information about the forthcoming attack. They were interrogated two or three times in all. On 31 March, Major Lenz, Chief of Staff to I Bavarian Reserve Corps, signed an intelligence report which went out on wide distribution:[73]

> "From statements by prisoners belonging to 2nd Canadian Division the following points have arisen:
> – The mission of the 2nd Canadian Division is to attack to the south of the road Neuville – Thélus – Farbus.
> – To its south it appears that 1st Canadian Division has been inserted between it and 51st [Highland] Division.
> – To the north are located 3rd and 4th Canadian Divisions in that order. 5th Canadian Division <u>may</u> be a designated reserve.[74]
> – The Arras – Souchez front is to be rolled up from south to north. If that succeeds, the cavalry will be released onto the [Douai] Plain . .
>
> .
>
> "The statements sound probable and fit well with the picture built up by the Corps concerning the direction of the [forthcoming] attack and the main break-in points. Divisional Infantry and Artillery counter-measures would seem to be indicated."

Reacting immediately, Generalmajor Freiherr von Pechmann, Commander of 1st Bavarian Reserve Division, issued an order later that day ordering various measures to raise the alert state within the Division.[75] These included identification of the likely main enemy thrusts, an order to accelerate the deployment in depth of available weapons and manpower and the production of the new obstacles and direction on the creation and placement of local reserves for each layer of command. The second of the reports relating to the 29 March raid[76] was dated 1 April 1917 then, the following day, a supplementary report was produced.[77] In the 1 April document the interrogators reported:

> "Units of [6 Canadian] Brigade conducted attack exercises between 13 and 23 March to the north of Grand Servin. Each day between 8.00 am and 1.00 pm drills were rehearsed and attacks were practised on a training area adapted to resemble the actual terrain of the attack. The target of the attack which was intended to be launched some time between 26 March and 6 April was announced to be Thélus and Farbus Wood [modern Bois de Berthonval]. The German trenches were marked out with white tapes and the communication trenches were represented by red flags. The roads Arras – Lille and Neuville – Thélus were marked with yellow flags. Blue flags were used to show the village of Thélus and the wire obstacle was indicated with two wires.
>
> "A small wood near the training area was used for Farbus Wood. Each exercise began with the troops advancing in 'diamond artillery formation', then the attack was conducted by the individual companies in three waves against Thélus and Farbus Wood. 27th Battalion had been designated to capture Thélus, whilst the 31st Battalion was intended to move through it and thrust towards Farbus Wood . . . "[78]

As far as the supplementary report was concerned, the main item of additional information was the fact that the forthcoming offensive would be launched on a front from Lens to Arras and that it would be preceded by a bombardment lasting six to ten days. The whereabouts of large stacks of ammunition and numerous gun pits was described, as was the fact that that twelve out of sixteen companies of 6 Brigade would participate in the attack on Thélus/Farbus, whilst the remainder would be in reserve. The exact tactics to be deployed and the reason behind them were volunteered in detail, as were numerous minor points of general interest.

In view of the latest information and the way the intelligence picture was developing on the Vimy Front at the end of March, Army Group Crown Prince Rupprecht called for a local assessment of the situation. Referring to it, the commander made a note in his diary on 31 March,[79] 'A question to I Bavarian Reserve Corps elicited the response that they expect the enemy offensive to be launched in approximately ten days. Unfortunately today we received a reply from the Army High Command concerning reinforcements for Sixth Army which did not correspond to what we had requested.' Vimy was clearly uppermost in his mind at the time because he returned to the subject the following day,[80] 'A captured Canadian has stated that the attack on Vimy Ridge will take place during the first half of this month after a preparatory bombardment lasting between six and ten days. It seems as though four Canadian divisions are now deployed along that front. In a further statement the captured Canadian said that gas cylinders have been dug in along that front . . .'

At the same time, the intensity of the preliminary bombardment increased very considerably. On 29 March, 79th Reserve Division noted in their Situation Report covering 28 March,[81] 'Approximate number of incoming artillery shells and mortar bombs: *Fischer* – 2,510 shells, 800 mortar bombs; *Zollern* – 1,100 shells, 140 mortar bombs; *Arnulf* – 7,850 shells, 400 mortar bombs. Casualties: Infantry – five killed, two seriously wounded, five slightly wounded; Artillery – three killed, five seriously wounded, seven slightly wounded; Mortars – two slightly wounded; Reinforcement Companies – two killed, one seriously wounded, one slightly wounded.' By the following day there was yet another increase in bombardment:[82] '*Fischer* – 1,802 shells, 775 mortar bombs; *Zollern* 4,900 shells, 540 mortar bombs; *Arnulf* (Northern Sub-Sector only) – 20,000 shells estimated, coupled with heavy mortar concentrations. Rear areas – 5,000 heavy and super-heavy shells.' Casualties continued to mount; raiding and patrolling took place during pauses in the bombardment and it became increasingly impossible to work on the positions, respond to Canadian pressure, or even to keep a count of incoming fire that was in any way close to the truth. This was an attritional battering outside the experience of all concerned.

Further north, in the 16th Bavarian Infantry Division sector, the decision had been made to attempt Operation Munich once more at 5.25 am on 1 April. On 31 March final preparations were made. The assault troops made ready, in accordance with the coordinating instructions issued by 9 Bavarian Brigade:[83]

> "Assault order: two water bottles per man are to be carried. There is to be large scale distribution of wire cutters, signal pistols and cartridges. Air panels, artillery flags, pennants to mark [captured] trenches and other identifying markers are to be carried. Engineers are to carry large sized wire cutters, picks and prepared demolition charges. Pay books are to be carried and identification marks are to be worn. No maps showing friendly positions and no diaries are to be taken!"

Orders to prevent straggling or avoiding the action were also issued:

> "Police posts are to be set up on the main communication trenches, in the Second Position and at all the aid posts. Men without orders, who have brought wounded to the rear, together with other shirkers, are to be intercepted, then, under the control of a reliable man, who is to be issued with a list of their names, is to escort them forward once more to the nearest company or command post."

The German artillery increased their rate of fire throughout the day, but it was dwarfed by the immense quantities being fired by the Allied guns. It was once more all in vain. At 9.30 pm 16th Bavarian Infantry Division postponed the operation yet again, citing the impassable state of the muddy ground. The decision came as a relief to all directly involved. Any sober assessment of the state of the ground and the strength of the Allied artillery would have had to have concluded that the chances of success were by now slight. So heavy was the weight of fire that night that German artillery commanders felt that, once more, the Canadians were preparing to beat off any attempt at an attack.

Despite this further setback, VI Reserve Corps persisted in its intention to launch Operation Munich. In response to a report and query by 16th Bavarian Infantry Division, its commander despatched a signal on 2 April, which left no room for doubt:[84]

> "To: 16th Bavarian Infantry Division
>
> Operation Munich is to be carried out, just as soon as the weather permits. Early execution is desirable, in order that reinforcing artillery may be allocated, as intended, to 56th Infantry Division and 80th Reserve Division. In view of the current divisional frontage, the temporary allocation of an infantry regiment does not seem to me to be an essential pre-requisite for the conduct of the operation. In an emergency one or two battalions belonging to other divisions of the Corps can be made available. The reinforcing mortars and Air Detachment 235 are to remain subordinated to the division for the time being. Any additional requests for ammunition for the guns or mortars are to be passed to corps headquarters in a timely manner."

The Army Group Commander was of the same opinion, outlining his concerns the following day, then again on 5 April:

Crown Prince Rupprecht of Bavaria: Diary Entry 3 April 1917 [85]

> "Because the enemy have driven numerous galleries under the *Gießler Höhe*, clearly with the intention of preceding the attack there with major mine explosions and because we are somewhat behind with our countermeasures (the enemy are able to drive their mine galleries forward horizontally from the foot of the hill, whereas we have to dig down deep to be able to counter their work), it seems to me to be highly desirable that 16th [Bavarian] Division's Operation Munich be launched as soon as possible. That way, capture of the enemy's trenches means that we shall be able to destroy the entrances to their galleries. So far it has been postponed because the rain has saturated the ground and made it impassable . . . "

Diary Entry 5 April 1917 [86]

> "Because a major enemy offensive against Sixth Army and more particularly against the front from Souchez to Tilloy, is to be launched in only a few days time, it would be a very good thing if Operation Munich could be conducted earlier. That would certainly get the ball rolling."

Having examined the directive from General der Infanterie Georg Wichura, the Corps Commander, Generalmajor Ritter von Möhl, Commander 16th Bavarian

Infantry Division, passed on his own order to 9 Bavarian Brigade the following day:[87]

> "Provided that the weather is fit, Operation Munich is to be executed in accordance with the existing plan by 7 April at the latest. The Brigade is free to adjust the allocation of troops to tasks."

The response from Generalmajor Großmann, Commander 9 Bavarian Brigade, came almost immediately:[88]

> "In view of the wet weather, which is still persisting today, I do not believe that it will be feasible to carry out an operation on 7 April. As a result I have directed that the troops manning the front line are to be relieved. Because of the fact that the battalions currently resting will have to be allowed time to prepare for their missions, Operation Munich cannot be executed before the morning of 10 April at the earliest."

Großmann then settled down to explain his reasoning in detail to Generalmajor Ritter von Möhl. Apart from the light this casts on any assessment of German determination to conduct a pre-emptive operation, the paper also serves as an illustration of the detailed staff work required to launch even the most minor of operations and how this could not be skimped, even in the middle of what was probably the heaviest preliminary bombardment in the history of warfare up until that time:[89]

> "Subject: Allocation of Troops to Tasks for Operation Munich
>
> If we proceed on the basis of a four day rotation between forward, support and resting battalions then, on the day that Munich is executed, we can launch the assault with three battalions fresh from three days' rest. [In order to achieve this], three of the forward and support battalions will have to spend four days in the line and the other three eight days. To spend eight days in the forward positions under heavy fire has such an effect on the troops involved that they cannot be regarded as fully fit to operate as an assault force. It seems to me appropriate, therefore, that the battalions manning the two sectors from which the attack will be launched, who will have already spent more than four days forward, should be withdrawn before the attack and that the two battalions from outside the division should be deployed in the Support Position.
>
> "If, for example, the attack takes place on 10 April, in order to give the two battalions involved two nights' rest, the two [reinforcing] battalions must be allocated to the Brigade from the night 7/8 [April] onward. These battalions should remain in support during the day of the attack as well, thus enabling the two battalions which have been withdrawn to remain in reserve right up until the evening of the day of the assault.
>
> "If we assume the most favourable outcome; namely, that the support battalions do not have to be deployed on the day of the attack itself then,

during the night following the attack, four battalions would be available as reserves or to act as reliefs. It would not be a good idea to relieve the assaulting force during the first night, but this would have to be planned for the second night. The only forces which could be considered for this task are either two battalions of the Brigade or the two [reinforcing] battalions, previously in support. The most that could be hoped for from the assaulting battalions is that they could be used to secure the previous position.

"After a further four days, the infantry of the Division, including the [reinforcing] battalions would be completely worn down. At that point it would no longer be possible to produce reliefs from within divisional resources because even those troops in Sector *Burg* would have been deployed forward, without relief, for either four or eight days. It would of course be possible to occupy Sector *Burg* with the two [reinforcing] battalions, but either the two battalions from [Bavarian] Reserve Infantry Regiment 21 would have to be transferred directly from the position into the new support location, or the attacking battalions, which had already spent eight days forward, would have to be left there for longer.

"For the execution of Operation Munich I request, therefore:
  – that the two battalions belonging to the neighbouring division be subordinated [to the Brigade] from the night 7/8 [April]. They will either be deployed in support in Sectors *Ansbach* and *Döberitz*, or be used as the forward and support battalions in Sector *Burg*.
  – that the assumption be made that, five or six days after the operation is launched, the entire infantry belonging to 16th [Bavarian] Infantry Division will have to be withdrawn from the position."

Of course, although it was not known at the time, all this planning and preparation was entirely nugatory. Elsewhere staffs were at full stretch as the various headquarters worked to put in place all the operational procedures which would be necessary if the forthcoming defensive operations were to be conducted efficiently. On 3 April, for example, with the bombardment of Vimy Ridge in full swing, I Bavarian Reserve Corps issued an order outlining the latest command arrangements and the deployment of the slender additional artillery assets which had been allocated to it.[90]

"From midday 3 April 1917 the southern Corps of the Army are to be known as 'Groups'. The various designations are as follows:

VI (VIII) Reserve Corps	Group Souchez
I Bavarian Reserve Corps	Group Vimy
IX Reserve Corps	Group Arras

" . . . Additional artillery has been placed at the disposal of Group Vimy:
  – Field Artillery Regiment 25 (six batteries of field guns). Together with a regimental staff and one artillery battalion of 79th Reserve Division, these guns will be subordinated to 1st Bavarian Reserve Division.

- From Field Artillery Regiment 600 (six batteries of light field howitzers) the regimental staff and one artillery battalion will deploy to 1st Bavarian Reserve Division. One battalion will deploy to 14th Infantry Division.
- Once the newly subordinated battalion from Field Artillery Regiment 600 is in position, 1st Bavarian Reserve Division is to release 2nd Battalion Field Artillery Regiment 9 to Group Arras.
- The batteries of these regiments are to be emplaced where they can superimpose their fire on the [most probable] break in points.

"From Foot Artillery Battalion 68 (100 mm guns) the regimental staff and two batteries are allocated to 14th Bavarian Infantry Division and one battery to 1st Bavarian Reserve Division. The 100 mm batteries of the two divisions must exploit their long range and be employed to fire gas shells at the enemy batteries which are outside the range of the howitzers.

"The heavy, low trajectory artillery of 1st Bavarian Reserve Division must be placed so as to be in a position to bring down flanking fire on a possible break in to the east of Souchez and that of 14th Bavarian Infantry Division to be able both to counter thrusts to the east of Neuville and to bring down harassing fire along the roads leading to Arras.

Signed: von Fasbender

So much for the attempts of higher headquarters to make the adjustments to deployments, procedures and tactics, in order to be able to counter the coming storm. What, however, of the defenders in the front line from Angres to St Laurent Blangy? How were they coping in the face of an unprecedented bombardment of savagely violent intensity? From the beginning of April it was no longer possible to make good the damage caused by the fire. Such was the effect of the heavy shells in conjunction with the overwhelmingly wet weather, that the positions were soon reduced to crater fields of glutinous mud, within which only a few of the dugouts survived the bombardment – and the majority of these were wrongly placed in the front line. Just to move a small load of ammunition trench stores or rations took the whole energy of a man for a complete night. These conditions created gigantic problems as far as ammunition resupply was concerned – especially for the artillery.

Wherever the wagons pulled by teams of eight horses were unable to go, manpower had to be substituted to haul forward the heavy loads. Despite all this, not only was it possible to move forward the daily requirements (on some days the artillery of 79th Reserve Division fired up to 2,000 rounds), but also plentiful ammunition was stockpiled in the fire positions in anticipation of the need to counter the anticipated attack. Although the constantly shot-up communications cables – even the cables buried two metres deep were broken again and again by direct hits – were supplemented by radio and light signalling stations, effective fire by the German artillery was constantly being disrupted, due to the destruction of observation posts and means of communications.

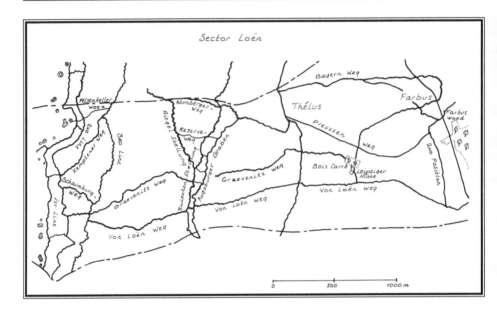

The numerical superiority of the British air squadrons made itself felt in a thoroughly unpleasant manner; this despite the fact that German airmen, above all the red aircraft of Rittmeister von Richthofen's [The Red Baron's] squadron, flung themselves into battle, frequently driving them off with serious losses. Between 4 and 8 April 1917, for example, the RFC lost no fewer than seventy five aircraft shot down and a further fifty six aircraft in accidents.[91] At that time the German Albatross, though only available in relatively small numbers over the Vimy area, was more than a match for any of the British fighter types. Not for nothing was that month known to the Royal Flying Corps as 'Bloody April'.

It was not only for the airmen that this was a period when casualties were mounting rapidly. Major Anton Maier, whose Bavarian Reserve Infantry Regiment 3 of 1st Bavarian Reserve Division had the task of defending the vital Thélus – Farbus area, produced a pair of reports in quick succession on 6 and 8 April to his Brigade Commander, Generalmajor Lamprecht, which must have made grim reading.

"Bavarian Reserve Infantry Regiment 3, 6 April 1917, 5.30 pm

"The enemy artillery fire and its effects have increased day after day. In none of the First, the Third, the Stop Lines or the *Zwischenstellung* [Intermediate Position] is it possible to speak of continuous lines of defence. For the most part the trench lines have been flattened, to such an extent that they are simply crater fields. The same is true of the approach routes. Due to crushing and burying of the dugouts, there has been an extraordinary reduction in the ability to provide protected accommodation for the troops.

"Enemy activity has the entire garrison on edge. Raids, both large and small, keep coming in; sometimes with artillery preparation; sometimes without; sometimes here; sometimes there. The usual artillery and mortar fire is often interrupted by repeated, violent and sudden concentrations, often in the strength of drum fire and lasting up to twenty minutes at a time. These concentrations appear to be lifted (by day) when white flares are fired.

"Deploying the battalions on the positions for eight days continuously, as has been the case up to now, cannot be continued in the present circumstances. But a rotation of two days in the front line and two days in support means that the reserve battalion can only have a rest period of two days at a time. This routine cannot be maintained for more than a few weeks. The allocation of a fourth battalion for each sector, as already requested, is urgently sought: [at the latest] at the time of the next relief."[92]

"Bavarian Reserve Infantry Regiment 3
Subject: Battleworthiness of the Troops

"Following on from my report of 6 April, 5.30 pm, I regard it as my duty to forward the enclosed report by the Regimental Medical Officer, concerning the current state of health, which he prepared for me on his own initiative. The trigger for this was my request for an explanation as to why thirty one men from 12th Company reported sick simultaneously and to make it clear to him that all men, except the most pressing medical cases, were to be directed back to their companies.

"Currently the troops in the sector are deployed as follows:

"Ten companies are manning the position: four companies in *Loën North*, four companies in *Loën South* and two companies in Bois Carré and the Second Position respectively (on high alert). Only two companies are resting. Each battalion has spent eight days manning the sub-sectors. Each company has spent four days in the Forward Position (First and Second Lines) and four days in support (North: Third Line and Stop Line; South: Third Line only). In this context, deployment in support is to be equated with service in the front line, because the Third Line, the Stop Line and the *Zwischenstellung* [Intermediate Position] are constantly under almost the same weight of fire as the First and Second Lines. There is no mortar fire, but this is replaced by large calibre shells from the enemy artillery.

"To this must be added the fact that the companies in support have already sent several sections to the forward companies, because their average strength (which has sunk to eighty men) is insufficient for the manning of company sub-sectors 350 metres wide.[93] When a battalion is relieved after eight days on the position, two companies move to the dugouts in Bois Carré and the Second Position, both of which are under constant fire. Only two companies are able to move into billets in Fresnoy.

"As a result, each company spends ten days on the positions; under constant fire and without a break. When this is coupled to the need to counter the daily enemy raids, both large and small, by day and night, it amounts to a commitment which leaves anything on the Somme or at Verdun in the shade; not, perhaps, in terms of casualties, but certainly in the demands it makes on the battleworthiness of the troops."

As Maier had stated, his Medical Officer, Dr Schwesinger, had indeed presented him with a worrying assessment which, after a lengthy sick parade, conducted on 7 April, he had immediately written.

"Subject: The State of Health of the Troops

"The 3rd Battalion sick parade occupied me until 5.30 pm yesterday.

As a result, it was not until 7.00 pm that I was able to despatch my report to Higher Authority. At the same time I forwarded an exact report concerning 3rd Battalion to the Commanding Officer. In view of the alarming figures it contained, I am certain that it would have been forwarded to Regimental Headquarters. Yesterday morning there were thirty six men on 'medicine and duties' and nineteen bedded down or receiving treatment. Amongst these was Leutnant Heninger 11th Company, suffering from nervous exhaustion. That day a further 130 men reported sick.

"One of these men was Leutnant Hiltner, psychologically disturbed and suffering from nervous exhaustion, such that he had to be evacuated to the field hospital. I then personally examined every single man, applying strictly objective medical criteria. 131 of them were fully justified in reporting sick. Of these, ninety two were placed on the sick list, thirty were retained for further treatment and nine (including six suspected gas poisoning cases, as a result of gas shelling on 4, 5 and 6 April) were transferred to hospital.

"Amongst the sick were fifty seven men suffering from heart conditions or nervous exhaustion. More than half of these were suffering from illnesses and injuries caused by the cold and eleven had acute dysentery. Out of the entire sick list, I have only hospitalised the gas cases. The remainder remain on strength and are being treated but, in view of the numbers involved, it has only been possible to bed down the dysentery cases; beds in Aid Post III had to be specially cleared for them. This place is being shelled so dangerously that apart from those who volunteered to remain there, the remainder have had to be placed in neighbouring dugouts.

"Their appearance, the objective diagnoses and the nature of the duties of the men involved has convinced [me] the Medical Officer that the majority of the sick personnel are unfit for duty. There was a striking number of men above the age of thirty nine amongst them. I am of the opinion that some of the exhausted men will be fit once more for duty after a few days of real rest, but that the great majority are no longer fit for active service. If the experience of the Somme is any guide, then a similar surge in cases of exhaustion is to be expected in the 1st and 2nd Battalions during the next few days and, which is worse, the reinforcements which have arrived were nowhere near enough to replace the casualties.

"The situation which has arisen in 3rd Battalion has developed exactly as it did in Martinpuich; only the incidence of dysentery was greater there. The Medical Officers of 1st and 2nd Battalions reported yesterday in their weekly summaries:

I.   Increasing numbers of cases of exhaustion are appearing.

II.   The following ailments have had to be treated: foot conditions, coughs and colds, a noticeably large number of skin complaints and many cases of nervous exhaustion

I reported to the senior Medical Officer, 1st Bavarian Reserve Division, yesterday by telephone and informed him about the regimental wastage [due to illness]: 'Overall state of health – poor. Numerous cases of nervous exhaustion. Many men with coughs and colds. No infectious diseases.'

"I have just been informed that another seventy three men of 10th Company have reported sick."

Reading between the lines of these reports, carefully couched in their sober, official language, it is easy to see the harsh reality which lies behind terms such as 'softening up the enemy'. Here is clear evidence of the effectiveness of this unprecedented preliminary bombardment. The approximate bayonet strength of the three regiments of 1st Bavarian Reserve Division on 9 April was: Bavarian Reserve Infantry Regiment 1 – 1,360; Bavarian Reserve Infantry Regiment 2 (which had suffered particularly from the effect of raids) – 850 and Bavarian Reserve Infantry Regiment 3 – 1,000.[94]

Just to the north the picture was very similar. Losses in men and equipment increased noticeably at the beginning of April. Just before Easter it was possible to make a final check on the fighting strength of those battalions of 79th Reserve Division which were stationed forward. The general situation was as follows. There were one to two companies forward in the first two lines of trenches. One or two companies were located in the third trench, in support and the rest were under command of the battalion commanders in the reserve role. The trench fighting strength of the companies varied from fifty to ninety riflemen, figures which were reduced even further during the final stages of the bombardment. Because the battalion reserves were reduced to a few small groups, the Division directed the move forward of one company from each of the resting battalions into the battle zone in order to form, along with engineer companies, a small reserve at the disposal of the regiments.

In fact, in at least one case, even this modest reserve had to be deployed before battle was joined. On 5 April, 2nd Battalion Reserve Infantry Regiment 262, having suffered sixty five casualties during the past few days, had to send forward eight sections of men from the Infantry Pionier [Engineer] Company to strengthen its forward companies.[95] The machine guns, including the six belonging to Machine Gun Sharp Shooter Troop 20, which were only deployed at the end of March, were arranged in depth in amongst the craters where, in conjunction with the few remaining undamaged mortars, they formed the backbone of the positions, which by now were only thinly held.[96]

The Allied superiority in materiel was overwhelming. The Germans believed that for each kilometre of front north of the Scarpe, approximately 140 guns and 50 mortars were firing. Sixth Army reported on 7 April that, 'during the past two weeks, fire has been observed coming from 679 different positions'.[97] As far as the 79th Reserve Division was concerned, this meant that the fire of over 400 guns and 150 mortars could be brought to bear against its positions. Against this, it could only deploy eighty nine guns and a few mortars, some of which were destroyed during the bombardment. It is little wonder that the soldiers in the forward trenches were left with the impression that they were being sacrificed unprotected to the destructive fire. In the face of all the Allied preparatory fire, it became increasingly difficult to transport sufficient food forward to the front line. Frequently the soldiers were reduced to bread and water which, contaminated though it was with gas or other filth, they were reduced to collecting from the shell holes.

Their psychological state was not improved either, because many of them believed that there was a strong chance that Allied mining operations meant they were occupying locations which might be blown up at any moment. In the event the Canadian view was that the ground in this sector of the front was already sufficiently difficult to traverse without adding to the number of craters already in existence. Nevertheless, all these pressures put together led to a noticeable decline in the strength and morale of the troops. In practical terms, this meant that the attack, when launched, would be going in against defenders who were well below their normal establishment, whose nerves were shattered, who were physically exhausted and frequently so ill that in any other circumstances they would have been in bed.

Increased incidence of illness was not the only way the strain of the past few weeks manifested itself. Reporting on 5 April to the Commander of Group Souchez [VIII Reserve Corps], the commander of 16th Bavarian Infantry Division, Generalmajor Ritter von Möhl, first described the state of the defences between Hill 145 and the *Gießler Höhe,* then went on to outline concerns about discipline in the front line:[98]

> "The bombardment, in combination with the weather conditions, has greatly reduced the defensive value of the position. Currently there is no continuity within the First or Second Lines because, in places, the trenches have been flattened. On the left flank of *Döberitz,* forward of the Third Line, [the defences] are reduced to sentry posts in craters. Large numbers of the dugouts have been buried and the approach routes are unusable in places.

"The constant heavy bombardment, the ceaseless high state of alert in a severely shot-up position, protected by only fragments of an obstacle, coupled with the endless work each night on positions which are generally destroyed again the following day, has naturally had a negative effect on the morale of the troops and has led to some isolated incidents . . . My oral report yesterday was somewhat limited, because I had just been informed about examples of gross insubordination within a regiment, in whose fighting ability I had previously had the highest trust."

Möhl did not choose to expand on this worrying situation, but is quite clear that men were at the end of their tether as the bombardment reached its climax. As far as the gunners of 79th Reserve Division could tell, there was no day when the divisional sector was hit by fewer than 12,000 rounds and on several days the figure went considerably higher. From 7 April attempts to keep an accurate check on the amount of ammunition fired were abandoned. 'The number of enemy shells fired cannot be determined . . . Mortar fire was broadly comparable to the previous few days', they reported that day.[99] Like a boxer trapped in the corner of the ring and forced to take punishment to which he can make only a limited reply, the defenders had no choice but to protect themselves as well as possible, to remain vigilant and to await the inevitable overwhelming assault.

That was the stark reality for the German defence all along Vimy Ridge during the final hours of the bombardment, but what was it like for the men actually manning the front line? One of the commanding officers of Bavarian Reserve Infantry Regiment 2, deployed in Sector *Wittelsbach*, gave a view at battalion level:

Major von Dittelsbach 1st Battalion Bavarian Reserve Infantry Regiment 2[100]

"The enemy had divided up the battlefield like a chessboard. Strip after strip was ploughed and torn up. The entire defensive works were to be demolished and the nerves of the defenders shredded. As it unfolded it made for dreadful scenes. The explosion of the massive shells ripped great craters out of the earth, sent their contents skywards then, as they fell to ground once more, repeated the process in chaotic confusion. The earth rocked, the air rushed like gusts of wind past the ears: thunderclap after thunderclap.

"In between were the light and medium calibre shells, fired from the front and the flanks to carry out their work all along the line, or to come down as harassing fire on the cold, wrecked slopes where the clouds of gas clung. New monsters crashed down on the front line: torpedo mines, 138 pounders, landing with massive effect; whilst, along the approach routes the long-barreled guns brought down hails of fire and claimed victims in the villages."

Hanging on to his wrecked position in Sector *Zollern*, in the centre of the 79th Reserve Division front, one company officer of Reserve Infantry Regiment 262 left an account of his experience during the bombardment in the La Folie area. Reading it, his increasing exhaustion and desperation at the pressure of events beyond his control is almost tangible. There can be little doubt that this time of trial was entirely typical of the experience of many others manning the Vimy front:[101]

"I exercise command over a crater field more than one kilometre in extent. At my disposal are: four platoons of infantry; one reserve platoon; six machine guns; three light mortars; one telegraph station and five telephone points. To that must be added assault groups, the artillery forward observation officer, reporting points, messengers and flare relay stations to pass on signals and so alert the artillery. We can only move in this crater field during the hours of darkness. During the day my time in my dugout is so full of the need to product reports and returns, sketches and defence plans that my head is buzzing. If everything goes perfectly, it takes me three hours to tour the sentry posts; if I add in the need to link up with the neighbouring sectors, this rises to six hours.

"I have created five independent mixed defensive teams. The men are magnificent. Every day half of them are buried [by the fire]. Sentry duty is an immense burden. The food is cold; even fetching it involves extraordinary exertion. The men are working until they are nearly dropping from exhaustion. But none of these brave young men are grumbling or complaining. Covered in clay and mud they can only snatch rests on the freezing cold ground, but their eyes light up at the thought of being able to give the Tommies what for. Mindful of our joint responsibility, they stick it out through the heaviest concentrations of fire. The demands they make are the minimum to sustain life – a shining example to the greedy drones back home. They have just gone thirty six hours with no food, but nobody is cursing about it. The wounded are stoical and are simply grateful for a cigarette which we place in their helpless lips.

"We have now been subjected to ceaseless drum fire for eight days and our casualties are severe. Yesterday the company lost nine men. All we could do was to drag them unconscious out of the trenches under the constant clatter of British [sic] machine gun fire. The British [sic] pressurise us indefatigably. Yesterday we had two men stabbed to death in their trench at 2.00 pm. Then there is the ceaseless fire: 600 mortar bombs and one hundred shells on the company sector in only twelve hours. We are enduring a second Battle of the Somme here. The battalion is already in an awful state. There has been no warm food for forty eight hours. The men are in a state of collapse. The British major offensive is about to begin. Here in the Second Line, I am down to only one section of men. I have been waiting since 9.00 pm for warm food for the company.

"The British are simply miles ahead of us in their superiority in mortars, artillery and technology, so we infantry just have to soldier on with no artillery support. But our men are truly outstanding. Because more and more dugouts are being collapsed every day, we shall all soon be forced to move out into the open. My dugout is full of the wounded; the trench outside of the dead. Nobody has come for them. My best men are either dead or wounded . . .

"My men are beyond all praise! The company commander expressly ordered the occupation of an essential sentry position that was in such a dangerous place that anybody manning it was certain to be more or less seriously wounded within a very short space of time. Not a man flinched and, sure enough, the dugout adjacent to that of the men waiting to go on duty has gradually filled up with seriously wounded men . . . "

Throughout the bombardment extensive use was made of gas. On 4 April, for example, there was a concentrated gas attack on *Zollern* North. Because some men moving forward in a relief operation removed their gas masks too early through impatience or difficulty in seeing to move at night, there were numerous gas casualties.

Reserve Leutnant Zeller 7th Company Reserve Infantry Regiment 262[102]

During the evening of 4 April my platoon was due to be relieved by another from 5th Company. The relief was to have started at midnight but suddenly, at 11.00 pm, the Tommies launched a gas attack. We were not totally surprised by the attack because we had heard the noise of the installation of cylinders over a period of several days. Being cautious, however, I ordered increased gas readiness as soon as the wind was favourable. In addition we were all outside in the trenches because the Canadians had attacked to our right a short while earlier. The Canadians released two gas clouds and it was possible for us to unmask in between the two waves. I remained unclear why the Canadians had released gas in this way without following it up by an attack. In the front line gas casualties were practically zero, but the relieving troops from 5th Company, who were underway, suffered worse. Some of them were gassed and had to turn about immediately and some men of the sections which completed the forward relief were affected the following day. As a result I, together with half my platoon, had to remain forward in the trenches for an extra day.

On 7 April the weight of artillery fire slackened noticeably, only to swell once more when the German batteries countered it fiercely. Then, on the afternoon of 8 April (Easter Sunday), it increased to violent drum fire which continued, sometimes at a lesser rate, sometimes at a higher one, throughout the following night. It was the start of the final softening up process and it was obvious that the attack on Vimy Ridge was imminent. The time for directives, instructions and contingency plans was past. The next task of all the headquarters, formations and units of

Group Vimy would be to fight for their continuing possession of this dominating landmark, for which so much blood had already been spilled. There remained one last piece to be placed in the jigsaw of preparation. It was time for an exhortation to the men who were going to have to try to make the defensive concept work.

"Group Vimy: Corps Order of the Day, Easter Sunday 1917[103]

Soldiers!

For days the enemy has been trying to wear you down through an immense weight of artillery fire. The enemy has succeeded in smashing our trenches and obstacles, but has made no impression on the steadfastness of our courageous infantry. Each time raids have been launched against our positions they have been repulsed bloodily and prisoners have been taken.

"Our excellent, strong, artillery has supported the infantry admirably. Each gunner understands that it is his duty and a matter of honour to come self-sacrificially to the aid of the infantry in its hour of need.

"Our airmen and anti-aircraft gunners have all performed brilliantly. During the past week twenty five enemy aircraft have fallen to the guns of the Richthofen Squadron and the anti-aircraft guns have brought down two more. The achievement and maintenance of air superiority is an essential pre-requisite for success.

"In battle and at the cost of huge labour, the engineers, mortar men and pioneer battalions have all played their part in supporting the infantry.

"Soldiers! The day of the decisive assault draws near! It will demand nothing less than a supreme performance from all ranks. Be ready at all times to begin the defence! The British must not be allowed to gain one single foot of ground. Wherever they succeed in breaking in they must ejected without delay.

"Do not forget that here we are facing *the* enemy which actually caused this dreadful war; who alone bears the guilt that it is still continuing.

"You all know what is at stake: Victory and Peace.

Signed: von Fasbender"

It is impossible to say how far this message permeated down through the ranks before battle was joined and even harder to judge what difference, if any, it made. It reads, in any case, as though the Corps Commander was trying to overcome his own misgivings and convince himself that all would be well.

The truth was about to be revealed.

Notes

1. Kriegsarchiv München A.O.K. 6 Bd 432 Nachrichten Offizier 3.1.17
2. Kriegsarchiv München A.O.K. 6 Bd 432 A.O.K. 6 1a. Nr. 85041 5.1.17
3. Heeresgruppe Kronprinz von Bayern Oberkommando Ia Nr. 2026 geh. *Vorschlag für die Operationen auf dem französischen Kriegsschauplatz im Frühjahr 1917* H.Qu., 15. Januar 1917. Quoted in Kronprinz Rupprecht *Mein Kriegstagebuch Dritter Band* pp 120–126
4. Kriegsarchiv München Pi. Btl. 17 Bd 9 Generalkommando VI. Reservekorps Ic Nr. 3847 K.H.Qu., den 14.2.1917
5. Kriegsarchiv München 1. R.I.B. Bd 37 A.O.K. 6 B. Nr. 8353 A.H.Qu., 13.2.17
6. HMT (formerly RMS) Olympic was the sister ship to the Titanic and belonged to the White Star Line. Her maiden voyage was in 1911, she served as a troop transport on the transatlantic run during the Great War, then returned to passenger service as RMS Olympic until she was withdrawn from service in 1935 and scrapped two years later.
7. The actual date of his desertion is not absolutely clear: 11, 12 and 13 February are all mentioned in the different reports.
8. Kriegsarchiv München A.O.K. 6 Bd 433 A.O.K. 6. B. Nr. 8581 2.3.17
9. Kriegsarchiv München Pi.Btl 17 Bd. 9 Generalkommando VI. Reservekorps Ic Nr. 3847 K.H.Qu., den 14.2.1917
10. Much of the story of Dörr's later life remains obscure. He was swiftly identified as a deserter when documents discovered after the capture of Vimy Ridge were recovered and examined. It transpired that he had signed on using the false name George McDonald and claiming to be an American citizen. It is highly probable that the main document involved was the interrogation report of VI Reserve Corps, dated 14 February 1917, which contains a great deal of personal information about Dörr and was given wide distribution for such a sensitive paper – sixty one copies in all – to relatively low-level headquarters. It is not known if he was permitted to fight in the German army, but he certainly survived the Great War. He re-crossed the Atlantic some years later as a passenger from Southampton on the Olympic (which was an interesting coincidence) and landed in the port of New York on 12 May 1931. At some stage he made his way back to Canada and lived for many years in Nanaimo, Vancouver Island, claiming to have served with the Royal Flying Corps. In the days before records were held on computer, cross-checking was very difficult, so he was clearly able to re-integrate fully into Canadian life and was First Principal of the Saskatchewan Grand Chapter of the Royal Arch Masons in 1961. At the time of his death at the age of ninety eight in July 1996, by which time he was a Life Member of the Lantzville Branch of the Royal Canadian Legion, he had been living in his adopted country, undetected, but with the constant risk of exposure, for sixty five years. Dörr was honoured after his death with a mention in the 'Last Post' section of the magazine of the Legion.
11. Dunzinger: History Bavarian Infantry Regiment 11 pp 45–46
12. Kriegsarchiv München 11.I.R. Bd. 16 No 377a K.9.Infanterie Brigade *Betreff Unternehmen am 13.2* Br.St.Qu., den 15.2.1917
13. Oberleutnant Anton Breher and Reserve Leutnant Friedrich Reuter are buried in the German cemetery at St Laurent Blangy in Block 1, Graves 323 and 329 respectively.
14. Canadian casualties during this raid were high. Fatal casualties were: 44th Battalion – five; 46th Battalion – seven; 47th Battalion – five and 50th Battalion

fourteen. In addition approximately 130 were apparently wounded. If true, this amounts to a casualty rate of 50%.

15. Kriegsarchiv München 1 R.I.B. Bd 37 Nachrichtenoffizier A.O.K.6 b. Nr. 8363 A.H.Qu., 14.2.17

16. History K.B. Infantry Regiment 14 p 215

17. Kriegsarchiv München Pi. Btl. 17 Bd 9 VI Res. Korps Ia/Ic4461 K.H.Qu., den 22.2.1917

18. Berton (*Vimy* p 131) states that large white boards were used to mark the routes forward through the Canadian wire for the attacking troops on 1 March and that the Germans had previously trained machine guns on the gaps. This is entirely feasible; machine guns firing on fixed lines at night had to be aimed at some sort of potentially useful target, but the linkage between the reported signs and machine guns is not made specifically in any of the German accounts.

19. Kriegsarchiv München 11 I.R. Bd 16 Bayer. 16. Inf. Div. 590/I Div. St. Qu. Den 20. Februar 1917

20. Kriegsarchiv München 11 I.R. Bd 16 11 Infanterie Regiment An 9.Infanterie Brigade *Betreff: Kampfabschitt Döberitz* R.St.Qu., 20.2.17

21. Kriegsarchiv München HGr Rupprecht Bd 122 *Beurteilung der Lage 24/2 17 6. Armee*

22. Kronprinz Rupprecht *Mein Kriegstagebuch Zweiter Band* p 106

23. Schwerin: History Reserve Infantry Regiment 261 p 125

24. Reserve Infantry Regiment 261 *Nachrichtenblatt Nr. 29* pp 2–3

25. The body of Major Frederick Lucas was recovered during the truce. He is buried at Villers Station CWGC cemetery in grave VI E 2.

26. Zickner was later killed as a Hauptmann on 16 August 1917 at Langemark.

27. This figure is somewhat inflated, though it is true that a great many bodies were recovered.

28. Kriegsarchiv München R.Pi.Kp.1 Bd 5 General–Kdo I. Bayer. Reserve Corps K.H.Qu. 2.3.17

29. Although this was a four battalion attack, one of the Canadian battalions attacked on the VI Reserve Corps front.

30. It has proved to be impossible to verify this statement from other sources. It is thought that the Canadians claimed to have captured some prisoners. Possibly they were from 16th Bavarian Infantry Division, VI Reserve Corps, on The Pimple.

31. Kriegsarchiv München A.O.K. 6 Bd 433 A.O.K. 6. B. Nr. 8590 3.März 1917. p 3

32. Dieterich: *Die 79. Reserve-Division in der Schlacht auf der Vimy-Höhe/April 1917* p 7

33. Kriegsarchiv München 1 R.Korps Bd 1 *Kriegstagebuch 1.3.17*

34. Kriegsarchiv München HGr Rupprecht Bd 125 A.O.K. 6. B. Nr. 8538 A.H.Qu., 27.2.17.

35. One of the consequences of all this bombardment was that three out of four guns of a battery of Reserve Field Artillery Regiment 63 were destroyed. Dieterich p 7

36. Kriegsarchiv München Pi.Btl.17 Bd 9 79. RESERVE-DIVISION *Nachrichtenblatt vom 1.3.1917*

37. Kriegsarchiv München A.O.K. 6 Bd 433 A.O.K. 6. B. Nr. 8590 3.März 1917. p 2

38. Berton: *op. cit.* p 135

39. Kriegsarchiv München Pi.Btl.17 Bd 9 79. RESERVE-DIVISION *Nachrichtenblatt vom 1.3.1917*

40. Leutnant Karl Lieser is buried in the German cemetery at Neuville St Vaast/Maison Blanche Block 9, Grave 533.

41. Reserve Infantry Regiment 261 *Nachrichtenblatt Nr. 37* pp 2–3
42. Gefreiter Oskar Pietzschke is buried close to Leutnant Lieser in the German cemetery at Neuville St Vaast/Maison Blanche in Block 9, Grave 537
43. He who meets his death in sacred battle / Though on foreign soil, is at rest in the Fatherland. Here Lauch is quoting the final couplet of the *Marschlied der Jäger* written in 1813 by A Methfessel (1785 – 1869).
44. Kriegsarchiv München HGr Rupprecht Bd 122 *Beurteilung der Lage 3/3 17 6. Armee*
45. Kriegsarchiv München HGr Rupprecht Bd 122 *AOK 6 Beurteilung der Lage 10.3. 17*
46. Kriegsarchiv München HGr Rupprecht Bd 149 *Oberkommando 6. Armee Ia No. 550 g. A.H.Qu.*, den 14.3.1917
47. Kronprinz Rupprecht *Mein Kriegstagebuch Zweiter Band* p 115
48. *ibid.* p 119
49. Kriegsarchiv München 14. I.R. Bd. 10 K.Bayer.9.Infanterie – Brigade Nr. 1075a B.St.Qu., den 4.4.1917 *Betreff: Unternehmen München*
50. After Vimy Ridge was captured, a copy of this order was discovered by the Canadians. Commenting on it, the War Diary of 176th Company RE homed in on the fact that one of the reasons for the attack was, 'an anxiety which our underground operations were causing the enemy.'
51. Kalb: History Bavarian Field Artillery Regiment 10 p 141
52. Kriegsarchiv München 14. I.R. Bd 10 K.Bayer.9.Infanterie – Brigade Nr. 1075a B.St.Qu., den 4.4.1917 *Betreff: Unternehmen München*
53. Kriegsarchiv München 14. I.R. Bd 10 K.Bayer.9.Infanterie – Brigade Nr. 1075a B.St.Qu., den 4.4.1917 *Betreff: Unternehmen München*
54. Divisional time was to be used to control the operation. 9 Bavarian Brigade was made responsible for obtaining the official time sufficiently far ahead of the attack to ensure that it was distributed forward early enough for regiments and detachments to synchronise watches.
55. Kriegsarchiv München A.O.K. 6 Bd 433 A.O.K. 6. B. Nr. 8783 18.3.17
56. Kriegsarchiv München: I R Korps Bd 147 Gruppe Vimy General-Kdo I Bayer.Res.Korps Abteilg. Ia No. 21 600 H.Qu., 2.7.1917 Beilage 2.
57. The notes expand on the requirement for guns: each regiment needed eighteen to twenty weapons. Although Machine Gun Sharpshooter Detachment 28 had arrived with eighteen guns, it was in need of rest and recuperation. There were still no light machine guns (i.e. Maxim 08/15) available.
58. Kriegsarchiv München 1 R. Korps Bd 1 *Kriegstagebuch 18.3.17*
59. The repeated postponement and ultimate cancellation of this operation must have had an adverse effect on the plan to produce these extra assets.
60. Lenz later added the remark, 'During the night 18/19 the situation clarified itself more in favour of [the assessment of] Corps Headquarters, when elements of 9th Division appeared along the Scarpe'.
61. Heinicke: History Reserve Infantry Regiment 263 pp 115 – 116
62. Fischer: History Reserve Infantry Regiment 262 p 105
63. Kriegsarchiv München A.O.K. 6 Bd 433 A.O.K. 6. B. Nr. 8752 16/3.17
64. Kriegsarchiv München 1 Res Division Bd 20 79. RESERVE-DIVISION *Nachrichtenblatt vom 20.3.1917* D.St.Qu., den 21.3.1917
65. Kriegsarchiv München 1 Res Division Bd 20 79. RESERVE-DIVISION *Nachrichtenblatt vom 21.3.1917* D.St.Qu., den 22.3.1917
66. Kriegsarchiv München 1 R. Korps *Betreff: Vorbereitungen für die Abwehrschlacht*

General-Kommando I. Bayer. Res. Korps Abteilung Ia No. 13 720 K.H.Qu., 21.3.1917

67. Original emphasis.

68. Kriegsarchiv München Pi.Btl.17 Bd 7 1.Bayer. Res.Div. Ia No 2341 Division. St. Qu., den 28. März 1917

69. Nasmith: *Canada's Sons and Great Britain in the World War* pp 305–306

70. These identifications are not accurate and it is hard to know how Bacmeister's staff made the mistake, bearing in mind that his division had been engaged against the 4th Canadian Division constantly since it had arrived in the area.

71. Kronprinz Rupprecht *Mein Kriegstagebuch Zweiter Band* p 124

72. Kalb: *op. cit.* p 142

73. Kriegsarchiv München 1 R.I.B. Bd 37 General-Kommando I. Bayer.Res.Korps Abteilung Chef No. 14 326 K.H.Qu., 31.3.1917

74. Original emphasis. The Germans constantly asked questions of prisoners concerning the whereabouts of a 5th Canadian Division, which of course never left the United Kingdom, was broken up later in 1918 and never saw active service. The precise reason for this incorrect assumption is not clear from the intelligence report.

75. Kriegsarchiv München Pi.Btl.17 Bd 7 1.Bayer. Res.Div. I No. 2430 Div. St. Qu., den 31.3.17

76. Kriegsarchiv München A.O.K. 6 Bd 433 A.O.K. 6. B. Nr. 8950 1.4.17

77. Kriegsarchiv München A.O.K. 6 Bd 433 A.O.K. 6. B. Nr. 8961 2.4.17

78. In the event, on 9 April 1917, once Les Tilleuls had been taken, 31st Battalion advanced to capture Thélus and 27th Battalion subsequently took Farbus Wood. However the procedure for the attack was quite clear already to the Germans.

79. Kronprinz Rupprecht *Mein Kriegstagebuch Zweiter Band* p 126

80. Kronprinz Rupprecht *ibid.* p 127

81. Kriegsarchiv München 1 Res Division Bd 20 79. RESERVE-DIVISION *Nachrichtenblatt vom 28.3.1917* D.St.Qu., den 29.3.1917

82. Kriegsarchiv München 1 Res Division Bd 20 79. RESERVE-DIVISION *Nachrichtenblatt vom 29.3.1917* D.St.Qu., den 30.3.1917

83. Kriegsarchiv München 14. I.R. Bd 10 K.Bayer.9.Infanterie – Brigade Nr. 1075a B.St.Qu., den 4.4.1917 *Betreff: Unternehmen München* p 7

84. Kriegsarchiv München 14. I.R. Bd 10 Generalkommando VI.Res.Korps Abt. Ia. Nr. 933 K.H.Qu., den 2.4.1917

85. Kronprinz Rupprecht *Mein Kriegstagebuch Zweiter Band* pp 128–129

86. Kronprinz Rupprecht *Mein Kriegstagebuch Zweiter Band* p 130

87. Kriegsarchiv München 14. I.R. Bd 10 16.Infanterie-Division 3.4.17 Nr. I/1735 G.R. zur 9.Inf.Brigade

88. Kriegsarchiv München 14. I.R. Bd 10 K.B.9.Infanterie-Brigade 4.4.17 Nr. 1074 a

89. Kriegsarchiv München 11. I.R. Bd 16 K Bayer.9.Inf-Brigade Nr. 1088a Brig.St.Qu., den 5.4.1917 *Betreff: Kräfteeinsatz für 'München'*

90. Kriegsarchiv München Pi. Btl. 17 Bd 7 Gruppe Vimy Abt I a /Art No. 14 553 K.H.Qu., den 3.4.17

91. Jones: *The War in the Air Vol III* pp 334–335

92. Kriegsarchiv München R.I.R. 3 Bd. 3 Nr 5154 Bayer.Res.Inf.Regt. Nr. 3 6.4.1917 5.30 abds.

93. Bearing in mind that there was no time to rectify this situation before the offensive opened, it is small wonder that rapid progress was made on a front reduced in defenders to less than one man every five metres.

94. Kriegsarchiv München OP 38887 1 Res.Inf.Brigade Nr. 9340 *Gefechtsbericht über die Ereignisse am 9., 10. und 11. April 1917 Brig.St.Qu., 6.6.17*

95. Fischer: *op. cit.* p 109

96. Dieterich: *op. cit.* p 10

97. Kriegsarchiv München: HGr Rupprecht Bd 122 *AOK 6 No 239 7/4 Beurteilung der Lage.*

98. Kriegsarchiv München 16. Inf. Div. Bd. 4 Bayer 16. Infanterie-Division Ia,. No. 1767 *Wochenbericht für die Zeit vom 29. März 1917 – 5. April 1917* Division.St.Qu., den 5. April 17

99. Kriegsarchiv München 1 Res Division Bd 20 79. RESERVE-DIVISION *Nachrichtenblatt vom 6.4.1917* D.St.Qu., den 7.4.1917

100. Behrmann: *Die Osterschlacht bei Arras 1917 I.Teil* pp 30–31

101. Fischer: *op. cit.* pp 109–110

102. *ibid.* p 109

103. Kriegsarchiv München: R.Pi.Kp. 1 Bd. 5 Gruppe Vimy Korpstagesbefehl H.Qu., Ostersonntag 1917

CHAPTER SEVEN

The Battle of Vimy Ridge
April 1917

When day dawned, wet and cold, at 5.30 am on 9 April, a storm of fire, unparalleled in anyone's experience, crashed down over the German positions. Its impacts were like the deafening roar and tossing of a sea lashed by a hurricane. Everywhere great fountains of earth rose in the air. The earth seemed to quake. Whilst the front line was engaged primarily with light guns and mortars, supported by massed machine guns, the support lines and battery positions came under fire from medium, heavy and super-heavy guns, as well as being drenched with gas. The fumes and smoke which hung over the German positions grew into dark masses of cloud, which glowed red. All the roads which the reserves moving forward would need to use were lashed by fire. Yellow flares rose all along the German lines, but before the defending batteries could begin to bring down defensive fire, the hail of fire lifted from the front lines, only to fall with increased violence on the depth positions. Even the curtains of machine gun fire, which had been raking the German front line parapets, permitting the sentries only to observe by the use of periscopes, lifted. In many places the earth itself opened as mines and subway exits were blown.

Simultaneously, as an icy wind and squalls of sleet lashed the muddy scene, from out of the trenches and craters rose the rested, well fed and supplied Canadian assault divisions who rushed towards the German trenches. In the lead were groups armed with hand grenades and pistols and behind them, in one dense mass after another, came infantrymen, with their weapons slung and carrying large spades. In those places where the preparatory drum fire and exploding mines had extinguished all resistance, the German lines were soon overrun. But wherever German rifles and machine guns could bring fire to bear, the attackers were checked and their dead mounted up. Whenever bullets and grenades ran out, or where machine guns, clogged with mud, failed, fighting continued with bayonets. Down to the south of Thélus, where groups of tanks crawled forward along the roads radiating from Arras, the German First and Second Positions were taken, whilst along the Arras-Douai road and in the valley of the Scarpe, the Third Position was also captured. Opposite Arras a gap twelve kilometres wide and temporarily practically devoid of defenders was created. This could only be closed gradually as reserves were rushed forward, from neighbouring sectors unaffected by the attack, to meet the emergency but, due to poor positioning, the arrival of reserve divisions could not be expected before 10 April.

The greatest Allied advance of the day by far was made on the left flank of Group Vimy, just north of the Scarpe in the sector of 14th Bavarian Infantry

Division, which was attacked by the British 34th Division. The 14th Division was later the subject of sharp criticism for its failure to put up stronger resistance, but of more immediate importance as far as the defence of Vimy Ridge itself was concerned was the fate of 1st Bavarian Reserve Division, deployed just to the south of 79th Reserve Division in Sectors *Loën*, *Wittelsbach* and *Rupprecht*. Immediately south of Reserve Infantry Regiment 263, on the northern flank of 1st Bavarian Reserve Division, was Reserve Infantry Regiment 3, commanded by Major Anton Meier from a dugout known as *Leipziger Hütte* [Leipzig Cottage], located just south of the present day Bois Carré Cemetery.

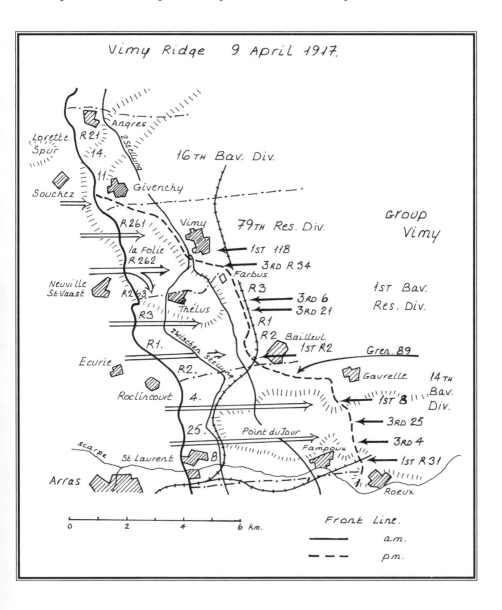

Major Meier was on the missing list after the battle, so it fell to Major von Poschinger to describe the events of the day, when his regiment was attacked by the 1st Canadian Division, in his brief initial after-action report:[1]

"9.4.1917. . . . Of the battalions deployed on the position, the 1st Battalion had relieved the 3rd Battalion during the night 7/8 April, whilst 2nd Battalion had already been located forward on the position from 4 April. The uncommitted companies (11th and 12th) were back at Fresnoy in reserve. After extremely heavy artillery and mortar fire came down on the sector during the night 8/9April, just as it had for the past few days, destroying almost all of the dugouts of the First Position, at 5.30 am 9 April drum fire started coming down all along the divisional sector.

"From this moment onwards all contact was lost with the front line. After the heaviest imaginable drum fire by artillery and mortars, lasting a quarter of an hour, the enemy infantry began its attack in great waves. Opposite Sub-Sectors *L[oën] 3* and *L4* the enemy used flamethrowers and, at the moment of the attack, two enemy aircraft were in the air above the position.

"Despite constant demands for defensive fire, the response of our artillery was extremely weak. As a result, the tiny garrison of the First and Second Lines (the companies averaged only a bayonet strength of sixty men) was simply overrun. The main enemy break in point was along the road Neuville – Thélus. It appears that the enemy broke straight through here to the Third Line in the first rush; at least no more reports were received by the regiment from 5th Company, which was deployed there – none of the runners despatched there ever returned.

"In *L[oën]* South the enemy was checked for a considerable time by small arms fire, but gradually they made progress here too, breaking down the resistance of the weakened companies of 1st Battalion once they had advanced in the neighbouring sectors. At 5.45 am the two companies of 3rd Battalion located in Fresnoy, which had only just been relieved at 2.00 am in Bois Carré and the Second Position by 9th and 10th Companies, were alerted and ordered to move forward with two machine guns to Bois Carré . . .

"In the meantime the garrison of the *Riegel-Stellung* [Stop Line] (8th Company assisted by survivors from the first three lines) maintained obstinate resistance, holding up the enemy for approximately three hours. About 10.00 am, after the *Riegel-Stellung* had been completely smashed, the British [*sic*] succeeded in penetrating its northern part, from the Neuville-Thélus road. At the same time the enemy managed to force a way into the centre of Thélus, whose western edge was still being held by elements of 79th Reserve Division.

"Whilst artillery fire came down on the trenches around Bois Carré, at about 10.30 dense skirmishing lines of British [*sic*] soldiers advanced on Thélus East and Bois Carré. Here 9th Company, with about forty riflemen and two machine guns and led by the Regimental Commander, was still holding out. The staff of 2nd Battalion Reserve Infantry Regiment 3 was also here, having been forced to withdraw once the enemy had advanced over the *Riegel-Stellung* towards *Augsburger-Weg* [Augsburg Way].

"Despite suffering heavy casualties from rifle and machine gun fire, the enemy worked their way forward to Bois Carré, [helped by the fact] that resistance had ceased north of the Thélus – Bailleul road. Once the enemy had begun advancing along *Preussen-Weg* [Prussian Way] and were threatening the rear of 9th Company located between Bois Carré and *Leipziger-Haus* [*sic – Hütte*], it was ordered at 11.30 am to withdraw along *Loën-Weg* to the Second position, in order to avoid being cut off. Once *Leipziger-Haus* had been destroyed by fire, the regimental staff moved their command post to the dugout of an aid post at the southwest corner of Farbus Wood.[2] Throughout the morning the Second Position, which was manned by 11th and 12th Companies, was under extremely heavy artillery fire.

"At about 12.45 pm the British [*sic*] launched forward in dense masses from *Preussen-Weg* against the Second Position. Despite obstinate resistance they succeeded in penetrating the left flank of the regiment from *Weisses Haus* [White House] and simultaneously to outflank, then to encircle, the right flank of the regiment from the northwest, once Infantry Regiment 261 [*sic – Reserve Infantry Regiment 263*] had withdrawn to the railway embankment east of Vimy/Farbus. Those elements of 3rd Battalion (which by now incorporated survivors of the other two battalions) who managed to break clean of the enemy – nobody returned from 10th Company – moved after 1.30 pm to occupy the railway embankment east of Farbus, in extension of the line of Infantry Regiment 261 [*sic*].

Once the Second Position had fallen, the British [*sic*] pushed forward initially only to the eastern edge of Farbus Wood. About 4.00 pm they attempted, using cavalry, to break through to the east. Of a twelve man patrol which rode forward along the road Farbus – Willerval, six were shot by rifle and machine gun fire and two men were captured in Willerval. The remainder escaped. Of another which pushed along the line of the railway embankment towards Bailleul all, bar two, were shot down.

"Once the full weight of enemy artillery fire began coming down on the railway embankment, this was simply held by security outposts. The line was pulled back seventy metres and everyone began to dig in. Here the remnants of the companies were relieved at 7.30 pm by elements of Bavarian Infantry Regiments 6 and 21 . . . "

Despite the severe reverses on the ground, which led to one of the regimental commanders of 1st Bavarian Reserve Division being declared missing and a second (Oberstleutnant Brunner of Bavarian Reserve Infantry Regiment 2) being captured,[3] some aspects of the command and control remained intact even in this area. The surviving battle log of Bavarian 1 Reserve Brigade, commanded by Generalmajor Lamprecht,[4] makes clear that there was two-way passage of information between Brigade and Regimental Headquarters throughout the day. Accurate descriptions of the situation were given, reserves and resupply were arranged and Headquarters 1st Bavarian Reserve Division was kept fully informed. The problem for the defence was the speed of events. The Divisional Commander, Generalmajor Freiherr von Pechmann, issued at least six abbreviated operation orders during the day (at 8.00 am, 9.00 am, 11.00 am, 11.45 am, 12.00 pm, 3.00 pm and 10.50 pm),[5] but such was the tempo of operations that even swift staff work meant that the German decision cycle was simply unable to react decisively to events until the Canadian attacks with their limited objectives had run their course.

To the north of Thélus, where on Vimy Ridge the regiments of the 79th Reserve Division waited, nerves on edge, in mud-filled trenches and craters for the start of the offensive, the Canadian attack poured down on them with extreme violence. On the left flank, manning the forward trenches and with their machine guns all destroyed or out of action, were the men of Reserve Infantry Regiment 263, commanded by Oberstleutnant von Behr. Severely weakened by the intense bombardment, only a few of them were still fit to fight, but not until after they had mounted an obstinate defence with hand grenades were they finally overwhelmed. Manning the Third Line of the First Position in Sector *Arnulf* North was one of its company commanders, waiting for dawn to break.

Reserve Leutnant Bittkau Reserve Infantry Regiment 263[6]

"Gradually the first streaks of dawn began to light up the darkness. Light squalls of snow blew across the cratered landscape. There was a striking stillness. Suddenly between Arras and Lens came great flashes and wild arcs of light in the sky: signal flares? Mine explosions? All of a sudden, as though at a single word of command, down came drum fire from thousands of large and small calibre muzzles. Shell fire rose to crazy heights. It was impossible to distinguish the firing signatures from the shell bursts. It was just one mass of fire amidst an extraordinary racket.

"It was like the final intake of breath before a race. Nerves were stretched to breaking point as we took in these scenes, which were like a painting of terrible beauty. Standing there for just a few seconds, a shell landed just to my left and a fragment hit my left side at chest height. My nerves took another knock! My heart was like lead, the gorge rose in my throats; blood ran into my mouth, taking my breath away. I was at the end of my strength; ready to faint. Suddenly came a thin shout, seemingly from far off, 'The British [sic]! Get out! Get out!'

"They were coming from the left, through the hollow, heading directly for Bonval Wood. Battle was joined: rifle shots – shouts – hand grenades. Hans Voigt, the drummer, came running up carrying ammunition and information, whilst down below secret documents were being burned. 'They are coming from the left – here they are!' a man was pulled down inside moaning . . . stomach wound. He lay there completely still. More bawling and shouting. 'They are right above us!' Then it was quieter – completely quiet until a strange voice called down [in English], 'Come out!'

"The light flickered . . . thoughts ran through my numbed head: what were they going to do? Throw down hand grenades? Smash my skull? No, better to shoot myself. But the revolver was lying on the table and I could not move. Should I wait for a counter-attack? . . . A Tommy came through the tunnel, looked carefully round the corner, a large revolver in his hand. 'Officer?' he asked, then left to fetch his comrades."

The Commanding Officer of its 1st Battalion, located in rear of his forward companies, later described the early stages of the attack:

Major Meyer 1st Battalion Reserve Infantry Regiment 263[7]

"At 5.30 am on 9 April enemy drum fire, supplemented by machine gun fire, came down. It was impossible to make out the position and in fact it was almost impossible to make out signal flares amidst the clouds of smoke and dirt thrown up by the shells. At 6.30 am heavy small arms fire could be heard and, at that moment, a message was sent by light signal to the rear, 'Heavy enemy attack.' About half an hour later the wounded Musketier Hagemann happened to pass Battalion Head-quarters, reporting that the British [*sic*] had broken into the battalion position from the right and were already occupying the Third Line. According to members of 9th Company Reserve Infantry Regiment 263, the British [*sic*] had overrun the right flank of 1st Bavarian Reserve Division and had then attacked our battalion in great strength from the left and rear.

"Unfortunately Musketier Hagemann's statements were soon confirmed when the battalion staff spotted that British [*sic*] infantry were already closing in and were mounting a machine gun in the remains of a ruined house. Because there were no reserves of any sort available for a counter-attack, the officers and men of the battalion staff left the in-defensible command post and pulled back to the Intermediate Position in order to conduct the subsequent defence as far as possible from there. On the way there two officers and all the other ranks bar two runners and three signallers were killed or wounded."

Along with many of his men, Leutnant Runge, commander of 11th Company Reserve Infantry Regiment 263, was killed as he fought standing up above the parapet of his front line trench. Meanwhile resistance continued along the second line. The combined fire of the 12th Company and parts of the 10th Company brought the Canadian attack to a halt, whilst from the *Felsenkeller* [a mined dugout and command post of *KTK South* of Sector *Arnulf*] to the rear, the reserve platoon of the 10th Company under Vizefeldwebel Borcherding, stormed forward over the cratered landscape to boost the resistance of their comrades. Gradually, however, the deep break in to the sector of 1st Bavarian Reserve Division by the 1st Canadian Division south of Les Tilleuls began to have an effect on Sector *Arnulf*. Constantly reinforced, masses of Canadian attackers advancing from the Arras-Lens road, forced their way against the flanks and rear of the 263rd, rolling them up from the south and surrounding them from the rear. The dead and wounded amongst the German ranks increased. Fighting back bravely at the head of the 4th and 10th Companies, Leutnants Patschek and Korb fell. The courageous Leutnant Zipp, who had rushed forward with his machine gun from the *Zwischenstellung* [Intermediate Position], was also mortally wounded and, nearby, Leutnant Hitzschke also met his death as he attempted to stem the Canadian break in with his machine gun.

It proved to be impossible to hold on to the First Position and, with it, went the Intermediate Position of the Regiment which ran from Thélus to Vimy. The mortars and grenade launchers there fired on for a further twenty minutes, then fell silent. No member of their crews returned. At the very last minute, Major Meyer (commander of the 1st Battalion) and his staff succeeded in breaking through to the railway embankment. In the meantime, led by the regimental commander, Oberstleutnant von Behr, the 8th Company which was in reserve, and remnants of the Engineer Company took up a blocking position south of Vimy. Here the attack was held up for hours. Leutnant von Rohrscheidt, commander of the 8th Company, together with many other courageous defenders was killed. Finally, the very last of the defenders – five men under an Offizierstellvertreter – withdrew to link up with reinforcements which had arrived at the railway embankment to the south of the Vimy-Acheville underpass.

At the *Felsenkeller* a desperate battle was waged by Hauptmann Geuinzius and Hauptmann Schmidt–Eberstein and the staffs of the 2nd and 3rd Battalions, (because of a gas alarm and the onset of the final intense drum fire, the staff of the 2nd Battalion, which had been relieved that morning, had been unable to get away). They hoped constantly that a counter-attack would come to their rescue, but once one man after another was killed or rendered unfit to fight and machine gun after machine gun was wrecked, the last of the defenders were forced in the face of overwhelming hand grenade attacks back into the *Felsenkeller*, where a battle for possession of the final remaining usable exit raged. Two men armed with rifles and grenades kept watch there constantly. When one of the men guarding the entrance was killed or collapsed wounded, he was immediately replaced by one of his comrades, but the number of men fit to fight declined steadily. When on one occasion both men were knocked out simultaneously and were not immediately replaced, the attackers succeeded in forcing a way in. A vigorous intervention with hand grenades by Hauptmann Gueinzius and Hauptmann Schmidt-Eberstein themselves succeeded in driving out the attackers once more. The battle went on for hours, even though the many wounded in the mined dugout nearly suffocated as a result of the poisonous fumes of smoke grenades which the attackers dropped down a ventilation shaft. Not until around 11.30 am, when all the grenades had been thrown and there was no longer any prospect of timely relief, did the remainder of the garrison decide, reluctantly, to surrender. The final resistance in Sector *Arnulf* had been overcome.

Writing about the events of the day later, Major Meyer, commanding officer of 1st Battalion Reserve Infantry Regiment 263, whose command post in the *Schwabentunnel* in Sector *Arnulf North* was quickly rendered untenable by the outflanking manoeuvres to his south, reported:

Major Meyer Commanding Officer 1st Battalion Reserve Infantry Regiment 263[8]

"The regimental commander [Oberstleutnant von Behr] was briefed in person by the battalion commander. Major Meyer then received orders, together with Oberleutnant Heinicke, to take 6th Company Reserve Infantry Regiment 261, ten machine guns of Reserve Infantry Regiment 263, three companies of 2nd Battalion Reserve Infantry Regiment 263 and approximately fifty men of 1st Battalion Reserve Infantry Regiment 263 (who were back with the heavy baggage) and move to defend the line of the railway embankment to the east of Vimy. The vulnerable point of this position was at Farbus Wood, where the Canadians could close up to the embankment using covered routes. If they were to succeed in crossing the embankment the danger was that its entire length could be enfiladed by machine gun fire and therefore become untenable.

"Temporarily there was a similar danger for the right flank at Vimy Station, but this was removed through the deployment of 'Detachment von Block' (1st Battalion Infantry Regiment 118 and elements of Reserve Infantry Regiment 262), which subsequently succeeded in counterattacking as far as the slopes of the so-called Telegraph Hill. During the afternoon of 9 April, large masses of Canadian soldiers were observed assembling in Farbus village, apparently in order to conduct an assault on the railway embankment. At that the battalion commander directed two machine guns into action at the southern underpass where they could bring enfilade fire down on Farbus Wood. In addition the deployment of 6th Company Reserve Infantry Regiment 261 and a platoon from 2nd Battalion Reserve Infantry Regiment 263, which had thus far been held back, meant that the left flank could be extended to a point to the south of Farbus Wood. The regimental commander was also requested to make forces available to reinforce and thus improve the security of the threatened left flank.

"A little while later enemy cavalry was observed in the area of Willerval. At approximately the same time two companies (10th and 12th Companies Reserve Fusilier Regiment 34) arrived. One company was deployed to strengthen the left flank, whilst the other company remained concentrated behind the right flank in case the enemy succeeded in breaking through at Vimy. In the meantime the enemy kept the railway embankment and the two flanks in particular under fire by heavy shells and shrapnel. Towards evening Oberstleutnant von Behr arrived once more at the railway embankment in order to direct a counter-attack. This was to sweep round the flank of Detachment von Block, roughly in the area of Petit Vimy, then was to be directed against Telegraph Hill. The troops which had been subordinated to Major Meyer were initially to support his attack by means of machine gun fire, then to undertake a frontal attack. This action was begun, but had to be halted when information arrived that the Bavarians had not succeeded in recapturing Farbus; that it was still in Canadian hands, which meant that the left flank of the attack would have been in acute danger.

"During the night the companies were withdrawn to the railway embankment. They were reinforced by, amongst other units, elements of Reserve Infantry Regiment 224, which had been placed at the disposal of 1st Bavarian Reserve Division, but which had strayed rather too far to the right as they advanced and so had become mixed up with the battle line of Detachment Meyer. To the left 12th Company Reserve Infantry Regiment 34 was now deployed, with its left flank resting on the road Willerval – Farbus Station. To its south there was a gap of 800 metres for which no troops were available to fill. Also that same night two machine guns were deployed in the area of the windmill at the south-western exit of Vimy. Their role was to secure the left flank of Detachment von Block, which was located around the Vimy crossroads. During the morning of 10 April, Oberstleutnant von Behr, to whom Detachment von Block was also subordinated, withdrew on order of brigade to the cross roads about 1,200 metres further to the east. Two newly-arrived companies of Infantry Regiment 64 were deployed in the second line to the east of Farbus in order to improve the security of the railway embankment.

"A short time later 9th Company Reserve Infantry Regiment 34 arrived at the railway embankment. Two of its platoons were used to occupy the southern edge of Vimy and so improve the security of the left flank of Detachment von Block and one platoon was deployed to the north of Vimy Station to secure up to the right. Towards the afternoon a weak enemy force attacked the left flank near to Farbus Wood, but was easily repulsed. During the evening Hauptmann Lüters, commander of 1st Battalion Infantry Regiment 118, who was in telephone contact with Major Meyer but not Hauptmann von Block, told the former that he had been attacked by strong forces and had been forced back into the Second Position. He had suffered about 30% casualties and required reinforcements, small arms ammunition and grenades. Because links to regiment were destroyed, Major Meyer allocated to Hauptmann Lüters 1st Battalion Reserve Infantry Regiment 262, 10th and 12th Companies Reserve Infantry Regiment 34 and 3rd Platoon 9th Company Reserve Infantry Regiment 34. This information was passed immediately to brigade and later, when communications were restored, to the regiment. Patrols launched by 3rd Battalion Reserve Infantry Regiment 34 established that the enemy was digging in along the wood edge to the south of Vimy. Weak sallies from this location were beaten off easily. The ground between the villages of Farbus and Vimy was free of enemy troops."

In Sector *Zollern*, which was defended by Reserve Infantry Regiment 262, the assault by the 3rd Canadian Division was preceded with massive mine explosions, which carried off much of the garrison of the front line. The few remaining defenders deployed in other positions were too few in number and could only put up temporary resistance. The attackers were not halted until just before the third line. As they then began to fall back in the face of the murderous fire laid down by the 262nd, masses more descended upon the flanks and rear of the defenders and forced them back in turn. Putting up a determined defence, Leutnant Niekutowski fell at the head of the 6th Company, along with many courageous grenadiers of the 2nd Battalion. Leutnant Wilke too was killed, together with many of his fusiliers. Isolated pockets of resistance were able to hold out temporarily, whilst other groups were able to break through to the rear, bearing reports of the imminent loss of the First Position.

The commanders of the engaged battalions – the Fusilier [3rd] and 2nd – deployed their weak reserves (the 10th and elements of the 7th Companies) in a counter-stroke. Major Reschke, commander of the Fusilier Battalion, soon found himself engaged, along with his staff and a few fusiliers, in hand to hand fighting. After a desperate struggle, he fell into the hands of the enemy, along with his few remaining men, almost all of whom were wounded. Command of the remainder of his battalion was assumed by Oberleutnant Freiherr von Richthofen. Further to the south the elements of the 7th and 10th Companies, which had launched a hasty attack, armed with hand grenades, succeeded in pushing the attackers back about 100 metres and in beating back repeated thrusts. Along with his adjutant, Leutnant Uhlhorn, Hauptmann Kröber, commander of the 2nd Battalion, was seriously wounded. He died a few days later in a field hospital. The reserves of the regimental commander, Major Freiherr von Rotenhan, which arrived at about 8.00 am (9th Company and the machine gun reserves, which had rushed forward from Drocourt), were able in the course of a bloody struggle to hold on to the eastern edge of the ridge. Immediately to the soldiers' front the ruins of the chateau at La Folie could be seen being blown skywards.

The main characteristic of the battle that day at trench level was confusion.

The experience of a front line soldier of Reserve Infantry Regiment 262 must have been typical of many other defenders that day. Writing after the war, he recorded:

Grenadier Otto Schröder 12th Company Reserve Infantry Regiment 262[9]

"That night [8/9 April] we lay down, tired after night sentry duty, saying, 'Wouldn't it be nice to pull the blankets over our heads and go to sleep?' Suddenly heavy drum fire came down. The day sentries all bawled, 'Get out. Here come the British! [*sic*]. We leapt up, all tiredness forgotten, then it was a life or death fight for the Fatherland. Every man was in his appointed place. As I was quickly passing up hand grenades, the entire trench was already full of firing. The British – they were Canadian troops – had broken through to our left, in the area of Bavarian Reserve Infantry Regiment 3 and, coming along the line of the road, were already rolling up our position. My section commander ordered me to go down into the dugout and fetch up the box of egg-shaped grenades. I immediately carried out his order, but once I was about half way up the thirty two steps of the dugout, my section commander suddenly shouted. 'Come up at once. The Canadians have already pressed on beyond the trench on the left.'

"I quickly threw the egg-shaped grenades back down into the dugout and raced upwards into the trench. As I did so, I discovered that I was alone in the trench, accompanied only by a dead comrade, who lay there with his legs drawn up as though he was trying to launch himself up the wall of the trench. I knew only that he came from Hessen; I had quite forgotten his name. I risked climbing up onto the parapet and noticed that to the left, right and front there was nothing but enemy soldiers. In their 'straw hats' [steel helmets], they looked as though they were hunting hares. As I later noted, they seemed to have drunk a lot of schnaps. I had to do something, but what? I dragged the dead comrade into a shell hole and lay down next to him as though I was dead. In the meantime the waves of attackers swept on past us. A long time went by.

"Suddenly a very tall Canadian arrived and jabbed his fixed bayonet into the dead comrade. It was for me the most terrifying moment of my life. I moved and the Tommy shouted 'Come on!' At that I climbed up out of the shell hole (taking silent leave of my comrade). He then pointed his bayonet at my chest and asked me something. I did not understand him, so I just shrugged my shoulders. As quickly as he had appeared, he disappeared once more. Now I was once more all alone, so I raced off in the direction of the *Gießlerhöhe* [*sic*], where the Reserve Infantry Regiment 261 positions were.[10] As I was running past a parapet, a Canadian soldier jumped out and shot at me, hitting me in the upper arm. As I was running around wounded and confused, my friend Cordes leapt up. He had been hidden away unwounded in cover. The joy of meeting up with a good comrade whilst surrounded by the enemy can only be imagined by someone who has experienced the same thing.

"We linked hands and raced aimlessly amongst the fallen who had been mowed down here by machine gun fire. They included both our comrades and Canadian soldiers. We arrived at a dugout and settled down on the stairs to shelter from the heavy fire that was falling on the ridge. At that point the German artillery brought the ridge under heavy calibre fire. Then we tried to solve the mystery. Where were we: in our positions or those of the Canadians? My mate thought that we were in the enemy position, I that we were in our own. I said, 'Let's sit and wait until our division launches a counter-attack, then we shall be saved!'

"Whilst we were discussing this, a door opened in a dug out and a Canadian came out. We were amazed to discover that there were six enemy soldiers sitting in this dugout. They were not taking part in the assaults which were occurring up above, but were leaving the war to its own devices and were happily playing cards. Initially they did not notice us and continued to play cards calmly. When their game was over a Canadian medical orderly came over to me and said: 'Hallo Fritz, how are you? Are you wounded?' I nodded; he examined me and said 'No gout' [*sic*]. He then bandaged me up and gave me something to eat and drink. A few more of our regimental comrades turned up. Once I felt stronger, the Canadian soldier took my hand and led me back to an advanced dressing station where I was examined by a doctor. Then a Tommy took me back to the nearest village. Here I saw the British reserves, some of whom were black. It was obvious to me that everything was going to be done to hold on to Vimy Ridge. Behind the front I arrived at a large prisoner collection point, where I met up with several comrades, including my former company commander, Leutnant Schulz."

Leutnant Kopka, who with the 2nd Machine Gun Company of Reserve Infantry Regiment 261 had been located in Vimy, was put at the disposal of Reserve Infantry Regiment 262 to help meet the crisis and was killed in the front line by a shot to the head.[11] The left flank of the regiment, which hung in the air, was constantly threatened. However, thanks to the courageous defence put up by the 262nd, it was maintained for a considerable time, despite all assaults. To the north, on the right flank of the division, in Sector *Fischer*, the defence was the responsibility of Reserve Infantry Regiment 261.

Feldwebel and Offizierstellvertreter Paul Radschun 3rd Company Reserve Infantry Regiment 261[12]

"Foggy, grey and dull, Easter Monday dawned to an icy wind and squalls of snow. Relief was due to take place that night. Suddenly, in the early dawn, thousands of British guns opened up as one, pouring their thunderous hail of iron on our positions. For the regiment a bombardment of such violence was totally unprecedented. In all directions an endless dense series of fountains of clay shot upwards. Rocks were reduced to dark dust and tiles into red dust clouds. There was a constant terrible banging and crashing and, now and again, enormous thunderclaps, which could be heard above everything else, as ammunition dumps blew up. Impassively, but tense, von Goerne's regiment stuck it out in its trenches, completely surrounded by dreadful circles of roaring, blood-red fire, but with hands clutching the butts of the weapons tightly, determined to defend every last foot of ground to the last, in accordance with Prussian tradition.

"Then the British [*sic.*] came. As the fire which had been coming down intensely for hours lifted to the rear, the sentries of Reserve Infantry Regiment 261, peering through the dark blanket of mist and mud, caught sight of dense columns trudging forward through the clinging clay of No Man's Land with their rifles slung around them. At long last! Now it was going to be a matter of a battle with the same weapons; shot for shot, throw for throw. As the enemy came up to the barbed wire, there was a sudden burst of fire as Goerne's Grenadiers opened up on them, strengthened by their tough, firm and knightly soldierly spirit. The machine guns and rifles of the grenadiers crashed constantly. The dense British [*sic.*] columns were broken up and scattered by this determined defensive front. Heaps of khaki-clad bodies began to pile up in front in front of the trenches. Unfortunately, on the left flank the heavy enemy fire had destroyed almost all the machine guns. Only here did the enemy have it easy. Favoured by the bumps and dips of the craters, they succeeded in breaking through along the boundary with our neighbouring unit and were able to threaten our left flank and rear.

"Hand grenades fell in dreadful numbers among the brown-clad enemy. Finding themselves embroiled in the toughest of defensive battles, the flanking companies began to bleed to death. Only a few men succeeded in breaking out and some survivors fell into the hands of the enemy. But the British [*sic.*] also succeeded in breaking through on the right boundary. Once again there was bitterly hard fighting everywhere. The cracks of the infantry small arms were mixed with the drum beats of the hand grenades and, roaring above it all, was the thunder of the guns. Heroism and faithful duty escalated to titanic heights. Heavily outnumbered, the German grenadiers fought on. The weather conditions, namely the damp and the cold, caused stoppages in the feed mechanisms of the machine guns. Sometimes it was possible to clear them quickly, but at other times no amount of blows, shaking or rattling would free the damp belts of these precious weapons and they remained silent, to be replaced by the use of grenades and the bayonet. In the meantime the enemy losses rose steeply, but again and again new brown masses surged forward, threatening to encircle the regiment, which fought on in a superhuman way. Everywhere the battle had broken down into a dreadful close-quarter battle, man against man."

Here in Sector *Fischer* the front line was held by 3rd Company (Balla), 1st Company (Wittkop), 11th Company (Wagner) and 9th Company (Neumann). Immediately to their front the great surging Canadian attack was halted forward in No Man's Land but, as has been noted, it had achieved greater success left and right in the adjacent sectors *Zollern* and *Döberitz*. In those sectors penetrations were made as far back as the third defensive line and preparations were made to roll up the first position from the rear. Hauptmann Zickner, who was in command of the so-called 'Island Fischer,'[13] immediately launched a counter-attack by 2nd Company (Hoppe) and 4th Company (Ketzlick) from the *Potsdamer Riegel* [Postdam Stop Line]. The assault troops made almost immediate contact with the enemy in *Potsdamer Graben* [Potsdam Trench], capturing thirty men (including one officer) and a machine gun. They succeeded in pushing back the enemy lines as far as the crater field to the right of *Prinz-Heinrich-Weg* [Prince Henry's Way].

One platoon of 5th Company, commanded by the company commander, Reserve Leutnant Osthold, forced its way though to the 3rd Company, which was locked in heavy fighting, whilst two and a half sections under Leutnant Degenhorst stayed back in *Potsdamer Riegel* to secure it. In the meantime the front line was sealed off by a party under Offizierstellvertreter Stracke, along the line of *Hanseatenweg* [Hanseatic Way]. Together with the last remaining section of 11th Company, commanded by Vizefeldwebel Rittershausen of 1st Company, they continued to beat off frontal attacks and, by means of a series of thrusts, succeeded in clearing the front line trench as far as 9th Company.

The situation remained essentially unchanged for hours. It was certainly extremely dangerous though, had sufficient reserves been on hand, certainly not hopeless. Up where Reserve Infantry Regiment 261 was still clinging on, the few machine gunners and riflemen who had escaped destruction brought down a hail of fire against the enemy. They fought like men possessed; some of them from a standing position, to bring fire to bear. The attack petered out bloodily in front of the regiment. But there was greater danger to the flanks. A flood of soldiers bore down from the south, from Sector *Zollern*, threatening to envelop the left flank of the Fusilier Battalion and to roll it up. Despatched forward by the battalion commander, Major von Knobelsdorff, in a powerful counter-stroke, the reserves (10th and elements of the 12th Company) succeeded at the cost of heavy losses in sealing off the enemy break in from the south.

Feldwebel and Offizierstellvertreter Paul Radschun 3rd Company Reserve Infantry Regiment 261[14]

"In the meantime the enemy losses rose steeply, but again new brown masses surged forward, threatening to encircle the regiment, which fought on in a superhuman way. Everywhere the battle had broken down into a dreadful close-quarter battle, man against man. Without being able to help, my company commander, Leutnant Balla, had to look on, whilst his company was reduced to a tiny handful of men. Smoke, noise, wild shouts gradually died away in the evil, muddy battlefield. It was all over! Honour these heroes, who hoped to cheat death! Through the iron curtain, the fusiliers of the regiment, together with elements of 5th Company and the Infantry Engineer Company, continued to fight on and before this fresh defensive wall, which was inspired by the same spirit as the remainder, the last waves of the British [sic.] burnt out and the dreadful storm of steel ebbed away. A circling infantry cooperation pilot was able to make out the message of the signalling panels: 'We are holding the line.' During the morning of the following day came the moment of relief. The regiment lost twenty officers and 860 NCOs and men during this tough battle. It had not yielded. It had defended its appointed place to the last drop of blood; worthy of its fathers; worthy of its parent formation the Prussian Guard; worthy of the heroic spirit of its beloved commander, who had always taught it to stand firm against the odds in all circumstances."

Leutnant Koschmieder, one of the last of the officers of Reserve Infantry Regiment 261 still on his feet, was mortally wounded as he brought a machine gun into action and by his side many brave infantrymen of the regiment also fell. Nevertheless the few remaining fit officers, NCOs and fusiliers held on grimly to the newly-won position. Captured Lewis guns reinforced their firepower. From the north too, the enemy, after blowing up large craters in the right hand neighbouring Sector *Döberitz*, broke in and swung south in large numbers to threaten encirclement. The right flank of the 1st Battalion was locked for hours in bitter hand to hand fighting against constantly reinforced groups. Here Leutnant Klabisch was killed amidst his faithful comrades, but one of the counter-attacks by the 2nd and 4th Companies which the battalion commander, Hauptmann Zickner, launched, drove the Canadians attackers back in the course of a lengthy and bloody struggle. The success was dearly bought. Along with many grenadiers, Leutnant Ketzlick, the commander of 4th Company and one of his platoon commanders, Leutnant Lehmann, were killed.

Hauptmann Behrmann Reserve Infantry Regiment 261[15]

"While the soldierly fate of the right flank companies was being deter-mined, great masses of British [sic] soldiers broke in along the boundary between Reserve Infantry Regiment 261 and Bavarian Infantry Regiment 11 (16th Bavarian Infantry Division). This caused an immediate break in the desperate defence. Whilst the main thrust continued to the east, strong forces swung south, falling against the flank of the 1st Company (Reserve Leutnant Wittkop) and 3rd Company

(Reserve Leutnant Balla). In this area, too, all the machine guns were out of order. The first serious resistance did not come until the enemy hit the *Berliner-Riegel* [Berlin Stop Line], where the weapon of Gefreiter Neumann was still in full working order.

"Of the first three British [*sic*] waves, almost nothing remained, but then there was a stoppage which could not be cleared. Frantic efforts, shaking and pulling could achieve nothing. Having soaked up dirt and moisture for days, the belt was jammed and could not be freed. Shot through the head, Gefreiter Neumann fell, as did the rest of his crew, together with a large group manning the trench. Some brave lads rescued the machine gun and carried it into an adjacent post. To the front the enemy, who had been pressing strongly, were pinned down in the muddy craters by the fire of the remaining infantrymen."

In view of the vigorous resistance they had encountered, the Canadian 4th Division did not attempt further frontal assaults throughout the afternoon. However, when it went dark, a further massed attack was launched further to the north against Sector *Döberitz*, forcing back the line which, weakened because of previous counter thrusts, had to withdraw from the craters. After Leutnant Hoppe was wounded and Leutnants Ketzlich and Lehmann were killed, command devolved on Reserve Leutnant Fladt, who had suffered a head wound. His force conducted a fighting withdrawal towards the *Potsdamer Riegel* [Potsdam Stop Line] and the Intermediate Position (North). It was not possible for the battalion to respond to the urgent requests of Leutnant Balla for reinforcement, which had been brought through an area which was teeming with Canadian troops by the runners Gefreiters Pilorz and Siefert.

Still the regiment clung on to the forward trenches in the centre with the remnants of the 3rd, 1st, 11th and 9th Companies, acting like a breakwater, but continuing attempts by the Canadians to break down this 261st wedge through the constant deployment of fresh forces meant that the fighting power of the defence reduced more and more. When the crater belonging to Leutnant Balla, commander of the 3rd Company, was surrounded by a bombing party throwing grenades from a range of thirty to thirty five metres, the German grenadiers found that they were so exhausted that they could only throw theirs fifteen metres; it was as though their arms were paralysed. At one point the Canadians were kept at bay by the fire of a single rifleman who, lying behind a firing shield, maintained his fire for hours, reporting after every shot, 'Yet another!' During this battle, the courageous Vizefeldwebel Stracke was killed close by Leutnant Balla. During the morning a British aircraft appeared with the intention of attempting to deal with the craters that were still holding out by dropping bombs on them. By a lucky chance the Germans fired white flares at it, whereupon it flew away without dropping bombs. White flares, apparently, were the recognition signal for friendly forces that day.

Hauptmann Behrmann Reserve Infantry Regiment 261[16]

"Bringing down concentrated fire against the forces pushing down from the east were the machine guns, echeloned back towards the rear and the remainder of the garrison under Leutnant Balla. British [*sic*] losses were heavy, but ever more groups kept streaming forward through the gap which existed between us and our left hand neighbouring division. Forward, elements of 3rd Company under Leutnant Klabisch hung on grimly, regardless of their casualties. They fought with the desperation of the heroes of yesteryear, but without being able fully to beat back the troops who were able to take cover in the numerous shell holes. Firing from the rim of a crater, Gefreiter Siefert shot at every worthwhile target, whilst the British [*sic*] threw grenades from a range of thirty to thirty five metres. One by one these throwers were picked off. 'Yet another', the courageous [Siefert] would shout after each shot.

"Unteroffizier Becker was despatched to Battalion Headquarters with a report on the situation, upon which piece of paper each of their valuable lives depended. Becker was never seen again and, minute by minute, the daring little band that was 3rd Company reduced in numbers. A few more shots, a last grenade then, in one final desperate effort, Leutnant Klabisch and his grenadiers fixed bayonets and charged the enemy. Wild shouts were drowned in the noise of British [*sic*] grenades exploding, there was a final flurry of hand to hand fighting and the flickering shadows disappeared into the mud like ghosts. It was all over. Honour the memory of these men who, staring certain death in the face, nevertheless hoped to cheat it."

During the afternoon reinforcements arrived at last. Oberstleutnant von Goerne despatched two platoons from his final reserve, the 5th Company, to the Fusilier [3rd] Battalion and, with their help, it was possible to secure the link to Reserve Infantry Regiment 262. One platoon under Leutnant Osthold, which was sent to the 1st Battalion, pushed forward to Leutnant Balla and was able to join in the life and death struggle there. A short pause in the battle meant that many lightly wounded could be sent to the rear and the severely wounded moved into the mined dugouts. But the question on everyone's mind was, would a counter-stroke in strength be launched?

As the drum fire of a violence never before experienced worked its way back towards its command post during the early hours of 9 April, 79 Reserve Brigade alerted the battalions which were resting. Immediately after that the Division ordered an increased state of alert for the entire area. During the early fighting, until 7.00 am and, in some cases, until 8.30 am, the divisional artillery, despite heavy losses, maintained its defensive and destructive fire. However, because the situation in the infantry front line was unclear, it had to continue to fire on its previous defensive fire zones. The batteries which were deployed in Sector *Arnulf*, at least those whose positions were west of the railway embankment, were drawn into the close quarter battle and for a long period had to beat off infantry attacks, firing over open sights or using rifles and hand grenades. 3rd and 8th Batteries, Reserve Artillery Regiment 63, succeeded in pulling their guns out of action in the midst of small arms fire and took up new positions to the east of the railway embankment. The 1st and 6th Batteries, against whom the enemy had succeeded in closing right up to the barbed wire obstacle to their front, had to blow up their guns after they had fired their final rounds. Two heavy field howitzer batteries – 10th and 11th Foot Artillery Regiment 10 – which were located in Sector *Zollern*, were assaulted by infantry, but with friendly infantry support were able to maintain their fire positions, despite fighting at close quarters.

Many of the guns were swiftly overrun. Hundreds of horses were killed in the initial gas attack, so there was no means of dragging them to the rear when they were threatened and in any case their frequently unfavourable fire positions increased their vulnerability. Nevertheless some guns were able to continue the battle, doing great execution to the stalled 4th Canadian Division attack on the western slopes of Hill 145.

Leutnant Hauser 1st Battalion Bavarian Field Artillery Regiment 10[17]

"It was 5.30 am on Easter Monday. There was a dazzling flash and terrible mine explosions made the whole ground shake. Then, with a dreadful series of crashes, enemy drum fire started coming down amongst us. 'Barrage fire all along the front!' shouted our observer down the voice tube. The telephone was already ringing – battery – regiment. All the batteries were under fire. The dugout was trembling with all the impacts. The British had blown mines in Sector *Döberitz*; there was no other information . . . The telephone rang again, then a voice said, 'Good morning. There seems to be a bit of an attack.' [!].

"By 6.00 am the first of the stragglers were gathering around the command post – with and without weapons. They had even brought a machine gun with them. 'The British [*sic*] are advancing along the road Givenchy – La Coulette.' There was fog and smoke everywhere; but no, things could not have moved that quickly. Anyone who participated regularly in major battles will recognise these sad individuals: men who were quick to see themselves as forced back, only to be spinning great yarns later when they were on leave! These shirkers were as much a part of major battles as the bloody casualties.

"Of course it must be remembered that nerves were shattered by ten days of continuous destructive fire which smashed the trenches. Now came the mine explosions, the drum fire. It was in fact a miracle that not more men failed; that there were so many who possessed an iron will and would dispute and defend every centimetre of ground. It was 6.20 am. The drum fire crept closer, especially heavy on Sectors

Döberitz, Fischer and further to the south. The rattle of machine guns was mixed with the crash of exploding shells. A heavy infantry battle was in progress. Our batteries brought down defensive fire. It was a time of troubled uncertainty and contradictory messages. 'The enemy has broken into Givenchy!' 'Attack in *Döberitz* beaten back short of the Second Line!' 'To the left the enemy is advancing along the road Arras – Lens!' 'The machine gun fire in Sector *Fischer* is increasing all the time!' Then the worrying impression began to build that the batteries to the south, those of 79th Reserve Division, were suspiciously silent.

"Even without having received specific reports, it was obvious that there was danger to the left. The fire of all batteries was needed in that direction. At 8.40 the picture clarified somewhat. In sectors *Ansbach* and *Burg* the front line was in our hands. In *Döberitz* and *Fischer*, the enemy was occupying part of our old front line and part of our second. Fighting was continuing everywhere. The fire of [Artillery] Groups *Döberitz* and *Bahndamm* [Railway Embankment] was now laid on our former front line in Sector *Döberitz*. By 11.45 am the enemy had worked their way forward to the third line in Sector *Döberitz*. It was reported that in Sectors *Fischer* and *Zollern* they had pushed on to our Second Position.[18] Bavarian Infantry Regiment 11 was holding the western approaches to Givenchy, but the following night there was a large gap between 16th Bavarian Infantry Division and 79th Reserve Division.

"Visibility had improved and now we could observe from our Group Command Post. We could see movement on Vimy Ridge in La Folie Wood. The batteries had also spotted this from their own positions. 'The enemy is advancing over the Ridge, individually and in columns – wave after attacking wave.' The artillery of 79th Reserve Division was either knocked out or could not see the enemy. Not a single shell was being directed there. Naturally our batteries began bringing down fire on the British [*sic*] on their own initiative, but then the Group divided the area to be engaged between the batteries with observation over it: 3rd Battery Bavarian Field Artillery Regiment 10, 4th and 6th Batteries Reserve Field Artillery Regiment 66, as well as 1st Battery Bavarian Field Artillery Regiment 10 and 3rd Battery Bavarian Field Artillery Regiment 8 of Group *Burg*.

"Ammunition began to run short. In broad daylight, despite the aircraft, despite the enemy on Vimy Ridge, despite all the fire, the ammunition columns drove forward, bringing up the much needed ammunition. The Kriegsfreiwilliger Unteroffizier Deschermeier of 1st Battery Field Artillery Regiment 10 drove forward one loaded ammunition wagon after another. Numerous horses were killed or wounded, but they were simply unharnessed and he carried on. Deschermeier, as small and unprepossessing as he was, was full of energy and undying love for his Fatherland. That very day he had received the Bravery Medal in Gold for his service during the Battle of the Somme in September 1916. On 9 April he did enough to have earned another.

"Despite being under heavy fire, 3rd Battery Bavarian Field Artillery Regiment 10, under the direction of Reserve Oberleutnant Florschütz, assisted by Leutnant Syller, who were working from an observation post alongside the gun positions, continued to bring down their own fire. How they slaved away: the gunners, gun commanders, Unteroffiziers Dan and Hohlhut and the Section Commander Sergeant Puchta. Shell after shell crashed down in the immediate vicinity of the guns, falling just in front or just behind the battery position. One gun was buried, one man wounded, but the battery went on firing with three guns. The range (2,000 metres) meant that the traverse of the dug in guns was too small. They were pulled out into an open position.

"Observing in the front line was Sergeant Lippert, known as 'Lippert's Franz'. He was a cool man. He had little luck with his telephone line that day, but sent back a stream of valuable messages by runner. On the far side of the Avion – Givenchy road, not far from 3rd Battery Bavarian Field Artillery Regiment 10, was the 1st Battery of the same regiment. It was linked by a land line with 3rd Battery, but this kept being cut where it crossed the road. Gunners Lauterbach, Korn and Lochner of 3rd Battery and Emmert of 1st Battery ignored all the fire and went out constantly to repair both it and the line back to the battalion. Leutnant Vogg commanded the 1st Battery.[19] The individual guns and ammunition stores were linked by narrow covered passages. The powder smoke, which could not be dispersed from these places, caused several men, already exhausted from the strenuous efforts of the past few weeks, to lose consciousness, but the iron will and energy of its commander permeated the entire battery . . .

"1st and 3rd Batteries fired 1,590 and 1,408 shells respectively that day, sending a hail of iron at the British [*sic*], who were attempting to advance over Vimy Ridge and remorselessly slowing them. We also passed orders to 3rd Battery Bavarian Field Artillery Regiment 8 – via 1st Battery, because they had no link to Group *Burg*. 1st and 3rd Batteries Field Artillery Regiment 69 were too far off, as was the Angres Section – ½ 2nd Battery Bavarian Field Artillery Regiment 10. The telephone lines to them kept breaking. Runners and despatch riders were the only answer. They were kept rushing backwards and forwards between the command post and the batteries. Clearly they could not dismount or seek protection from shell splinters in the trenches. The only way was to ride above ground and as quickly as possible. The horses became utterly exhausted, but the object was achieved.

"Despite the fact that roads were swept by heavy fire, we did not have a single casualty amongst the despatch riders. I still see them before me as ghostly figures – amongst them the tall Landwehr Gefreiter Thomas

Hoffmann of 2nd Battery Bavarian Field Artillery Regiment 10, with his tanned face and black hair who was seemingly too large to fit into a dugout. We used him whenever the task was especially difficult or particularly important. No fire could dissuade him; he always delivered the orders to their destinations in the shortest possible time. The Angres Section (½ 2nd Battery Bavarian Field Artillery Regiment 10), commanded by Leutnant Wagner, who was killed in spring 1918, had a field day. After bringing down defensive fire in the morning, they spent the rest of the day bringing aimed fire down in amongst the enemy reserves . . .

"The section fired in enfilade against the British [*sic*] attack. From Angres, Leutnant Wagner could see behind Vimy Ridge [i.e. the western side] and so had a long view right back into the enemy approach routes. The extent to which this fire troubled the British [*sic*] may be seen from their Daily Communiqué which mentioned, 'Flanking fire from Angres very much affected the forward movement of the reserves.' In fact the only guns there were Wagner's two gun section. Between them these two guns fired 1,000 shells and, although heavy fire came down near them, they were completely untouched.

"Similarly, in Sector *Döberitz* the fire of our batteries played a large part in keeping the enemy back from the western edge of Givenchy. Observed fire into Sectors *Fischer* and *Zollern* made it difficult for the British [*sic*] to exploit further their successes there. The left flank of 16th Bavarian Infantry Division was effectively protected and the attack neutralised. At 6.30 pm our fire was used to support a counter-attack by 1st Battalion Bavarian Infantry Regiment 14 in Sector *Döberitz,* but the attack made very little difference to the overall situation. 1st Battalion Bavarian Reserve Infantry Regiment 21 was deployed to close the gap between 16th Bavarian Infantry Division and 79th Reserve Division and succeeded in achieving a link up that night; 79th Reserve Division holding positions between the old Third Line and the Second Position."

It was little wonder, bearing in mind the difficulties faced in mounting it, that the counter-attack into Sector *Döberitz*, held by Bavarian Infantry Regiment 11, 'made very little difference'. Although after the battle the main German enquiry was into the failure to deploy and manoeuvre the operational reserves correctly, the effect of the comprehensive, complex fire plan designed for the Canadian Corps by Major Alan Brooke RA[20] meant that local command and control, not to mention use of what reserves were to hand, was rendered extremely difficult. The passage of information was a major problem – one runner, for example, took three and a half hours during the morning of 9 April to carry a single message the two and a half kilometres from Hill 145 to Headquarters Reserve Infantry Regiment 261 just to the north of Vimy village. One of the company commanders involved in the attempted counter-attack later wrote a comprehensive description, which illustrates clearly the problems experienced by the defence that day. The immediate reserves of 16th Bavarian Infantry Division hung around for hours, then had to rush to try to get in positions and spent the night floundering about in the mud and the dark.

Reserve Oberleutnant Trummert 4th Company Bavarian Infantry Regiment 14[21]

"We were rudely awakened from our sleep during the early hours of Easter Monday. An unimaginable increase in enemy fire to the densest drum fire, coupled with the noise of several mine explosions and the roar of our own defensive fire set in so swiftly that no more effective alarm system to wake us could possibly be devised. Within a few moments, more or less equipped for battle, we were assembled in our companies and ready to move on the road in front of the miners' cottages at Méricourt. There we stood, whilst every man wondered why our services had not been called on. There was a simple explanation why the Divison did not make use of us or 3rd Battalion Bavarian Reserve Infantry Regiment 11, located in Hénin Liétard, which formed the other part of the reserve. It was because the first information concerning the attack, which had occurred at 5.00 am, did not arrive at Divisional Headquarters until 8.00 am and, when it did, unfortunately it did not make the situation clear.

"As a result, initially we had several hours at our disposal to prepare ourselves for what was to come, distribute coffee, then issue ammunition, hand grenades and rations. Towards 10.00 am the Battalion received orders to move forward as brigade reserve. Because the roads were packed with ammunition wagons, transport for the wounded etc., we advanced along previously reconnoitred trackways. We soon found that even these routes were swept with artillery fire, which forced us to make numerous time-consuming detours, but had no other effect. Nevertheless, by about midday, we arrived at La Coulotte. We spent the first part of the afternoon there whilst the battalion Commander went to find out what the situation was. It transpired that the morning attack had been limited to Vimy Ridge, but that a large part of the First Position had been lost.

"Bavarian Infantry Regiment 14 had maintained its positions on the *Gießler Höhe,* however, which meant that there was a dangerous gap to its left which had to be closed. Towards 6.00 pm the expected order arrived from Brigade. The Battalion was to launch a counter-attack in Sector *Döberitz* which would enable Bavarian Infantry Regiment 14 to hold on to its positions. The battalion ordered the following dispositions: 3rd Company *Sandgrube* [Sand Pit] 3; 4th Company *Sandgrube* 2; 2nd Company Givenchy north of the track to Souchez and 1st Company to the south of the same track. From these assembly areas, the further advance was to begin at 8.00 pm and, because the companies were not able to set off until 6.30 pm, timings were tight.

"In addition a number of other circumstances made matters even more difficult: the difficult going underfoot, the snow squalls which meant that darkness fell early, lack of knowledge of the route and the terrain and last, but by no means least, the considerable amount of enemy fire. As a result, it was not until 11.00 pm that it could be reported that all companies were in position. This in turn meant that the advance could not begin until midnight: the line to be achieved was defined as one linking Bavarian Infantry Regiment 14 with weak elements of Bavarian Infantry Regiment 11, who were holding out near the *Sachsen Lager.*

"For my 4th Company the objective was in the former Third Line in the area *Souchez Weg – Koch Weg* [Souchez – and Cook Ways]. Between my start line, the *Hamburgergraben* [Hamburg Trench] and *Souchez Weg* lay the 500 metre wide *Givenchy Mulde* [Givenchy Hollow], which was always wet and, as a result of the winter weather and years of shelling, had become a bottomless crater field. Founded mostly on Jurassic chalk, the entire re-entrant was as good as impassable. As a result not one single communications track led forward from Givenchy in the direction of Souchez across it. Now across this terrain, which was completely unknown to them, 3rd and 4th Companies had to advance, through snow squalls and the pitch black night.

"From *Hamburgergraben* the ground dropped away sharply to the base of the hollow, which was located much closer to this trench than to *Souchezweg.* I set off with two platoons leading and one following up, right rear, with the task of maintaining contact with 3rd Company. To begin with the formation was maintained quite well, but the closer we got to the base of the hollow the swampier the ground became. With each step we sank up to our knees. We were no longer advancing; this was mere staggering forward. Anybody who had chosen to wear jackboots rather than the more practical lace-up boots with puttees was extremely lucky not to lose them. Many were in this predicament and unable to continue. The remainder waded gallantly on, some moving faster, some slower, encumbered as they were by the heavy weight of ammunition, hand grenades, rations and other items.

"As a result the company was soon strung out. Flares which helped us to maintain direction and cohesion were only fired occasionally, but there were continuous salvoes of enemy artillery fire in the Hollow, interspersed with bursts of enemy machine gun fire. I was in the lead with my so-called company staff (two runners and my brave Sanitäts-Unteroffizier Schönberger). Because there was no sign of the enemy, we made our way forward as quickly as possible, reasoning that the platoons would be following close behind. After what seemed to be a very long time, we arrived, dog-tired and pouring with sweat at a collapsed trench, which from its direction and dimensions could only be *Souchezweg*. Here we realised for the first time that we had lost all contact with our platoons.

"We lurked there for some time, our eyes straining to pierce the darkness. We seemed to be entirely alone. Certainly there was not a trace of the enemy, our company or any other. I despatched my runners to find the platoons and remained there with Unteroffizier Schönberger. More time passed without us seeing another person, so we moved further on, in order to reach the Third Line. Suddenly we saw steel helmets sticking up out of the mud very close. It was impossible to tell if they were the flat British helmets or the coal-scuttle shaped German ones. The wearers were not moving any more than we were, so I attempted to contact them in a neutral manner, by giving a quiet whistle. Now there was some movement. The whistles were returned and to my joy I realised that we had German helmets in front of us.

"It was the commander of 1st Company who, together with some of his men, had moved to find us. Oberleutnant Völk was in a similar situation to me, He too had pressed on with a few men in advance of his company. Soon we were joined by some sections of 2nd Company Bavarian Infantry Regiment 14 under Reserve Leutnant Türk. Before the remainder of the Battalion arrived we came across a few men of Bavarian Infantry Regiment 11 in an almost totally collapsed dugout, but of the enemy there was no sign. Soon, moving along either side of the communication trench, came 1st and 2nd Companies, more or less complete, then a platoon of my 4th Company under Vizefeldwebel Rupp turned up. To our left 3rd Battalion Bavarian Infantry Regiment 11 had moved strong forces forward into the Third Line, which now seemed to be held in sufficient strength.

"In the circumstances my platoon and I could be spared, so after a discussion with Oberleutnant Völk I headed back to the start point, collecting the other two platoons of my company on the way. They had got lost in the hollow and were stuck. Back at the assembly area I met up with 3rd Company, which had swung round so much during its advance that it ended up in Sector *Burg* [i.e. on the right flank of the divisional frontage, rather than the left!]. I went to Command Post *Augsburg* in Givenchy, which was occupied by the commanding officers of our battalion and that of 3rd Battalion Bavarian Infantry Regiment 11, where I made a written report concerning the results of the night's operation and the current situation in the Third Line. Both commanders were of the opinion that as much had been achieved with the forces available as had been expected."

Elsewhere, earlier in the day, once the alert state had been increased, the reserves of 79th Reserve Division, comprising 2nd Battalion Reserve Infantry Regiment 261 (5th Company regimental reserve in the Lower Slope Position), 1st

Battalion Reserve Infantry Regiment 262 (2nd Company regimental reserve in and around Vimy) and 2nd Battalion Reserve Infantry Regiment 263, which had just been relieved in the forward position (8th Company regimental reserve in Vimy; Staff and 5th Company not yet returned from the First Position), were ordered by the Brigade Commander, Generalleutnant Dieterich, to move closer to the battle zone. Whilst they were on the march, news arrived that the enemy had succeeded in penetrating the area of 1st Bavarian Reserve Division to the south and that they had taken the First Position. Soon information came in that the enemy had also succeeded in breaking in on the left flank of the 79th Reserve Division and was rolling up the position from south to north. It was also reported that there had been a further break in north of the Division. The Brigade then gave orders to the forces at its disposal (2nd Battalion Reserve Infantry Regiment 261 under Hauptmann von Goerne and 2nd Battalion Reserve Infantry Regiment 263 led by Oberleutnant Heinicke), to head in the direction of the railway embankment south of Vimy and to send their machine gun companies ahead at the double. 2nd Battalion Reserve Infantry Regiment 262 under Hauptmann von Block was despatched to the cross tracks at La Gueule d'Ours, east of Vimy, as divisional reserve.

The first of the reserves who were hurrying forward to arrive was a Machine Gun Company of Reserve Infantry Regiment 261, which was greeted joyfully at the railway embankment and deployed to reinforce the weak forces from Reserve Infantry Regiment 263 who were already there. They were followed by 2nd Battalion Reserve Infantry Regiment 263, which was completely exhausted, 6th Company Reserve Infantry Regiment 261 and later by a company from Reserve Infantry Regiment 262. The other elements of the Brigade Reserve, namely 7th and 8th Companies Reserve Infantry Regiment 261, together with the 2nd Machine Gun Company Reserve Infantry Regiment 263, were despatched by Brigade to Reserve Infantry Regiment 261, with orders to hold the Second Position at all costs and make contact with Reserve Infantry Regiment 262. (According to radio and light messages, which had so far been received, it had to be assumed that the enemy had already outflanked and encircled Reserve Infantry Regiment 262 and that it was effectively unable to exercise command and control of the battle.) The 2nd Machine Gun Company, which had been located in Vimy had, as has already been mentioned, placed itself on its own initiative at the disposal of Reserve Infantry Regiment 262. Altogether this meant that at least the most urgently required support had been secured for the troops who were being most heavily pressed. Unfortunately the reserves available were insufficient and too weak to carry out an immediate counter-stroke to restore the situation.

Sergeant Dorrmann 6th Company, Reserve Infantry Regiment 261[22]

"During the early hours of Easter Monday a dull rumbling from the front woke us. Soon we received the order, 'Get your assault order on. Everything else must stay here!' Each man was to take a piece of bread with him. The most senior of the NCOs were placed in charge of sections of soldiers and then the company set off, leading the battalion. The field artillery was going into positions to the left and right, with British shells landing in amongst us. Nevertheless we reached the railway embankment near Vimy unscathed. The 210 mm howitzers of a Saxon foot artillery regiment were in position here. My group took up position near some of these monsters. With each shot I thought that my eardrums would burst. In addition shell fragments and pieces of ballast from the embankment were flying everywhere and hitting our helmets. Later the Tommies lifted their fire more to the rear areas, where I could observe the approach of our ammunition columns. A gunner standing jacketless by one of the guns stopped a wagon and swiftly unloaded it. Then, just like a baker placing loaves of bread in the oven, he loaded one shell after the other into his gun, which was readjusted right and left after each shell. If I had been allowed to leave my post I would have run over to this comrade to express my appreciation.

As things became a little calmer we left sentries up on the embankment and took cover in the dugouts of the artillery. Towards 9.00 pm, we were ordered forward. I went with Leutnant Rahlfs at the head of our platoon. The artillery fire of both sides hindered our movement. Wearing our gasmasks, we leapt from one crater to another, dodging the falling gas and phosphorous shells. In the meantime the sky had darkened so much that it was impossible to see the next man, even if was possible to touch him. There was then a shower of hail which, even though it was thoroughly unpleasant, saved us. We were not far off from the howitzer position, which had once been German, when we came under fire from there. Because our flanks were hanging in the air, we were later ordered back to our jumping off point. Unfortunately two men were missing and we never heard anything of them again. Towards 4.00 am we were meant to be launching another assault, but this was cancelled later.

Gradually we began to feel hungry, because we had each only brought a piece of bread forward with us. The gunners and our sister regiment 263, to whom we had been allocated, gave us something to eat; the number of casualties meant that not all the rations had been consumed. During the morning [presumably 10 April], heavy fire continued to fall on the rear areas and during the afternoon on our position too. A shell wounded the sentry in front of our dugout and we took him to the medical dugout at the railway underpass. I then went and checked on the sentries, noticing that Grenadier W., who was always very fearful when he had not had a drink, was flinching whenever a shell landed. I moved him ten metres to the left and said, 'Keep your chin up, they're not shooting at the place where you are standing now.'

The sentry who had been relieved and I continued on, when suddenly a shell exploded, we flew through the air like dolls and found ourselves

lying on our stomachs with wounds to the shoulder and arm. We moved
to the medical dugout where we were bandaged and had the well-known
labels attached to us. I reported to the company commander and
requested to be allowed to stay with the company, but he said, 'My dear
Dorrmann, you are the father of a family and wounded. Even though
your wound may not be very severe go where you are sent. Nobody
knows what is going to happen here, or even if anyone will come out of
it alive!' We parted with a powerful handshake and, with his good wishes
ringing in my ears, I made my way to the medical company.

Towards midday, orders arrived at 79th Reserve Division from Headquarters
Group Vimy that the lost Third Line was to be recaptured. At the same time information was received that two fresh battalions – 1st Battalion Infantry Regiment
118 (56th Division) and 3rd Battalion Reserve Infantry Regiment 34 (80th
Reserve Division) were on their way. Orders had arrived in Billy Montigny just
before noon and the mens' midday meal had to be left steaming away in their
field kitchens. There was no time to waste as they hurried forward, seeking what
shelter they could against continual showers of shrapnel balls.[23] General von
Bacmeister, who in the meantime had been able to obtain a more-or-less clear
picture of the overall situation, now decided to fill the wide gap which had opened
up between Reserve Infantry Regiment 262 and I Bavarian Reserve Division and
to recapture Telegraph Hill [Hill 135, north of Thélus] by means of a counter-
attack. For this purpose, he allocated 1st Battalion Infantry Regiment 118 and
one company of Machine Gun Sharpshooter Detachment 20 to the Brigade.

From 1.40 pm the Brigade Staff had been located at La Gueule d'Ours, the
cross tracks three kilometres to the east of the centre of Vimy. It issued an order
which placed Oberstleutnant von Behr in charge of the attack and allocated the
following forces to Hauptmann von Block: 1st Battalion Infantry Regiment 118,
1st Battalion Reserve Infantry Regiment 262 (less two companies) and one
company of Machine Gun Sharpshooter Detachment 20. Block was ordered to
launch the attack against Telegraph Hill from the area of the foundry (north of
Vimy) along the line of the road Lens-Arras and to link up with Reserve Infantry
Regiment 262 on the right. Oberleutnant Heinicke, with the forces from Reserve
Infantry Regiment 263 which were located at the railway embankment, was to
attack Telegraph Hill frontally from the south of Vimy, conforming to von Block's
assault and linking up with the assaulting troops of 1st Bavarian Reserve
Division. Whilst the artillery was firing a preliminary bombardment against the
heights north of Thélus in support of the counter-attack, the battalions which
had been allocated to the division began to arrive at the ridge to the east of Vimy.
Because of the increasing quantity of artillery fire which was coming down there,
they were forced to cross this in widely dispersed formations. Not until about
6.00 pm could Hauptmann von Block's attacking force traverse Vimy.

A combination of darkness and snow squalls hindered a swift conduct of the
attack which, having cleared the Canadians out of the ruined village, could not

cross the Second Position, its right flank linked up with the left flank of Reserve Infantry Regiment 262 and its left anchored on La Compte Wood [the northwest extension of Goulot Wood], until late evening. Because the assault force from 1st Bavarian Reserve Division advancing to the south was well to the rear, the counter-attack of the left assault group, advancing from the railway embankment, also made only slow progress and finally stalled along the track Vimy-Farbus due to heavy artillery fire. Completely out of contact in the constant flurries of snow, the regimental commander withdrew them to the embankment once more. At a result, during the night, the Brigade allocated Oberstleutnant von Behr 3rd Battalion Reserve Infantry Regiment 34 (less two companies) and some machine guns, so that he was able to occupy the southern edge of Vimy and establish contact with von Block's group. Despite great difficulties, as well as the fact that Vimy was under heavy fire with both conventional and gas shells, these courageous troops succeeded in achieving this by morning. There was still a wide gap to the left hand neighbouring division, which could not be closed during the hours of darkness. As a result, the Brigade allocated the reserves which had arrived, namely one company Reserve Infantry Regiment 34 and two engineer mining companies, to Reserve Infantry Regiment 263 in order to strengthen its left flank.

As it went dark up on Vimy Ridge, fresh Canadian troops renewed their violent assault on the narrow salient of Reserve Infantry Regiment 261 which stuck out well forward. It had proved to be out of the question for further runners (commanded by Unteroffizier Kremer, 1st Company) to break through to Leutnant Balla and his command, which had been almost wiped out by mortar fire, with instructions; nevertheless they succeeded in bringing in some Canadian prisoners. Pressed in by overwhelming forces, the garrison had to surrender the position which it had succeeded in holding until evening. Leutnants Balla, Wittkop and Osthold (severely wounded) were captured, along with the remnants of the 1st and 3rd Companies, which had been involved in constant close quarter grenade and bayonet fighting. Offizierstellvertreter Stracke (1st Company), Leutnant Klabisch (3rd Company), Leutnants Lehmann and Ketzlich (4th Company) had been killed, together with a large number of the most courageous NCOs and men. Three machine guns, which were no longer capable of being fired, were destroyed with hand grenades. The light mortars of the regiment, which had fired off all their ammunition, were buried and the crews continued the fight with rifles.

Once the last of the grenades had been thrown and the final bullets fired, the commanders decided to give orders for a withdrawal to the next position to the rear but no sooner had the last of the fighters leapt out of the craters in order to race towards their objective, than they were caught by a sudden concentration of fire from the British guns, which scattered them. Some of them became prisoners of war of the Canadians. The fate of one of these men provides a dramatic impression of the scene at the end of the day. Leutnant Balla, having with a heavy heart given the order to withdraw from the positions which had been held with such sacrificial courage, lost his footing in the darkness and fell into a huge shell hole which was full of water. In order to avoid sinking, he hauled himself with his last reserves of strength up the side of the crater, where he lay, unable to move or even, without outside assistance, to free himself from the mud. There he lay totally exhausted until he was found and rescued by some Canadian soldiers. Only a very few defenders made their way back and were able to bring news about the final stages of the day's fighting.

The deployment of the last of the troops of Reserve Infantry Regiment 261 meant that the Intermediate Position on the eastern edge of the ridge could be held. That night the first relief came with the arrival of 3rd Company Engineer Battalion 18, which was sent forward by Brigade. The bitter fighting continued during the night on the front of Reserve Infantry Regiment 262. An energetic thrust led by Oberleutnant von Richthofen succeeded in winning some terrain back from the Canadian 3rd Division. Fighting was particularly heavy on the left flank of the regiment until the advance of Hauptmann von Block removed the risk of encirclement. The following morning brought further relief when a company of Reserve Infantry Regiment 34 arrived. All along the battlefront there was a shortage of small-arms ammunition, hand grenades, flares and barbed wire, but resupply took place that night. The northern sector was supplied from the ammunition depot in Bétricourt via the narrow gauge railway which led to the railway embankment; the southern by trucks, which were unloaded under heavy fire.

The divisional batteries suffered heavy casualties in exactly the same way as the infantry which fought with their very last reserves of strength. By the evening of 9th April, out of twelve field batteries [i.e. forty eight guns], only seventeen guns were battleworthy. In order best to meet the demands of the battle, they were organised into two groups; Group North under Major von Pressentin and Group South under Hauptmann Döring. Three of the batteries of Reserve Field Artillery Regiment 63, which had been withdrawn from the battle zone west of the railway embankment, took up positions by Brigade Headquarters at La Gueule d'Ours. They were joined by 3rd Battery Field Artillery Regiment 25, which had been allocated by Headquarters 79th Reserve Division. Major von Pressentin moved his headquarters to the area of 2nd Battery Reserve Field Artillery Regiment 63 by the railway embankment, where he was followed during the morning of 10th April by the staffs of Reserve Infantry Regiment 261 and Reserve Infantry Regiment 262. Hauptmann Döring moved to the cross tracks, near to which the staff of Reserve Infantry Regiment 263 and the Heavy Artillery were also located. This made it possible for the Brigade to conduct the infantry battle in close coordination with the artillery groups. By order of 79th Reserve Division, the British battery positions around Neuville were engaged with gas shells and the villages of Les Tilleuls, Thélus and Farbus, along with the roads leading to the German battle positions, were kept under heavy fire.

In the meantime, thanks to the resistance put up by the forward defenders, the Germans felt that the immediate crisis of the battle had been overcome. Already during the late evening two battalions of 111th Infantry Division, which was moving up, had arrived at Acheville and Arleux to occupy the third line. They were followed on 10 April by the remaining units of the division, which were at the disposal of Group Vimy and went into bivouac in the built up areas behind the Third Position. During the early morning, Major Müllenhoff's 2nd Battalion Infantry Regiment 73 and 3rd (composite) Battalion Infantry Regiment 164 were subordinated to 79th Reserve Division, which immediately allocated them to the Brigade. After an exceedingly strenuous and difficult approach, first through snow and then in clear weather which exposed them to observation from Vimy Ridge, they arrived at La Gueule d'Ours at 10.00 am, where their arrival had been eagerly anticipated. Two companies and some machine guns were immediately despatched forward to each of the exhausted fighting regiments. The Brigade retained half of 3rd Battalion Infantry Regiment 164 as a reserve which, together with eight machine guns, was readied to protect the left flank of the division.

Reserve Hauptmann Mierzinsky 3rd Battalion Infantry Regiment 164[24]

"The next objective was a small rise in the ground about three kilometres away. There I ordered a halt and the preparation of hasty defences whilst I went to the Brigade Command Post, which was located further forward in a deep chalk pit. I wished to report in so that I could be given further orders and be briefed on the situation. After we had covered another kilometre the snow stopped, the skies cleared and it was a bright, sunny day. The enemy must have been able to see us clearly from Vimy Ridge, but apparently the observers must have had bad communications with their guns. There was absolutely no cover and we just had to go on hurrying forward because the situation to the front was known to be grave.

"We were still about 1,000 meters from our destination when very heavy enemy shrapnel fire came down. It would have accounted for all of us had it not been directed too far to our rear. We were also lucky again because a thick snow squall came down before the enemy guns could home in on us. In the meantime the companies were able to dig in for protection behind a fold in the ground. The ground was one morass, but soft clay and chalk were accepted as the price to pay and there were no casualties. Together with Leutnant Reinhardt and six runners I reached the chalk pit where the Brigade staff was located and reported our arrival.

"I experienced a great feeling of relief because three quarters of an hour previously, when we left Rouvroy and moved into the open ground, I had not believed that it would be possible to move the Battalion forward so easily and with no casualties . . . The Brigade Commander General Dieterich, whose headquarters was situated in a weakly constructed dugout in the chalk pit, was highly delighted at our arrival. There was still a further 1,500 metres to the front line, but this was only weakly held. The enemy could very easily have overrun us and captured the brigade staff. However everybody who was still occupying holes in and around the chalk pit was under clear orders from the Brigade Commanders and was determined to defend it to the last.

"The general himself gave the briefing and the orders, not leaving it to his adjutant or orderly officer. The orders were very specific. 1st and 3rd Companies were to take over protection of the left flank from the weak forces currently manning the railway embankment there and were to be echeloned in depth. 11th and 12th Companies were to act as divisional reserve: 12th Company providing further protection on the left flank and 11th Company remaining in the area of the chalk pit. It was recommended that I used one of the dugouts in the chalk pit for my own command post because, in the event of an attack from the endangered left flank, I should be able personally to observe the ground from there.

"Together with the company commanders I reconnoitred the ground, which was under shrapnel fire. Two hours later, split into small groups to avoid casualties and taking advantage of the snow squalls, the companies could be led forward to their appointed locations. Because the field kitchen would not be arriving until the following morning, I authorised the consumption of the iron rations."

Even though there was no attack, it was a grim day for the troops, Unteroffizier Schwarze of 3rd Company noting, 'From 9.00 am until the evening we lay there in the snow and dug in. We then pulled our groundsheets around us. Freezing and numb with cold we crouched down in our holes. During the night we dug in again further forward on the left flank near a sunken road.' The front in the area where the break in had occurred now ran as follows: western edge of the village of Givenchy – eastern edge of Vimy Ridge – south of Vimy to the railway embankment – from there south of Bailleul eastwards, bending backwards along the western edges of the villages of Gavrelle, Monchy and Wancourt. The deployment of new and complete divisions either side of the Scarpe removed the most immediate danger and the occupation of the rearward positions by fresh battalions and batteries strengthened the defence further. As a result, subsequent attempts by the Canadians to push forward on 10 April were not believed to represent a serious threat. A British attack supported by tanks via Bailleul – Farbus during the afternoon and directed at the rear of 79th Reserve Division was halted by concentrated counter fire, including that of the left flank of 79th Reserve Division. Much the same happened to an attempt to break through south of the Scarpe.

Towards evening heavy fighting broke out on Vimy Ridge once more, during which its eastern edge (which, despite an heroic defence, had been temporarily lost) was retaken by an immediate counter-stroke. Everywhere the performance of the German troops, including those from outside 79th Reserve Division, was notably effective. Alongside many brave NCOs and men of Reserve Infantry

Regiment 261, Leutnants Florenz and Schnioffsky were killed. Leutnant Wiese, who was severely wounded, was captured by the Canadians. He died of his wounds on 17 May. Within a short time the situation of 1st Battalion Reserve Infantry Regiment 261 was extremely critical, as constantly reinforced masses pressed in on it from the flanks.

Nevertheless it could not bring itself to withdraw from the ridge and drop down to the Second Position. It remained manning *Potsdamer Graben* [Potsdam Trench] and the Intermediate Position (North), as the Canadians dug in to its front. Its hopes of reinforcement were met to a limited extent. Between 2.00 and 3.00 am 3rd Company Pionier Regiment 18 arrived, as did 6th Company Infantry Regiment 73, under Leutnant Gipkens, the following morning. Heavy fighting for the Intermediate Position, which was now the front line, took place. Suffering under heavy enemy and also [misdirected] German artillery fire, the decimated garrison, unable to find cover, pulled back to the *Sachsenlager* in the face of a massed Canadian attack. Unteroffizier Piesker, who had already distinguished himself through his outstanding courage, covered the withdrawal with the last remaining serviceable machine gun. Vizefeldwebel Petersen (4th Company) guarded the left flank, whilst the remainder, which had closed in around the battalion staff, barricaded themselves into *Sachsenweg* [Saxon Way], preventing the enemy from advancing further.

It was already evening when it became increasingly obvious that the battalion was completely outflanked, that the remainder of the slopes of Vimy Ridge were controlled by the Canadians and that there was no prospect of the arrival of reserves. Finally the battalion decided that there was nothing more they could do in order to save the Ridge so, in order to avoid further useless casualties, the decision was taken to exercise the discretion given it the previous evening and to pull back to the Second Position. Leaving behind deception forces, the remnants of the 1st Battalion and 1st Company Pionier Battalion 18 moved back across ground, swept by heavy shrapnel fire and gas, to the Second Position, taking with them all the wounded, the telephones and the reserve rations. There were pitifully few of them, because the companies had already left behind on the ridge, or evacuated to the rear, large numbers of wounded men.

The infantrymen of 79th Reserve Division had spent many days and nights in action, enduring snow, cold and mud, with insufficient food and sleep. Their battleworthiness had been stretched to the limit and would soon have been fully exhausted. General Headquarters decided, therefore, to give up the eastern edge of Vimy Ridge which up until then had been held, to withdraw the remnants of the battalions of the 79th Reserve Division during the night 10/11 April and to replace them in the Vimy Position with troops of 111th Infantry Division. Once 2nd Battalion Infantry Regiment 76 along with its regimental staff and 2nd Bn Infantry Regiment 164 had arrived, the relief of the 79th Reserve Division commenced, being controlled by Brigade.

The remnants of Reserve Infantry Regiment 261 were so weak by this stage that Infantry Regiment 76 only had to deploy 7th and 8th Companies forward in the Second Position; 5th and 6th Companies, together with the 2nd Machine Gun Company, remained in reserve to the east of the railway embankment. Infantry Regiment 76 spent an uncomfortable few hours here, under constant fire and holding muddy, half collapsed trenches without dugouts.[25]It would, of course, have been preferable to have been able to carry out this entire operation sooner, but such was the confusion caused by the late despatch of the operational reserves that they had to be fed piecemeal into the battle. The experience of one of the battalions of Fusilier Regiment 73 is instructive. It should have moving forward no later than 8 April, but twelve hours into the battle it was still in its billets. Its commanding officer, Rittmeister Böckelmann, was temporarily absent, so the move was controlled by one of the company commanders.

Reserve Leutnant Schmidt 1st Battalion Fusilier Regiment 73[26]

> "At 5.00 pm on Easter Monday we were stood to in a telephone call from the regiment then, at 6.30 pm, came the order to be ready, less our heavy equipment, to board a train at Seclin at 7.00 pm. That was impossible because it was nine kilometres away, so I managed to get the order changed to 'as soon as possible'. Our spirits were dampened by the weather; it began to snow hard and through it the battalion marched via Attiches to Seclin, prior to waiting a solid two hours at the station before we could be loaded.

> "We then sat for four hours in freezing cold carriages and it was not until 3.00 am 10 April that we alighted in Beaumont. After reporting in to 79th Reserve Division, we then began to look for billets, which were already full to overflowing with other troops. The company commanders raced around searching and, about an hour later, somewhere had been found for everybody. At 7.00 am we departed for Drocourt. Here I handed over command to Rittmeister Böckelmann, who had by now arrived and, a little later, the battalion headed off to Fresnoy."

Despite the greatest difficulties, before dawn on 11th April the sectors to the east of Vimy Ridge had been reorganised and the relieved battalions withdrawn. There remained in Sector *Zollern* on the eastern edge of Vimy Ridge, which was lightly covered with fresh snow, a weak force of Reserve Infantry Regiment 262, which it had not been possible to withdraw before dawn. On 11 April, too, they held on devotedly to their forward position, despite being pressed on all sides. Finally the last of the fighters was withdrawn on the night of 11/12 April from their positions along the heights, for which, in accordance with their orders, they had fought so hard. [27]

The battle line of the 79th Reserve Division now ran along the line of the Second Position, bending back from the south western corner of Vimy to the railway embankment. The divisional, brigade and sector commanders maintained command of their sectors and the troops of 111th Infantry Division, even after their own infantry had been relieved. During the night 10/11 April, when Vimy

Ridge was evacuated, the final batteries which were still deployed west of the railway embankment were withdrawn. Some took up new fire positions near La Gueule d'Ours; others behind the Third Position. A British attack against Vimy on 11 April was shot to a standstill by the defensive fire of the German artillery batteries, whose other preoccupation was to observe the Canadians up on the ridge and to harass the approach routes. After repairs and maintenance the number of available guns increased. By the evening of 11 April, twenty two field guns and twelve heavy guns were operating in front of the Third Position.

During these days, the main British assaults were along the line of the road Arras-Cambrai. Thanks to overwhelming firepower and the use of tanks, they were able in this way to take Monchy. The overall situation had developed in such a way that, in order to produce a more bearable situation, the Army Group decided to pull clear of the enemy and to withdraw to the Third Position along the line Lens-Avion-Méricourt-Acheville-Arleux-Oppy-Gavrelle. The bulk of the artillery had to take up fire positions behind this line during the night 11/12 April. Nevertheless, 79th Reserve Division left the Infantry Brigade two field batteries east of Vimy, in order that they could continue the close quarter battle. When day dawned on 13 April, the German Positions from Liévin via Vimy to Gavrelle had been evacuated. Only weak rearguards remained, to yield only when enemy pressure built up. Command of the former sector of 79th Reserve Division then passed to 111th Infantry Division and, on 14 April, the batteries of Reserve Field Artillery Regiment 63 were also withdrawn from the battle.

The withdrawal was handled skilfully and efficiently. Despite the pressure of events, clear orders had been prepared and issued. Those for 2nd Battalion Fusilier Regiment 73 are quite typical. They were simple, left no room for doubt and were entirely effective, despite the friction of war and the odd error caused by the difficulty in passage of information. Their war diary recorded the operation as follows:[28]

> "The front line was to be evacuated at 3.00 am and the railway embankment by 4.00 am. At 4.30 am, following the blowing of charges, the last of the patrols commanded by officers was to withdraw. The use of roads was to be avoided during the withdrawal. During the night we had an unpleasant surprise when our artillery began bringing down fire at 2.15 am on the embankment which was to have been denied until 4.00 am. The telephone system failed and it was some time before they could be stopped. Later, stage by stage, all the companies arrived safely in Rouvroy."

The main battle for Vimy Ridge might have been over, but there had been a sharp fight for The Pimple on 12 April. Bavarian Infantry Regiments 11 and 14 of the 16th Bavarian Infantry Division had suffered particularly heavily during the bombardment and the initial actions, so the decision was taken to move forward fresh troops from 4th Guards Division to reinforce, then relieve, the hard-pressed Bavarians, the survivors of which remained in support. They were soon to clash with the 46th, 50th and 44th Battalions of 12th Canadian Brigade.

The reorganisation meant that on 12 April, the Fusilier [3rd] Battalion Grenadier Guard Regiment 5 and 1st Battalion Reserve Infantry Regiment 93 were defending the forward part of this important feature. Arriving tired, unfed and thirsty in the area of Bavarian Infantry Regiment 14 at 2.00 am on 11 April, it took until 6.00 am for companies of Grenadier Guard Regiment 5 to deploy into

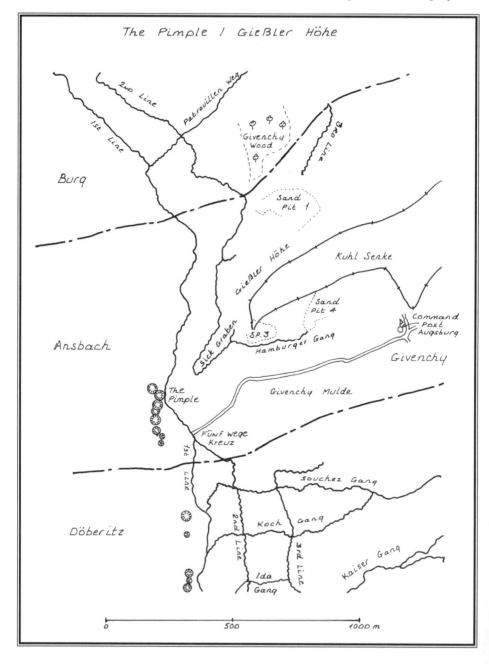

The Pimple / Gießler Höhe

position. 9th, 12th and 10th Companies occupied the front line, with the 11th behind them. In reserve was 2nd Battalion Bavarian Infantry Regiment 14. Battalion HQ was established back down at *Angres-Kreuz*.

The situation of Grenadier Guard Regiment 5 was anything but promising. The trenches were levelled and full of mud and icy water; the artillery fire rained down on the largely defenceless fusiliers.[29] Worst of all, lack of numbers meant that the front line contained several gaps, between one hundred and three hundred metres wide, which represented a disaster waiting to happen. No more troops could be made available, so the companies had to make the best of the situation. Communications were bad. There were no working telephone lines and light signalling was not possible. Runners maintained with great difficulty the link between battalion and companies, whilst to the rear messenger dogs and carrier pigeons were employed.

At midnight 11/12 April, artillery fire crashed down all over the positions, pounding the men, who had not been fed a hot meal for two days. Crouched in wet, muddy shell holes, worn out, soaking wet and freezing, the fusiliers could only sit and wait as casualties mounted. About 4.00 am the first of the assaults began. This was largely beaten back with small arms fire and grenades but, at 4.50 am, shielded by a snowstorm which cut the visibility to nothing and artillery fire which hammered the depth positions, a Canadian attack in considerable force came in behind a rolling barrage. Some of the Canadians were alleged to be wearing German steel helmets, rather than their own flat plate-shaped helmets as a deception measure.[30] Every third or fourth man of the leading wave was said to have been carrying a light machine gun.

German defensive fire, when it eventually arrived, was late and too light to cause the Canadians serious problems and they broke into the German positions with relative ease, exploiting the wide gaps. Isolated groups of German soldiers fought on with rifle and hand grenade until they were overrun. The remnants of 9th Company, commanded by Vizefeldwebel Bröker, for example, held out for some time until, reduced to four men still on their feet, Bröker ordered them to break out to the rear. Staying behind himself to cover the others, Bröker was killed. Of the whole company only Fusiliers Heinrichs, Koog and Palubitski made it back. That story was mirrored all over the *Gießlerhöhe* and Givenchy Wood, where small groups fought their way back via the various sand and gravel pits and the web of trenches, until eventually the survivors were forced back into Givenchy.[31]

In the later stages of the battle, men of 3rd Battalion Bavarian Infantry Regiment 14, who had come through the earlier fighting, became involved once more. One of their members left a description of the events around the gravel pits which, although couched in fairly lurid terms, is reasonably accurate.

Hauptmann G Marsching Bavarian Infantry Regiment 14[32]

"[On 12 April] it was hard to obtain a clear view forward. The sentries huddled deep into their coats. Suddenly the sound of hand grenades could be heard, together with rifle and machine gun fire. Then it was quiet once more for a time, before the noise increased again ... Up went the flare signals which brought down destructive fire from hundreds of guns. A few moments passed then a curtain of shell splinters, smoke and dust came down in front of our forward positions. A runner rushed past, 'They have been beaten off'.

" ... *Sandgrube* [Sand Pit] 4 was actually located well back as the fourth line of defence. To our front, forming the third line, was another sand pit. There and in the two forward trenches fought a battalion of the Fusilier Guards.[33] To the south the ground fell away into the bottomless muddy morass of the *Givenchy Mulde* [Hollow]. A few deep mined dugouts in the side of the sand pit had been crushed. In the centre of the workings were two shell holes, six meters wide and full of water and mud. In a corner to the left was a machine gun in an improvised firing position. Our machine guns gave us our best chance of holding on in the event of an attack. The second machine gun was still down in a dugout.

"Had all hell broken loose? An ear-splitting racket began and great crashes filled the air, continuing as the first of the 150 mm shells began landing in the pit. A dugout was crushed, but there was no time to dwell on it. Everybody stood to. Sleet and snowflakes whirled about until showers of shell splinters merged with them, ripping apart anything they touched. Our nerves were on edge. What was happening forward? The first of the wounded stumbled past. 'The Tommies have broken through!' We were enraged – impossible! But it was true. The fire slackened. Like a whirlwind the brave lads of 12th Company made their way forward through mud knee deep towards the shell-torn firing line.

"Two machine guns were swiftly mounted on the damaged stands. Come on then, Canadians! Two hundred metres from us and not a step further! Suddenly, lunging forward from Sand Pit 2, came the Canadian assault troops, disdaining to take cover. They assumed that their hellish fire had killed or buried us all. Suddenly fire was opened! Who gave the order? In no time the first Canadian wave was swept away. Had they just gone to ground? Fresh masses of troops launched forward. Our machine guns hammered away angrily and the second line sank bloodily into the deep mud. The ground to our front was clear of enemy. Some tens of wounded were dragged into the dugouts and we buried one dead man carefully by the entrance to one of them.

"Two runners rushed towards the command post. One of them got stuck in the mud and lost his boots, but the other delivered a short, sharp message to Major Utz [Commanding Officer 3rd Battalion Bavarian Infantry Regiment 14], 'Sand Pit 4 is firmly in our hands!' But they never gave up. Heavy flanking fire, rising to drum fire, started coming down from the Loos salient. We stood in this hellish rain for a whole hour, nerves stretched to breaking point. Suddenly the enemy fire was lifted.

At a shout our gallant little band rushed to man their positions and fired until their barrels glowed. The enemy were unable to start their attack. The morale of our men under their outstanding leader, Leutnant Link, was sky high. The price the enemy paid in blood was heavy. We watched as they attempted to dig in in the marshy ground, which had been ploughed up by shells. German fire had forced them to seek cover.

"Another message winged its way back to the *KTK*, 'Beaten off again!' It went on snowing, but our hearts were rejoicing. It was a day of honour for the Bavarian 3rd Battalion from Central Franken. They had been in drum fire for nine days, six of them with hardly anything to eat, taking cover far away from day light in their deep dugouts. It was a day of honour, too, for the entire regiment. None of its positions had been lost, not a foot of ground had been conceded to the enemy

On a day of serious casualties for 3rd Battalion Grenadier Guard Regiment 5, its battalion commander, Major Roosen, was killed later when his temporary command post was destroyed by a direct hit, killing also his dog handler and one of the two messenger dogs which had maintained the links to regimental head-quarters throughout the fighting. The company commanders of the 9th, 10th and 11th Companies (Leutnants Kurt Bronsch, Erich Riemke and Kurt Hühnerbein) were also killed, as was Leutnant Paul Schmidt, Roosen's orderly officer. Like almost every German casualty during the battles for Vimy Ridge, none of them has a known grave.[34]

1st Battalion Reserve Infantry Regiment 93, which was deployed to the south of Grenadier Guard Regiment 5, had a difficult day, but was never under the same degree of pressure as the Guards. One of the company commanders survived the battle and later produced a detailed account of the time he spent on the rear slopes of the Pimple to the south of the *Givenchy Mulde*:

Reserve Leutnant Ueckert 2nd Company Reserve Infantry Regiment 93[35]

"It was immediately obvious when we arrived at the appointed position that it had been the scene of heavy fighting. Those companies of the Bavarians which had not been completely wiped out were down to a strength of about ten men and they were completely intermingled along the main defensive line. The relief was extremely difficult to carry out because the front line trace varied throughout its length. Dawn was already appearing on the eastern horizon by the time the companies of the 1st Battalion had occupied their designated sector. The Givenchy salient was very like Thiepval. On the right flank, marked by the *Souchez-Gang* [Souchez Way], the Third Line was occupied by 1st Company, whilst the left flank was held by the 3rd Company, with sentry positions distributed from *Kaisergang* [Emperor's Way] down to the lower *Sachsenlager* [Saxon Dugouts].

"Forward at the most prominent part of the salient there was a large gap between the companies. This was because this point was already occupied by the enemy. To the 2nd Company fell the task of closing the gap. I made use of part of the existing *Koch-Gang* [Cook's Way], and caused a new line to be extended right through the crater field to the right flank of the 3rd Company. Fortunately this re-grouping went very well and was completed swiftly. As a result, by the time it was fully daylight the company was dug in all along the new line. Despite the extremely difficult situation in which we found ourselves, everyone was alert and ready for the coming operations. Most of 11 April was taken up with the exchange of considerable quantities of artillery fire on both the forward positions and routes to the rear.

"My main concern was the left flank of the company and the battalion, which was hanging in the air, because I expected an outflanking enemy attack from the south from La Folie Wood. [In 1917 the remains of this wood extended all the way into Sector *Fischer*.] In the event completely the opposite happened. It went dark early, because the skies were full of threatening snow clouds and an icy wind blew across the battlefield. Reinforced night sentries went on duty. The need for reliefs meant that there was little opportunity for rest in the dugouts. Those off duty had to lie there with their equipment on, helmets pushed back on their heads, rifles to hand; ready at any moment to be torn out of their slumbers by the shouts of alarm of the sentries in the trenches.

"In the enemy trenches all was quiet. There was no sign that any operation was to be undertaken that night. Suddenly, in the early hours of 12 April, the sentries raised the alarm. Within a minute the company was out of the dugouts and stood-to along the parapet. Squally snow showers blotted out the dawn and it was impossible to see more than five metres. Insanely violent drum fire came down on our trenches and the village of Givenchy. Under the protection of the driving snow, the enemy had attacked and had gained a lodgement in the sector of the Grenadier Guards. Suddenly the enemy appeared in *Koch-Gang* as well and began to roll up the company position, taking some prisoners. Everyone was taken by surprise by this sudden appearance of the Tommies in the trench. Nobody could explain it. Had the 1st Company been surprised?

"I immediately launched a counter-stroke. The Canadians left the trench rapidly, pulling back to the *Souchez-Graben*. In an instant the entire trench garrison of the *Koch-Graben* launched forward charging after the enemy. Within a few moments, Vizefeldwebel Beutel and his platoon had caught up with them, capturing two officers and nine men. The remainder of the enemy were scattered and the prisoners they had taken were freed. Other remnants of the enemy were captured by 1st Company. Meanwhile 2nd Company had returned to *Koch-Gang*. The snow squalls eased off and the drum fire died away gradually. The whole business had only lasted a few minutes. The entire company was elated.

One thing was clear: the Tommies had been given a bloody nose by 2nd Company.

"The same fate had befallen the enemy in front of 1st Company which, under the command of Leutnant Roland Müller, had energetically beaten them off. The 3rd Company was not involved in this attack. At the end of it the 1st Battalion was in complete control of the sector which it had taken over on 10 April. The situation was a good deal worse in the area of our right hand neighbours, the Grenadier Guards. Despite a vigorous defence the enemy had broken into the trench system and were working their way forward along *Souchez-Graben*. The enemy break-in had occurred to the north of *Fünf-Wege-Kreuz* [Five Way Junction]. We realised that the prisoners were very drunk. Later there was unanimous agreement the enemy assault troops were completely drunk.[36] The situation became serious for us once more. Enemy parties had worked their way forward about 300 metres along the *Souchez-Graben*. I ordered the company to occupy the whole of *Koch-Gang* and to block off *Souchez-Gang*, to avoid the risk of being cut off from Givenchy.

"This meant that the company was occupying a narrow wedge-shaped position, which meant that, gradually, it was having to defend two fronts. To our front there was the eerily silent, but ever present, threat from the salient further forward. Luckily the enemy did not seem to appreciate exactly where our positions lay and we were left alone from that direction. The entire attention of the company was directed towards the *Souchez-Gang* and the hollow to its rear. We could watch large scale enemy movements there and the sentries engaged them. Enemy patrols were constantly pushing forward in order to determine the size and shape of our positions.

"For the most part, these patrols were shot up by our grenadiers. This provided an important lesson to the infantryman, who in this way learnt once more to appreciate the value of their own weapons. Trench warfare had meant that the hand grenade had become the principal weapon, with the rifle playing only a subordinate role, but rifle fire could have a devastating effect on the enemy – even at short range. The whip-like crack of the shots, coupled with their sharp sound through the air, had a much greater demoralising effect on the enemy than the dull thuds of the hand grenades and so it was near Givenchy. Our well aimed rifle fire held the Tommies completely in check, forcing them to bring forward fresh troops in order to be able to continue the advance.

"By now the sky had cleared and the afternoon brought spring-like warmth from the sun. Our situation became ever more threatening as the arrival of enemy reinforcements increased the pressure on us. Towards 5.00 pm strong enemy columns were seen forming up, front facing south-east, behind the wire and level with *Fünf-Wege-Kreuz* [Five Way Junction]. Similar enemy detachments could be seen massing in the salient to our front and further to the south. In view of this perilous situation I immediately discussed fresh defensive measures with Leutnant Roland Müller. Then, at 5.30 pm, we were surprised to receive an order from the battalion, ordering a withdrawal by 1st and 3rd Companies to Givenchy then on to Avion. 2nd Company was to remain in position as rearguard.

"It would be no easy task to hold the position until 3.00 am, because a major enemy attack from north and south could be launched against Givenchy at any moment. The grenadiers, who had been absolutely staunch up until this point, began to get somewhat uneasy in view of the changed situation, but were nevertheless all prepared to defend themselves and their position to the utmost. Shortly before 7.00 pm, 1st and 3rd Companies withdrew from their positions and pulled back to Givenchy, where they occupied positions in the *Souchez-Gang* left and right of Battalion Headquarters.[37] My grenadiers suddenly felt an oppressive feeling of being isolated. I had to take immediate measures because the enemy, who had spotted the withdrawal of 1st Company, immediately began to tighten the noose around us by occupying the abandoned trenches south of *Souchez-Gang.*

"2nd Company, every man of which was stood-to, brought the groups of enemy under fire. I had stops erected in the trenches to block off the trench to the north and south. In *Souchez-Gang* things remained lively, with the grenadiers bringing down rapid rifle fire whenever they detected the flat helmets of the Tommies. It was absolutely vital that our blocks were not overrun, otherwise the line of our withdrawal to the village would have been cut. The enemy columns were assembled like gathering thunder clouds on the heights to the east of *Fünf-Wege-Kreuz*, ready to launch an attack on Givenchy. The masses increased in size before our eyes and we waited tensely for the moment when they would launch forward. Then, about 6.30 pm, a runner arrived from the battalion bearing the following order: '2nd Company is to pull back to Command Post *Augsburg*. Only the rearguard will remain in *Koch-Graben*. (Enemy about to launch an attack.)' Everybody heaved a sigh of relief as I directed the company to prepare to move out. Leaving one platoon behind as a rearguard in *Koch-Graben*, the other two pulled back to Givenchy. The withdrawal was spotted by the enemy, but although we came under heavy fire we had no casualties. It now fell to the 1st Battalion to hold the village of Givenchy until 9.00 pm.

"Shortly after 7.00 pm the enemy columns attacked with the evening sun behind them from their positions east of *Fünf-Wege-Kreuz*. At that the final rearguard pulled back from *Koch-Gang*. Firing from a small heap of rubbish near the command post, four machine guns from the 1st Machine Gun Company, under Leutnant Jeibmann and supported by some rifle sections from 1st and 2nd Companies, brought down a torrent of rapid fire on the unsuspecting enemy. There was complete confusion.

The attackers all went to ground and stretcherbearers came forward to carry back the wounded. The attack was beaten off without the aid of a single German gun, but the British artillery lost no time in bringing down revenge fire.

"Heavy shells crashed down around the firing positions and they had to be abandoned. It was now 9.00 pm and high time to depart if the battalion was not to be surrounded; the enemy was already in Givenchy and in rear of the 93rd. Finally the companies began to fall back. First to go was 3rd Company, followed at fifteen minute intervals by the 2nd, 1st and 4th. Enemy artillery fire increased minute by minute to drum fire. The enemy seemed to be preparing for another attack. At the double we pulled back along *Souchez-Gang* to the *Kronprinzen-Lager* [Crown Prince Dugouts], straight through a hail of British shells. An intense box barrage sealed off the rear of the village. Near the church everything was in flames. We were witnessing the funeral pyre of Leutnant Jaap of 4th Company, who met his end at that time.

"He had intended to blow up his dugout and, to facilitate that, had carried sacks of powder and mortar bombs into it. When it was time to go he ordered everyone out, placed several packets of flares on the charge and lit the fuse. As he raced up the stairs, he saw that the entrance was blocked by his men who were unwilling to brave the move into the open and the hell of the British drum fire. A heavy shell suddenly crashed down into the entrance of the dugout collapsing the timber framework of the entrance and hurling several of the men at the top of the stairs (including Leutnant Jaap) back down. Simultaneously the charge went off with a dreadful crash. Flames, metres long, roared up, engulfing both the men and their commander. All attempts at rescue were in vain."[38]

With the skilfully conducted evacuation of Givenchy, the final scenes of the battle for Vimy Ridge were played out. 1st Battalion Reserve Infantry Regiment 93 was fortunate, emerging with casualties of only nine killed, sixty eight wounded and twelve missing, seven of whom were accounted for when six men died with Leutnant Jaap in the dugout. Reserve Infantry Regiment 93 was lucky not to be at the main focus of the fighting, but its companies had been forced effectively out of their trenches. Out-manoeuvred and ultimately out-fought, the German defenders who had borne the brunt of the fighting for Vimy Ridge were withdrawn to rest, recuperate and count their losses, which were high. The survivors of 79th Reserve Division were proud ever after to be counted as *Vimykämpfer*. They felt that they had given a good account of themselves against the odds and the name Vimy appeared in the place of honour on their regimental banners after the war.

Amongst the many honours and awards given for service on Vimy Ridge was the *Pour le Mérite* presented to the commander of Reserve Infantry Regiment

261, Oberstleutnant Wilhelm von Goerne, whose humanity had led to the truce following the disastrous raid of 1 March. His citation reads:

> "For outstanding leadership, distinguished military planning and successful operations during the 1917 British offensive. The award was also given in recognition of distinction in action during the Battle of Arras and especially the fierce fighting at Vimy Ridge when Reserve Infantry Regiment 261 prevented a British [sic] breakthrough and for distinguished military planning and successful operations between 9 and 13 April 1917."[39]

Their devotion to duty had cost them dear. Following the withdrawal of its formations from the battle, I Bavarian Reserve Corps reported to Sixth Army and Army Group Crown Prince Rupprecht that casualty figures for Group Vimy were:[40] '79th Reserve Division: forty five officers, 4,000 other ranks, twenty machine guns, thirty mortars and thirteen guns, one of which was heavy; 1st Bavarian Reserve Division forty five officers, 3,000 other ranks, twenty eight machine guns, thirty five mortars and thirty eight guns, of which twelve were heavy; 14th Bavarian Infantry Division seventy officers, 3,500 other ranks, twenty four machine guns, twelve mortars and sixty nine guns, of which thirty were heavy.' Of course these initial figures would later be revised downwards when all stragglers, walking wounded and similar personnel had been accounted for correctly. The corrected combined figures of killed , wounded and missing for 1st Bavarian Reserve Division, for example, were later computed to be: Officers ninety three, other ranks, 2,679 – an initial severe underestimate of officer casualties and an overestimate of eleven percent for other ranks.[41] Nevertheless these were serious losses, which more or less matched those of their Canadian opponents.

Paying a final tribute to their comrades, whom they had had to leave amongst the fallen on the ridge, Reserve Infantry Regiment 262 turned to poetry:[42]

> *Sie ruhen und schlafen aus von der Not*
> *Vom Leid und der Mühsal im Kriege*
> *Und küßt ihre Gräber das Morgenrot*
> *Dann träumen sie lächelnd vom Siege*

> They rest and sleep free from danger
> From the pain and the trials of war's history
> When the red of the dawn comes and kisses their graves
> Then they dream with a smile of the victory

> Strötgen

In truth of course there was no German victory to celebrate at Vimy. For two and a half years they had battled valiantly and fought well to retain Vimy Ridge, but this, the final act of a long campaign, was a Canadian triumph, which nothing could disguise. Writing in his diary on 9 April, the Army Group Commander, Crown Prince Rupprecht of Bavaria, noted pessimistically, 'It is questionable if we can hold on in the face of artillery fire of this increasing intensity. This prompts the further question: In these circumstances, is there any point in continuing to prosecute the war?'[43] Generalfeldmarschall von Hindenburg, writing in his memoirs, admitted that 9 April cast a mood of gloom across the birthday of Ludendorff, which fell on that day. Ludendorff himself was greatly depressed by the turn of events. He later recorded,[44] 'I had anticipated the expected offensive, confident that all would be well and now I felt deeply depressed. Was that really the result that we had earned after all the worry and care we had taken during the past half of a year? Had all our writings on the defensive battle been based on false premises and, if that was so, what were we to do about it?' It fell to Hindenburg to shake him out of this negative frame of mind. [45]

> "On 9 April the evening briefing painted a dismal picture. There was much shadow and little light. Nevertheless it is essential to look for light in cases like that. There was one ray of sunshine, even though its outlines were a little unclear. The British did not seem to understand how to exploit their success to the full.[46] On this occasion that was lucky for us, as it had been on occasion before. After the briefing was over I shook my First Quartermaster General [Ludendorff] by the hand and said, 'Well, we have lived through worse situations than today together.' Today, on his birthday! My trust remained unshaken. I knew that we had fresh troops marching on to the battlefield and that trains were rolling in its direction as well. The crisis would be overcome. As far as I was concerned, it was already over. The battle would continue."

In one sense Hindenburg was justified in his confidence. Under the positive, decisive direction of Oberst Fritz von Loßberg, the newly appointed Chief of Staff Sixth Army, the German defenders withdrew rapidly five to six kilometres to their Third Position, which had already been partially prepared in anticipation of such an eventuality. There they were located sufficiently far to the east to neutralise the advantage that possession of Vimy Ridge gave the Allies and there the front stuck for weeks and months to come, whilst the German chain of command analysed this shock reverse and devised the tactics they would later use at Ypres when the Passchendaele campaign opened three and a half months later.

Notes
1. Kriegsarchiv München 1 R.I.B. Bd 30: Bayer.Res.Inf.Regt. Nr. 3 *Gefechtsbericht über die Kämpfe am 9. und 10. April 1917*
2. This was a point very close to the Commandant's House on the extreme right of the Canadian Corps sector.
3. Brunner's capture was controversial. The circumstances were investigated postwar by a court of enquiry which absolved him of any blame. The full record of the court proceedings is available in the Kriegsarchiv München OP 38887.

4. Kriegsarchiv München 1R.I.Brig Bd 29 *Gefechtsnotizen der 1. Reserve – Infanterie-Brigade vom 9 April 1917*
5. Kriegsarchiv München 1. Res. Div. Bd 21 *Divisionsbefehle 9.4.17*
6. Behrmann: *Die Osterschlacht bei Arras 1917 I.Teil* p 37
7. Heinicke: History Reserve Infantry Regiment 263 pp 116–117
8. Heinicke: History Reserve Infantry Regiment 263 pp 117–119
9. Fischer: History Reserve Infantry Regiment 262 pp 118–120
10. This is an error. Schröder must have headed towards Hill 145.
11. Leutnant Peter Kopka is one of the very few German fatal casualties of 9 April 1917 who has a known grave. He is buried in the *Kamradengrab* of the German cemetery at Neuville St Vaast/Maison Blanche.
12. Reserve Infantry Regiment 261 *Nachrichtenblatt Nr. 49* pp 3–4
13. For some reason the terms *'Island Fischer'* and *'Falkland Fischer'* were used (at least by Reserve Infantry Regiment 261 and possibly more generally) to describe Sub-Sectors *Fischer North* and *Fischer South* respectively. Apart from the fact that *Island* [Iceland] is in the North Atlantic and *Falkland* [The Falkland Islands] are in the South Atlantic, it is difficult to make a connection. It is additionally confusing because Fischer was split officially into three sub-sectors.
14. Reserve Infantry Regiment 261 *Nachrichtenblatt Nr. 49* pp 3–4
15. Reserve Infantry Regiment 261 *Nachrichtenblatt Nr. 45* pp 5–7
16. Reserve Infantry Regiment 261 *Nachrichtenblatt Nr. 45* pp 5–7
17. Delmensingen: *Das Bayernbuch vom Weltkriege* pp 409–412
18. This was an over-pessimistic report. Progress had been made, but not as far as the Second Position at the foot of the eastern slopes of Vimy Ridge.
19. Arthur Vogg was killed as a Hauptmann on 27 March 1918 during the German offensive. He is buried at the German cemetery at Ecourt St Quentin Block 3 Grave 1.
20. Brooke was one of the greatest gunners the British Army has ever produced, rising to command the School of Artillery between the wars and to become Chief of the Imperial General Staff during the Second World War. A well-deserved tribute by Patrick Brennan to his role in planning the fire support for the assault on Vimy Ridge may be found at pp 98–100 of Hayes et.al. *Vimy Ridge: A Canadian Reassessment.*
21. History Bavarian Infantry Regiment 14 pp 226 – 230
22. Reserve Infantry Regiment 261 *Nachrichtenblatt Nr. 41* pp 3–4
23. Freund: History Infantry Regiment 118 pp 178 – 180
24. History Infantry Regiment 164 pp 361–362
25. Sydow: History Infantry Regiment 76 p 128
26. Voigt: History Fusilier Regiment 73 pp 480–481
27. Fischer: History Reserve Infantry Regiment 262 pp 122
28. Voigt: History Fusilier Regiment 73 p 483
29. Because these men were from the 3rd [Fusilier] Battalion of the regiment, the private soldiers were known as fusiliers, rather than grenadiers.
30. It is impossible to judge the truth of this statement. It is possible but, equally, a man wearing a German helmet in poor visibility ran the risk of being shot by his own side.
31. Stosch: History Grenadier Guard Regiment 5 pp 367–369
32. Delmensingen: *Das Bayernbuch vom Weltkriege* pp 408 – 409
33. Marsching is incorrect. The unit involved was 3rd Battalion Grenadier Guard Regiment 5. The Fusilier Guards were not involved in the Battle of Arras until

later and were then deployed south of the Scarpe. The confusion probably arose because the 3rd Battalion of the regiment, in common with other Guard and Reserve Guard Regiments, was known as the Fusilier Battalion.

34. Stosch: History Grenadier Guard Regiment 5 p 370
35. Sievers: History Reserve Infantry Regiment 93 pp 182 – 188
36. This accusation occurs repeatedly in German personal accounts of the battles of the Great War. Certainly large tots of high proof rum were given before battle, so men would have had the smell of it on their breath, but drunkenness in the trenches was severely frowned on and the veracity of these reports is at least questionable.
37. There must be something wrong with the timings at this stage of the report, but the course of events is nevertheless clear.
38. Given the reported circumstances of his death, it is hard to credit that Leutnant Jaap is believed to be buried in the *Kamaradengrab* of the German cemetery at Neuville St Vaast/Maison Blanche. Nevertheless, his is an unusual name and the German *Volksbund* is satisfied that he lies there. The name Jaap appears on one of the bronze panels which list the names of the identified occupants of the mass graves.
39. Quoted by Godefroy Andrew, *The German Army at Vimy Ridge* in Hayes (Ed.) *Vimy Ridge A Canadian Reassessment* p 233
40. Kriegsarchiv München HGr. Rupprecht Bd. 93 *A.O.K. 6 541 11/4 gruppe vimy meldet an heeresgruppe kr Rupprecht – voraussichtliche verluste in den kaempfen vom 9/4 17*
41. Kriegsarchiv München OP 38887 Nr. 9340 1.Res.Inf.Brigade *Gefechtsbericht über die Ereignisse am 9., 10. und 11 April 1917* Brig.St.Qu., 6.6.1917.
42. Fischer: History Reserve Infantry Regiment 262 p 125
43. Kronprinz Rupprecht *Mein Kriegstagebuch Zweiter Band* p 136
44. Ludendorff: *Meine Kriegserinnerungen* p 334
45. Hindenburg: *Aus meinem Leben* p 192
46. The German chain of command never seemed fully to appreciate that the capture of Vimy Ridge was designed to exploit the potential of a 'bite and hold' operation, intended primarily to secure the northern flank of the Arras offensive. Equally, all were unanimous subsequently that a vigorous large-scale follow up, pushing on to the east of Vimy Ridge, would have been extremely difficult to counter. The logistic challenge of attempting such an operation across the devastated Vimy Ridge in the immediate wake of its capture would, of course, have been immense, especially at a time when priority had to be given to active operations which were being conducted elsewhere on the Arras front.

CHAPTER EIGHT

Epilogue

T he loss of Vimy Ridge was a serious blow to the German army and the recriminations began immediately. Sixth Army had been issued with six days' stocks of artillery and mortar ammunition at the beginning of April, but had failed to engage the Allied preparations with destructive fire – why? Enemy artillery batteries were meant to be drenched with gas when they began the final drum fire before the assault, but this had not happened – why not? It had been repeatedly reported that the morale of the forward regiments was intact and that they were in sufficient strength to hold the initial attack – what had gone wrong? The move forward of reserve divisions had been ordered days before the offensive opened – why were they not in position when they were needed?

Within a very short time of the arrival at the Army High Command of the first of the reports outlining the major reverses suffered on the Arras front, demands by Ludendorff for an explanation were flashing down the chain of command. Whilst the Battle for Vimy Ridge was still being decided, Ludendorff, possibly at the instigation of Crown Prince Rupprecht, had already made up his mind that there had been serious failures at Sixth Army and he sacked both the Chief of Staff and the Head of Operations, who departed the Headquarters on 11 April. Generaloberst Freiherr von Falkenhausen also tendered his resignation. This was refused by the Kaiser, who expressed renewed confidence in him, but Crown Prince Rupprecht was less sure. 'The Generaloberst', he recorded, 'who, belying his seventy three years, was extraordinarily fresh and energetic, has now become apathetic under the pressure of the defeat.'[1]

The following day, whilst the fighting for The Pimple and Givenchy en Gohelle was still continuing, the first of the initial impression reports were being circulated. Then, as the Battle of Arras continued to rage, headquarters at all levels had to contend not only with fighting the battle, but also with preparing explanations concerning their part in the disastrous opening phase of operations. Such was the pressure on the staff that, in some cases, divisions were tasked directly by Army Group Crown Prince Rupprecht, especially if, as in the case of 79th Reserve Division, they had been withdrawn and transferred to another Army. Generalleutnant Alfred Dieterich, Commander 79th Reserve Brigade, explained on 22 April[2] that:

> "The reason why 79th Reserve Division had a relatively large number of missing is the fact that the enemy succeeded along the road Neuville – Thélus in overrunning our own positions and, to the south of the road, those of the neighbouring division. They then swung northeast, cutting

off the southern regiment in [Sector] *Arnulf* and elements of the centre regiment [Sector] *Zollern*. The losses in the southern regiment alone account for half of the total number of missing. The attempt by means of an immediate counter-stroke to release the cut off regiment had to be abandoned because, in view of the width of the enemy breakthrough, there were insufficient reserves available to launch such an operation sufficiently powerfully to offer a good chance of success.

"As far as the centre and northern regiments were concerned, the enemy did not succeed in overrunning them frontally in one rush. The regiments held on to the heights, launching one counter-stroke after another to throw back the attacking enemy until, during the evening of 10 April, they withdrew to the second position on order of the Group [Vimy]. It has proved to be impossible to establish the extent of the bloody casualties caused during these battles, because the regiments were not able to move the greater part of their dead and wounded to the rear.

"The large numbers reported as missing are explained by the fact that they embrace all those wounded and dead who could not be recovered and, therefore, have had to be reported as missing. Because, according to reports from officers and men who returned, nobody wanted to surrender to the Canadians without a fight, it must be assumed that a large percentage of dead and wounded were amongst those reported missing."

More generally the usual reporting chain was used to filter the information; each succeeding headquarters adding in its own assessment until, on 21 April, the Army Group Commander was able to issue two documents. One was a preliminary report, classified secret and the other a top secret supplement which dealt with use of reserves, evaluation of the battleworthiness of the troops, artillery operations and anti-tank measures. In his preliminary report, he acknowledged a number of difficulties faced by the Sixth Army during the days leading up to 9 April, but then homed in on what he considered to be the major issue:

Crown Prince Rupprecht of Bavaria, Army Group Commander[3]

"Decisive for the unfavourable outcome on 9 April was the non-appearance [original emphasis] of the reserves. Had they been at the right place at the right time, it is probable that they would have succeeded in largely balancing out the disadvantages caused by other circumstances. The British [*sic*], in the general judgement of the eye-witnesses, performed with such lack of skill following the break-ins that timely counter-strokes would have ejected them once more, or at least held them.

"Already in my written order of 2 April, I had directed that the five divisions in reserve were to be moved to positions in rear of Groups

Souchez, Vimy and Arras. Headquarters Sixth Army was given the mission of ensuring that the divisions were called forward in good time. Army Headquarters demurred, reporting by signal on 5 April, which arrived here on 6 April, that, 'it did not consider it to be appropriate to move the divisions at the moment. It would disrupt training and lead to over-concentration of forces in the forward area.' I was of the opposite opinion and sent an order the same day by signal directing that the designated divisions, 'were to be moved forward immediately [original emphasis] into position behind your Group [sectors].' This order arrived at Sixth Army on 6 April.

"On 7 April the Chief of the General Staff of the Army Group [General der Infanterie Hermann von Kuhl] telephoned to check that the order was being carried out. From Major [Rudolf Ritter] von Xylander [Head of Operations Branch, Sixth Army] he received the information that, '18th Division and the Guards Reserve Corps would be moved forward today, the 26th [Division] tomorrow'. In the Sixth Army daily situation report concerning the state of reliefs and reserves as at the evening of 7 April, it was stated that the divisions, with the exception of 26th Infantry Division, were moving. Direction was immediately passed by telephone that this division, too, was to be moved up straight away. In actual fact the divisions did not all begin their movement in a timely manner. The Guards Reserve Corps did not even begin to move until 9 April. It has been reported verbally that this was due to a misunderstanding. A full report has been demanded; it has still not arrived.[4]

"It appears that during that time Headquarters Sixth Army did not expect the attack to occur as soon as it did, whereas I, on the basis of reports obtained directly from the individual Groups by officers of my staff, believed it to be imminent and this impression I communicated to Headquarters Sixth Army."

It is not possible to check every statement in the Army Group Commander's version of events. Inevitably there are some gaps in the documentary record and much was done by word of mouth: in person, by telephone or liaison officer visit. His diary is of some help in this respect. It is quite obvious, for example, that by 6 April Army Group Headquarters was convinced about the timing and extent of Allied plans. 'All the signs indicate that an attack against the Sixth Army on the Arras front is imminent',[5] he wrote that day. On the other hand, an objective reading of the Sixth Army Appreciation, classified secret, dated 7 April,[6] reveals a strange mixture of certainty at that level about some aspects of the situation, coupled with lack of clarity about others. It is a poor piece of staff work which, because it seemed to be fixated on only one possible Allied course of action, fails to draw the correct conclusions from intelligence available to the Headquarters. In short, it reveals confusion and uncertainty at a critical time, when decisive action was called for.

"Appreciation of the Situation

" . . . South of the [La Bassée] Canal enemy preparations for the offensive have made further progress. The artillery appears to have been reinforced, albeit only slightly. In the Loos salient there has been no increase in infantry. On the other hand, this is certainly the case south of Angres. Here there is no doubt that not only have all four Canadian divisions been deployed to the front, it is fairly certain that there is a new British division around Souchez. On the Canadian southern flank there are also probably new British troops. There are still dense concentrations of troops around Arras. Not until the area south of Beaurains are the divisional sectors wider. Here the enemy have closed up towards our *Siegfriedstellung* [Hindenburg Line] in a series of what have been, for them, costly front line actions, but they are not ready to launch an attack, despite having moved their artillery forward.

"Enemy planned destructive fire, which has involved very great quantities of ammunition, has badly damaged the positions from the *Gießler Höhe* to Tilloy. Initially the fire was directed mainly at the sectors west of Givenchy and Vimy and it is still heaviest there, reducing the position to craters in places. Since 4 April, it has spread to the entire front and has been directed onto the rear areas. Villages and towns far to the rear have become targets. In contrast counter-battery fire has remained low-key, not achieving results until 6 April and the losses were very meagre in relation to the expenditure of ammunition. Despite the brilliant defensive work of our pilots, the British airmen, who have been somewhat reserved in their operations, have begun to undertake long distance bombing sorties. There has not been much of an increase in balloons.[7]

"So far the enemy infantry have not been very active. [!] Their operations have been restricted to discovering what effect the British fire has had and what new forces we have deployed. There has been another increase in the number of enemy billets and other accommodation west of Arras. Nothing certain is known about fresh enemy reserves. It appears that cavalry is located west of Arras.

"Judging from this, there is now no doubt that the moment of the defensive battle is approaching; there could even be a major enemy offensive [original emphasis] imminent. It would be hard to understand if the British continued such heavy artillery operations, which have already been going on for a long time, without launching an attack. But the frontage of the attack from Angres to Tilloy is not wide enough for a major attempt at a breakthrough. A further extension is, of course, possible. This would be most probable in the Loos salient.

"In view of the overall situation the highly desirable introduction of 111th Infantry Division cannot take place.[8]

"Because the enemy are not deployed there [presumably around Loos] in the way they are further south and because it is improbable that they will suddenly deploy strong forces here for an attack, it must be assumed that the British wish, above all, to conduct a local [original emphasis] attack, in order to prepare favourable preconditions for a later break-through. The capture of Vimy Ridge would be a rewarding target in this context. Activity south of the Scarpe does not entirely support this, because it cannot be regarded as merely diversionary. The capture of Tilloy, without a further continuation of the offensive, would not have the significance of the occupation of Vimy Ridge.

"As a result, enemy intentions are still unclear, especially because there was a reduction in enemy activity all along the attack frontage on 7 April."

At the height of the crisis, Oberst Fritz von Loßberg, whose name was a byword for calm, energetic competence, was appointed Chief of Staff to Sixth Army. In passing on the news of his appointment, Ludendorff told him: 'His Majesty the Kaiser has appointed you as Chief of Staff Sixth Army. Take over your new duties immediately. Due to the large loss of terrain following the British [sic] major assault of 9 April the Sixth Army is in a dangerous situation. I trust you to master the situation.'[9] 'If anything at all can be done about it', remarked General der Infanterie Hermann von Kuhl to Crown Prince Rupprecht at the time, 'then he can do it.'[10] So it proved and within days the situation was back under control.

Later (although he had no need to do so) when he came to write his memoirs, Loßberg chose to spring to the defence of Sixth Army.

Oberst Fritz von Loßberg Chief of Staff Sixth Army[11]

"In order that the reasons for the failure of Sixth Army on 9 April may be properly understood, I should like to outline the following points, which are derived from my reading of the files of the Headquarters:

"From the beginning of March the Army had constantly reported that preparations were underway for a major British offensive directed against the Army. On 31 March it reported to the Army Group that the assault could begin at any time. Long before that Higher Headquarters had been informed repeatedly, not only about the large scale of enemy artillery operations, but also the exact situation as far as friendly destructive and defensive fire was concerned. Because sufficient quantities of ammunition were available the artillery battle was to be conducted without consideration of the amount of ammunition being expended. Heavy losses amongst the artillery did not occur until 9 April. Despite urgent representations, reinforcement of the artillery did not take place until 2 April. On 9 April there was still a shortfall of forty five of the approved batteries. Despite constant urging by Army Headquarters, gas shells required for the gassing of Arras had still not arrived on 9 April.

"On 5 April Army Headquarters sent the Army Group a very urgent request that the reinforcement divisions be moved forward by railway. This was not approved until the evening of 6 April and not until 7 April, by which time Sixth Army had reported that the offensive was imminent, did the Army Group direct that the following formations were to *march* [original emphasis] forward to Sixth Army:[12]

- 111th Division, located in the area of Group Loos. This division was so slow to get underway that by 9 April only four of its battalions, together with some batteries, had arrived on the battlefield.
- Guards Reserve Corps (1st Guards Reserve Division and 4th Guards Division) to move on 8 and 9 April, with leading elements along the line of the road Lille – Douai.
- 17th and 18th Divisions to move on 7 April into the Group Vimy area with leading elements at Douai. The 17th Division was to work on the construction of a rearward position, with one third [working] in the area of Sixth Army and two thirds in the area of First Army. The 17th Division was not to be at the disposal of Sixth Army until after it had been relieved by 47th Landwehr Division on 10 April.
- 26th Division to move on 8 April into the area of Group Arras with leading elements along the road Douai – Cambrai.

"Therefore, on 9 April, only the following [formations] were available: 111th Division, 1st Guards Reserve Division, 4th Guards Division, 18th and 26th Divisions. Of these five divisions, the 18th and 26th were temporarily subordinated to First Army. According to the Army Group order, all of the allocated divisions were not to be used for operational purposes, but were only to serve the *purpose of relief* [original emphasis]. Counter-strokes and counter-attacks were to be conducted by the forces already in the forward area from their own reserves.

"Headquarters Sixth Army had requested two divisions *more* [original emphasis] than had been approved. On 9 April, it had, at its disposal, no formed *Eingreif* [counter-stroke/counter-attack] divisions and merely two Infantry Regiments hastily assembled by the two northerly corps. The transfer of these two regiments from the northern flank to the main battlefield by truck had been thoroughly prepared and occurred during the morning of 9 April.

"According to the results of reconnaissance, twelve German divisions (with 108 battalions) deployed south of the canal at La Bassée were opposed by 19 British divisions (with 228 battalions). In addition the British artillery enjoyed a three-fold superiority. The battle situation of Sixth Army on 9 April was very serious, therefore. The British had already begun their preparations for battle at the end of March. To begin with these were directed primarily against the German artillery but, from the beginning of April, they were directed against the German infantry positions which were shot to ruins. On 8 April the British artillery bombardment increased to drum fire throughout the entire German battle zone. Almost all the German dugouts were destroyed and the wire obstacles were flattened. Simultaneously, all the German artillery positions from the right flank of Group Vimy to the left flank of Group Arras were drenched with gas. The effect of the gas was to hinder seriously both German artillery operations as well as the resupply of ammunition.

"At 5.00 am on 9 April very heavy drum fire came down came down on the German artillery and infantry positions either side of Arras, in the Givenchy – Neuville sector and on the northern flank of First Army. At 7.00 am, preceded everywhere by a rolling barrage, the British offensive opened against the entire Group Vimy front and between the Scarpe and Neuville. Group Souchez managed to hold on the *right hand half* [original emphasis] of its positions. In the centre and on the left flank of Group Vimy there were British breakthroughs to the west of Thélus and around St Laurent. Between the Scarpe and Tilloy, where numerous British tanks were deployed, there was considerable loss of terrain. At the breakthrough points the British rolled up the German battle lines and forced their way into Vimy and Farbus. Further south, our battle line was thrown back to the line Gavrelle – Roeux and to the village of Monchy. Vimy was retaken in a counter-attack. Only three battalions from 1st Bavarian Reserve Division and the leading regiment of 111th Division were able to participate in these attacks.

"During the evening of 9 April the front line ran: Givenchy – southern edge of Vimy – railway embankment Vimy to Farbus – southern edge of Bailleul – Gavrelle – Fampoux – west of Monchy – western edge Wancourt – Hindenburg Line. Sixth Army ordered that this line was to be held. All the divisions which had been allocated *only to conduct reliefs* [original emphasis] were called forward . . . When, on 11 April, the former chief of staff of Sixth Army, General von Nagel and his head of operations, Major von Xylander, were relieved, the Commander in Chief, Generaloberst Freiherr von Falkenhausen, tendered his resignation, but this was refused immediately and very graciously in a telegram from the Kaiser . . . "

This account, which reads as a robust defence of Sixth Army, flatly contradicts elements of Crown Prince Rupprecht's version of events. One of his contemporary diary notes, in which he expresses disquiet about the Sixth Army performance, is significant:

Crown Prince Rupprecht of Bavaria: Diary Entry 6 April 1917[13]

"In view of the forthcoming enemy offensive, Sixth Army was issued with five days' supply of ammunition. Although they were informed that they would constantly be adequately re-supplied with ammunition, so far they have delayed bringing down destructive fire against the enemy artillery and particularly against enemy trenches and approach routes to the main attack frontage. This is possibly because the infantry feared that it might encourage increased artillery fire against their trenches. As far as the gas ammunition, the allocation of which has been especially generous, is concerned, the Army High Command has directed that it is not to be dispersed amongst normal fire missions, but is to be used to gas the enemy batteries; the Army High Command has apparently received indications that the enemy intends to use gas against our batteries at the start of their attack."

Unfortunately, Loßberg does not list his sources and his account is not completely supported by the surviving documentary record. Other witnesses, whilst acknowledging the relieving role of the five divisions, did not regard that fact as incompatible with their potential use in counter-strokes or counter-attacks.

Generalleutnant Alfred Dieterich Commander 79th Reserve Brigade[14]

"On 6 April Headquarters Sixth Army was directed by Army Group Crown Prince Rupprecht to move *the divisions earmarked for the initial relief of the front line divisions*[15] closer to the threatened Angres – Wancourt sector. The move forward of these divisions, however, was so delayed that they were not in position to launch a counter-stroke on 9 April."

The question of reserves was also raised in a Sixth Army signal regarding the situation on 7 April, which in several ways was wide of the mark. Note that only one division is discussed. There, in its report to Army Group Crown Prince Rupprecht, part of its paragraph, 'Overall Impression', reads:[16]

" . . . An offensive, launched from south of Angres to the area of Neuville, may be imminent. South of Neuville Vitasse the enemy have worked their way forward, but are not ready as yet to launch an attack. On the other hand, it is still possible that the enemy will initially strive only to capture Vimy Ridge and not yet attempt to achieve a major break-through, for which the front to be attacked is too narrow. In this case, however, the extensive preparations against Tilloy are not entirely understandable, because a local attack here would not have the same significance as one against Vimy Ridge . . .

"It has not been established if the enemy have already concentrated strong reserves behind the front. First indications of the presence of cavalry were noted on 6 April, so it must be assumed that an attempt at a major breakthrough will be made fairly soon – in which case the attack frontage will be extended. This is most probable in the Loos Salient, so the Army requests that 111th Infantry Division be deployed there where it can prepare and shake out . . . "

The same appreciation also paints an over optimistic picture of the ability of the forward troops to withstand the forthcoming offensive. Commenting on the Allied counter-battery fire in the Vimy Area, it reported that,

> "Since 4 April heavy fire has extended all over the area, although the main weight has still been falling west of Givenchy – La Folie, where the positions are reduced to [clusters of] craters. Other sectors have also suffered severely and the positions are ripe for attack. The infantry is now in a difficult position. On the other hand counter-battery fire against our artillery has made little progress. Only during 6 April did the enemy achieve some success and that has had no effect on the battleworthiness of our artillery . . . [17]

> "The following divisions are fully battleworthy: 3rd Bavarian Infantry Division, 49th Reserve Division, 6th Bavarian Reserve Division, 7th and 8th Infantry Divisions, 80th Reserve Division, 56th Infantry Division, 16th Bavarian Infantry Division, 11th Infantry Division, 17th Reserve Division, 18th Reserve Division. As far as 79th Reserve Division, 1st Bavarian Reserve Division and 14th Bavarian Infantry Division are concerned, it cannot be denied that there has been a certain reduction in physical and mental robustness as a result of the bombardment of the past few days, *but the divisions are still sufficiently battleworthy to withstand a major assault* [author's emphasis].

It seems probable that this Sixth Army assessment drew on a report of Group Vimy dated 6 April:[18]

> "4 April may be regarded as the first day of the defensive battle. The enemy work of destruction and attrition, which has been reported previously has – together with simultaneous extension to the sector of 14th Bavarian Infantry Division – increased to such an extent that it is to be regarded as the preparation for an imminent attack. In all the sectors, the First and Intermediate Positions, namely the trenches and obstacles, have suffered very badly during the bombardment of the previous days. In that respect the position is ripe for assault.

> "On the other hand *the spirit of the troops manning the positions is still unbroken* [author's emphasis], as can be seen from their bearing when they beat off enemy thrusts and raids. So far the artillery positions have suffered relatively little damage. The opening of the enemy attack can only be a matter of days now."

It is clear that the Corps did not want to be seen to be in command of a group of formations whose morale and ability to resist was very low, so its report puts the best possible gloss on the situation. However, it is hard to see why Sixth Army further strengthened their version of events and so suggested to Headquarters Army Group Crown Prince Rupprecht that there was no immediate cause for concern when the offensive opened, especially when information must have been arriving from Group Souchez, based on sources such as the 16th Bavarian Infantry Division Weekly Report dated 5 April, which specifically drew attention to a morale problem within the division.[19] In one of his reports of 21 April, Crown Prince Rupprecht himself drew attention to the difficulty of assessing battleworthiness.[20]

> "A division, whose battleworthiness had previously only been viewed favourably [14th Bavarian Infantry Division] and which had spent three weeks behind the lines in February, failed rapidly at the moment of the enemy infantry attack. The reasons have not been fully established. This shows that the battleworthiness of the troops – divisional, army artillery and special formations – needs to be evaluated almost every day. The best judgement would be obtained by despatching officers from the command staffs forward. It is often difficult for commanders to be able to judge if complaints concerning exhaustion etc. of the troops are fully justified . . . "

Difficult it may have been, but it had to be achieved if defensive operations were to be conducted successfully in future and it was, in any case, no excuse, as the Army Group Commander made clear in his concluding remarks.

Crown Prince Rupprecht of Bavaria, Army Group Commander[21]

> "14th Bavarian Infantry Division has clearly failed; both the troops and the commanders.[22] As late as 7 April Headquarters [Sixth] Army stated that 14th Bavarian Infantry Division was, 'still battleworthy in the event of a major assault' and that 11th Infantry Division was 'fully battleworthy.' 14th Bavarian Infantry Division had performed well near Serre during the winter and had had a three week period of rest and recuperation in February. On 9 April it had kept its reserve back in Douai, that is to say, up to twenty kilometres behind the front line.
>
> "In conclusion, it must be stated that certain unfavourable circumstances, beyond the control of Sixth Army, had an influence on the course of events on 9 April, but that the most important reasons for the failure were:
>
> – Insufficient artillery action against the enemy
> – The failure to call forward reserves in accordance with orders[23]
>
> These two facts amount to serious negligence."

By early May further discussion about who, or what, was responsible for the initial setbacks during the Battle of Vimy Ridge and Arras more generally had run its course. Dwelling on failure was something in which the German army never indulged. The setbacks at Vimy Ridge and elsewhere during what was in fact only the first phase of the Arras offensive were behind them. The more important matter was to draw the lessons of Vimy and the weeks of fierce fighting which followed it. On 25 April Headquarters Army Group Crown Prince Rupprecht tasked all subordinate headquarters down to Group level to provide papers concerning lessons learned.[24] Group Vimy and Sixth Army in turn concentrated on placement of reserves, mobile defence in depth and aggressive use of mobile artillery, all of which had proved to be extremely successful on 23 and 28 April in particular.

Once all the material had been studied by the staff at the Headquarters of the Army Group, on 13 May Crown Prince Rupprecht signed off a paper on this subject, distributing it to the Army High Command, together with all Armies and Groups under his command. It is of considerable interest, because it contains the germs of several ideas which informed the German preparations for the fighting later that summer and autumn in the Messines – Ypres sector.

Crown Prince Rupprecht of Bavaria, Army Group Commander[25]

"The mobile offensive battle conducted in and around the depth of the positions contributed largely to the success of the battles near Arras on 3 May. In evaluating this method of defence, it must be borne in mind that it is based on a <u>particular</u>[26] situation and therefore may not simply be transferred to other cases. The battles for the strong *Siegfried-Stellung* [Hindenburg Line] are of a different nature to those in open territory astride the Arras – Cambrai road. Wherever the rear area limits the movement of reserves, such as is the case, for example, in and around Lens, the aim in some sectors must be standard defence . . .

"Mobile operations, which have now proved themselves in three severe battles, arose in an <u>emergency situation</u>, where it was necessary to prepare to conduct a defence against imminent attack in an area where little or no fixed defences were available. There was no question of being able to produce strong defences against which the enemy attacks could be broken – the time and necessary means were both lacking. In such a situation the defensive main effort is entirely dependent on the <u>fighting ability of the troops</u>. To that end they must be <u>deployed in depth</u> from the start.

"It is crucial, therefore, to create <u>a deep zone of defence</u> swiftly, ensuring that the lack of strength of individual positions is balanced out by <u>concealing</u> them as far as possible. All natural cover from view must be exploited then, when positions are improved and extended, obvious changes, such as vertical or sharp-angled constructions must be avoided. The enemy airmen must be given as few means of locating our positions as possible. This principle rules out the digging of <u>continuous trenches</u> in the forward area. Where they existed, especially in chalky soil, they acted as dangerous magnets for fire. On the other hand they made good dummy positions. My previous [directive] *Ic 2941 secret* disputed the necessity for continuous trench lines further to the rear. It is also the case that continuous trenches are not even required for conventional positional warfare . . .

"The creation of positions, which are as invisible as possible, not only provides a degree of protection in the event of planned enemy artillery fire; they also make enemy attacks thrusts in to the unknown. Instead of coming up against fixed, previously identified, lines they are confronted by mobile defenders who exploit <u>surprise</u> to counter them. It is clear that this requires <u>improved training of both our troops and their commanders</u>. Against the British [*sic*], in particular, these tactics offer the prospect of success, even when they have numerical superiority. During <u>training</u> in the rear areas, increased numbers of exercises in the context of offensive defence are going to have to be conducted. These must concentrate on the handling of detachments of all sizes on the ground, together with their deployment and launching to conduct swift counter-strokes. They will contribute to the further consolidation of our advantage in the standard of training of commanders and men. The troops have a real sense of this superiority and take pleasure in bringing it to bear against these, our most dangerous opponents.

"The original assumption that this style of battle would be accompanied by increased casualties has happily not been confirmed. The overall figures, with the exception of painfully high officer casualties have, in fact, been maintained within limits considerably lower than was the case during the Battle of the Somme. A summary of the comparison, which is just about to be distributed, will make this clear. It is a remarkable fact that we have taken far more prisoners than we have lost during these recent battles. The capture of entire trench garrisons in their dugouts played a large part in this!

"<u>Fighting in built up areas</u> on the other hand has proved once more to be costly. Despite all sacrifices it was often not possible under the weight of heavy enemy fire to hold on to villages when they were outflanked, nor to recapture them later. In each case it is important to decide if the possession of a particular village is of such importance that the defender is justified in deploying forces for village fighting which will generate high casualties. It would appear that in only a few instances is this the case and that, in other circumstances, it is better as far as possible not to incorporate villages into the defence plan. No definitive judgement can yet be made about this subject.

"Alongside the advantages of mobile defence, some <u>disadvantages</u> have been noted. All movement on and behind the positions is made considerably more difficult, but this can and must be accepted by battle-tested, well-trained troops. Because of the rigidity of the British artillery, careful study of its planned harassing fire means that it is often possible to identify strips of ground which are entirely free of artillery fire, or barely affected by it. This permits movement to continue even without approach trenches.

"Notice has already been given in my *Ic 2941 Secret* about the fact that the massing of previously spread out troops for counter-attacks creates a vulnerable moment of weakness. However, up to now the British have not succeeded in exploiting the situation by deploying swiftly and launching fresh attacks. Nevertheless, it is the bounden duty of commanders at all levels to act with all possible energy in such situations, in order to bring about a rapid return to defence in depth. Holding reserves near to the front, constant readiness for battle, lack of protected accommodation, the counter-attacks and the close-quarter battle will all lead to rapid wastage which cannot be avoided. It will be impossible, therefore, to avoid a quick turnover of reliefs. It must be borne in mind that this necessity should not be as a result of excessive casualties and rather be caused by exhaustion and intermingling of units. That way the relieved divisions can recuperate relatively rapidly.

"The artillery played a crucial role in the successes of 3 May. It supported the infantry excellently, causing the attackers very heavy casualties. It was better able to achieve this because it had not suffered badly from attrition. Right until the end it could call on eighty to ninety percent serviceable guns; whereas, during the Battle of the Somme, equipment losses often reached fifty per cent. The reasons for this striking outcome have not yet been established . . . A partial solution may be the fact that the operations of our fighter squadrons meant that the enemy only slowly established where our guns were located . . . it is unlikely that this error will be repeated. Certainly it is true that there has been a considerable increase in counter-battery fire during the past few days.

"In view of the hasty construction of positions which only offer cover from aerial observation, only frequent moves between alternate fire positions offer protection against planned bombardments. These must be so planned that fresh positions, which also offer cover from view, can be occupied without delay. The firing of rigid defensive fire missions, often accompanied by large, unfruitful expenditure of ammunition, have no place in this style of mobile battle where offensive spirit is to the fore. Defensive fire zones [each fired by a four gun battery] can be 250 to 300 metres wide, provided that divisions and Groups have mobile artillery reserves at their disposal – [a procedure] which has proved itself outstandingly during the recent battles.

"Mobile artillery reserves can carry out a wide variety of tasks. Their priorities are to deploy to counter major enemy break-in points, to fire on particularly favourable targets and to operate in support of our counter-attacks. In certain circumstances they may also be used to reinforce artillery in the line, or to fill gaps which have arisen during battles. On numerous occasions mobile artillery has been placed under command of the infantry commander responsible for the conduct of a major counter-attack. It is necessary to provide our infantry commanders with the opportunity to practise this behind the lines. It has proved successful to allocate about one section of guns and some ammunition wagons to each infantry regiment sector. These form the smallest components of the mobile artillery reserve and are intended to be used in the anti-tank role or for other opportunity targets.

"Successful deployment of mobile artillery demands careful preparation and, above all, detailed reconnaissance of the entire battlefield or approach routes and points of observation. Thought must also be given to the rapid re-supply of ammunition . . . Most of all, surprise deployment demands very skilful leadership and use of ground. Training behind the front and on artillery training areas must concentrate on this.

"Surprise intervention by mobile artillery against the British [sic] will always hold the promise of success; British [sic] fire control has repeatedly proved itself to be too inflexible to be able to counter swiftly and surely enemies who appear unexpectedly."

Many of these ideas were those of Oberst Fritz von Loßberg who, having overcome the crisis of confidence in the staff at Sixth Army and successfully masterminded the defensive battle during the remainder of the Battle of Arras, until it ground to a halt later in the spring, was moved on 13 June to take over as Chief of Staff Fourth Army. There he applied the lessons bought in blood on and around Vimy Ridge earlier in the year to the problems of the *Flandernschlacht* [Third Battle of Ypres], which was probably his defensive masterpiece.

Aggressive defence in depth, careful placement of well-trained *Eingreif* Divisions and deployment of mobile artillery all played an important role for the defence during the three months leading up to the Battle of the Menin Road Ridge in late September 1917. There, large-scale use of 'Bite and Hold' tactics which had been premiered at Vimy Ridge and practised once more at Hill 70, stymied the new procedures and posed the German defenders serious problems for the remainder of that battle. How ironic that the methods that had led to the triumph at Vimy in April should provide the key once more to the capture of Passchendaele by the Canadian Corps in November.

Notes

1. Kronprinz Rupprecht *Mein Kriegstagebuch Zweiter Band* p 141 In the event von Falkenhausen was replaced on 23 April by General der Infanterie **Otto** von Below (not to be confused with General der Infanterie **Fritz** von Below, successively Commander of Second then First Army).
2. Kriegsarchiv München Heeresgruppe Kronprinz Rupprecht Bd 93 *79. Reserve Division Ia/No 546/17. geh. Zu H.Gr.Kr.R.Ic/2850 geh. A.O.K. No 313/4* Div.St.Qu., den 22.4.1917

3. Kriegsarchiv München Heeresgruppe Kronprinz Rupprecht Bd 93 Oberkommando Ia/No. 2857 geh. H.Qu., den 21. April 1917

4. Here the Crown Prince was striving to portray his own interventions in the best possible way. During the evening of 9 April, he had written in his diary (Kronprinz Rupprecht *Mein Kriegstagebuch Zweiter Band* p 135): 'I cannot spare myself the rebuke that I ought to have ordered the Commander, Sixth Army to move his reserves closer.' He does not expand on this remark, but he may have meant that although he had directed that reserves were to be moved forward, he may not have specified how close they were to be placed. He returned to the subject the following day (Kronprinz Rupprecht *Mein Kriegstagebuch Zweiter Band* p 138): 'To ease my conscience, I called for the orders relating to the move forward of reserves to be placed in front of me. From [study of them] it transpired that on the evening of 6 April Sixth Army sent a report, which did not arrive at the headquarters of the Army Group until the morning of 7 April, stating that in order not to interfere with the training of the divisions located more to the rear and in order not to concentrate too many men in the forward villages, they did not wish to call forward their allocated divisions. At that I replied on 7 April that they were, nevertheless, to call forward the Guards Reserve Corps and IX Corps. Of course nobody could have anticipated that the expected attack would gain ground as rapidly as it did.'

5. Kronprinz Rupprecht *Mein Kriegstagebuch Zweiter Band* p 131

6. Kriegsarchiv München 1.Res.Korps Bd 135 Oberkommando der 6. Armee Ia No. 1500. *Beurteilung der Lage 7.4.1917*

7. This brief comment suggests that Commander of Air Operations 6, whose branch formed part of Headquarters Sixth Army, had very little input into this report. His Weekly Report for 31 March – 7 April 1917 contains several clues about future enemy intentions, as derived from analysis of Allied air operations. These include the very significant fact that, 'Enemy air operations in the Lens – Arras area have increased [original emphasis] even more. There is hardly any activity [original emphasis] on other sectors of the front.' See Kriegsarchiv München 1.R.Korps Bd. 135 Kommandeur der Flieger 6 Nr. 25500 *Wochentlicher Taetigkeitsbericht vom 31.3. mit 7.4.1917* A.H.Qu., den 7.4.1917.

8. This remark, which is not qualified, is the only mention of any type of the uncommitted divisions in the area.

9. Loßberg: *Meine Tätigkeit im Weltkriege 1914–1918* p 280

10. Kronprinz Rupprecht *Mein Kriegstagebuch Zweiter Band* p 140

11. Loßberg: *Meine Tätigkeit im Weltkriege 1914–1918* pp 284 – 287

12. It is difficult to interpret why Loßberg chose to emphasise this word. The original was *vormaschieren,* which is a neutral verb meaning no more than 'to advance' or 'to move forward'. It has been translated here as 'march', because the context – the word juxtaposed with the earlier Sixth Army request for railway transport – seems to imply that the request was denied and that the movement was to be conducted on foot. However it is stressed that this is no more than an informed guess.

13. Kronprinz Rupprecht *Mein Kriegstagebuch Zweiter Band* p 131

14. Dieterich: *Die 79. Reserve-Division in der Schlacht auf der Vimy-Höhe/April 1917* p 10

15. Author's emphasis. The original describes them as, *die zur ersten Ablösung der Frontdivisionen bestimmten Divisionen.*

16. Kriegsarchiv München HGr Rupprecht Bd 122 *AOK 6 No 239 7/4 Beurteilung der Lage*

17. This statement concerning the relative ineffectiveness of Canadian counter-battery fire during most of the bombardment is also confirmed by Oberst Graf von Zech auf Neuhosen, Bavarian Artillery Commander Nr. 13 from 26 Feb 17 in his report 1368/I to 1st Bavarian Reserve Division dated 4.6.1917 : Kriegsarchiv München OP 38887: '. . . It was striking that our battery positions were not brought under definite destructive fire. Instead they were only subjected to the same heavy harassing fire which was spread all over the rear areas. Not until 4.4 were some battery positions brought under planned bombardment, which increased on 6.4 to massed fire directed against the batteries and Farbus [village]. The two final days of the bombardment were marked by a noticeable slackening of enemy artillery fire; not until late afternoon on 8.4 did the enemy fire begin to come down heavily once more against the Intermediate and Second Positions. The batteries were subject only to harassing fire.' This statement is borne out by the weapons state on 9 April as reported in the same reference. Serviceable were: field guns 19 from 24; light field howitzers 17 from 24; heavy field howitzers 14 from 16; heavy howitzers 6 from 6; 100 mm guns 3 from 4; 120 mm guns 3 from 4; heavy 150 mm guns 3 from 3. Furthermore, two additional field howitzer batteries arrived as replacements/reinforcements during the night 8/9 April, but had not had time to range in prior to the attack. Each gun had two days' stocks of ammunition dumped forward on the positions. On the 79th Reserve Division and 1st Bavarian Reserve Division fronts the weak response by the defending artillery on 9 April had little to do with pre-battle counter-battery fire and a great deal to do with the quality of neutralising fire that morning and the speed with which the gun lines, many of which had, perforce, to be located west of Vimy Ridge, were overrun by the Canadian infantry. The inability of the defence to get more of the guns away, was attributed to the highly lethal gassing of the area when the attack was launched, which killed hundreds of draught horses.

18. Kriegsarchiv München 1 R. Korps Bd. 147 *Tätigkeit des General-Kdos I. Bayer.Res.Korps vor der Schlacht bei Arras und am 9. und 10.4.1917 2.7.1917*

19. Kriegsarchiv München 16. Inf. Div. Bd. 4 Bayer 16. Infanterie-Division Ia,. No. 1767 *Wochenbericht für die Zeit vom 29. März 1917 – 5. April 1917* Division.St.Qu., den 5. April 17

20. Kriegsarchiv München HGr Rupprecht Bd 93 Oberkommando Ia/No. 2853 geh. Streng Geheim! *Betreff: Erfahrungen u. Folgerungen aus den Kämpfen bei Arras am 9.4.17* H.Qu., den 21. April 1917

21. Kriegsarchiv München Heeresgruppe Kronprinz Rupprecht Bd 93 Oberkommando Ia/No. 2857 geh. H.Qu., den 21. April 1917

22. Nevertheless this judgement does not seem to have affected the divisional commander's subsequent career. Generalleutnant Otto Ritter von Rauchenberger was honoured several times by Bavaria. He also received the *Pour le Mérite* on 6 September 1917 and an oak leaf to it on 19 October 1918.

23. General der Infanterie Hermann von Kuhl, admittedly Chief of Staff to Crown Prince Rupprecht and therefore in this particular instance not an entirely independent witness, remained of this opinion in later years. Virtually all of his post-war judgements in *Der Weltkrieg 1914/1918* are sound. His considered view, expressed in 1929, was that, '. . . the main reason for the failure was the fact that the reserves were held too far to the rear [original emphasis] and therefore were not in a position to launch counter-strokes, despite the fact that Crown Prince Rupprecht had pressed Sixth Army several times to move them closer. Despite all

the indicators, the [Army] believed that the offensive was not imminent.' See *Der Weltkrieg* pp 85–86

24. Kriegsarchiv München 1.R.Korps Bd 12 Gruppe Vimy General-Kdo I Bayer.Res.Korps Chef No 16 922 Zu H.Gr. Ic. No 2881 v. 25.4.17 *Erfahrungen aus den Kämpfen bei Arras am 9., 23. u. 28.5.17* H.Qu., 30.4.1917

25. Kriegsarchiv München A.O.K. 6 Bd. 419 Heeresgruppe Kronprinz Rupprecht Oberkommando <u>Ic No. 3023 geh</u>. *Weitere Erfahrungen aus den Kämpfen bei Arras* H.Qu., den 13. 5. 1917

26. All underlined words are emphasised in the original.

German – British Comparison of Ranks

Generalfeldmarschall	Field Marshal
General der Infanterie	General of Infantry ⎫ General
General der Kavallerie	General of Cavalry ⎭

N.B. The holder of any of these last two ranks was at least a corps commander and might have been an army commander.

Generalleutnant	Lieutenant General.

N.B. The holder of this rank could be the commander of a formation ranging in size from a brigade to a corps. From 1732 onwards Prussian officers of the rank of Generalleutnant or higher, who had sufficient seniority, were referred to as *'Exzellenz'* [Excellency].

Generalmajor	Major General
Oberst	Colonel
Oberstleutnant	Lieutenant Colonel
Major	Major
Hauptmann	Captain
Rittmeister	Captain (mounted unit such as cavalry, horse artillery or transport) It was also retained by officers of this senority serving with the German Flying Corps
Oberleutnant	Lieutenant
Leutnant	Second Lieutenant
Feldwebelleutnant	Sergeant Major Lieutenant
Offizierstellvertreter	Officer Deputy

N.B. This was an appointment, rather than a substantive rank.

Feldwebel	Sergeant Major
Wachtmeister	Sergeant Major (mounted unit)
Vizefeldwebel	Staff Sergeant
Vizewachtmeister	Staff Sergeant (mounted unit)

Sergeant	Sergeant
Unteroffizier	Corporal
Korporal	Corporal (Bavarian units)
Gefreiter	Lance Corporal

Musketier	
Grenadier	
Garde-Füsilier	N.B. These ranks all equate to Private
Füsilier	Soldier (infantry). The differences in
Schütze	nomenclature are due to tradition, the
Infanterist	type of unit involved, or the class of
Jäger	conscript to which the individual
Wehrmann	belonged.
Landsturmmann	
Soldat	
Ersatz-Reservist	

Kriegsfreiwilliger	Wartime Volunteer. This equates to Private Soldier.

Kanonier	Gunner	
Pionier	Sapper	N.B. These ranks
Fahrer	Driver	all equate to
Hornist	Trumpeter	Private Soldier.
Tambour	Drummer	

Medical Personnel

Oberstabsarzt	Major (or higher)
Stabsarzt	Captain
Oberarzt	Lieutenant
Assistenzarzt	Second Lieutenant
	N.B. These individuals were also referred to by their appointments; for example, *Bataillonsarzt* or *Regimentsarzt* [Battalion or Regimental Medical Officer]. Such usage, which varied in the different contingents which made up the imperial German army, is no indicator of rank.
Sanitäter	Medical Assistant ⎱ N.B. These two ranks both
Krankenträger	Stretcherbearer ⎰ equate to Private Soldier.

Frequently the prefix 'Sanitäts-' appears in front of a normal NCO rank, such as Gefreiter or Unteroffizier. This simply indicates that a man of that particular seniority was part of the medical services.

German Outline Order of Battle 9 April 1917

(Angres to the Scarpe)

Army Group Crown Prince Rupprecht
Commander: Generalfeldmarschall Crown Prince Rupprecht of Bavaria
Chief of Staff: Generalleutnant Hermann von Kuhl

Sixth Army
Commander: Generaloberst Ludwig Freiherr von Falkenhausen
Chief of Staff: Generalmajor Karl Freiherr von Nagel zu Aichberg

Group Souchez (VIII Reserve Corps)
Commander: General der Infanterie Georg Karl Wichura

16th Bavarian Infantry Division
Commander: Generalmajor Arnold Ritter von Möhl

9th Bavarian Infantry Brigade
Commander: Generalmajor August Großmann

Artillery Command 16
Commander: Generalmajor Treutlein-Mördes

Bavarian Infantry Regiment 11
Commander: Major Maximilian Ritter von Braun

Bavarian Infantry Regiment 14
Commander: Oberstleutnant Prenner

Bavarian Reserve Infantry Regiment 21
Commander: Oberstleutnant Walter Freiherr von Ruffin

Bavarian Field Artillery Regiment 8
Commander: Major z.D. Stöber

Group Vimy (I Bavarian Reserve Corps)
Commander: General der Infanterie Karl Ritter von Fasbender
Chief of Staff: Major Hermann Ritter von Lenz

79th Reserve Division
Commander: Generalleutnant Ernst August Marx von Bacmeister

79th Reserve Brigade
Commander: Generalleutnant Alfred Dieterich

79th Reserve Field Artillery Brigade
Commander: Oberst Bleidorn

Reserve Infantry Regiment 261
Commander: Oberstleutnant Wilhelm von Goerne

Reserve Infantry Regiment 262
Commander: Major Freiherr von Rotenhan

Reserve Infantry Regiment 263
Commander: Oberstleutnant von Behr

Reserve Field Artillery Regiment 63
2nd Battalion Field Artillery Regiment 69
Commander: Major Cropp

1st Bavarian Reserve Division
Commander: Generalmajor Friedrich Freiherr von Pechmann

1st Bavarian Reserve Brigade
Commander: Generalmajor Lamprecht

Artillery Command 13
Commander: Oberst Graf von Zech auf Neuhofen

Bavarian Reserve Infantry Regiment 1
Commander: Oberstleutnant Otto Ritter von Füger

Bavarian Reserve Infantry Regiment 2
Commander: Oberstleutnant Ernst Ritter von Brunner

Bavarian Reserve Infantry Regiment 3
Commander: Major Anton Meier

Bavarian Reserve Field Artillery Regiment 1
Commander: Major Werner Freiherr von und zu Auffeß

14th Bavarian Infantry Division
Commander: Generalleutnant Otto Ritter von Rauchenberger

8th Bavarian Infantry Brigade
Commander: Generalmajor Karl von Reck

Artillery Command 14
Commander: Oberst Gartmayr

Bavarian Infantry Regiment 4
Commander: Major Hoderlein

Bavarian Infantry Regiment 8
Commander: Oberst von Rücker

Bavarian Infantry Regiment 25
Commander: Oberstleutnant Seemüller

Bavarian Field Artillery Regiment 23
Commander: Oberstleutnant Theodor Ritter von Hermann

Other assets of Group Vimy included Corps artillery – 9th and 69th Field Artillery Regiments; 25th and 66th Reserve Field Artillery Regiments and three batteries of 300 mm naval guns; engineer assets and machine gun sharp shooter detachments.

Bibliography

Unpublished Sources

Kriegsarchiv München

HS 1962	*Das kgl. bayr. 2. Infanterie-Regiment 'Kronprinz' am 28. Januar 1916 bei Vimy.*
HS 1992/3	*Die 5. Bayerische Reserve-Division Oktober 1914 bis Mai 1915*
HS 1992/5	*Das VIII (Rheinische) Armeekorps auf der Vimyhöhe vom 15. Mai bis 15./19/ Juni 1915*
HS 1992/10	*Schlußbetrachtung zur Ersten Schlacht bei Arras*
OP 38887	*Nr. 9340 1. Res.Inf.Brigade Gefechtsbericht über die Ereignisse am 9., 10. und 11. April 1917 Brig.St.Qu., 6.6.1917*
OP 38887	*Bayer.Art.Kdeur.Nr.13 <u>Nr. 1368 I</u> An <u>K.B.1.Res.Division Betreff:</u> Schlacht am 9.4.1917. zu Div.V.v. 2.6.17 Nr. 4151/I St.Qu., 4.6.1917.*
H Gr Ruppr. Bd 93	*aok 6. 541 11/4 = gruppe vimy meldet = an heeresgruppe kr rupprecht = voraussichtliche verluste in den kaempfen vom 9/4 17*
H Gr Ruppr. Bd 93	*Heeresgruppe Kronprinz Rupprecht Oberkommando Ia No. 2853 geh. <u>Streng Geheim!</u> Betreff: <u>Erfahrungen u. Folgerungen aus den Kämpfen bei Arras am 9.4.17.</u> An A.O.K. 2, 4, 6 H.Qu., 21.4.1917*
H Gr Ruppr. Bd 93	*Heeresgruppe Kronprinz Rupprecht Oberkommando <u>Ia/No. 2857 geh</u>. H.Qu., den 21. April 1917 An O.H.L.*
H Gr Ruppr. Bd 122	*Beurteilung der Lage 24/2 17 6. Armee*
H Gr Ruppr. Bd 122	*Beurteilung der Lage 3/3 17 6. Armee*
H Gr Ruppr. Bd 122	*AOK 6 Beurteilung der Lage 10.3 17.*
H Gr Ruppr. Bd 122	*AOK 6 No 239 7/4 Beurteilung der Lage*
H Gr Ruppr. Bd 149	*Oberkommando 6. Armee. Ia No. 550 g Betreff: Unternehmen gegen die englischen Stellungen östlich Souchez A.H.Qu., den 14.3.1917*
AOK 6 Bd 419	*Heeresgruppe Kronprinz Rupprecht Oberkommando. Ic No 3023 geh. Betreff: Weitere Erfahrungen aus den Kämpfen bei Arras H.Qu., den 13.5.1917*

AOK 6 Bd 432	*Nachrichtenoffizier A.O.K. 6 Geheim! 3.1.17*
AOK 6 Bd 432	*A.O.K. 6 1a 85041 Betreff: Offensivmöglichkeiten der Entente A.H.Qu., den 5.1.17*
AOK 6 Bd 433	*Aussagen eines Mannes des I.R. 97 (153. Brig.) 77. Div. übergelaufen am 19.1 südwestlich Givenchy hart südlich Höhe 119 N.O. A.O.K. 6 B. Nr. 4048 A.H.Qu., 22.1.1916.*
AOK 6 Bd 433	*Aussagen von 82 Gefangenen vom I.R. 226 (139. Brig.) 70 Div. N.O. A.O.K. 6. B. No. 4202 A.H.Qu. 9.2.1916*
AOK 6 Bd 433	*Aussagen von 11 englischen Gefangenen der 170. Mining Comp. Roy. Engineers N.O. A.O.K. 6. B. No. 4459 22.3.16*
AOK 6 Bd 433	*Aussage eines Mannes v. V/S.Staffordsh. (D Komp.) 137. Brig. 46. Div. N.O. A.O.K. B. No 4533 A.H.Qu. 6.4.1916*
AOK 6 Bd 433	*Aussagen eines Gefreiten vom VI/Seaforth Highl. (A Komp.): NO A.O.K. 6 B. No 4677 A H Qu 29.4.1916*
AOK 6 Bd 433	*Aussagen von 20 Gefangenen. Gefangen genommen am 11.V.16. 8 Uhr abends, oestlich Vermelles N.O. A.O.K. 6 B. No. 4792 13. Mai.1916*
AOK 6 Bd 433	*Aussagen von 4 Gefangenen vom 58. Inf. Batl. (c-Komp) 7. kan. Brig 3.kan Div A.O.K. 6. B. Nr. 7400. 30.11.16*
AOK 6 Bd 433	*Aussagen von 2 Gefangenen vom 49. Inf. Batl. (a-Komp) 9. kan. Brig 4.kan Div A.O.K. 6. B. Nr. 7757. 24.12.16*
AOK 6 Bd 433	*Aussagen von 1 Leutnant und 2 Mann vom 46. Inf. Batl. (South Saskatchewan) 10. kan. Brig 3.kan Div A.O.K. 6. B. Nr. 7616. 15.12.16*
AOK 6 Bd 433	*Aussagen eines Ueberläufers vom R.Can.Regt. 3.kan.Div. gefangen genommen am 12.2.17 nordöstlich Neuville-St.Vaast A.O.K. 6. B. Nr. 8581 A.H.Qu., den 2.3.17*
AOK 6 Bd 433	*Aussagen von 2 Uoffz. Und 6 Mann vom 75. Inf. Batl (b u. c Komp) 11. kan. Brig. 2 Uoffz. Und 8 Mann vom 72. Inf. Batl. (a u. b Komp) 12. kan. Brig. 4. kan. Div. gefangen genommen am 1.3 morgens bei dem englischen Unternehmen südwestlich Givenchy-en-Gohelle. A.O.K. 6 B. Nr. 8590 A.H.Qu., den 3. März 1917*
AOK 6 Bd 433	*Aussagen von 2 Mann vom 43. Inf. Batl. 9. kan. Brig. 3. Kan. Division gefangen genommen bei dem deutschen Patrouillenunternehmen am 15.3*

	morgens nordoestlich Neuville-St-Vaast bei La
	Folie Ferme. A.O.K. B. Nr. 8752 A.H.Qu., 16/3.17
AOK 6 Bd 433	*Aussagen von 2 Verwundeten des <u>VIII/Arg. u.</u>*
	<u>*Suth'd Highrs.*</u> *152 <u>Brig. 51 Div.</u> gefangen*
	genommen am 17.3.17 nordöstlich Roclincourt
	A.O.K. 6 B. Nr. 8783 A.H.Qu., den 18.3.17
AOK 6 Bd 433	<u>*Aussagen*</u> *von 4 Mann des 31. Batls. <u>6. kan. Brig 2.</u>*
	<u>*kan. Div.*</u> *gefangen genommen im Abscnitt A 3 zu*
	beiden Seiten der Strasse Neuville-Thélus A.O.K. 6
	B. Nr. 8950 A.H.Qu., 1.4.17
AOK 6 Bd 433	*Ergänzende Aussagen der am 29.3 abends nördlich*
	der Strasse Neuville-Thélus gefangen genommen 4
	Mann vom 31. Inf. Batl. <u>6. kan. Brig 2. kan. Div.</u>
	gefangen A.O.K. 6 B. Nr. 8961 A.H.Qu., 2.4.17
I. Res. Korps Bd 1	*Kriegstagebuch 1.3.17*
I. Res. Korps Bd 12	*Gruppe Vimy General-Kdo I.Bayer.Res.Korps Chef*
	No. 16 922 An A.O.K. 6. Zu H.Gr. Ic No. 2881 v.
	25.4.17 H.Qu., 30.4.1917
I. Res. Korps Bd 135	*Oberkommando der 6. Armee. <u>Ia No 1500.</u>*
	Beurteilung der Lage A.H.Qu., den 7.4.1917
I. Res. Korps Bd 135	*Kommandeur der Flieger 6 Nr. 25500.*
	<u>*Wochentlicher Taetigkeitsbericht*</u> *vom 31.3. mit*
	7.4.1917 A.H.Qu., den 7.4.1917
I. Res. Korps Bd 147	*Generalkommando VI. Reservekorps: Kurze*
	Charakteristik des Abschnitts des VI. R.Ks. (Stand
	vom 10.1.1917)
I. Res. Korps Bd 147	*Betreff: Vorbereitungen für die Abwehrschlacht*
	General-Kdo I Bayer.Res.Korps. Abteilung Ia No.
	13 720 K.H.Qu., 21.3.1917
I. Res. Korps Bd 147	*Tätigkeit des General-Kdos I. Bayer.Res.Korps vor*
	der Schlacht bei Arras und am 9. und 10.4.1917
	Gruppe Vimy General-Kdo I.Bayer.Res.Korps
	Abteilg.Ia No. 21 600 H.Qu., 2.7.1917
16. Inf. Div. Bd 4	*Ia No. 1260 WOCHENBERICHT für die Zeit vom 8.3.*
	1917 – 15. März 1917
16. Inf. Div. Bd 4	*Mineur-Kommandeur 16. b.I.D. Wochenbericht*
	(Beurteilung der Lage) zu Div. Kdo. Verfg. V.
	9.2.17. Nr. 2173.Z.4 28. 3
16. Inf. Div. Bd 4	*Mineur-Kommandeur 16. b.I.D. Wochenbericht*
	über die Arbeitstätigkeit im Minenkrieg für die Zeit
	vom 22.3. bis 28.3.17 Nr. 161/III 28.3
16. Inf. Div. Bd. 4	Bayer 16. Infanterie-Division Ia,. No. 1767
	Wochenbericht für die Zeit vom 29. März 1917 – 5.
	April 1917 Div.St.Qu., den 5. April 17

1. Res. Div. Bd 20	*79th Reserve Division Nachrichtenblatt* *7.3.1917(173); 10.3.1917(235); 11.3.1917(257);* *12.3.1917(277); 13.3.1917(299); 21.3.1917(92);* *22.3.1917 (116); 29.3.1917(424); 30.3.1917 (454);* *7.4.1917(343)*
1. Res. Div. Bd 21	*Divisionsbefehl 8.00, 9.00, 11.00 und 11.45 am,* *12.00, 3.00 and 10.50 pm 1.Reserve Division* *Division. St. Qu., 9.4.1917*
1. Res. Div. Bd 45	*N.O. Armee-Oberkommando 6. Armee B. Nr. 3509* *16.11.15 Auszug aus dem Notizbuch eines* *Offiziers.*
1. Res. Div. Bd 45	*Vernehmung des am 31.5.15 . . . übergelaufenen* *Turkos Mohamed ben Hamed . . . Br. B. No 1032* *A.H.Qu. 2.6.15*
1. Res. Div. Bd 45	*Aussagen von 4 Ueberläufern des frz. I.R. 78 (45.* *Brig. 23. Div.) A.H. Qu. 20.11.15*
1. Res. Div. Bd 45	*Aussagen eines Mannes des I.R. 63 (45.Brig) 23.* *Division übergelaufen am 19.1 nachts nördlich* *Ecurie N.O. A.O.K. 6 B. Nr. 4058 22.1.1916*
1. Res. Div. Bd 45	*Ausssagen der am 23.1. früh nördlich Roclincourt* *gefangenen 71 Franzosen des I.R. 107 (46. Brig.)* *23. Div. N.O. A.O.K. 6 B. Nr. 4079. 26.1.1916*
1. Res. Div. Bd 45	*Aussage eines Überläufers vom I.R. 88 (34.* *Division) XVII A.K. N.O. IV., I. Bayer. U. IX Res.* *Korps 22. Januar 1916*
1. Res. Div. Bd 45	*Aussagen von 17 Gefangenen vom I.R. 226 (139.* *Brig.) 70 Div. N.O. A.O.K. 6 B. Nr 4118 A.H.Qu.* *31.1.1916*
1. Res. Div. Bd 45	*Aussagen von 1 Sergeanten, 1 U'ffz. & 10 Mann* *vom V/Gordon Highl. (d comp) 153 Brig. 51* *Division 28.III.1916*
1. Res. Div. Bd 45	*I. Vorläufiges Ergebnis der Vernehmung* *nachstehend aufgeführter am 21. Mai östlich* *'Cabaret Rouge' gef. genommener Engländer. N.O.* *A.O.K. 6. B. No 4860 23 Mai 1916*
1. Res. Div. Bd 45	*Aussagen von Mannschaften von Sonder-* *Formationen, gefangen genommen am 21.5.16* *östlich Cabaret Rouge N.O. A.O.K. 6. B. No. 4863* *24.5.16*
1. Res. Div. Bd 45	*II. Zusammenfassende Ergänzung (zu B. No 4860)* *der vorläufigen Vernehmung (I. vom. 23.5) von* *gefangenen Offizieren und Manschaften vom VI.,* *VII., VIII., and XX /London R. N.O. A.O.K. 6. B. No.* *4870 25 Mai 1916*

1. Res. Div. Bd 45	*III. Zusammenfassende Ergänzung (zu B No 4860/63 und 4870) der vorläufigen Vernehmung (I. vom 23.5.) von 11 Gefangenen vom X/Cheshire, (D-Comp)*
1. Res. Div. Bd 45	*Nachtrag zu den Aussagen der am 21. Mai östlich Cabaret-Rouge gefangen genommen englischen Offiziere. N.O. A.O.K. 6 B. No. 4884 25.V.1916*
1. Res. Div. Bd 45	*Aussagen von 3 Telephonisten vom VIII/London R. (140. Brig. 47. Division) gefangen genommen am 21 Mai 16 östlich Cabaret-Rouge N.O. A.O.K. 6. B. No. 4892 26. Mai 1916*
1. Res. Div. Bd 45	*II Nachtrag zu den Aussagen der am 21 Mai 1916 östlich Cabaret Rouge gefangen genommen englischen Offiziere. (I Nachtrag v 25 5 B No 4884) N.O. A.O.K. 6 B No 4909 29 Mai 1916*
1. R.I.B. Bd. 29	*Gefechtsnotizen der 1. Reserve-Infanterie-Brigade vom 9. April 1917*
1. R.I.B. Bd. 30	*Zu Nr. 127 a. Bayer.Res.Inf.Regt.Nr.3 Gefechtsbericht über die Kämpfe am 9. und 10. April 1917.*
1. R.I.B. Bd. 37	*Aussagen eines Überläufers vom R.Can.Rgt., 7.kan.Brig. 3.kan.Div. gefangen genommen am 12.2.17 nordöstlich Neuville-St. Vaast. A.O.K. 6 B. Nr. 8353 A.H.Qu., 13.2.17*
1. R.I.B. Bd. 37	*Aussagen eines Sergeanten vom 44. Inf.Batl. (Winnipeg) 10. kan. Brig. 4.kan. Div. gefangen genommen mit 4. Schwerverwundeten vom 46. u. 50. Inf.Batl der eigenen Brigade, am 13.2. morgens bei dem englischen Unternehmen südöstl. Souchez. Nachrichtenoffizier A.O.K. 6 B. Nr. 8363 A.H.Qu., 14.2.17*
11. I R Bd 16	*Bayerische 16 Infanterie-Division: Divisions Befehl 590/I 20 Februar 1917*
11. I R Bd 16	*11. Infanterie Regiment An 9. Infanterie Brigade Betreff: Kampfabschnitt Döberitz R.St.Qu., 20.2.17*
11. I R Bd 16	*Nr. 1088a K Bayer.9.Inf-Brigade An den Herrn Kommandeur K.Bayer.16.Infanterie Division Betreff: Kräfteinsatz für München Brig.St.Qu., den 5.4.1917*
14. I R Bd. 10	*Generalkommando VI.Res.Korps. Abt. Ia. Nr. 993 Zum Schreiben v. 1.4.17 Ia. Nr. 1680 An 16.bay.Inf. Division. K.H.Qu., den 2.4.1917*
14. I R Bd. 10	*16.Infanterie-Division 3.4.17 Nr. I/1735 G.R. zur 9.Inf.Brigade*

14. I R Bd. 10	*K.B.9.Infanterie-Brigade 4.4.17 Nr. 1074 a*
14. I R Bd. 10	*Betreff: Unternehmen 'München' Tritt anstelle des Befehls vom 26.3.17 Nr. 971a, der zu vernichten ist. Nr. 1075a. K.Bayer.9.Infanterie-Brigade Br.St.Qu., den 4.4.1917*
R.I.R. 3 Bd. 3	*Nr 5154 Bayer. Res.Inf.Regt Nr 3 An K.1.Res. Brigade 6.4.1917 5.30 abds*
R.I.R. 3 Bd. 3	*Nr. 2190 R.I.R. 3 An 1.Res.Inf.Brig. Betreff: Kampfwert der Truppe 8.4.17*
R.I.R. 16	*Übergabe des Abschnitts Fischer an II. b.R.I.R. 16 am 18.10.16*
Pi. Btl 1 Bd 4	*Erfahrungen im Minenkrieg No. 2271. Kommandeur der Pioniere I.B.A.K. 24.10.15*
Pi. Btl 1 Bd 5	*2. Feld-Pion.Komp. I B.A.K Beilage: 34a. 24.1.1916 Betreff: Teilnahme d. 2.F.Pion.Kp an der Unternehmung 'Rupprecht' I am 23.1.16*
Pi. Btl. 1 Bd 5	*Kommandeur der Pioniere I.B.A.K. An General der Pioniere b.A.O.K. 6. Betreff: <u>Horchgeräte 14.2.1916</u>*
Pi. Btl 1 Bd 5	*Bildung der Mineur-Kompanie No. 3 I. B.A.K. No. 5459 7.4.1916*
Pi. Btl. 17 Bd 6	*Kommandeur der Pioniere I. B.R.K. Abendmeldungen v. 5./6.5.15 6.5.15 und 17.5.15*
Pi. Btl. 17 Bd 7	*Betreff: Stellungsbau 1. Bayer. Reserve-Division Ia No. 2341 Div. St. Qu., den 28. Mårz 1917*
Pi. Btl. 17 Bd 7	*Teilweise Erhöhung der Gefechtsbereitschaft 1. bayr. Reserve- Division I No. 2430 Div. St. Qu., den 31.3.17*
Pi. Btl. 17 Bd 7	*Korpsbefehl Gruppe Vimy Gen. Kdo. I. bayr. R.K. Abt Ia/Art. No. 14. 553 K.H.Qu., den 3.4.17*
Pi. Btl. 17 Bd 9	*Nachrichtenblatt vom 1.3.1917 79. Reserve-Division D.St.Qu. den 2. März 1917*
Pi. Btl. 17 Bd 9	*Aussage des am 16. April Mittags bei Beaurains übergelaufenen Soldaten William Holmes vom VI./Yorkshire-Rgt. General-Kdo. I. Bayer. Res. Korps K.H.Qu. 18. April 1916*
Pi. Btl. 17 Bd 9	*1 Canadier, übergelaufen am 13.2.1917 beim R.I.R. 23 nordöstlich Neuville St Vaast, gehört der C. Komp. des <u>R.Can.Regts.</u> der 7.can. Brig. Der. 3. can. Div. an. Generalkommando VI. Reservekorps Ic Nr. 3847 K.H.Qu., den 14.2.1917*
Pi. Btl. 17 Bd 9	*Nachrichten über den Feind VI Res. Korps Generalkommando <u>Ia/Ic4461</u> K.H.Qu., den 22.2.1917*
R.Komp Bd 200	*Die Herbstschlacht bei la Bassée und Arras vom*

	25. September bis 13. Oktober 1915 A.O.K. 6. Ib Nr.
	58385
R. Pi. Kp. 1 Bd. 1	*Kriegstagebuch 6 Mai – 30 Juni 1915*
R. Pi. Kp. 1 Bd. 1	*Spreng-Trichter April – Mai 1915*
R. Pi. Kp. 1 Bd. 5	*General-Kdo I.Bayer. Reserve Korps K.H.Qu.*
	2.3.1917 Korpstagesbefehl
R. Pi. Kp. 1 Bd. 5	*Gruppe Vimy General-Kdo I.Bayer. Reserve Korps*
	Abteilg. Ia. H.Qu. Ostersonntag 1917
	Korpstagesbefehl

Robinson Collection

Personal communication Herr Olaf Grieben 15.1.1989

Printed Works (German: Author known)

Auenmüller Oberst a.D. Leo *Das Kgl. Sächs. 8. Infanterie-Regiment 'Prinz Johann Georg' Nr. 107 während des Weltkrieges 1914 – 1918* Dresden 1928

Bamberg Hauptmann Georg *Das Kgl. Sächs. Res.-Inf.-Regiment Nr. 106* Dresden 1925

Baumgarten-Crusius Generalmajor Artur *Sachsen in großer Zeit Band II* Leipzig 1919; *Band III* Leipzig 1920

Behrmann Franz *Die Osterschlacht bei Arras 1917 I. Teil Zwischen Lens und Scarpe (Schlachten des Weltkrieges Band 28)* Oldenburg 1929

Beumelburg Werner *Loretto (Schlachten des Weltkrieges Band 17)* Oldenburg 1927

Bezzel Oberst a.D. Dr. Oskar *Das Königlich Bayerische Reserve-Infanterie-Regiment Nr. 6* München 1938

Bose Königl. Preuß. Major a.D. Thilo von *Das Kaiser Alexander Garde-Grenadier-Regiment Nr. 1 im Weltkriege 1914–1918* Zeulenroda 1932

Braun Generalmajor a.D. Julius Ritter von *Das K.B. Reserve-Infanterie-Regiment Nr. 21* München 1923

Burchardi Oberst a.D. Karl *Das Füsilier-Regiment Generalfeldmarschall Graf Moltke (Schlesisches) Nr. 38* Oldenburg 1928

Collenberg Oberstleutnant a.D. Karl Freiherr von *Das 3. Garde-Feldartillerie-Regiment Seine Geschichte* Berlin 1931

Delmensingen General der Artillerie Kraft von and Feeser Generalmajor a.D.

Friedrichfranz *Das Bayernbuch vom Weltkriege 1914–1918* Stuttgart 1930

Demmler Major a.D. Ernst, Wucher Oberstleutnant a.D. Karl Ritter von and Leupold Generalmajor a.D. Ludwig *Das K.B. Reserve-Infanterie-Regiment 12* München 1934

Dieterich Generalleutnant a.D. *Die 79. Reserve-Division in der Schlacht auf der Vimy-Höhe/April 1917* Magdeburg 1917

Dunzinger Hauptmann a.D. Albert *Das K.B. 11. Infanterie-Regiment von der Tann* München 1921

Eitel Friedrich Prinz von Preußen and Katte Hauptmann a.D. von *Das Erste Garderegiment zu Fuß im Weltkrieg 1914–18* Berlin 1934

Falkenstein Major a.D. Hans Trüzschler v. *Das Anhaltische Infanterie-Regiment Nr. 93 im Weltkriege (Erster Teil)* Oldenburg 1929

Fischer Hauptmann d.R. *Das Reserve-Infanterie-Regiment Nr. 262 1914–1918* Zeulenroda 1936

Flies Major a.D. Otto, Dittmar Hauptmann Kurt *5. Hannoversches Infanterie-Regiment Nr 165 im Weltkriege* Oldenburg 1927

Freund Leutnant d.R. a.D. Hans *Geschichte des Infanterie-Regiments Prinz Carl (4. Großh. Hess.) Nr. 118 m Weltkrieg* Groß-Gerau 1930

Freydorf Oberstleutnant a.D. Rudolf von *Das 1. Badische Leib-Grenadier-Regiment Nr. 109 im Weltkrieg 1914 1918* Karlsruhe 1927

Fromm Oberst z.D. *Das Württembergische Reserve-Infanterie-Regiment Nr. 120 im Weltkrieg 1914 – 1918* Stuttgart 1920

Gropp Offizier-Stellvertreter Hugo *Hanseaten im Kampf – Erlebnisse bei dem Res. – Inf. – Rgt. 76 im Weltkriege 1914/18* Hamburg 1934

Großmann Generalleutnant a.D. August *Das K.B. Reserve-Infanterie-Regiment Nr. 17* München 1923

Guhr Generalmajor a.D. *Das 4.Schlesische Infanterie-Regiment Nr 157im Frieden und im Kriege 1897 – 1919* Zeulenroda 1934

Hasselbach Major a.D. von and Strodzki Hptm. d.Res. a.D. *Das Reserve-Infanterie-Regiment Nr. 38* Zeulenroda 1934

Haupt Oberleutnant a.D. Dr. Karl *Das K.B. 15. Infanterie-Regiment König Friedrich August von Sachsen* München 1922

Heinicke Lt. d.Res. a.D. Karl and Bethge Lt. d.Res. a.D. Bruno *Das Reserve-Infanterie-Regiment Nr. 263 in Ost und West* Oldenburg 1926

Hindenburg Generalfeldmarschall von *Aus meinem Leben* Leipzig 1934

Hottenroth Oberst a.D. Johann Edmund *Sachsen in großer Zeit Band I* Leipzig 1920

Kaiser Generalmajor a.D. Franz *Das Königl. Preuß. Infanterie-Regiment Nr. 63 (4. Oberschlesisches)* Berlin 1940

Kalb Oberstleutnant a.D. Georg *Das K.B. 10. Feldartillerie-Regiment* München 1934

Karitzky Hauptmann d.Res. a.D. Erich *Reserve-Jäger-Bataillon Nr. 9* Oldenburg 1925

Klitzsch Kgl. Sächs. Hauptmann a.D. Johannes *Kriegstagebuch 1914 – 1918 des Kgl. Sächs. Reserve-Infanterie-Regiment Nr. 101* Dresden 1934

Kuhl General d.Inf a.D. Hermann von *Der Weltkrieg 1914 – 1918 Band II* Berlin 1929

Lehmann Generalleutnant a.D. August *Das K.B. Pionier-Regiment* München 1927

Loebell Hauptmann Egon von *Mit dem 3. Garde-Regiment z.F. im Weltkriege 1914/18* Berlin 1920

Loßberg General der Infanterie z.V. *Meine Tätigkeit im Weltkriege 1914 – 1918* Berlin 1939

Ludendorff Erich *Meine Kriegserinnerungen 1914 –1918* Berlin 1919

Martin Leutnant d.R. a.D. Dr. Phil. A. Das Königl. Sächs. Grenadier-Reserve-Regiment Nr. 100* Dresden 1924

Meier-Gesees Karl *Vater Wills Kriegstagebuch* Bayreuth 1931

Müller Major d.R Paul, Fabeck Oberst a.D. Hans von & Riesel Oberstleutn. a.D. Richard *Geschichte des Reserve-Infanterie-Regiments Nr. 99* Zeulenroda 1936

Niebelschutz Major Günther von *Reserve-Infanterie-Regiment Nr. 230* Oldenburg 1926

Nollau Oberstleutnant a.D. Herbert *Geschichte des Königlich Preußischen 4. Niederschlesischen Infanterie-Regiments Nr. 51* Berlin 1931

Pache Oberleutnant d.R. a.D. Alexander *Das Kgl. Sächs. 16. Infanterie-Regiment Nr. 182 I. Teil 'Die beiden Jahre an der Westfront'* Dresden 1924

Poetter Hauptmann *Infanterie-Regiment Nr. 55* Oldenburg 1922

Poland Hauptmann a.D. Franz Theodor *Das Kgl. Sächs. Reserve-Infanterie-Regiment Nr. 103* Dresden 1922

Reinhard Königl. Preuß. Oberst a.D. Wilhelm *Das 4. Garde-Regiment zu Fuß* Oldenburg 1924

Reymann Oberleutnant a.D. H *Das 3. Oberschlesische Infanterie-Regiment Nr. 62* Zeulenroda 1930

Rieben Oberstleutnant a.D. Oberarchivrat Dr. von *Kaiser Franz Garde-Grenadier-Regiment Nr. 2* Oldenburg 1929

Rieben Oberstleutnant a.D. Oberarchivrat Dr. von *Das 2. Garde-Regiment zu Fuß* Zeulenroda 1934

Riebensahm Generalleutnant a.D. Gustav *Infanterie-Regiment Prinz Friedrich der Niederlande (2. Westfälisches) Nr. 15 im Weltkriege 1914 – 18* Minden 1931

Ritter Oberstleutnant a.D. Holger *Geschichte des Schleswig-Holsteinischen Infanterie-Regiments Nr. 163* Hamburg 1926

Rogge Oberst a.D. Walter *Das Königl. Preuß. 2. Nassauische Infanterie-Regiment Nr. 88* Berlin 1936

Rosenberg-Lipinsky Hauptmann Hans-Oskar von *Das Königin Elisabeth Garde-Grenadier-Regiment Nr. 3 im Weltkriege 1914–1918* Zeulenroda 1935

Rupprecht Kronprinz von Bayern *In Treue Fest. Mein Kriegstagebuch, Erster Band* München 1929, *Zweiter Band* München 1929, *Dritter Band* München 1929

Schmidt Oberstleutnant a.D. Walther *Das 7. Badische Infanterie-Regiment Nr. 142 im Weltkrieg 1914/18* Freiburg im Breisgau 1927

Schmidt-Oswald Kgl. Preuß. Major a.D. *Das Altenburger Regiment (8. Thüringisches Infanterie-Regiment Nr. 153) im Weltkriege* Oldenburg 1927

Schütz Generalmajor a.D. & Hochbaum Leutnant *Das Grenadier-Regiment König Friedrich Wilhelm II (1. Schles. Nr. 10)* Oldenburg 1924

Schwerin Rittmeister a.D. C. von and Schmidt Oberleutnant d.R. a.D. Dr. Karl *Reserve-Inf-Regiment 261 in Ost und West* Berlin 1932

Seiler Major a.D. Reinhard *10. Rheinisches Infanterie-Regiment Nr. 161(II. Band)* Zeulenroda 1939

Sievers Leutnant d.R. Adolf *R.I.R. 93 Geschichte eines Regiments im Weltkriege* Wilster in Holstein 1934

Speck Justizinspektor William *Das Königlich Preußische Reserve-Infanterie-Regiment 84* Zeulenroda 1937

Stammberger Oberleutnant d.Res. a.D. Ludwig *Das K.B. Reserve-Infanterie-Regiment 13* München 1921

Staubwasser Generalmajor a.D. Otto *Das K.B. 2. Infanterie-Regiment Kronprinz* München 1924

Stegemann Hermann *Geschichte des Krieges: Dritter Band* Stuttgart 1919

Stosch Oberstleutnant a.D. Albrecht von *Das Garde-Grenadier-Regiment Nr. 5 1897 – 1918* Oldenburg 1925

Stosch Oberstleutnant a.D. Albrecht von *Das Königl. Preuß. 5. Garde-Regiment zu Fuß 1897 – 1918* Berlin 1930

Sydow Hauptmann a.D. v. *Das Infanterie-Regiment Hamburg (2. Hanseatisches) Nr. 76 im Weltkriege 1914/18* Oldenburg 1922

Trümper-Bödemann Leutnant der Landwehr a.D. *Das Königl. Sächs. ReserveInfanterie-Regiment Nr. 102* Chemnitz 1929

Voigt Oblt. d. Res. Hans *Geschichte des Füsilier-Regiments Generalfeldmarschall Prinz Albrecht von Preußen (Hann.) Nr. 73* Berlin 1938

Voigt Leutnant. d. Res Julius *Das Garde-Reserve-Infanterie-Regiment Nr. 64 im Weltkriege* Oldenburg 1925

Werner Leutnant. d. Res. Dr Bernhard *Das Königlich Preußische Inf.-Rgt. Prinz Louis Ferdinand von Preußen (2. Magdeb.) Nr. 27 im Weltkriege 1914 – 1918* Berlin 1933

Wiederich Leutnant d.R. Dr. Alfons *Das Reserve-Infanterie-Regiment Nr. 229* Berlin 1929

Windhorst Major d.R. a.D. Karl *Das Mindensche Feldartillerie-Regiment Nr. 58 im Weltkriege 1914–1918* Dortmund 1930

Zahn Oberstlt a. D. Th. *Das Infanterie-Regiment Markgraf Ludwig Wilhelm (3. Badisches) Nr. 111 im Weltkriege 1914 – 1918* Wiesbaden 1936

Zastrow Oberstleutnant a.D. Maximilian von *3. Badisches Feldartillerie-Regiment Nr 50* Oldenburg 1929

Printed Works (German: Author unknown)

Reichsarchiv / Reichskriegsministerium / Oberkommando des Heeres
Der Weltkrieg 1914 – 1918

— *Fünfter Band: Der Herbst-Feldzug 1914* Berlin 1929
— *Achter Band: Die Operationen des Jahres 1915(Die Ereignisse im Westen im Frühjahr und Sommer, im Osten vom Frühjahr bis zum Jahresschluß)* Berlin 1932
— *Neunter Band: Die Operationen des Jahres1915(Die Ereignisse im Westen und auf dem Balkan vom Sommer bis zum Jahresschluß)* Berlin 1933
— *Zehnter Band: Die Operationen des Jahres1916 bis zum Wechsel in der Obersten Heeresleitung.* Berlin 1936
— *Elfter Band: Die Kriegführung im Herbst 1916 und im Winter 1916/17 vom Wechsel in der Obersten Heeresleitung bis zum Entschluss zum Rückzug in der Siegfried-Stellung* Berlin 1938
— *Zwölfter Band: Die Kriegführung im Frühjahr 1917* Berlin 1939
Geschichte des Feldartillerie-Regiments von Peucker (1. Schles.) Nr. 6 1914 – 1918 Breslau 1932
Das K.B. 1. Infanterie-Regiment König München 1922
Das K.B.12. Infanterie-Regiment Prinz Arnulf München 1929
Das K.B. 14. Infanterie-Regiment Hartmann München 1931
Das Füsilier-Regiment Prinz Heinrich von Preußen (Brandenburgisches) Nr. 35 im Weltkriege Berlin 1929
Infanterie-Regiment Graf Bülow von Dennewitz (6. Westfälisches) Nr. 55 im Weltkriege Detmold 1928
Geschichte des 6.Badischen Infanterie-Regiments Kaiser Friedrich III. Nr. 114 im Weltkrieg 1914 bis 1918 Zeulenroda 1938
Geschichte des 9. Rhein. Infanterie-Regiments Nr. 160 im Weltkriege 1914 – 1918 Zeulenroda 1931
Geschichte des 4. Hannoverschen Infanterie-Regiments Nr. 164 und seines Stammtruppenteils des 2. Königlich Hannoverschen Regiments Kassel 1932
Das Königlich Sächsische 13. Infanterie-Regiment Nr. 178 Kamenz 1935
Reserve Infantry Regiment 261 Nachrichtenblatt Nr. 29 Berlin Jan./März 1927
Reserve Infantry Regiment 261 Nachrichtenblatt Nr. 37 Berlin Jan./März 1929
Reserve Infantry Regiment 261 Nachrichtenblatt Nr. 41 Berlin Jan./März 1930
Reserve Infantry Regiment 261 Nachrichtenblatt Nr. 45 Berlin Jan./März 1931
Reserve Infantry Regiment 261 Nachrichtenblatt Nr. 49 Berlin Jan./März 1932
Unsere Pioniere im Weltkrieg Berlin 1925

Printed Works (French)

Ministère de la Guerre *Les Armées Françaises dans la Grande Guerre:*
— *Tome Premier, Quatrième Volume* Paris 1934
— *Tome II* Paris 1930
— *Tome III* Paris 1923
— *Tome III Annexes – 2e Volume* Paris 1925
— *Tome IV, Premier Volume* Paris 1927

Printed Works (English)

Barris Ted *Victory at Vimy: Canada Comes of Age* Toronto 2007

Berton Pierre *Vimy* Barnsley 2003

Cave Nigel *Vimy Ridge* Barnsley 1996

Edmonds Brigadier General Sir James E *Military Operations France and Belgium 1916 Sir Douglas Haig's Command to the 1st July: Battle of the Somme* London 1932

Falls Captain Cyril *Military Operations France and Belgium 1917 The German Retreat to the Hindenburg Line and the Battles of Arras* London 1940

Hart Peter *Bloody April: Slaughter in the Skies over Arras* London 2005

Hayes Geoffrey, Iarocci Andrew and Bechthold Mike (Eds.) *Vimy Ridge: A Canadian Reassessment* Waterloo Ontario 2007

Jones H A *The War in the Air: Being the Story of the part played in the Great War by the Royal Air Force Vol III* Oxford 1931

Jones Simon *World War I Gas Warfare Tactics and Equipment* Oxford 2007

Nasmith Col. George G *Canada's Sons and Great Britain in the World War* Toronto 1919

Sheldon Jack and Cave Nigel *The Battle for Vimy Ridge 1917* Barnsley 2007

Turner Alexander *Vimy Ridge 1917* Oxford 2005

Index